UNIVERSAL FATHER

UNIVERSAL FATHER

A Life of Pope John Paul II

GARRY O'CONNOR

BLOOMSBURY

Published by Bloomsbury Publishing, New York and London
Distributed to the trade by Holtzbrinck Publishers

Every reasonable effort has been made to contact copyright holders of material
reproduced in this book. If any have been inadvertently overlooked the publishers
would be glad to hear from them and to make good in future editions any errors or
omissions brought to their attention.

For legal purposes the Acknowledgements and Picture Credits pages constitute a
continuation of this copyright page.

All papers used by Bloomsbury Publishing are natural, recyclable products made from
wood grown in well-managed forests. The manufacturing processes conform to the
environmental regulations of the country of origin.

Library of Congress Cataloging-in-Publication Data has been applied for.

ISBN 1-59691-096-8
ISBN-13 978-1-59691-096-6

First U.S. Edition 2005

3 5 7 9 10 8 6 4 2

Typeset by Hewer Text Ltd, Edinburgh
Printed in the United States of America by Quebecor World Fairfield

This book is dedicated to the memory of my mother,
Rita O'Connor (née Odoli), 1907–2004

The Christian does not live in a state of equilibrium, like the sages of old, but in a state of conflict . . . Even Christ was tempted. And from the intellectual point of view, what a heroic stimulus for the mind is there for us in all those revelations which we have got to understand!

Paul Claudel
Letter to André Gide

Availing myself of the solemn occasion of my meeting with the representatives of the nations of the earth, I wish above all to send my greetings to all the men and women living on this planet.

Pope John Paul II
Addressing the 34th General Assembly
of the United Nations
2 October 1979

Contents

Part Three

THE POPE OF THIS DISTRACTED GLOBE (1978–90)

Part Four

THE NEARER WE ARE TO THE MOUNTAIN,
THE SMALLER WE ARE (1990–2005)

List of Illustrations
with Picture Credits

POLAND in 1939

National boundaries as at 31 August 1938
Nazi-Soviet Frontier 28 September 1939
Territory incorporated into the Reich
General Government
Territory occupied by Soviet Russia

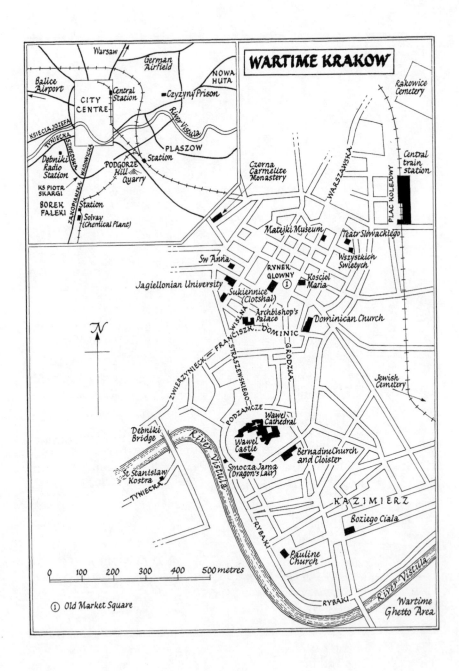

Preface

Universal Father is written as much for doubters and disbelievers as for believers of all faiths and denominations, but especially for those caught up in the maelstrom or turmoil of the many arguments and conflicts which beset not only the Catholic church, but all forms of contemporary religious belief.

Popes are paradoxes. As divine autocrats ruling the Catholic church of over a billion souls, not only do they confront the universal issues but they are expected to be authorities, if not infallible, in their pronouncements on the most sensitive aspects of human existence. Having renounced so much for their faith, how can they know what they know? 'This hermit buried in the Vatican cave,' Graham Greene observed, is, 'addressing a special audience of newly married couples on the heroic energy required in everyday life, the boredom and frustrations and torn nerves of two people living under one roof.' He tells his audience, 'One should remember during a chilly dispute that it is better to keep quiet, to keep in check a complaint, or to use a milder word instead of stronger, because one knows that the stronger word, once it is out, will relieve, it is true, the tension of the irritated nerves, but will also leave its darkening shadow behind.'

These words are not – as they well might be – a statement from the subject of this biography, but from Pope Pius XII, an earlier, long-serving and wartime pope, generally considered an aloof and remote figure. In contrast to that earlier pope, however, the courage and breadth of spirit of Karol Wojtyla, Pope John Paul II, have never been in dispute. 'They try to understand me from the outside,' he has said of the many books and biographies written about him. 'But I can only be understood from the inside.'

Here, then, is a different approach, an attempt – in relation to the epic story of his life – to convey the feelings, heart, soul and thoughts of the man, to understand him from the inside.

The Harvard philosopher Stanley Cavell ruminates, in his study of Samuel Beckett's *Endgame*, that humanity seems no longer to know what it is, the reason why it is here, or where it is going:

> Shall we blame Beckett because he cannot keep still? Then blame Hamlet because he cannot keep going? Won't somebody stop us, or start us? Perhaps we've got something to complain about, and maybe it has got to do with our efforts first to create and then to destroy our Gods. Nietzsche said we will have to become like Gods ourselves to withstand the consequences of such deeds, Camus said we will never be men until we give up trying to be God. Que voulez-vous, Monsieur? Which do you pick? – We hang between.

Karol Wojtyla lived through many endgames, but one in particular dwarfed the others: the loss of the purpose and meaning of life in advanced, pluralistic societies. In *Crossing the Threshold of Hope*, Wojtyla cites André Malraux saying 'that he was certainly right when he said that the twenty-first century would be the century of religion or it would not be at all'. All through his life Wojtyla addressed himself to this universal endgame, and applied himself to its solution.

The election of a Pole as pope is itself of especial significance because it underlines Wojtyla's own and very specific Polish Christian vision of history. The Nazis, when they took over Poland in 1939, exterminated the intelligentsia and murdered a sixth of the priests with the intention of destroying the spiritual consciousness of the country. The vision of history which Wojtyla and his countrymen share is that man should not be reduced to an instrument of power or utilitarian wealth, but judged continually against the criteria of morality and spirituality, and with these as aspirations find a new and different freedom and self-expression. In this very different view of the struggle or drama of history it is God who is the protagonist.

Popes believe there is a purpose in human life beyond the grave: Karol Wojtyla is universal in his appeal and in his humanity, and at least part of the fascination of looking at his life is that we are also looking at ourselves in a mirror, and confronting the problems that are common to everyone.

Part One

A SLAV TROUBADOUR
IN TROUBLED TIMES

Had Pilsudski . . . and Weygand [General Maxim Weygand, French military adviser to the Polish general staff] failed to arrest the triumphant advance of the Soviet Army at the Battle of Warsaw in 1920, not only would Christianity have experienced a dangerous reverse, but the very existence of Western civilisation would have been imperilled.

Lord d'Aberon

I am convinced that sometime in the future we will be able to see a statue of the Virgin looking down over Moscow from the top of the Kremlin.

Maximilian Kolbe

I

Like Death, Beyond Comprehension

(1920–29)

Nothing in this world . . . is ready-made. Each of us is born, then learns to crawl, then attends the first grade, then matures.
Speech by Metropolitan Archbishop Wojtyla,
7 March 1964

When the new Polish republic was born in 1918, Wadowice was a very ordinary, nondescript town, except for the fact that it was relatively homogenous in race and religion. Of its population, estimated at between five and six thousand, more than four-fifths were Polish Roman Catholics, while 700 were Jewish. By comparison, in Polish Ukraine, where Joseph Conrad (an early favourite of Wojtyla's) was born, the people were of four different ethnic origins, speaking four different languages. Set in the foothills of the Carpathian Mountains, in the province of Galicia, Wadowice was a remarkably balanced, even-tempered place.

Progress seemed to have passed it by. Although only thirty miles south-west of the historic cathedral city and one-time capital of Krakow, it possessed no great magnets for visitors, no shrines for pilgrims, no ambitious industrial enterprises. By the mid-1930s, when Karol was in his teens, Wadowice still had only a half-dozen or so cars, the prize being a Skoda Rapide owned by a local landowner. Even bicycles were rare.

'Horse-drawn buggies . . . remained common. The open platform truck was preferred for hauling goods, its driver balanced on spread feet and holding the reins of a sturdy draught horse.' Social differences were marked, as a school friend of Karol's reported many years later:

'men and women in red-and-white peasant garb – the women in long, hem-embroidered skirts – and red-faced from a life of cold, wind, and sun – kept to themselves. Shopkeepers and professional men invariably wore sober suits.'

Mr Kluk, the mayor, owned the Rynek complex, just south of the town church of St Mary of Perpetual Succour, a combined restaurant and consumer-goods emporium. Like a comic character from a novel by Elias Canetti or Jaroslav Hasek, he was famous locally for having two pairs of shoes from Mr Bata's Footwear made especially for his dog. As the county seat Wadowice had the district court and local-government offices, a teachers' college, good-quality secondary schools and mostly literate citizens employed in education, government or the military. It provided a quiet and genteel atmosphere for Karol's early life.

Jews, earlier in time debarred by Polish law from owning land, owned 40 per cent of the shops, yet even so they had much better relations with the Catholics than was typical elsewhere in Poland. Crime was virtually non-existent, while the only judicial killing that took place during Karol's teen years was that of the notorious murderer, Nikifor Maruszeczko, who was hanged at the prison on Slowackiego Street. His last words were, 'It's a beautiful life!'

Wadowice possessed one cinema, the Kino Wysoglada, but it had three amateur theatres, two of them part of Catholic establishments. Krakow, with its many cultural attractions, was within easy reach by train. Karol's mother, Emilia, had grown up in Krakow, and she often visited her three sisters who still lived there.

Karol's brother, Edmund (nicknamed Mundek), was born in 1906. Eight years later, Emilia gave birth to Olga, but she lived, it is believed, only a few days or weeks. The cause of her death is unknown. Karol Jozef was born on 18 May 1920. He was loyally given his father's indigenous Polish name, with the addition of Jozef because Emilia wanted him called after Christ's father. The army chaplain, Father Zak, baptised him over the road in St Mary of Perpetual Succour. Local rumour has it that Emilia, whom her second son much resembled, would tell neighbours while pushing his pram or chatting in their central courtyard that he would one day become a great man.

Karol (whose nickname was Lolek, a variant of 'Lolus' from Carolus) and his family lived in Rynek Street in a modest, rented, middle-class flat in the centre of Wadowice. Karol's father worked in the army's quartermaster stores, and rose to the rank of lieutenant, retiring on a small pension in 1927 but continuing to serve part-time in the recruitment office. His family stock was of 'hortulanus' – small farmers or tradesmen – similar in station to Emilia, whose family owned a saddlery.

The Wojtylas' flat was owned by a Jewish merchant, Balamuth Chaim, whose crystal-and-glass store occupied the front of the building. Situated on the second floor 'up a crooked flight of stone steps with iron handrail', it had three rooms, including a kitchen through which one entered, and overlooked a central private courtyard where children played and neighbours chatted. By the front door was a holy-water stoop in which the family would dip their fingers and make the sign of the cross as they passed in and out. Balamuth Chaim was not the only Jewish presence in the building: among the other tenants were the Beer family. In later years the Pope recalled his closeness to this Jewish community: 'Man lives on the basis of his own experiences. I belong to the generation for which relationships with Jews were a daily occurrence.'

The first seven years of Karol's life were an undisturbed idyll. He had quiet, a solitude of the kind to develop within him the creative soul, the romantic poet, the fierce devourer, even at such an early age, of myth and ritual. By the time Karol began at Marcin Wadowita elementary school, his studious and ambitious brother Mundek was studying at the Jagiellonian University, Krakow, to become a doctor. Karol had his mother's full and undivided attention. In their living room they had a prie-dieu to encourage family prayers. Before school each morning, Karol attended mass (school was behind the church), while after school Emilia read to him from the New Testament.

His mother's devotion was important, for he learned to listen and concentrate carefully on others. And the quietness of the age – the absence of the constant media, cartoons, advertisements and relentless peer pressure that is the lot of most small children in the Western world today – meant that Karol's childhood must have more re-sembled the life of an early Christian than that of a child born, say, into the jazz era celebrated by Scott Fitzgerald, or one of Europe's great cities. The small provincial town had its villains, its criminals, its madmen and its cantankerous characters – such as Mrs Anna Hup-pert, the rich Jewish lady (she owned eleven buildings with 210

tenants), or, at the other end of the scale, the penniless postman who
spent everything he had on vodka. Everything and everyone had a
human scale.

Everyone too was aware of their rank and position in this class-
ridden society. An instinctive and constant assertion of dignity stems
in Karol's case from being more or less in the position of an only child
enjoying the full attention of his mother. Psychologists often suggest
that the capacity to be alone in adult life originates with the infant's
experience of being alone in the presence of the mother. Donald
Winnicott, for example, suggests that without the sufficiency of being
alone in the presence of someone, the capacity to be alone cannot
develop: 'It is only when alone . . . (that is to say, in the presence of
someone) that the infant can discover his personal life.' This would
seem to have happened in the case of Karol. In early photographs of
Karol his face and posture emanate a sense of power and self-confidence. He was, records a childhood friend, very much a physical
presence, a handsome blond boy with large-boned Slavic features and
blue eyes, stronger and taller than most, habitually cheerful.

Beyond and within him, ever deepening, was preserved that sense of
his mother's undivided love, recorded in many forms throughout
Karol's life. In a series of poems he delineates how Jesus was taken
from his mother: John the Apostle says to Mary,

> Your arms now remember His space, the little head
> snuggling to your shoulder,
> for the space has remained in You,
> for it was taken from You.

It is revealing that he should depict Mary's amazement at Jesus,
mentioning the 'luminous silence' of his presence that she experienced.

> In that little town, where they knew us together
> you called me mother; but no one had eyes to see
> the astounding events as they took place day by day.

And again,

> How attentive your stillness: it will always be part of me.
> I lift myself towards it . . .

A sense of wonder, a capacity for stillness, a direct and continuous experience of maternal tenderness with its comforting physical warmth: all these are evident in Karol's early relationship with his mother – and remained strong enough to become permanently part of him.

Motherhood is also centred in that personality which is, or becomes so for many, divinely inspired. This further influence of motherhood is symbolised in an early poem written by Wojtyla when John breaks the bread to give the sacrament to Mary, and says:

> I stood for a moment amazed as I saw
> the whole truth through one single tear
> in your eye.

And in his play *The Radiation of Fatherhood* (1964) he reveals a profound physical sense of what it means to be a mother. Adam tells his daughter Monica that when she was conceived:

> first you had to penetrate the depths of her body, then to tear yourself out of it with the first impulse of independent life . . .

Karol underlines his early identification with the family of Jesus, with the Virgin's devotion to her only son. Except that, in his case, in the real terms of his life, the roles were to become tragically reversed.

In childhood, with a warmth of emotional contacts with neighbours and friends, Karol lived through untroubled years. Poland, too, passed through a halcyon period that gave its historically down-trodden and subjected people unexpected hope for the future. A symbol lives in the hearts and feelings. Symbols, both of nation and of soul, surrounded him on all sides: the flag of the new Polish republic, horizontal white above and red below in equal bands, was one; the emblem of the white eagle and crown, another (although the post-Second World War communists took off the crown). The Black Madonna of Czestocho-wa, 'Queen of Poland', an icon painted on lime-tree timber, symbo-lised the Polish soul; the shrine of St Stanislaw, Poland's patron saint, in Krakow's Wawel Cathedral, the Zygmunt Bell, the Szczerbiec or Jagged Sword used for coronations of Polish kings . . . the list becomes endless. The Roman Catholic churches too were full of symbol and ritual magic. In terms of the patriotic Poles themselves, in the consciousness of Karol senior, as transmitted to his son in these early years, this creation of a new Poland, a phoenix rising from the ashes, was a miracle.

Even after the 1919 treaty, fighting had gone on between Russia and Poland. In the summer of 1920, three months after Karol was born, the Red Army stood at the gates of Warsaw again. The second Polish republic, independent for the first time since the kingdom of 1795, was in the earliest months of its resurrection about to be crushed. But now there was a difference. The Red Army cavalry, commanded by General Budennyi, met its match in Marshal Jozef Pilsudski's army. Pilsudski had defeated the Red Army at Kiev ten days before Karol's birth in an attempt to drive the Russians from the Polish Ukraine, but then suffered serious reverses, before outmanoeuvring the Russians at the Battle of the Vistula. Here daringly, with few casualties, the Polish army routed a force which threatened not only to repeat the tragic domination, but to instil a puppet communist regime under the terror of the Cheka, the Soviet secret police.

In Poland this battle became known as 'the miracle of the Vistula'. It took deep root in patriotic national consciousness. The date of the victory, 15 August, was also the feast of the Assumption of Our Lady, and this coincidence of time and place became, in the mind of the young Karol, no doubt elaborated and embroidered on by his devout father, the first intercession in his life of the Divine Virgin, Our Lady, who was traditionally the 'Queen of Poland'.

To understand the character of twentieth-century Poland, it is important to appreciate the historic grandeur of its past. 'To Poland,' Wojtyla said shortly after becoming pope, 'the Church brought Christ, the key to understanding the great and fundamental reality that is man.' Few countries – except perhaps Israel or Russia – had such a theocratic vision of history. Established as a Roman Catholic kingdom in the eleventh century, Poland was at the height of its power and influence from the early part of the fifteenth century until the last quarter of the seventeenth, when it played a crucial part in the defeat of the Muslim Turks at the Battle of Vienna in 1683. The Polish cavalry – the winged Hussars – led by King Jan III Sobieski, won lasting military glory.

The Battle of Vienna was a turning-point, and from then on Poland became afflicted by its historic curse. In the eighteenth century its powerful neighbours – Prussia, Russia and Austria – invaded it three times, in what is now known as the Three Partitions – dismembering and devouring it, shifting its boundaries, its people, but fomenting an inner cultural war and resistance against their hegemony.

Early in the nineteenth century, with Napoleon's invasion of the East, hopes were raised for national revival, but in spite of Poland fighting bravely on the side of the French, Napoleon had fed a dream that turned out to be another transient fantasy. Poland, adapting the Romantic literary tradition prevalent in the rest of a Europe to which it always felt it belonged spiritually, 'elevated sacrifice and sorrow to sublime heights. Poland was compared to the Christ among nations, redeeming through suffering not only the Polish nation but mankind. Poland had a sacred mission to fulfil: to break the chains of absolutism and bring about universal freedom.' These were the grand sentiments of the revolutionary Apollo Korzeniowski, the father of Joseph Conrad.

The reality of the heroic Polish struggle for independence even became a playwright's and novelist's joke. Three nineteenth-century insurrections, in 1830, 1846 and 1863 – all of them heroic and ill-advised – cemented the legend that most Polish men dreamed of dying in a hail of rifle fire while leading a cavalry charge in a hopeless attack on foreign invaders. 'Show a precipice to a Pole and he'll make a leap,' wrote Honoré de Balzac in *Cousin Bette*. 'As a nation they are like cavalrymen; they think they can overcome all obstacles and emerge victorious.'

D.H. Lawrence wrote in *The Rainbow* of the aftermath of the 1863 insurrection, when his characters Lydia Lensky and her husband flee to England: '. . . they were very patriotic: and . . . at the same time, very "European" . . . Lensky, very ardent and full of words, went about inciting his countrymen. Little Poles flamed down the streets of Warsaw, on the way to shoot every Muscovite.' Alfred Jarry's *Ubu Roi* (1899), fore-runner of the drama of the absurd, contained a stage direction for an imaginary country: 'En Pologne, c'est à dire nulle part' ('In Poland, namely nowhere').

These many defeats and residual griefs lived on in the national soul, confronting each young educated Pole as he or she grew up. One such defeat and decline concerned especially the *szlachta*, the Polish nobility. The *szlachta*'s knightly code was based on peacock pride in a supposedly exclusive ancestry, but 'was grotesquely unsuited to their miserable decline'. They became 'the laughing-stock of Europe, the butt which every radical wit from Defoe to Cobden could mock'. Their noble Republic became, in Carlyle's cruel words, 'a beautifully phosphorescent rot-heap', while they were 'the parasites who swarmed upon it'.

In exile the Pole often felt deeply alone and marked as an outsider. The 'Count' in Iris Murdoch's *Nuns and Soldiers*, for example, passes his childhood in an ardent endeavour to become English: he was not displeased by his honorary title, considering it as a little English jest 'which bound him to his surroundings and gave him a shared identity'. When strangers sometimes took him for a real count 'never sure if this was a charade or not . . . he increasingly felt, in every cell of his being, an alien'.

Emilia became ill when Karol was seven: his father, as reported by some, taking premature retirement from the Polish army at the age of forty-eight, to care for her and raise Karol; by others, as retiring early through ill-health. Emilia, who had suffered from kidney disease and a weak heart since childhood, when, as fifth in a family of nine children, she had helped raise her younger siblings, had been severely demoralised by the death of her only daughter. Emilia had trained as a teacher and taught in primary school for a short period; she had taken in sewing to supplement the meagre family income, but in Karol's early years she was seriously ill and she became virtually paralysed from her congenital weak heart and the kidney disease. It is said he wanted to stay with her when she went into hospital. She often refused to let Karol see her as she feared she could not hide her pain.

On 13 April 1929, with the official reason given as myocarditis nephritis, Emilia died at the age of 45. Three days later as her funeral mass began Karol faced her coffin before the altar of St Mary of Perpetual Succour. The three men in her family sat side by side in a front pew. Karol senior was fifty, Edmund twenty-three and Karol was soon to be nine. 'Eye has not seen, nor ear heard, nor the heart of man conceived, what God has prepared for those who love him,' the priest, Canon Prochownik declaimed. Later, when Wojtyla was consecrated bishop in 1958, her remains were taken to Krakow to be buried alongside those of her husband in the eastern sector of Rakowice Cemetery.

From now it was sadness and intelligence that became more etched in Karol's face, rather than plumpness and radiant optimism. Nine years later, when he and his father moved to Krakow, Karol commemorated Emilia's passing in a very simple poem of three stanzas, in which he referred to the passage of time and her white grave.

> Over this your white grave
> Covered for years, there is a stir
> in the air, something uplifting
> and, like death, beyond comprehension.

He cannot even then make full sense of it and perhaps will never be able to, as it appears, as it must have been, an unfinished love which will only be completed in the future when he rejoins her.

The First World War had now been over for ten years, and as the ensign told his young son, a million Poles, conscripted into the opposing powers of Russia and the Austro-Hungarian German axis, had died, often fighting each other. According to some historians the collapse of the Tsarist regime in Russia in 1917 had led to a larger and more independent Poland whose very existence became a threat and humiliation to Germany in the aftermath of the war. On 4 June 1917, before the October Revolution led by Lenin, Kerensky's provisional government recognised an independent Poland; France had raised an army of Poles in exile, and on 3 June 1918 proclaimed the creation of a powerful Polish state a primary objective.

But the Versailles Peace Treaty of 1919 had a calamitous effect in the long term. In particular, in the ceding of the Silesian provinces, the imposition of a Polish corridor on Prussia leading to its break-up and a redrawing of German–Polish boundaries would, it was feared, provoke future war. During June 1919 Lloyd George, the British prime minister, tried to mitigate the severity of the terms, and in doing so ended the *entente cordiale* between Britain and France. The French were set on revenge, and through Clemenceau's negotiation fostered the creation of a 'big' Poland, the occupation of the Rhineland, and huge reparations imposed on Germany. President Wilson refused sensible advice, especially from Maynard Keynes, the Cambridge economist, on the economic issues at stake. Keynes resigned as a delegate at the peace conference, considering the Treaty was a formula for economic disaster and future war. He wrote to Chamberlain, 'How can you expect me to assist at this tragic farce any longer?' He told Lloyd George, 'I am slipping away from this scene of nightmare.'

For Poland the economic problems came first. As a worldwide depression took hold in the wake of the Wall Street crash, father and son became aware of the expense of daily life, especially of any item from abroad. At the same time they witnessed ominous signs of the future conflict between Communism and Fascism, which would soon strike on both sides of Poland's long territorial frontiers.

For the moment Poland held its head high 'raised for ever for a sign'. But what was the sign, and when would it be seen? For every maturing child, such as Karol Wojtyla, life was severely politicised.

2

I Became a Motherless Only Child

(1929–34)

Lieutenant Wojtyla, who had risen through the ranks, had years of experience of old-fashioned army regimentation. As quartermaster he had experienced an area of army life where pilfering, bribery and corruption of all kinds flourish. Wojtyla had commendable reports from his superiors on his qualities of character, but the Polish army was not a philanthropic institution, and officers who have risen through the ranks generally tend to have an extra toughness about them which reinforces the maintenance of discipline in the unit they serve. They become, more often than not, sticklers for rules. Karol himself said his father was a hard man, but 'So hard on himself that he had no need to be hard on me; his example alone was sufficient to inculcate discipline and a sense of duty'.

Karol was seven when his father quitted the army to look after Emilia. Karol senior had to take upon himself many of the functions of mother as well as father: no doubt the mentality formed in years of military service remained influential in the home. 'There was a moment, like a flash,' wrote Karol later in another dramatic work, in which he explored a fatherhood theme,

> when I wanted to tear out of myself the meaning of the word 'father' . . .
> . . . Is it not true that in the word 'father'
> There is also fear?

Although Karol did not fear his father unduly, he could well have felt, in the formation of spirit and character, that strength built on fear had nothing wrong or bad about it. It is reasonable to assume that Karol began to reflect at an early age on the nature of his parents, to see his father's shortcomings as well as his virtues, and above all to become curious about what these two human beings meant to him, and how what they were and had been might become important to his own life and future.

Freud asserted that 'Many women who have chosen their husband on the model of their father, or have put him in their father's place, nevertheless repeat towards him, in their married life, their bad relations with their mother'. Perhaps, reversing the sexual roles, this could be applied to Karol's choice of career in the church. To take the place of his mother he marries the church by becoming a priest; and as a priest he repeats not the bad but the *good* relationship he had with his father.

Again, as Freud observes, a child will replace both parents by grander people, but in doing so, 'these new parents . . . are equipped with attributes that are derived entirely from real recollections of the actual and humble ones', so that the child is not getting rid of his father but exalting him. The whole of Karol's childhood was severely restricted, not only by a small income, but also by the narrow scope of the 'freedoms' on offer in Wadowice society, so that he had little else to do than follow his studies assiduously. Yet he followed Freud's observation by selecting and following exemplary father and mother figures who were not only selfless but celibate.

What direct reminiscences from this period do we have? The lieutenant – having trained as a tailor before joining what was then the Austrian army in Krakow – re-cut and sewed the fine materials of his military uniforms to enable his son to look better dressed than other boys. A railwayman's son reminiscences that 'Karol and I were growing so fast that what fitted us today would be too short and too tight in six months'. Karol senior was also highly literate, fluent in German as well as Polish, and typed quickly. Others would say that when Emilia died he lost some of his fervour, his hair turned white, and he would collect his son from the houses of friends, not speaking to anyone.

But one friend was taught to swim by Karol senior, who cooked his son breakfast, took him daily to the restaurant of Alojzy Banas only yards away from their front door (*pierogi* are named as the speciality), then gave him supper. Father and son played football in the now-abandoned parlour of their flat (no television or radio in those days, and they had no garden). Karol had a narrow escape when Boguslaw Banas, a younger friend, picked up a loaded revolver which a policeman took off with his belt and left lying by the cash register of his parents' restaurant. Banas loosened it from its holster, aimed at Karol in sport, then fired, not knowing the safety catch was off. The bullet flew past him, narrowly missing, and smashed a window pane. 'My God, I might have killed the Pope,' said Banas later.

Football, the national game, was pursued further and in greater earnest at the Marcin Wadowita state secondary school, a single-sex high school that Karol joined in autumn 1930. At this age Karol had already visited with his father the Carmelite monastery just outside Wadowice, where the monks heard their confessions and presented young Karol with the scapular of Our Lady of Mount Carmel, which is two holy pictures joined by strings which he would wear next to his skin for the rest of his life. The privacy and indeed maturity of Wojtyla's home life saved him from undignified exposures and humiliations, and his boyhood would seem to have been without them. He does record he was reproved by his father for not paying enough attention to the Holy Spirit, which stimulated him to rectify this in later life. 'When I was 10 or 12 years old I was a choirboy,' John Paul told André Frossard, the French author who became his friend and closest literary confidant,

'but I wasn't very dedicated, I must confess. My mother wasn't with us anymore . . . but my father, when he noticed my lack of diligence, said to me one day: "You are not being a very good choirboy. You don't pray to the Holy Spirit enough. You ought to pray to him." And he taught me a prayer to say.'

'And you haven't forgotten it.'

'I certainly haven't. That was a major spiritual lesson, longer lasting and more powerful than anything I got from my reading or from the courses I took later on. What conviction his voice held as he told me that! I can still hear his voice saying those words, even today.'

To a person living in the secular world of today the fervent attention to religious duty will seem strange, even primitive. After his wife's death Karol senior prayed constantly, as his son would much later attest:

> I had not yet made my first Holy Communion when I lost my mother: I was barely nine years old. So I do not have a clear awareness of her contribution which must have been great, to my religious training . . . Day after day I was able to observe the austere way in which [my father] lived . . . Sometimes I would wake up during the night and find my father on his knees, just as I would always see him kneeling in the parish church.

The piety was unforced, however, and everywhere the religious symbolism was evident; holy images on the walls, inside and outside the flat, a small altar in the parlour, the small font with holy water outside the front door. Laughter, too, accompanied prayer; learning was worn lightly. Karol senior delighted in historical parody, and backed this with a powerful gift for mimicry (able to convey the humanity of his target, a friend observed, as well as the ridiculous). The Marcin Wadowita secondary school teacher of Greek, Tadeusz Szeliski, becomes a vile kind of barley soup, 'Krupa'; when he denounces the use of tobacco, Karol mimics him chucking the forbidden substance discovered in class out of the window; the Latin teacher, affectionately mocked as 'Damazy' for his horror of perfume, comes in for similar treatment, while the German lady, Dr Sabina Rottenberg, good-looking, flirtatious and Jewish, appears to provoke adolescent hearts (and more), pursing her lips into a pout and letting fall on her pupils her 'big, dark eyes . . . a delicious torture'. Karol remains motionless, bemused at this onslaught, but his friend Jerzy Kluger drops paper on the floor, falls to hands and knees and pretends to look up provocative Sabina's skirt. They laugh and the teacher responds, 'Ruhe, ruhe,' which Karol later impersonates perfectly, achieving just the right contralto pitch.

In these early teenage years Karol made his reputation as a goal-keeper, gaining the nickname of Martyna, a star Polish footballer. Mainly he kept goal for the 'Cathos', although sometimes he would play for the Jewish team if their keeper, Poldek Goldburger, was not available. While elsewhere in Poland Jewish football teams often encountered attack and abuse from Gentiles, in Wadowice the racial harmony on the whole is markedly present. Canon Prochownik was prominently pro-Jewish while in the town's schools Catholics and Jews competed side by side or individually without outwardly at least showing any religious distinction.

There was, for all children, such a wealth of pastimes to choose from, 'that it was as if God had made that world for the young'. They swam in summer, in the Skawa, or walked to Grandmother Huppert's farm to pick cherries and gorge on them until their stomachs ached. In winter, they would take advantage of any good weather to hike into the hills for a few hours of skiing. Officers from the Twelfth Infantry who drilled and lectured the boys, rigged up a kind of trampoline to practise ski-jumping. Often Lolek, as his friends called him, and Jerzy Kluger, his Jewish friend, with the wooden, hand-fashioned slats on their shoulders, would wander off, far enough to worry about wolves, then race each other home as darkness fell (as early as three o'clock in January). 'Any frozen pond invited a makeshift hockey game, with sticks snapped from trees and a block of wood for a puck.'

On the far bank of the Skawa stood Venezia, a restaurant that was Italian in name only and was rather romantic, with a beautiful garden in summer and its own tennis court. It was a popular family gathering spot. On icy winter evenings, the court was flooded to make a rink and strung with coloured lights, and patrons skated to waltzes from a gramophone.

We may picture in scenes what happened next in Karol's life, and its impact on him in these years. Father and son visited 'Zebrzydowski's Calvary', a replica of the biblical Jerusalem, set among the hills a short railway or road distance from Wadowice. Built in the early seventeenth century by Mikolaj Zebrzydowski, a pious governor of Krakow, after his wife reportedly had a vision of Christ, the Calvary brought home to Karol the abstractions of Christianity, in the words of Shakespeare, about 'giving to aery nothings a local habitation and a name'. Pathways ran from a Bernardine monastery to forty-one stations following the way of the cross, depicting scenes from the Passion, death and resurrection. It was all very dramatically posed and, after its success, led the monks to construct a second circuit, of the life of the Virgin. The scale was such as to appeal to children, 'a prototype of Disneyland . . . with religion as its theme, and Christ and the Virgin the stars for an age of believers', although it was a completely free and non-commercial enterprise maintained by the Bernardine brothers.

Here Karol senior often brought Karol during religious festivals, and here the image of his dead mother, as he prayed devoutly to her, was omnipresent to him, deepening the idea of a Mary who was not only the Redeemer's mother but a queen of Poland. 'Every child's desire to build a playhouse and a secret garden is here fulfilled in the form of these little buildings [often not more than a hut with a single window at child's height] except that as each is keyed to the Holy Mother's life, the idea of a supreme, embracing maternal presence also settles on the mind of child and adult alike.' At Kalwaria Zebrzy-dowska the incipient poet learned early to address those who were absent, and to look for replies or answers in non-verbal signs.

In this place of refuge and source of hope we may imagine the twelve-year-old Karol, then, proudly telling his mother Emilia of his brother Mundek's progress as a doctor, for he was now fully qualified and had left Krakow for good. He worked in a hospital in Bielsko, a place which father and son found easier to visit.

Mundek was applauded for his high-spirited playfulness and his ability – shared with his father and younger brother – to entertain with his mimicry. While fourteen years separated the brothers, each saw much of himself in the other, sharing broad open highland faces and a facility in the local mountain dialect, and drawn together very closely by their mother's early demise. But in 1932 a scarlet-fever epidemic struck the town of Bielsko and in selfless, round-the-clock care on the wards for his patients Edmund succumbed to the killer disease, diagnosing in himself first the severely sore throat, then the red spots. The fever isolated him and, although he was cared for intensively by other members of hospital staff, he died at the end of the year, on 5 December.

The death, only three years after that of his mother, struck a further shattering blow to Karol. He and his father placed a notice in a Krakow newspaper, thanking the doctors and nurses for their care of Edmund, while Karol viewed his death as a gesture of self-sacrifice towards the sick and dying. 'But how much more could the young boy take?' was the sentiment of friends and neighbours. He was as yet unable to join suffering with love, and at this moment the suffering dominated: 'When I was young sick people used to intimidate me,' he remarked many years later, so that he would shy away from looking at people who were in agonising pain, for they 'bore in their bodies a dread mystery'.

With a catch of recalled suffering in his delivery, speaking as pope on a visit to Jagiellonian University in 1979, John Paul mentioned Edmund: 'These are events that became deeply engraved in my memory, my brother's death perhaps even deeper than my mother's death – equally because of the special circumstances, one may say tragic ones, and in view of my greater maturity at the time.' He kept his brother's stethoscope all his life as a relic, taking it with him to the Vatican.

Life at school was tough and disciplined, a training for harsh times ahead. Karol wore a dark-blue uniform with 374, his school number, on it, at all times, both in and out of school. In summer it was compulsory to be indoors by nine at night – eight in the winter – and in the months following Mundek's death, Karol's class divided into two camps: one side, led by the cheerful Piotrowski twins, formed a Revellers' Club, dedicated to turn every possible occasion into a party. While not averse to parties, Karol led the opposing side, forming and leading a Circle of Abstinents, who took oaths not to drink alcohol or smoke but remain in physical and intellectual control of their faculties.

There was little to ameliorate the suddenness, as well as the sadness, of Mundek's death. But the influence of his father (exerting over him the consolatory power of the Holy Spirit) perhaps now gave way to a greater influence, someone whom Karol called in later years (as archbishop in 1964) 'the guide of my young and rather complicated soul'.

Father Kazimierz Figlewicz, a young bespectacled catechist and assistant at St Mary's, had become his confessor when Karol was just ten. Figlewicz recalls him as 'a rather tall boy, but rather on the fat side . . . very lively, very talented, very quick and very good. He had an optimistic nature, though, after a more careful look, one could discern the shadow of early orphanage'.

Karol became a fervent ministrant at the altar – 'Thanks to him I grew closer to the parish, became an altar server, and had a hand in organising the group of altar servers.' Figlewicz left Wadowice to go to Krakow Cathedral in the old Royal Castle of Wawel. Karol remained in contact. During the boy's fifth year of secondary school Figlewicz invited him to Krakow 'to take part in the Sacred Tridum, beginning with the Tenebrae service on the afternoon of Wednesday of Holy Week. The experience made a profound impression on me.'

From the study of Latin and Greek authors, and with his rapid facility for learning, Karol broadened his mind, memory and understanding of the European culture into which he had been born. Over the school gate through which he passed each day was written, in Latin, 'Come with pure robes, and with unsullied hands drink water from the source' ('Para cum veste venite, et minibus puris sumite fortis aquam'). Ever-present was the fusion of classical discipline with Christian purity.

The influence of a pre-Christian Rome and Greece became an integral component of his developing character. Roger Scruton, the English philosopher, outlines how Christianity is a creed community with a difference because from its beginnings in the Roman Empire, 'it internalised some of the ideas of imperial government; in particular . . . adopted and immortalised the greatest of all Roman achievements . . . the universal system of law as a means for the resolution of conflicts and the administration of distant provinces'. Scruton emphasises how St Paul, as a Roman citizen versed in the law, transformed the ascetic and self-denying religion of Christ 'into an organised form of worship . . . [and] shaped the early church through the legal idea of the *universitas*, or corporation'. Karol identified at once with both the structure of Roman law as incorporated into Christianity, and its foundation in the mystery and drama of the Passion.

Behind, or underpinning, the law was the power of the word. Karol deeply appreciated the power of the word in his literary and linguistic studies: 'The word, before it is ever spoken on the stage, is already present in human history as a fundamental dimension of man's spiritual experience. Ultimately, the mystery of language brings us back to the inscrutable mystery of God himself.' He inevitably drew closer to 'the mystery of the Word of which we speak every day in the Angelus: "And the Word became flesh and dwelt among us"'.

With his gift for the word, both in its use and in his precocious power of linguistic memory, Karol established himself as a star pupil at school, an exemplary scholar and leader in every respect. In records kept of his school year 1933/34 we glimpse him at meetings of the school chapter of the Anti-Aircraft and Gas Weapons Defence League, where he trained with rescue teams. The training was conducted by Boleslaw Drozdowski from the eighth-year class. Karol gave, notably, a presentation on 'Defending the City Against Gas Weapons'.

They held, so aware were they of national self-defence, an Anti-Aircraft and Gas Weapons Defence League week from 3–10 June 1934. Here Karol performed in a programme consisting of 1/ A

medley of songs (performed by the school orchestra), 2/ An indoc-
trination lecture (given by W. Balon), 3/ School choir, 4/ Poetry
recitation (K. Wojtyla), 5/ Chemical Warfare Defence Exercises in
the school courtyard.

On 14 June 1934 he completed his fourth year with the grade of
'Very Good' in all subjects. A notation by the grade for Religion reads:
'exhibits special predilection for the subject'. 'Religion' and 'Chemical
Warfare Defence Exercises' emphasise the semi-mobilised spirit of his
secondary education.

But of all the influences and early formative pressures on the young
Wojtyla, in the end we come back to his father. Now in his fifties, bald
and ageing fast, the 'Captain', as he was now generally known,
pursued his large appetite for Polish republican culture. He had
not been educated beyond the age of thirteen, when he left school;
and, brought up under the heel of an occupying empire, had had no
access to Polish history, language or literature, which were forbidden
subjects. Now, with the flowering of Polish nationalism, the glories of
the Habsburg empire (which were drummed into his ears during the
many years of military service – he won the Iron Cross of Merit during
the First World War for his part in the defence of Krakow against the
Russians) faded before the exploits of Polish patriots, their martyrdom, bravery and the resurrection of the country. He would ask his
son and their friends what they were reading. 'Ah, the wars against the
Swedes! Have you read Sienkiewicz? Do you want to hear about how
we survived the Thirty Years War?' And so on.

Karol senior was an excellent raconteur, setting scene after scene.
He brought to life 'the saintly Queen Jadwiga, who . . . united Poland
with Europe's last un-Christian nation, Lithuania, and made her
country into a bulwark against the Turks, and for a while, a European
power'. He reminded his listeners that the tombs of these great Poles
were on their doorstep in Wawel Cathedral. They saw a very different,
more extrovert, Karol senior from the widower who was a solitary,
devout and pious communicant who never remarried. He told also, his
baritone voice rising and falling with dramatic inflection, stories of
Ancient Greece and Rome – 'how Aeneas carried his father, Anchises,
piggyback through the burning ruins of Troy on their way to an
escape by sea that led him to found Rome. Every story conveyed some
character isolated by a deed.'

Perhaps what Karol learned most from his remarkable father was the idea of the 'creative interaction' of persons. He meant by this that we become ourselves by virtue of our relationships with others. In terms of father and mother he believes that, although both are separate entities, they 'give birth' to each other as they assume motherhood and fatherhood. He imbibed from his own father 'the nucleus of a drama. One could argue that all dramas in the world describe the course of interaction – the creative one and the destructive one.'

From boyhood on Wojtyla saw life as drama. For the isolated child, communication became of paramount importance. He also saw fatherhood as of supreme value, asserting in *The Radiation of Fatherhood*, for example:

> If you are to be born of your father, you must first penetrate
> the depths of his will . . .

During his father's life, Karol never once spoke to him about a vocation to the priesthood, but later acknowledged that 'his example was in a way my first seminary, a kind of domestic seminary'.

His father taught him to be outward-looking and open to the world, to renounce the idea that anything is 'mine'. He could distil later from his extraordinary memory the feelings his father awoke in him, learning through him 'what it means to be a father; it means having the strongest bonds with the world . . . so let us shape the world together!'

If one lost 'faith in one's own fatherhood [think, child],/then only pain is possible'; he understood also, in that dramatic sense of interaction, how 'Fathers return through their children'; and how 'The father always revives in the soil of a child's soul'; he was

> embedded in me with his roots, *like another, parallel, tree trunk . . .*
> everything grows out of one system, out of common roots.
> So did father grow in me through mother,
> and I was their unity.

Karol senior functioned not only as his son's first seminary, he was also his son's first playhouse. For here, bold in its appeal, was the direction his son followed in the next few years – the theatre.

3

When the Ship Is Sinking, What Is Private?

(1934–39)

The internal difficulties of the new Poland, a third of whose thirty million people belonged to racial minorities (the largest being four and a half million Ukrainians), grew enormously during the first five years of Karol's secondary education, and strongly affected his mental outlook.

The million white Russians (Belorussians) in the north-east, and the 750,000 ethnic Germans in the west threatened Poland's uneasy peace, for either of her powerful neighbours could foment trouble on their behalf.

The three and a half million Jews, spread all over Poland, had no power base inside the country, and no patron foreign power to support their rights and interests, so, as elsewhere in Western Europe in the worsening financial situation, they increasingly became targets of prejudice, and on a national and personal level blamed and attacked as scapegoats. Poland was also riven by active class distinctions, and its people's own extreme awareness of rank and hierarchy. Although a backward society, mainly agrarian and poor, it possessed an intellectual élite with strong cultural and political aspirations. The new constitution in principle introduced democracy, but ninety-two officially registered political parties had resulted in fourteen separate governments between 1918 and 1925 ('Three Poles,' runs the joke, 'four parties'). In 1926, after two days of heavy fighting with government forces, fourteen regiments under Marshal Pilsudski took over the country. Pilsudski exercised power benevolently, introducing reforms

and allowing highly articulate and hostile opposition groups to
continue in an elected parliament of heavily curtailed powers.

Pilsudski led an army which was tolerant of Jews and many officers
were Jewish, fiercely patriotic, at the same time retentive of their
religious practices. On the right of society there flourished a neo-
fascist, patriotic National Democratic Party. This stigmatised Jews as
foreign and Christ-killers. On the extreme left was a small but
vociferous communist party, containing paradoxically many Jews.

Marshal Jozef Pilsudski died of liver and stomach cancer in 1935.
As decreed in his will, his heart was removed and taken to Vilnius, to
be placed alongside his mother's remains, while his brain was sent to
Warsaw's Institute of Anatomy for research purposes. The remainder
of his body was buried in Wawel Cathedral alongside the kings of
Poland. There was national mourning. While Pilsudski was criticised
heavily on all sides, notably by Archbishop Prince Sapieha in the
Catholic hierarchy, for his 1926 *coup d'état*, after his death Poland
sank into internecine conflict.

He had towered above other Polish leaders. He was the military
hero and leader of stature, the *de facto* dictator (he took the title of
defence minister) during the first decade and a half of Karol's life.
Most of those fifteen years were stable, while for any young man of
strong patriotic pride and deep religious devotion, Pilsudski must have
remained a strong example. But in the 1930s the life of politics and the
exalted life of the national myth were diverging too far. Karol drew a
conclusion, perhaps only later when he reflected on it, from the
example of Pilsudski, namely that a successful national leader has
to have a vision to capture the secret imagination of his people, and so
foster and enhance the vitality of his nation. Pilsudski, a severe realist
who considered throughout his life that the relationships with France
and Great Britain were illusory, 'exotic' alliances, had no such vision.
He did not embody the fantasy or aspirations of the nation and create
a republic which was to last after his death. Karol, in search of heroes,
did not find them among dictators or military leaders or, it must be
said, democratic leaders such as he saw around him in Poland.
Already attuning himself to modern thought, by the age of seventeen
he was reading Karl Marx's *Das Kapital* in German.

One of the bases of the 1920 republic had been Catholic-Jewish
union and co-operation. In September 1935 the Nuremberg Laws
proclaimed in Germany abolished German citizenship for Jews, de-

fined as people who had three Jewish grandparents. These laws forbade sexual contact and marriage between Aryans and Jews, reducing the latter to the status of a subject race. Jews, as for some time in practice, now legally could not be civil servants, doctors, journalists, farmers, teachers, actors, artists, writers, bankers, administrators or politicians.

The effects of this intolerance reverberated through Poland: the expression of the violent prejudice was no longer taboo. In the year following Pilsudski's death, as Poland drifted towards disintegration, Augustin Hlond, the cardinal primate of Poland, argued in a pastoral letter that there would be a Jewish problem as long as Jews remained in Poland: that it was a 'fact that the Jews are fighting against the Catholic Church, persisting in free thinking, and are the vanguard of godlessness, Bolshevism, subversion . . . It is a fact that the Jews deceive, levy interest, and are pimps. It is a fact that the religious and ethical influence of the Jewish young people on Polish people is a negative one.'

Marshal Edward Smigly-Rydz led the junta that took over power from Pilsudski with nationalist and Catholic support. Their popular calls to unity underlined the growth of the anti-Semitic virus that was now rapidly infecting Catholic-Jewish co-operation. Typical of the mood was the cartoon of a rapacious, bald-headed Jew with enormous nose, claws for hands, striped trousers and swallow-tailed coat of a banker, chucking an evicted Gentile family into a muddy ditch: it appealed to fellow countrymen that they were being murdered by Jews and yet kept supporting them. Polish consciousness had to wake up. 'Let the innocent blood of our comrades stand before you when you are about to commit a deed calling for God's revenge, when you are about to carry money to a Jew . . . Avoid your enemy the Jew.'

In a private meeting in December 1937 between French and Polish foreign ministers, Jozef Beck, who had fallen for the deceptive German call for *rapprochement* with Poland, raised the matter of his country's desire to be rid of her Jews, suggesting Madagascar as a possible refuge.

On the other hand the pro-Jewish Canon Prochownik (who had buried Karol's mother, Emilia) had a very different message for Karol. Now pastor of St Mary's, he spoke out against the economic boycott of Jews, insisting that to be anti-Semitic was to be anti-Christian. So did Pope Pius XI, a former Hebrew scholar and man of cultural distinction who had also written a book on mountain-climbing. He denounced anti-Semitism both in his measured encyclical *With a Burning Doubt* (specially published in German as *Mit brennender Sorge* instead of Latin) – 'Whoever exalts race, or the people, or the state distorts and prevents an order of the world created by God' (14 March 1937) – and in informal, angry outbursts as he did before Belgian pilgrims on 6 September 1938: 'It is not possible for Christians to participate in anti-Semitism. Spiritually we are Semites!'

Despite such attempts at conciliation, an atmosphere of mistrust and isolation took hold. Karol's friend Jerzy was the son of the lawyer known as the head of the local Jewish community, and following new regulations he was obliged to print his name in Hebrew on his office door, to identify him as someone to be avoided by good Polish Catholics. While some in Karol and Kluger's class were anti-Jewish, mainly with the belief that Jews were Bolsheviks, tolerance remained the dominant note of Wadowice's religious and historical instruction. But even here the situation could suddenly deteriorate. When in the spring of 1938 Radical Nationalist thugs smashed Jewish shop-fronts in the Rynek, threatening those who did not boycott the shops, Professor Gebhardt, Karol's history teacher, a socialist who wore a bright red cravat (Poland, land of symbols again), severely charged his class not to be intimidated.

The Janus face of Poland was dramatically demonstrated by Kalwaria Zebrzydowska, to which father and son went at Easter and for the August Feast of the Assumption. The Polish version of the Easter passion play in particular, featuring the children of Abraham and Moses as Christ's killers, and the anti-Jewish Good Friday observances were often followed by violence against Jews. As Kluger reports, 'As with all melodrama, the touchstone of audience reaction is the loathsome villain.' While Wadowice itself remained more quiet, 'Jews in surrounding villages and towns dreaded Holy Week as a time that was sure to bring out the latent contempt and hostility among some members of the Catholic majority.' And in the passion play, without any basis in Scripture these inflammatory words were given to Christ: 'I have planted for thee My most beautiful vineyard: and thou has proved very bitter to Me; for in My thirst thou gavest Me vinegar to drink; and with a spear thou has pierced the side of thy Saviour.'

In the main church of the Bernardine monastery in Kalwaria a large, anonymous, seventeenth-century painting was another Holy Week attraction for anti-Semitic Catholics. Each year its macabre imagery, prominently positioned, affected thousands, either repelling them or inciting them to racial feeling.

> It showed Christ falling under his cross as a throng of Jews, made to look like animals – with claws for hands, stained, jagged teeth, and evil eyes – tore, kicked, and spat at him. After seeing this enacted on the stage, its image burned in the minds of pilgrims as they took their journeys homeward. That was when the trouble always started.

The Wojtylas traditionally attended the passion play, so we can be sure Karol saw and registered an experience which affected him profoundly.

Another extreme aspect of Polish religious life that engraved itself on Karol's memory and remained with him as an influence was the Mariavite schismatic church. Founded by a Sister of St Clare, Felicja Kozlowska, in Plock, a small town on the Vistula north of Warsaw, this movement strove in its veneration of the Holy Sacrament to emulate Mary. It crossed over into heresy when its one-eyed foundress, from the miraculous visions and instruction she claimed to have received from God in 1893, furthered the idea of 'spiritual marriages' between nuns and priests (sexuality being conceived as a means of advancing their spirituality). In 1906 Pius X excommunicated the new order, which was now under the direction of a Father Jan Kowalski, but as a schismatic church it grew, continued to think of itself as Catholic, and three years later the Old Catholic Church of Utrecht, under its archbishops, received the 200,000 Mariavites into communion, while the Russian religious authority recognised them as a valid church.

Kowalski, ordained as bishop by the Archbishop of Utrecht in 1909, and now married, became with his wife progressively more heretical, celebrating the 'mystic' union between priests and nuns in the actual marriage ceremony, ordaining, in 1928, nuns as priests. In their sacrilegious idealism the Mariavites believed in immaculate conception for themselves, and a new and sinless race of angelic beings. The Old Catholic Church of Utrecht repudiated its tie with the Mariavites, and later, when persecution of the Mariavites increased, Kowalski ordained more and more women and abolished confession and the use of holy water.

This episode, directly experienced by the devout Karol in early life, ended in savage suppression by the Nazis, who sent Kowalski to Dachau, where he died. From the start of Karol's life the ordination of women carried dramatic associations of heresy, persecution and unending religious conflict.

'Tell me who influences you and I will tell you who you are,' wrote Jean-Louis Barrault, the French actor who famously played Baptiste in *Les Enfants du Paradis*, but also incarnated the French poet and dramatist Paul Claudel's Catholic heroes in the French theatre from the 1920s to the 1940s. From the age of fourteen or thereabouts, Karol fell under the spell of the spoken word and the theatre.

Mundek had introduced him to Mieczyslaw Kotlarczyk, a Polish teacher who had a passion for theatre. But it was not until 1934 that Karol visited Kotlarczyk at home to find stage sets, people dressed in costumes, handling props and speaking in assumed voices. He sat in on a rehearsal, at once mesmerised, then joined Kotlarczyk's youth theatre group. From this time on, his leisure hours and entertainment were mainly filled by his own representations, in voice and action, of heroes and villains.

Yet from the beginning religious conviction shaped Karol's view of art and of the theatre. No more powerful expression of this conviction in a writer can be found than in a letter written in 1905 by Claudel to André Gide; 'As for what people call "Art" and "Beauty",' Claudel tells Gide, 'I had rather that they perished a thousand times over than that we should prefer such creatures to their Creator and the futile constructions of our imagination to the reality in which alone we may find delight.'

Claudel chastises Gide for 'the preferring of things for their own sake, and the considering of them as nothing more than that, and the liking of them for what they are not . . .' and sees the basis of a whole art, brilliant and generous, in the chapter in Proverbs when the Spirit of God moves over chaos in sublime liberty. Art is 'an exclamation and an acclamation, a counting and a conferring of Graces, like the Canticle of the young men in the fiery furnace, like St Francis of Assisi's Canticle of the Sun'.

Claudel scorns modern art, 'from which everything of real substance has been taken away, and with it that powerful source of youth inherent only in the heavenly *naturalness* that animates Homeric poetry, for example . . .' The classical education Karol received at school, the symbolism of Polish art and literature, the ritual drama of Catholic religious observance: all these propelled Karol towards developing similar feelings. In particular the 'great ethical power of the theatre' – as well as the actor's art of mimesis, of putting oneself into the skin of another and speaking in, and impersonating, a different identity – seized Karol from the very beginning. This power, as he says, is most manifest in *Hamlet*'s play within the play, when by depicting the murder of Gonzago by his brother he provokes Claudius's guilt and catches 'the conscience of the king'.

The friendship between Mieczyslaw Kotlarczyk and Karol flourished. Eight years older than Karol, Kotlarczyk was born in 1912 in Wadowice. By education a philologist, he was student, then master and doctor of Polish philology at the Jagiellonian. Karol said how he enriched, with his enthusiasm and original approach to drama – first of all in amateur theatre – the cultural life of Wadowice. Karol recalls Kotlarczyk went to Salzburg one summer festival to see *Jedermann* and *Faust*.

'In the same period he was awarded a doctorate for his thesis about the critical work of the X Society [a Warsaw group of theatre critics who from 1815–19 signed their reviews with the pseudonymous X], and his interests in religious theatre took shape.'

Kotlarczyk taught at the Carmelite Fathers' high school for girls. Temperamentally fierce, he answered a need in Karol for a more immediate passion and commitment than that which the church supplied. Kotlarczyk's father ran one of Wadowice's amateur theatres in which the son acted. From the start Kotlarczyk picked Karol to play leads. In his flat Kotlarczyk coached the sixteen-year-old Halina Krolikiewicz, daughter of Karol's headmaster, who became his most frequent leading lady. Kotlarczyk's sister describes her brother giving demonstrations of how speeches should be recited, walking up and down the apartment while Karol followed, trying but not always succeeding in copying him.

'I got to know him,' said Karol later, 'as the pioneer of an original theatre, in the noblest sense of the word; as an exponent of the true Polish and Christian traditions of that art, traditions passed on to us by all our literature, and especially by the great romantic and neoromantic literature.'

The well-known poet dramatists who became so much in vogue in the early days of the new Polish republic, such as Adam Mickiewicz,

Juliusz Slowacki, and Cyprian Norwid, had much in common with Shakespeare and other patriotic English poets in Elizabethan times; by the standards of the West today, they can appear transcendental, high-flown and dangerously nationalistic. Mickiewicz's poetic drama *Dziady* (*Forefather's Eve*), for example, identified Poland's destiny through its redemptive sufferings, as the Messiah among nations. Slowacki shared a mysticism of spirit with Mickiewicz, but he also had the gift of prophecy, foretelling a future Slav pope who – unlike the Italian Pius IX, who in 1848 ran away from Rome in disguise – would not abandon Poland:

> Amid discord God strikes
> At a bell immense,
> For a Slavic Pope,
> He opened the throne.
> This one will not flee the sword,
> Like that Italian.
> Like God, He will bravely face the sword,
> For Him, world is dust . . .
> So behold, here comes the Slavic Pope,
> A brother of the people.

Cyprian Norwid attracted Karol by his more quiet and searching intellectuality. He, like Claudel, rejected art for art's sake: 'A man is born on this planet to give testimony to truth,' he writes in the prologue to *Promethidion* – and the 'great truth' that has to be witnessed is that 'Christ had led man out of the realm of fatality and into the realm of freedom'. Literature was a means of seeking and testing the truth of reality. Through such works as *Portrait of an Artist* and *Promethidion*, a poetic exaltation of Polish freedom, Norwid became more of a lasting influence on Karol than Mickiewicz and Slowacki, for he had more of a philosophical, enquiring bent of mind. According to Jerzy Kluger, Wojtyla senior read aloud to them Norwid's critical essays on Chopin's music (mazurkas, polonaises and of course the famous marching song that became Poland's national anthem in 1920 – 'Poland has not vanished so long as we live').

Influenced by his father, John Paul II retained a lifelong affection and respect for Norwid, regretting in later life that the playwright had fallen into neglect. But the autodidact father interspersed his readings with war stories, and interrogations on Polish history dates. As the Pope tells André Frossard, not without a touch perhaps of ruefulness – for how could he escape them or their influence? – 'during all my childhood, I listened to veterans of World War One, talking about endless horrors of battle.'

While still at school, Karol performed in ten plays between 1934 and 1938, invariably as the male lead, and he also, according to his Polish teacher, Kazimierz Forys, did much of the directing. As well as the two roles, chorus and hero, he played in Slowacki's *Balladyna*, he took over the prompting in Aleksander Fredro's *Virgins' Vows*, although still playing the lead, as he knew all the parts by heart (and therefore did not need the book). He acted Haemon in Sophocles' *Antigone* and the Apostle-narrator in a version of *St John's Apocalypse*; he played the poet-hero Count Henryk in *The Un-Divine Comedy* by Zygmunt Krasinski, the title roles in *Kordian* by Slowacki and *Sulkowski* by Stefan Zeromski: all three, plays of revolution and national liberation. He enjoyed comedy, playing the leading roles in Fredro's *Lady and Hussars* as well as *Virgins' Vows*, but he returned to serious romantic drama as the Polish king whose marriage to a commoner is opposed by the nobility (*King Sigismund Augustus*, by Stanislaw Wyspianski).

Finally he performed the title role in *Judas Iscariot* by Karol Hubert Rostworowski, whose mixture of verse and psychology with mystery and morality-play procedures caught his imagination and influenced him when he came to write plays of his own, which he began to do in his eighteenth year. He learned and performed two big parts a year and at such an early age this provided a formidable education in itself. Destiny had at once singled him out as a heavyweight.

The theatre also provided the backdrop for Karol's first romantic – and apparently platonic – link with a girl: Regina, the daughter of the Beers family who lived alongside the Wojtylas at No. 2 Rynek.

Ginka was two years older than Karol – black-eyed, beautiful and reputedly the most brilliant girl in her year at the high school. Living in such close proximity they must always have known one another, but the friendship reached a high point when the director cast Karol as Gucio opposite Ginka: she recalls, 'There was a lot of excitement in our building when, still a school-girl, I auditioned for the leading female role of a lover in a French [-influenced] play (*Virgins' Vows*). After I was chosen I heard Lolek also decided to try his luck. He was good-looking and as a result was given the lead as my stage lover.'

On stage she was impressive, with a talent for comedy and satire in particular; off-stage she was irrepressible. 'Her wit, her laughter that bubbled like a pot on the boil, the tiny space between her teeth – everything' – to Jerzy Kluger, at least three years her junior – 'was entrancing.' Top scholar in science, she hoped to follow in the footsteps of Maria Sklodowska (better known as Mme Curie). Ginka's heroine was her headmistress, a war hero from the 1920 campaign and it seemed in Karol's homeland that women had a status, a list of achievements in science and warfare to their credit, that put them well ahead of their Anglo-Saxon equivalents in Karol's developing awareness of society and the world.

Ginka organised the school theatrical club into a thriving regional theatre, inviting well-known professionals to come down and judge and award prizes for performances. Together with Karol she was the driving force behind the productions. Ginka's husband in later years claims that 'Karol was crazy about her' – this out of earshot of his wife – but Ginka demurely observed: 'I must admit that I enjoyed his company, but of course there was no question of a romance. What girl of eighteen thinks of a boy of sixteen in that direction? Anyway, he was a Catholic and I never forgot I was Jewish, which was very important to me.'

They did enjoy playing passionate scenes together in *Virgins' Vows*. They were described in Wadowice's *The Voice of the Young* as 'an absolute success. Gucio (Mr Wojtyla) and Aniela were most convincing as young lovers.' This witty, Molièresque play, written in 1833, toured locally, giving rise possibly to part of the later rumours, just after Karol was elected pope, that he had a love affair in his youth. This 'investigation' of a mooted affair, by two Italians, was published in their *Il Pastore Venutu* and featured on the front page of the *Corriere della Sera*. It was even suggested that Wojtyla married at this time. Yet, aside from these rumours, forcefully dismissed, Karol knew both directly and indirectly through the parts he played and those he played them with, the feelings of being in love.

Ginka applied to study medicine at the Jagiellonian in Krakow, but but there was now increasing pressure to exclude Jews; formerly a quarter of the university population was Jewish, but towards the end of the 1930s only those with special privileges or connections were admitted. The school headmistress lobbied for Ginka, and as she had fought in Pilsudski's Legion and been decorated with the Virtuti

Militari, the highest Polish military decoration, she prevailed. Ginka left to study, but shortly was back, for the girl she shared lodgings with in Krakow had a communist boyfriend, and one day he was followed by the police back to their rooms, where he was arrested. She felt guilt by association and feared action by the authorities against her.

Ginka obtained permission to go and work in Palestine, so she took her chance among the panic flight of thousands of Jews. South American countries were tightening immigration controls, so was the United States – 'Fewer than seven thousand Jews, a figure that included both Catholics and Jews, succeeded in obtaining visas to emigrate there during the late 1930s.' You survived where you could.

She had to tell Karol she was leaving but felt deep reluctance, knowing how popular she was with Polish boys and girls. 'There was only one family,' she said, 'who never showed any racial hostility toward us, and that was Lolek and his dad.' When she went to say goodbye to Lolek and his father,

> Mr Wojtyla was upset about my departure, and when he asked me why, I told him. Again and again he said to me, 'Not all Poles are anti-Semitic. You know I am not!'
>
> I spoke to him frankly and said that very few Poles were like him. He was very upset. But Lolek was even more upset than his father. He did not say a word, but his face went very red. I said farewell to him as kindly as I could, but he was so moved that he could not find a single word in reply. So I just shook the father's hand and left.

Ginka and Karol met again in the late 1980s when, as pope, at a general audience in St Peter's Square, he heard her name shouted out by fellow Wadowiceans who came to pay him homage. His recall was instant and when he summoned her she asked if he really remembered her: 'Of course I do,' he answered. 'You are Regina. We lived in the same house. How is your sister, Helen?'

She had to tell him that Helen and her mother died in Oswiecim (Auschwitz – which was only thirty miles from Krakow and thirty-five miles from Wadowice), while her father was killed in the Soviet Union.

'He just looked at me, and there was deep compassion in his eyes . . . He took both my hands and for almost two minutes he blessed me and prayed before me, just holding my hands in his hands. There were thousands of people in the Square, but for just a few seconds there were just the two of us.' In another report she described how 'Like the 16-year-old in Wadowice, again he was lost for words. As he turned back to face me I sensed immediately that he was as moved as I was to meet again. The expression in his eyes also told me that he was the same lovely Lolek whom I used to walk with to and from the theatre.'

Kasia Zak was another member of the drama club; her attractive looks and aura of mystery tantalised the boys in the group and in audiences; while apparently her vagueness suited the abstract poetic quality of much of the Polish-Romantic repertoire they performed. Kotlarczyk's sister Janina described Kasia as having 'a sunburnt complexion, beautiful long blond hair, and very blue eyes'. In Slowacki's *Balladyna* in 1937 Kasia played love scenes with Karol, who played the hero. According to Janina, Karol ended one scene saying, 'I wish this was real.' Kasia gave him a high-spirited brush-off, 'Potrzebuje Tego' – 'This is just what I need!' – flattering Karol with her rejection.

Although there is scant evidence as to how deeply they were involved with one another, Halina Krolikiewicz was his most frequently mentioned girlfriend. She played many more leading roles opposite Karol than Ginka. Four months older than him, Halina was blonde and statuesque, and she projected a precocious dignity similar to Karol's. Her father was headmaster of Karol's school, and he also taught Karol Greek. He was, according to Halina, a very severe and exacting man who would never countenance his daughter becoming a professional. When Halina and Karol were also rehearsing for *Balladyna*, the boy playing Kostryn, the evil villain, threatened to shoot one of the teachers at school if he gave him a low grade. Halina's father expelled the boy.

Halina recalls that this suspension forty-eight hours before they were due to open wreaked havoc and dismay among the cast. 'Lolek suggested quietly, blushing with embarrassment, that he could play both roles because the noble Kirkor dies rather early, and he would have time to change costumes and to play the ignoble Kostryn.' She asked him how he could learn the role: 'Oh,' he told her. 'It's easy. I know it already.' It seemed he had all the parts memorised, as if this was any actor's normal preparation. 'So it may be,' she told him, 'for you!'

Halina, like Ginka, denied any special romantic attachment, but it seems Karol came closer to her than to any other young woman.

Halina tells us only that 'Once he was asked to play the part of a seducer with me as the girl who fell for his charms.' Both decided to study Polish literature at Krakow University. 'We liked being together. We talked very much walking along the River Vistula, which crosses Krakow. Our conversations were mostly about the theatre.'

How close or how deep the contact went is a matter for speculation. English journalist and editor Charles Moore, after a papal interview, claimed that Wojtyla surely had a direct experience of a love affair in his early years. A Roman journalist went even further, telling Moore, 'This pope – good-looking bloke and all that. He must have slept with a girl, mustn't he?' Biographers assure us that the answer to the question is 'no', added Moore, 'but the remark strikes me as a sort of compliment. This pope is in no sense worldly, but he is a man for whom the world, human flesh and blood, is utterly real.' Paul Johnson, in a book about the Pope published in 1982, guessed the same; exploring how little his upbringing had been sheltered, and how wide his experience became, Johnson goes on to speculate: 'He had girlfriends. He experienced the normal emotional relationships of a virile and exceptionally gifted and intelligent young man. After recognizing his vocation he embraced chastity.' The implication, plainly, is that before he became a priest he had some knowledge of the opposite sex from personal involvement. This would seem to be so.

Later, powerful and important relationships with women continued, although entirely chastely, yet this fired up the erotic energy, which was not acted upon but certainly there, and which was closely bound up with his creative power. The first were with female students with whom, after he took holy orders in 1946, he went on camping trips in the mountains, and with whom he held explicit discussions about sex. From the start it was always clear to everyone with whom he came into contact that Karol's attitude to women was far from that of the stereotype male who relegated women to the kitchen and the nursery. Always the centre of attention for admiring women of all ages, the intense 'cross-gender' friendships he formed in those years were to continue throughout his life, and become centred on personal and intellectual preoccupations instead of the theatre. Unlike many who were to surround him later in the Vatican, he was a man before he was a priest.

There was of course nothing wrong with a celibate priest feeling desire. Was he proving to himself that in steering carefully through the perilous waters of desire, his celibacy was trustworthy? Was he testing himself? There was no reason to believe he put himself deliberately into occasions of sin. Yet as we shall see – and even as Nietzsche wrote – the degree and kind of a person's sexuality has repercussions on the very summits of his or her spirituality.

From 1936 to 1938 Wojtyla presided over his school branch of Marian Sodality, a religious body of persons established for devotions to the cult of the Virgin Mary. This began a very personal and lifelong commitment to the belief that everything could be entrusted to Mary because she was the 'sign of the woman' spoken of in the Book of Revelation. She was the sign of salvation for the history of the world. But there was nothing strident, or even very public, about Karol's commitment to faith. A classmate recalls him saying how, when asked, he was not going to become a priest – 'Non sum dignus' – 'I am not worthy' – while even a year or two later he told a historian that he decisively rejected the notion. A mixture of devotion, national service – he did this compulsorily in 1938, working the summer on the roads – theatrical activity, and a host of other interests such as music and learning foreign languages was forming a very complex human being.

He began, too, at this time, to compose poetry. He was to remark, much later, on the publication of a collection of poems by priests, that 'Poetry is a great lady to whom one must completely devote oneself: I fear that I haven't been entirely correct toward her.'

Marek Skwarnicki, a poet and journalist from Krakow who first met Karol in 1957 as poetry editor of *Tygodnik Powszechny*, believes Karol began to write poems in high school: 'A few poems of the kind any high school's graduate might write'. But the subjects were far removed from today's adolescent preoccupations. One, 'Ballads of the Beskidy', centres on the mountain chain rising beyond Wadowice, others, on a religious sculptor called Wowro who lived in the Carpathian Mountains.

At the end of his school years in Wadowice both father and son decided to move to Krakow, where Karol was to take up a place at the Jagiellonian University. Before they left, the Metropolitan Archbishop of Krakow, Prince Adam Stefan Sapieha, visited the parish of Wadowice: this was Karol's first encounter with this influencial cleric.

My religion teacher, Father Edward Zacher [he said later], chose me to give the address of welcome. It was the first time I had the opportunity of being in the presence of that man who was so highly regarded by everyone. I know that after my speech the Archbishop asked the religion teacher what university course I would be taking upon completion of secondary school. Father Zacher replied: 'He will study Polish language and letters.' The Archbishop apparently replied: 'A pity it is not theology.'

(Sapieha also in May 1938, a fortnight before his eighteenth birthday, confirmed him in St Mary's Church.)

During his last years at school while others thought of military careers he had often thought of becoming a priest. Several of his classmates had already enrolled in the Polish army: 'I believe the first to die in the war,' he said later, 'was the youngest member of our class.' Whatever he was doing, whether it was play, study or sport, he broke off constantly for prayer: a school friend Antoni Bohdanowicz reports in a memoir, 'after completing the assignment in each subject Lolek would leave the kitchen, going into the next room, and returning after a few minutes. Once the door was not closed well, and I saw that Lolek was on a prieu-dieu kneeling in prayer.' One day his classmate Danuta Michalowska pinned a card to his desk on which was written 'Karol Wojtyla Apprentice Saint'. Yet at this time Karol still felt that his *vocation to the priesthood had not yet matured* (his italics). Many people around him thought that he should enter a seminary. But he had other interests. Perhaps some people thought that if a young person with such evident religious inclinations did not enter the seminary, it had to be a sign that there were other loves or interests involved.

'Certainly,' he said, 'I knew many girls from school and, involved as I was in the school drama club, I had many opportunities to get together with other young people. But this was not the issue. At that time I was completely absorbed by a passion for *literature*, especially *dramatic literature*, and for the *theatre*.' (Wojtyla's italics)

By the standards of today to take your father with you to college seems ludicrous and restrictive, for university has become, in the rites of passage, the first flight from the parental nest, the first taste of independence. Financial considerations must have loomed large in

Karol's and his father's decision to move to Krakow together. They owned no property, Karol senior had a meagre pension, and although Karol had a scholarship to the Jagiellonian University, it covered only tuition, not board and lodging.

Living in Krakow in 1938, among its quarter of a million inhabitants, Karol had no fear of impending catastrophe. In Poland there seemed little awareness of the sinister undertow of the powerful but unseen current towards war. Perhaps it was blind and deliberate euphoria, or a 'sufficient unto the day are the evils thereof' attitude. For Poles the 1934 bilateral pact made with Hitler still held good and reassured the Poles of Germany's peaceful intentions. When the Germans marched into Czechoslovakia in 1938 the Poles annexed the rest of Cieszyn, the Silesian region, the larger part of which was theirs.

Krakow was a small but relatively important intellectual and cultural centre, similar to Oxford in England. Like Oxford, Krakow was a blend of the old and the new. Like Oxford it had aristocratic and royal connections, ecclesiastical traditions, and a host of businesses and even industrial enterprises. It, too, was built astride a river, the Vistula, which flowed towards the country's capital city.

Unlike Oxford, however, Krakow had a thirteenth-century royal castle which dominated its skyline, and a fourteenth-century cathedral in which, for two centuries, before the royal capital moved to Warsaw, kings and queens of Poland's past patriotic glory – such as Queen Jadwiga, and Kazimierz the Great – were crowned and buried; the writers Adam Mickiewicz and Juliusz Slowacki were buried there too. This cathedral embodied 'the inextricable bonds between literature and religion, symbolizing how in the Polish sensibility, patriotism, piety, and poetry – along with music and art – intermingle as a single phenomenon'.

The significance of this affected young Wojtyla strongly: 'The sanctuary of the nation . . . [which] cannot be entered without an inner trembling, without an awe, for here – as in few cathedrals of the world – is contained a vast greatness which speaks to us of the history of Poland, of all our past.'

Not far from these sublime embodiments of Poland's past, in Tyniecka Street, which borders the west bank of the Vistula just before the wide river makes a dramatic turn to the north, father and son moved into a very humble dwelling. Number 10, owned by Robert Kaczorowski, Karol's bachelor uncle, brother of his mother

Emilia, who was a master leather craftsman, was less than twenty years old. Built by Robert himself, who lived with Anna and Rudolfina, his two unmarried sisters, on the two upper floors, it incorporated old brick materials and discarded doors and window frames. It turned out to be a substantial house with a gabled tiled roof and two chimneys, a sizeable garden, and with trees fronting on to the street that overlooks the Vistula.

Karol's flat was in the basement, reached by its own front door under the staircase up to the rest of the house. This comprised two rooms – one large, one small – a narrow kitchen, and a bathroom. The two households did not have much to do with one another; presumably, with the meagre army pension and no other work, the Wojtylas were the poor relations, and little or no rent was demanded. Perhaps the maternal relations looked down on the unfortunate, death-blighted household of father and son, but if so, or if Karol regretted not receiving more help from them, nothing much is known of this, and no reference made to them in future years. All three had died by 1962, leaving the house empty and without an inheritor.

Straitened circumstances apart, it was a magnificent and stimulating position in which to be, five minutes' walk from the Debnicki bridge, where the attractive mixed working- and middle-class suburb of Debnicki begins, and twenty minutes' walk from the centre of town and the university.

Karol now owned only one crumpled black jacket, a long tweed overcoat for winter days, and rough-cloth trousers. His shoes, repaired and maintained by his father, were in reasonable shape, but from his own inclination he never wore a tie. The bohemian look was crowned by the black short-visor cap perched jauntily on his now-darkened blond locks. A romantic poet, sporting the 'Slowacki look' – after the raffish poet sometimes known as 'the Satan of poetry'.

Founded in the late fourteenth century by King Kazimierz the Great, Krakow had long been a centre of international learning. During his reign Kazimierz, paradoxically, brought from Germany around 50,000 refugee Jews, fleeing anti-Semitic persecution. He placed them under royal protection so firmly that they thrived and became the progenitors of the three and a half million Jews who were to be liquidated during the occupation. The Dr Faustus legend originated in Krakow, while among its distinguished scholars there figured in the late fifteenth century Nicolaus Kopernik (or Copernicus in Latinised form), the Polish astronomer who discovered that the earth revolves round the sun and brought about the revolution in scientific thought that shook the world and the Catholic church to its very foundations.

As John Donne expressed it:

> And new Philosophy calls all in doubt,
> The Element of fire is quite put out . . .
> And freely men confess that this world's spent
> When in the Planets and the Firmament,
> They seek so many new.

When Karol moved to Krakow it had possibly the greatest concentration of theologians and priests in northern Europe. There were sixty Catholic churches and numerous synagogues for its 50,000 Jewish citizens. Karol attended mass daily at St Stanislaw Kostra, the Debnicki parish church three minutes away from his flat. Determined because of his love of literature to study Polish philology, he enrolled in the Philosophy Faculty of the university, which was housed at No. 20 Golebia Street. Here the overwhelming majority of students were women (again a contrast to Oxford and Cambridge in the 1930s), one of whom was his friend Halina. With her he resumed attending plays and poetry readings, and the theatrical activities they engaged in together at school.

His first-year curriculum was daunting:

Principles of Polish Entymology; Elements of Polish Phonetics; Theatre and Drama in Poland Since the Mid-Eighteenth Century, Including 'Spring of Peoples' Literature; Analysis of the Theory of Drama; Novels, Memoirs, and Letters of Stanislaw Brzozowski; Literature of the Polish Middle Ages; Exercises in Old Polish Literature; Dramatic Interpretation of Stanislaw Wyspianski; Russian Language Beginner's Course; Interpretation of Contemporary Lyricism; Polish History and Geography; Humour, Comicality, and Irony and Their Role in Literary Work; Exercises in the History of Polish Literature; Grammar of Old Church Slavonic [the language in which St Cyril and St Methodius preached in the ninth century, bringing Byzantine-rite Christianity to the Balkans and Russia]; Introduction to Russian Literature; and Character of Literary Antiquities.

Having taken up private study and tuition in French, he prepared and submitted a paper on Madame de Staël as a 'Theoretician of Romanticism'; he attended lectures outside his syllabus: one, for example, on the legend of St Alexis; another, significantly, on German schools of Christian ethics, which included an examination of the works of Max Scheler. St Alexis represented for Wojtyla his future apostolic development; Scheler, an influential Austrian phenomenologist, his philosophical bent.

So, in this halcyon year, intellectual horizons expanded with accelerated force. But Wojtyla, neither then nor later, was merely a solitary scholar: always poorly dressed, according to Danuta Michalowska, he appeared like a village boy 'socially unpolished but of strong character'. He had numerous friends but they were conspicuously more self-assured and gregarious. Notably he accompanied Anka Weber, a Jew, to protect her from potential aggression by members of the Pan-Polish Union. He revived his old ties with Father Figlewicz who had moved to Wawel Cathedral and who again became his confessor. How much part his ashen-faced father regularly played in these myriad activities is a moot point. His father, who remained his domestic base and anchor even when for a while Karol lodged in a student dormitory, no doubt with gratitude to God participated in his son's progress, and otherwise engaged in his reading and spiritual devotions. The static potentiality of the father gave impetus to Karol's growth.

But we are impressed at once by the excess of energy, the superabundance of passion, emotion and intellectual power in the son. He is quiet, he is private, he has – almost – a sardonic sense of humour not without its sly mocking quality. Everything goes into his study or the objects of his devotion. Caught up as he is in philological investigation of the roots of Polish language and literature, he writes more poetry, which he reads aloud at literary circles, collecting together a volume of verse he calls *The Renaissance Psalter: a Slav Book*, in which is a hymn, 'Magnificat', his own version of the canticle ascribed traditionally to the Virgin Mary. It is a rousing paean of praise, spoken in the voice of the spirit of Poland, an early indicator, if in deliberately antiquated metre and form, of his power to express broad feelings, to reach out to the universal.

> A Slav troubadour, I walk Your roads and play
> to maidens at the solstice, to shepherds with their flock,

> but, wide as this vale, my song of prayer
> I throw for You only, before your throne of oak.

Karol's birth-sign was that of Taurus, the Bull. It may appear frivolous to pursue this line of enquiry but specifically for 18 May, his birthday, the horoscope shows 'A steadfast and persevering personality. A strong healthy body coupled with good recuperative powers . . . generally Taureans have natural soothing and healing powers; they make a good partner for one with a highly strung nervous system' (the Catholic church, for example?). Taureans can also have – this one for future critics perhaps – a 'dominant obstinate nature, inbred with the idea that what they say must go. Conservative in their mannerisms and habits.'

How much he saw the popular traits of his star sign in himself may be glimpsed when Studio 39, his experimental university dramatic club, in 1939 staged the farce called *Knight of the Moon* by Nizynski for eight evening performances outdoors in the courtyard of the Collegium Maius, Krakow. With Halina, he and ten others played characters from the zodiac. Karol was cast as his birth-sign and, according to Halina, roaring and frolicking behind his huge horned, papier-mâché mask he became so engrossed that he persisted after the show was over, still in the Taurus mask, running around and bellowing, 'I am Taurus! I am the Bull.'

Halina, never to be daunted by anyone, reminded him that Taureans were reputed to show among their other characteristics stubbornness to the point of obstinacy. She reports that he did not appear to mind, even delighting in this, as if to say 'So I am!'

This much-applauded diversion, with its improvised skits on local personalities, delighted audiences. One night, Juliusz Osterwa, Poland's leading actor, sat in the audience and warmly applauded. But the mood in midsummer began to darken, as intelligence reports of troop movements brought the prospect of war nearer.

Students at Karol's university hanged and burnt Adolf Hitler in effigy at anti-Nazi rallies – but these were more about Hitler's threats against Poland and the derogatory Nazi characterisations of all Slavic peoples than Germany's treatment of Jews. Exalting as they did the Aryan race – whatever that was supposed to be – the Germans 'intensified racial consciousness everywhere, although it must be said that the racialist idea, a product of distorted Darwinism, had been in vogue long before anyone had ever heard of Hitler'.

Karol's own enthusiasm for Slavs, for instance, exhibited innocently enough in 'Magnificat' with its celebration of Slavic tribal customs and traditions – reverence for acorns and fantasies concerning whose hides in the old days made better thongs – had parallels within every European ethnic group as legitimate pride, too long crushed in Poland.

> The difference between young Wojtyla's ethnic pride and Hitlerism was as vast as the difference between love and hate, or as wide as the gap between Christ and Nietzsche. One had to do with love, the other with racial superiority and the hate that results from it. To love the little platoon into which one is born, as Edmund Burke phrased it, is the first germ of public, or human affections. Trouble begins when that platoon vilifies others and takes up the gun.

But fantastic self-deceptions were also at work, while the approach of death encouraged dancing and lovemaking.

In successive summer camps, with the 7th Battalion of the 9th Company of youth works, based at Zubrzyca Gorna, Karol worked building a road and performed chores such as potato-peeling. In Krakow, on 5 and 6 August 1939, just weeks before its crushing humiliation, the Polish army celebrated the twenty-fifth anniversary of the forming of the very first detachment of Pilsudski's Legion. A military parade and march-past was held, during which Marshal Smigly-Rydz received from Krakow's children a wooden cannon and doll in army nurse's uniform.

Each evening in *Knight of the Moon* for an audience of Poland's military élite Karol in his bull mask played Taurus. On the penultimate day of the same month Karol reported at the Headquarters of the Academic Legion, with whom he had trained at summer camp to hand in the four-cornered cap, cloth puttees and infantry trousers, linen foot clouts, leather brogans and belt of the full military uniform he was never to wear again. These were needed urgently by the overstretched, under-equipped Polish army. In view of the deprivation to come he had reason to regret their loss.

4

Vita Cracoviensis

(1939)

Early in the morning of the first day of war, Karol and his father heard the drone of bombers and the explosion of bombs falling on the railroad yards and other industrial targets in the suburbs of Krakow. It was Karol's habit to attend mass on the first Friday of every month in echo or commemoration of Good Friday, so he still set out for Wawel Cathedral to confess, join in the mass, receive the Host. Karol's bald statement of what happened hides unspoken emotion: 'I will never forget the day of 1 September 1939: it was the first Friday of the month. I had gone to Wawel for confession; the Cathedral was completely empty. That was perhaps the last time that I was able to enter the church freely.'

The sudden but well-prepared German invasion of Poland began on three fronts, two from the west, and the other from the south. The Soviet invasion from the east was soon to follow. Over the next years the Germans killed nearly one fifth of the population, over six million Poles in all, Jews and Gentiles in roughly equal proportions.

The Polish army had reasonable plans for defence, but with the Molotov-Ribbentrop non-intervention pact allying the Russians to the Germans, and the French and British failing to respond by attacking Germany from the west, as they had promised, the combination of blitzkrieg air and armoured-column attacks overwhelmed the heroic Polish defence.

During Karol's Friday mass the Luftwaffe returned. Father Figlewicz wrote: 'This first wartime Mass, before the altar of the Crucified Christ and in the midst of the scream of sirens and the thud of explosions, has remained forever in my memory.' Mass over, Karol walked on to the flat of friends, the Kydrynskis, more centrally situated than his own, where he and his fellow actor Juliusz started on plans to help move some belongings to a safer location. As they sought a handcart from neighbours, they took shelter when another raid began. They watched the unopposed Stukas swooping down to deliver their bombs, then retreated well inside the building. Kydrynski reports: 'We stood inside the house as it trembled on its foundations, and Karol was absolutely calm, not showing the slightest fear.' They silently faced one another, each with his back against a wall. 'But even if Karol was praying, he was praying in his soul, not even crossing himself. He stood there, very serious and calm.'

After returning to his father, whom Karol was fearful of leaving on his own, Karol senior and he discussed the future. They decided to leave Krakow, hopeful they would find temporary asylum and safety in the territory to the east, which would be behind the lines of the retreating Polish army. In spite of a weakened heart the 'Captain' was keen to go. He was mindful of the atrocities committed by the Germans only twenty or so years before in torching the town of Kalisz in central Poland, and others in Belgium, as well as the recent orchestrations of hate towards Poles. He had a good idea of what might be in store. With Karol carrying as much as they could take in a single suitcase, they left on foot the following day, determined to use what form of transport they could find on the way.

In the week that followed, while they trudged eastwards, the full impact of the German terror – savagely aimed at devastating by every means the identity of the Polish soul, its pride, its nationhood, its culture and church – descended on the west of Poland, soon to become requisitioned and brutally incorporated into the Third Reich. The Nazis closed down all schools, even elementary ones, and all the universities, murdering and pillaging at random, but also system-atically choosing and targeting high-ranking Polish figures in all walks of life in order to inflict maximum humiliation and mayhem.

In the northern town of Bydgoszcz, for one example, the mayor, Mr Barciszewski, had been ordered by the Polish government at the beginning of the war to leave and carry to Warsaw city funds and important municipal documents. Finding him gone the German authorities accused him of stealing the funds, so Barciszewski decided to return to defend himself against the charges. Granted safe conduct, and provided with authorisation to travel, he was subjected to a rigged trial, then sentenced to be shot. Before the set date for this he was bestially tortured, humiliated and forced in public to lick the mud off a Gestapo car with his tongue; for two days, with insulting inscriptions and the announcement of his execution hung around his neck, he was paraded in a cart through the streets of Bydgoszcz.

They massacred more than 100 high-school boys and scouts aged twelve to sixteen years of the same town, mowing them down with machine guns on the steps of the Jesuit church in the market place. As the boys died they sang the Polish national hymn: 'God who protects Poland'. They murdered whole families, laying out the bodies in the form of the swastika, 'The father constituting one arm, the mother a second arm, whilst the others were formed by the bodies of the children and relations.' All this killing the Germans justified with that peculiarly Nazi definition of the *raison d'être* of law: as Hans Frank, who became the Governor-General based in Krakow for the occupied territories known as the 'General Government', declared: 'Law is all that which serves the German people. Illegality is all that which is harmful to the people.'

On the roads running eastward from south and central Poland, on which the 'Captain' and Karol took their chance, the destruction of life was less systematic, more random. German planes bombed villages and country roads that had no strategic significance, then strafed men, women, and children as they fled. Over 100,000 people perished in this way, so the sights witnessed by father and son on the road, when they weren't dodging the attacks themselves, must have been horrific. Later Karol as pope would issue a modest disclaimer as to how little he had suffered compared to others.

In the land they occupied in those early days, the Nazis did not wait to knock down, mutilate, or chuck into rivers the crosses and crucifixes which were a common sight on crossroads and at the side of the roads. They smashed into fragments or desecrated statues of Jesus and the Virgin. The favourite holy place of Czestochowa, with its miraculous Black Madonna in the Cathedral of the Most Holy Family, which father and son had often visited in pilgrimage, became the scene of almost inconceivable outrages. On 4 September the Gestapo and SS drove between seven and eight hundred Polish and Jewish men and women into the surrounds of the cathedral and ordered them to stand with arms raised for two hours: those that fainted or lowered their arms were kicked and beaten by soldiers.

When evening fell they were locked into the cathedral and kept there for two days and nights without food or sanitation. At the same time, claiming they had been fired on, German troops hunted and shot civilians, setting fire to houses and refusing to allow those inside to leave. They forbade the burial or removal of corpses. Another substantial number of people, including priests, were rounded up and placed against a wall, compelled to stand there with raised arms, waiting for a pretended order for execution. The guards forced them to lie down, then fired hundreds of rounds of ammunition over their heads; some died of heart failure, some went mad. Kept without food, they were sent to prison, not allowed to eat or drink, while a German soldier of Silesian-Polish origin who permitted them to have food was shot dead on the spot.

Five or six days after their exit from Krakow the Wojtylas gave up. There were still ten days to go before the Russians – although they had signed a non-aggression or at least a non-invasion pact also with Poland – crossed the eastern borders in vast numbers and with mechanised columns; they cunningly exhorted Polish forces to lay down their arms and join with them in defence against 'the common enemy of the Slavs'. Their weapons would soon be returned to them, they were told. The Poles were stunned and exhausted: resisting the Soviets while being routed by the Germans was just not an option. Who was the worst enemy? Poles said, 'The Germans will take our body – the Soviets will take our soul.' Had Karol persisted in his flight he might well have been temporarily interned, then released and trained to fight in the Polish army the Russians subsequently formed when the Germans invaded Russia. This happened to some of his school friends.

Karol senior could not go on. A hundred or more miles east of Krakow, having passed the town of Rzeszlow, but before reaching Tarnobrzeg, on the banks of the River San in the direction of Lwow, they abandoned their journey. They slogged back the whole distance to Krakow but at least they had somewhere tangible to go. On their return Karol explained in a letter to Mieciu Kotlarczyk in Wadowice, which in the breakdown of postal services Halina carried as courier, that 'my father, small wonder, could no longer stand that hard trek . . . He was enormously tired.'

The Skawa River, west of Krakow, was now the border between the General Government and the territory incorporated into the Reich (which included Oswiecim or Auschwitz). East of that border, in the city itself, although plans had been laid to draft 800,000 men from this new colony to work in Germany as slave labour, Krakow, as its new capital, had a greater chance of self-preservation and survival than Warsaw, in the north, much of whose architectural wealth, culture and population, if not already destroyed, was doomed to be savagely targeted.

But back at home Karol's mood was strong; he responded to Mieciu, giving us almost a sense of ebullient sociability:

> The theatre is in operation. Maybe you already know about this, because supposedly you do get the 'Courier'. *The March Cavalier* (Karbowski), *Mrs Dulska* (Korecka), now *Lobzowianie* and *By Domestic Drum*, also *Ladies and Hussars* and *Queen of the Suburb*. So vaudeville is well. I am not surprised. I spoke with Woznik about some position in the theatre, even as an extra. He was very gracious, even happy to see me in one piece, but of course he was not in the theatre at the appointed time. I will have to go again. And again after bread.
>
> Dobrowolski is here. He will conduct readings even though he was told that he would not get paid one cent; maybe I can arrange something with him. He's quite a decent chap and looks at these things from quite a different point of view, but then he also sees life quite distractedly and is forever running out of time. Well, now he has plenty of it. Czuprynowna and Danka are here. Only Kwiatkowski, after a long trek, has settled in Nadworna in the outer regions. Also, Kudlinski has returned.
>
> Nitsch [Kazimierz Nitsch, Professor of Polish Etymology], like a spectre who always returns to haunt the place to which fate ties him, has resumed pouring the nectar of Polish and Slavic literature into young minds (a minor seminar), and that 2 and ½ weeks before the official opening of the academic year.

Soon after he wrote this the Reich's authorities closed and pillaged the beautiful municipal theatre named after Slowacki. They wantonly toppled and destroyed the statue of the poet Mickiewicz on top of its monument in Krakow's central square; upon pain of dire penalties they forbade Wawel Royal Castle using its title 'Royal', and they installed beer parlours and lavatories in its historical chambers. Poles could speak Polish in Krakow, and use it for some official documents, but the publication of books in Polish was no longer allowed, nor were Polish-language broadcasts. The Nazis placed thousands of books on Polish culture or its recent history on an index of outlawed books. In the Reich territory it was far worse: they simply demolished all Polish libraries, destroyed all Polish books and punished the use of Polish in public, if overheard. Anyone heard praising England, or listening to English broadcasts, was summarily shot.

With the collapse of Poland Karol senior no longer had his full military pension, although for the present he collected 60 per cent of it. There were no other benefits. Karol could not find that job in the theatre, although some theatres remained open till November, and he had tried a second time in vain at the Slowacki Theatre. Leaving the damp, ill-lit 'catacomb' apartment in Debniki, Karol discovered that, in freezing temperatures, Poles formed queues to buy black bread at 4 a.m. Yet in its first stages, to a high-spirited young man, the occupation might well have seemed more a distraction than a reign of terror. In mid-September 1939, Karol wrote to Mieciu, who was still in Wadowice:

> 'Vita Cracoviensis' [The Krakow life]. Just think, think! It consists of standing in line for bread, or (rare) expeditions to find sugar. Ha! And also of a black longing for coal – and of reading. For us, life [once] consisted of evenings on the Dluga Street, of refined conversation, of dreams and longings. We dreamt away many an evening until midnight or beyond, but now . . .

That Karol's female friends such as Halina and other members of the dedicated circle of Polish patriots to which in time he came to belong, survived in Krakow was a testimony to their care and determination to maintain low visibility.

Cardinal Hlond, the Polish primate, notable for his expression of anti-Semitic sentiments, fled his homeland as Wojtyla and his father trudged back from the River San to Krakow. Hlond stayed first in Romania, but when threatened there moved to France in spring 1940, where he took up residence in the south, staying in so-called neutral Vichy France after the Nazi invasion in June. In 1944 he was arrested by the Germans and sent to Germany. Meanwhile he denounced, from the safety of flight, the atrocities in his homeland. Another voice was only partially forthright: 'The blood of innumerable human beings, even of non-combatants, evokes a poignant cry of sorrow, especially for the well-beloved nation of Poland, who, by her services in the defence of Christian civilisation, which are inscribed indelibly in the annals of history, has the right to the human fraternal sympathy of the world.'

This tepid outpouring of sympathy from the new pope, Pius XII, in his encyclical of October 1939, could not have failed in Krakow circles to cause incomprehension. While his predecessor, Pius XI, had been fiery in his denunciations of Hitler and Germany, Eugenio Pacelli, elected pope in March 1939, lost no time in dispatching a friendly letter to Hitler. When only weeks later the jackboots marched into Prague Pius did not raise any complaint against this, or the seizure of the whole country, where Catholics were a sizeable minority.

Karol, shut up in semi-hiding most of the time, perhaps making a quick dash from the house of one friend to another, had plenty of scope for thinking at this stage in the war. He thought much about Poland, about its culture, its church, its literature, its traditions. Day by day he could see all these things torn down around him. Practically he had much to do to support himself and his father, obtain food and fuel, keep the flat clean, avoid trouble.

Wojtyla's dedication, his focus, his single-mindedness of purpose were boundless. He was only nineteen. Jolted by the débâcle he confesses that the scales about his native land have fallen from his eyes. In a further letter to Kotlarczyk he says with some bitterness that up until that moment he had not understood Poland 'in her real truth'. He had failed to grasp the underlying 'atmosphere of ideas that should have surrounded in dignity the nation of Mickiewicz, Slowacki, Norwid and Wyspianski'.

He seemed, reading between the lines of this letter, to be saying that the pre-war Poland that had built up much of his hope and confidence had been a mirage hiding corruption, Fascism, and injustice: 'Today, after reflection, I understand with full clarity that the idea of Poland lived in us, as in the romantic generation, but in truth it did not exist because the peasant was killed and imprisoned for demanding his just rights from the government . . . He was right and he had law on his side, [but] the nation was misled and lied to . . .'

The 'peasant' – who suffered injustices like the 'true Pole' – was forced to be 'chased across the world like hostile winds, like in the days of the Partitions . . . so they would not rot in the motherland's prisons'.

If he expressed some of his analysis obscurely, he boldly stated what the answer to the problem was not: it was not Marxist, Communist, or materialist, capitalist or utilitarian. There was only one way. The liberation of the Polish people had to be through 'the gateway of Christ . . .' and he went on, 'I think of an Athenian Poland, but of an Athens immensely perfected by the greatness of Christianity. Bards and prophets of the Babylonian slavery thought of such an Athens. [This] Nation collapsed, like Israel, because it did not encounter [or presumably meet and live up to] the messianic ideal, its own ideal . . . that was not fulfilled.'

In October 1939 Karol and some of his young fellow patriots gathered in the apartment in central Krakow belonging to the Kydrynskis that Karol had visited on the first day of the war. As students, joined by a friend who had fought in the Polish army, then escaped from a German prison camp, they read together national works of literature and looked forward to the new term at the university; Karol even attended lectures before term began given by Kazimierz Nitsch, his professor of etymology.

But, on 6 November, a further blow fell. Two months after the invasion the authorities invited all the professors of the Jagiellonian University and the Mining Academy to a meeting in the University Aula to hear a lecture, by a German, on 'The attitude of the German Authorities to Science and Teaching'.

The lecturer was a Dr Meyer (who just happened to head the Krakow Gestapo). 'In view of the fact,' he began by saying, 'that (1) the professors of the university were intending to begin lectures; (2) they had not interrupted their work in the scientific institutes and seminaries; and (3) the University of Krakow had been a bastion of Polonism for more than five hundred years, all the professors in the Aula are arrested.'

Gestapo agents rushed on the shocked teaching staff, beat them and bundled them into cars. A total of 174 were arrested, and while a few were released on the grounds of age or ill-health, the remainder were transported first to Breslau, where they stayed a few weeks, then to Oranienburg-Sachsenhausen, where for three months they were fed on disgusting ersatz bread and turnip soup, living in unheated hutments where they had to sleep in pairs on wooden beds, head to foot.

Deprived of warm clothing they were forbidden books, paper and pencils. Reviled, beaten and tortured, denied medical attention, they were forced into several hot shower-baths in the course of the day, then in their thin ducks stood outside in the frost. These were Karol's teachers, whom he revered.

First to die was an elderly former rector of the university who had just refused presidency of a puppet Polish protectorate that the Nazis at one stage proposed to form. On hearing of his death his wife in Krakow also fell dead. More deaths followed, totalling seventeen in all, but 103 of the 174 professors were returned ultimately to Krakow, their release negotiated by Lucjana Frassati-Gawronska, the exotic and beautiful Italian wife of a Polish diplomat who now lived in Italy.

She visited Krakow, heard of the arrest and deportation, and intervened with Mussolini, a friend of hers, on behalf of the teaching staff. The Italian dictator brought up the matter with Hitler, who ordered this release. 'The news that the professors had returned from the concentration camp caused a tremendous impression', according to a document at the time. 'There were moving scenes, and women kissed the hands of professors they met in the streets.' But nearly fifty, including priests and some students, never came back; most of them were sent in April 1940 to hard labour at Dachau, where they died.

Karol knew and witnessed all this at first hand. His university days were over. The last Polish performance at the Slowacki Theatre had taken place on 11 November.

Meantime the authorities forbade worship at Wawel Cathedral. Archbishop Prince Sapieha, the most senior churchman in Poland since primate Hlond had fled, celebrated his last mass there on 29 October. The Germans allowed two masses only per month but with no congregation, and one German guard in attendance, a sole non-participant. This was part of Governor-General Frank's plan to tear nation and church apart; at the same time the seminary of the Krakow archdiocese was requisitioned to garrison SS shock troops.

By these and other means the occupiers drove Poland to the lowest point ever in its chequered and tragic history. But Karol Wojtyla's personal destiny, on its own way towards obliteration or revelation, still had some way to go before it reached rock bottom.

On the other hand, among those who trusted and loved each other, solidarity could never have been higher. Even if not fighting, or trying to blow up Adolf Hitler on a podium (as the Polish resistance vainly attempted when he came to Warsaw in October), or printing clandestine newspapers, Poles were bound together by an inner resistance.

At first the Nazis hoped for collaborators, as in France, or Quislings as in Norway, but there were virtually none. No structure could ever be formed to take the weight away from full-time active occupation. It drove the Germans to acts of greater and greater ferocity, no doubt, but their attitude too, hardening as time went by, was one of no compromise.

In this atmosphere, although no one knew when the next person might disappear, the next friend turn into a wayside corpse, the next edict condemning to labour or torture fall – so that of necessity one lived from day to day – there was a kind of freedom among those who knew that they had good, and as well the Catholic God, on their side. They knew that they would, one day, be liberated: if they were alive, that is, to see it.

At an intimate dinner in the Vatican in the nineties, given for ten Anglican bishops and ten English Catholic senior clerics, Cardinal Cormac Murphy-O'Connor, then a bishop, commenting perhaps on what he felt the Pope might consider the lukewarmness of English spirituality – but commenting not too seriously – said to the Pope: 'What we need in England is a bit of persecution.'

The Pope agreed and nodded vigorous assent; in his deep Polish accent he answered: 'Yes. Persecution.' He repeated, 'Persecution,' adding, 'you're tried under fire.'

In that winter of 1939 and the following spring it was a toss-up as to which of the twin torches of drama and religion would focus Karol's emotions and express his deepest spiritual aspiration. If he chose drama it would always have a strong religious content; if religion it too would have a powerfully dramatic structure.

But there was something in each choice too concentrated, contained, almost abstract – sensed or done at a distance from the reality – which suggests at once, pertinent and passionate although the choice of either was, that it would not, not yet anyway, realise the full man, the widest scope or arc of his ability.

He chose the theatre; through it he would express, even though veiled, his deepest preoccupations and those burdens he experienced in this dark period.

5

The Year of Three Plays

(1939–40)

Curiously enough this period of Karol's life (1939–40) had strong parallels with the life of another striking figure of his age, who although older and in exile, and known as 'Sam l'Irlandais', lived several years later in Nazi-occupied Paris, leading a clandestine existence as a *boîte de poste* and translator of secret intelligence for the resistance. Every day exposed to the daily loss of those he knew, the fear of betrayal, and the terror of death or extermination, this agent stayed in Paris until the Nazis broke up his cell and he fled with his wife to Vichy territory.

Waiting for Godot and *Endgame*, two masterpieces of eschatological doubt, had their source and took their power and consummate artistry from Samuel Beckett's immersion of body, soul and mind in confronting and surviving, at his own level, an almost unimaginable evil and negativism; Wojtyla, likewise, had little or no certainly that he would live to see the end of the war. But he possessed other certainties that Beckett, agonising in his doubts, would never come to accept and embrace.

The contrast is at once clear: that between the objective Pole, so far innocent of the influence of modernism and the subjective, solipsistic luxury of putting man first in everything, and the ascetic ex-Protestant Irishman from Dublin, hungry for faith but reluctant to abandon the seductive trappings and sensual luxury of what he saw as a decaying civilisation; this had now, with its modernism, arrived at a respectable idolatry – soon to become an established church – that of the hero-artist. Here action no longer meant anything, the new hero, the new focus of worship, was the artist themself.

Beckett was to become the 'religious' writer *par excellence* for a secular age, as witness how the young Iris Murdoch (after reading *Murphy*, his first novel) wrote him a fan letter calling it a 'sacred text'. The characters in Beckett's work were locked in themselves, unable to turn themselves out to the world. They would like to believe, to be good, to aspire to values. But those values have disappeared. Karol had the historical destiny of his country and the image of Christ in his mind when he faced similar doubt.

For a while Karol worked part-time as a storeman and messenger for a restaurant. In late 1939, as we know from letters to the late Mieczyslaw Kotlarczyk (which the director's widow preserved and made available after the latter's death in 1970), Karol embarked on an intensive period of writing plays. Only one other pope wrote drama and poetry, in this case before he took holy orders: Pius II, as Enea Silvio Piccolomini (1405–64), penned erotic poetry, a Boccaccian love story and verse comedy in the style of Terence and Plautus.

Karol had last performed in *Knight of the Moon* when as a spectacular Taurus he wore shorts, boxing-gloves, and on his head the mask of a bull. Staged in the medieval courtyard of the Jagiellonian University's Collegium Maius, this had been a popular and critical triumph. Now it belonged to a vanished golden age. The quality of laughter had changed for ever.

In marked contrast was Karol's first theatrical effort during wartime, a translation of *Oedipus Rex* by Sophocles which he undertook for Juliusz Osterwa, who was then fifty years of age, and well known for his Reduta theatre company which toured all over Poland, austerely presenting from the Polish romantic and neo-romantic repertoire classics for popular consumption. As theatre, universities, and secondary schools were now all closed Osterwa, out of work, planned for the future, and Karol and his friend Juliusz Kydrynski, with whom he had spent some of the first day of the war, met with him and performed acts or scenes from plays.

Osterwa approved of Karol's translation of *Oedipus*, which was faithful to the Greek, stageworthy and simple – as Karol wrote to Mieciu, 'so that every kitchen maid would understand'. The tragic national and moral theme of Sophocles influenced Karol. Exhorting his friend, on 2 November 1939, to come and live with them in Krakow, Karol wrote, 'Let theatre be a church where the national spirit will flourish'; he also observed, 'I have given much thought to the liberating force of suffering. It is on suffering that Christ's system rests, beginning with the cross and ending with the smallest human torment. This is the true Messiah.'

But Osterwa apparently then lost interest in the output of novices some thirty years his junior and their clandestine, restricted manner of presentation in the Kydrynskis' third-floor apartment. The Gestapo constantly threatened intervention; they turned up on one occasion an hour before a resistance talk was due to be held in secret, finding thirty chairs set out for the audience.

Kydrynski reports, 'My mother said we were preparing for a party. This seemed to satisfy them and they left. But that was a very close thing . . . If the Gestapo had arrived when there were people there . . . I would not be speaking today.'

David, who slew Goliath, became king and defeated the Philistines, then to the accompaniment of his lyre composed the Psalms. This was the subject of the verse drama Karol now turned to writing in December 1939. As well as its heroic theme Wojtyla's *David* – sadly the text has been lost – might also have dealt with more than what is generally suggested, namely one question that David laments in Psalm 13: 2 – 'How long shall I take counsel in my soul, having sorrow in my heart daily? How long shall my enemy be exalted over me?' No doubt this questioning of the hidden God whose face is obscured by suffering was an important part of Wojtyla's preoccupation: that the poet, unable to understand God's purpose in permitting horrors, had to search within himself for answers, which was an important theme too, of Beckett's *Endgame*. 'How long is the Philistine (German) tyranny to last?' was another important question.

Karol wrote to his friend Kotlarczyk that he had, in this first effort, which was partly biblical, partly rooted in Polish history, 'bared many things, many matters of my soul'. Among these matters may well have been Karol's own love life and sexual desire – also a preoccupation of the Psalmist – felt at first hand but again veiled in historical treatment.

Whatever the lost and secret content of *David* was – and we shall never know – Karol followed this, in the early months of 1940, with *Job*, about which he appears to his friends optimistic. His long summary, the first of the only two he ever made, is precise:

The point of departure in the plot is an event from the Old Testament:
. . . it goes like this. Job's neighbours come to a feast in his house. Job
welcomes them . . . [then] terrible messages arrive one after the other.
The terrified chorus of Guests disperse, to return as Mourners. (They
are convinced that Job's misfortunes are caused by his secret sins, for
they do not know of any open ones.) But before the Mourners arrive,
Job – after speaking a long monologue and sprinkling ashes over his
head – receives a visit from three of his friends. A dramatic exchange
with them begins to develop the idea that suffering is not always a
punishment but can sometimes be, often is, a presage.

Job still could not understand, Karol went on, why he, the just one,
was the object of God's punishment. The young prophet Elihu in his
presence has a prophetic vision: 'he sees Christ's Passion, the Garden
of Olives, Mount Calvary. Nobody except Job understands him. In
the end on the example of Christ's Passion, Elihu shows the positive
meaning of suffering (suffering as a presage) . . . we can see, in the
rising dawn, the outline of Mount Calvary and the Cross.'
Karol made this precocious and powerful judgement when he was
not yet twenty. However, putting to one side the early maturity of his
thought, his skilful combination of biblical source material, and his
preoccupation with both his personal plight and the fate of his
country, linking it to the first year of the war, what does *Job* reveal
of its author's own life? What is shown in the secret play, of the
unaffected inner life of the man?
Job is autobiographical, painful, extreme in expression and highly
dramatic in the immediacy and naked vulnerability of its protagonist's
utterances. The biblical Job is a vivid dramatic vehicle for any writer
who sees human life in highly coloured dramatic terms – as Karol
Wojtyla did from the very start – as a struggle between good and evil,
right and wrong, in terms, too, of suffering and redemption. Shakespeare often paraphrases or directly echoes parts of it, for example,
when Queen Gertrude tells Hamlet:

> Do not for ever . . .
> Seek for thy noble father in the dust

This echoes Job 7:21: 'Now shall I sleepe in the dust, and if thou
seekest me . . . I shall not be found.' Drama comes from conflict, from

doubt. Signs of doubt, like Job's, Abraham's, Peter's – and even Jesus's himself when feeling abandoned by God – occur and recur throughout Wojtyla's life.

It seems clear that many of his hero's utterances in the play express exactly what Karol felt about his own life. One example is when Job calls out that 'This day walks in nothing but wounds' (when his sons are discovered dead). At another time Job is described by the narrator:

> Thus he speaks; the voice quivering,
> he prays though he would fain blaspheme.
> But never does he cross the line –
> though a storm rages in his heart,
> though a storm transpires in his eyes.

'Never does he cross the line': like Job, but within limits, Karol is searching for reasons ('I search with my soul,/I look, I grope for the right way'). Yet he also complains loudly, using for the first time 'abyss', a word that was to be often brought into play by the future pope, even to describe man himself:

> I, who have been righteous in my life –
> see how He has hurled me into an abyss.

Although by the end of the play Elihu, the fair-faced youth with a dazzling presence, has his unexpected vision of Christ the Redeemer, and although it is claimed for those who are 'sent to the camps' (i.e. the concentration camps) who suffer, that '. . . The sacrificial circle closed/When the Lord's Word came to pass', we know that this is not really so, and that suffering is imposed to test man to the very limit.

So Karol has found a reason for the suffering: to justify it, to make it add up. He says he is satisfied with *Job*, telling Kotlarczyk, 'I have written a new drama, Greek in form, Christian in spirit, eternal in substance, like Everyman. A drama about suffering.'

Karol followed *Job* with an even more eloquent and powerful biblical drama. If *Job* established in the young playwright a strong sense of using theatre for clarifying ideas, as in a thesis, as well as expressing his intense emotions (the latter always well controlled) that suffering was not merely a curse, but a test imposed by God, Karol painted in *Jeremiah* an even more universal and national application.

Poland, as he sees it in the play, deserved the misery inflicted on her, for too much wickedness and abuse had been tolerated within her society, and her own internal weakness had brought about the ravages wrought upon her in history. Confronting Poland with full clarity, with full awareness, was not only to acknowledge her martyr status, but to understand her 'complex of strange disparities', so described in that earlier letter of 2 November to Kotlarczyk: 'next to outright mystic idealism, [her] buffoonery and Judas's pieces of silver, for which the nation's soul has been sold'.

In ordering his material to do justice to this theme, Karol connected the doom-prophesying Jeremiah with two seventeenth-century Polish priests, and a great Polish general and patriot who defeated the Russians and occupied the Kremlin. Father Peter, the first priest, is based on a well-known Jesuit, Piotr Skarga, a preacher at the royal court who warned often that Poland would fall if its house was not put in order. Karol himself identified most with this character.

The second priest is Brother Andrew, also based on a Jesuit, this time a missionary, Andrzej Bobola – murdered by rebellious Cossacks – who had been canonised in 1938 by Pope Pius XI.

Karol again summarised the action of *Jeremiah* (which he once thought of calling *The Covenant*), in a letter to Mieciu:

Act I takes place by the gate of a church (a cathedral) . . . Father Peter is praying [inside]. On the altar two White Angels, who hold the veil, are chatting. Through the window human shapes can be seen walking by outside: the 'earthly gods' on their way to Skarga's parliamentary sermon. Father Peter notices them . . . Statues come to life, and Jeremiah's exhortation to the elders of Judah is enacted.

This complicated mingling of vision and spiritual monologue, tied into Jeremiah's struggle with the elders of Israel and his prophecies, continues in Act II, when Father Peter delivers his sermon in the adjoining church. The martyred body of Jesus is identified with the Polish crusaders who first fight to save Jerusalem from destruction and then battle to save Poland itself from inner disintegration and foreign conquest. The many deaths and resurrections of Poland provide a potent analogy for the life of Jesus.

Finally, in Act III, Poland's enemies are defeated by the warrior Hetman. He and Father Peter hold their final council before the Hetman 'goes to [God's] judgment in a ray of light, and Peter takes up his final utterance and throws it into the empty church (into the filled auditorium)'.

Karol adds in his letter, 'Well, this is it . . . I have many other ideas . . . I see the "Covenant" quite clearly as part of a tetralogy. But it's a long way to go yet.'

'I think in theatrical images,' Karol remarked at this time: not only does this become true of him all through his life, but his power of marshalling, interweaving and co-ordinating these theatrical images in a complex yet integrated way is never better shown than in *Jeremiah*.

But while it was much more than a prefiguring of Poland's resurrection, and as such strongly influenced by Wyspianski's *Acropolis*, written in 1906, *Jeremiah*, like *Job*, has a very personal content. In the person of Father Peter, Wojtyla imagined and projected his whole future life as a priest hero. I am not of course claiming that this was conscious. Unconscious forces often have more power in life than conscious ones. Father Peter identifies with Jeremiah and the prophet in his person gathers new force. This is what was to happen to Wojtyla when later ordained as priest in 1946. He was to translate the following utterances from *Jeremiah* into many different forms in future statements and action. They remain germane, or central, to the core of the man's mission:

'You are in the clutches of the prophets,' claims Father Peter,

> your ears are fed with offending words –
> but I, rising in the morning,
> and unable to sleep at night,
> am put to shame because I bring
> unpleasant truth before your eyes.

And yet again

> One must throw truth across the path of lies.
> One must throw truth into the eye of a lie.

This man will be, he is saying, forever confrontational. And Karol sometimes registers direct personal experience of his own and Wojtyla senior's plight in a disintegrating Poland, as they fled wearily to the east, together with thousands of others:

> When the ship is sinking
> everyone counts and clings to his bundles,
> unmindful of the water that fills and sinks it.
> Fools! What will you do then with your bundles?
> when the ship is sinking, what is private?

Karol holds back much anger in *Jeremiah*, although even this bursts out at times when Father Peter calls for revenge, calls for power to be taken from the dead:

> Touch the coffin! – There is life;
> take the foetus to your womb;
> swear the oath ere you depart.
> Come spring, oath takes root in tomb.
> Rise! – Much must be done, avenged.
> In this act you all unite
> Work within you – God's revenge –

Although the key word 'within' is important, Karol was never far from asserting the positive aspects of hope ('overcome discord by love!'), and expresses very characteristic traits of himself as future priest. The Hetman, the warrior hero, the nobleman who, as Father Peter says, has an immense burden to carry, 'enter[s] the holy place in humility;/It is the humility that gives me strength', and while summoning and co-ordinating his forces to defeat the infidel he tells Father Peter: 'I have come here to listen, Father.'

Karol pours out agonies of doubt, he probes failure, in *Jeremiah*, and it is revealing that the protagonists in this play and its predecessor *Job*, while they never lose hope, do not get hooked up on dogma or blindly assert an unquestioning faith.

While Karol wrote plays Governor Frank had driven the Jews from 'Germanised' Krakow but now confined those who remained to the stinking, restricted Podgorze ghetto. Karol watched the progressive dehumanisation of his former landlord and family, his neighbours, and his Jewish friends in Wadowice, now their families were incarcerated in ghettos or forced to flee. Soon there would be no life for them at all. For example, Ida Elbinger, a vivacious Jewish girl he knew and with whom he acted at school, had thought of joining the secret underground theatre Karol and his friends were organising: one day she was shot on a Krakow street as she went to the aid of her mother who was being forced to clear snow.

In equal numbers non-Jewish Poles were also dying. Life took on a monstrous, unreal quality, and with the meagre rations doled out to Poles – half those allowed to Germans – everyone fiddled on the black market, so by definition every Pole became a criminal. It needed only one mistake to be put away.

Hope had flickered for a short while before the fall of France, where thousands of Poles had joined British forces, in June 1940. Afterwards there was none. The German lawmakers stipulated that Slavs could be tolerated as workers 'as long as they stick to their low biological and cultural status'; for Jews there was no place at all, 'they are *Vernichtung*, and they are dying at the rate of five thousand per month in the Warsaw ghetto, some of them reduced in the last resort, to cannibalism'.

But here we notice a remarkable thing about Karol Wojtyla: while others became haggard, anxious, full of doubt, eking out their lives, full of envy and hate, or endlessly tired and suffering the deprivations as personal afflictions, Karol Wojtyla saw the meagre rations, the daily potatoes and watery soup, the pain, suffering and death around him as a testing inspiration, as daily sustenance, as a sacrament.

'Whether food does you good or harm depends on your Ki, on your attitude! Have good attitude, any food good; have bad attitude, any food bad,' says Bo Lozoff's Aikido teacher in his book *We're All Doing Time*. Attempting to see in everyone as far as possible, even Nazis, the face of Christ, and in everything, even in the massive devastation, the hand of God, Karol did not, he could not, despair. It was perhaps this lack of resistance in his confrontation with circumstances that would finish off most people, that forged the connections in his mind, feelings, and personality into an unusual integrity.

This extraordinary process to a maturity few of us will ever know or experience – although we may be able to grasp and understand it in another person – began in Krakow, in that dark winter, which is why he could never in the future leave Krakow behind.

6

Equilibrium Which Love Learns Through Anger

(1940–41)

By the age of twenty Karol had incarnated ten patriotic Polish heroes, delivered in performance numerous sacred or patriotic texts, read all the powerful Polish literature, written three plays centred on David, Job and Jeremiah, three of the most tested and exposed biblical figures, and mingled these with Polish warriors and priests; but now was the moment of truth, now was the real testing. Now came the moment in Wojtyla's life when – like Thomas More standing up to Henry VIII, or Thomas à Becket choosing the path of martyrdom with Henry II, or Poland's own St Stanislaw with King Boleslaw – young Karol had to make his choice, find his own path.

It is crucial to observe that this happened in obscurity, before he held an important position in the church, before he was famous, that, in the most trying circumstances possible, as the English Protestant poet John Milton shows, conditions of mind and thought always precede significant action.

Milton wrote *Paradise Lost* 'to justify the ways of God to man'. Between 1941 and 1945 Karol justified those ways in the most gruesome and painful conditions possible. That he could have been arrested at any moment was surely an immense and horrible drama of suspense in itself: that uncertainty, living in that stressed limbo, was itself the real test. But he already sensed the role he was to be given, that of witness. He placed himself near his priestly mentors and confessors – exemplary men. These included Father Figlewicz, Archbishop Sapieha, the elderly 'unbroken prince', the clerics Fathers

Mazerski and Matlak in his local Debniki church, where he attended mass every day. Typically for Karol, however, he also sought out and pursued a more colourful or direct character, a lay preacher, such as you might find in Dickens or Thornton Wilder (or Conrad), who caught his imagination.

This was an eccentric tailor, Jan Leopold Tyranowski, who was forty years old when Karol met him. Described variously as 'sprung from the pages of Dostoevsky', a 'holy fool', a 'spiritual alpinist', 'irritating, pompous and obsessive', he stood, when Karol first saw him, outside the Silesian church of St Stanislaw Kostra in Debniki on the steps, importuning for the faith and recruiting for his Living Rosary Circle – 'Good morning, may I talk to you. I have noticed you at mass' – a common enough introduction.

Karol attended meetings and was impressed. Tyranowski lived in an apartment that in one room contained a bed, a sewing machine and odd bits of material, and in the second room a burgundy-coloured piano. He urged daily meditation and a rigorous menu of devotions – and that in a notebook one should account for every hour of one's life; he prayed while he worked cutting and sewing: 'laborare est orare'. Some of Karol's friends, who attended with him, such as an engineering student Mieczyslaw Malinski, who later wrote about the Pope, spoke to him sceptically of Tyranowski's methods, calling him 'importunate and bossy'.

But Karol, while conceding he was 'formal' and 'old-fashioned', told Malinski: 'yet he lives close to God, or rather with God.' He responded in particular to Tyranowski's capacity to strip away the abstract from observance and contemplation, and bring the facts of spiritual life close to each person. Souls were shaped not by limitation but by opening up in the presence of God, and the charisma of this spiritual leader, who formed and developed his Living Rosary Circles into coherent and well-organised units of fifteen people each over the years of occupation, appealed in particular to Karol's contemporaries. He emanated, according to Wojtyla in a 1949 tribute a 'sort of strange relentlessness' that resulted in a 'bowstring of tension between the master and his disciples', proving 'that one could not only inquire about God but that one could live with God'.

Later Wojtyla would emphasise this in his memoir *Gift and Mystery*: 'I learned the basic methods of self-formation which would later be confirmed and developed . . . Tyranowski, whose own spiritual formation was based on the writings of Saint John of the Cross and Saint Teresa of Avila, helped me to read their works, something uncommon for a person my age.'

Here was a gentle mystic to counterbalance and compensate for the harsh reality of the German occupation.

Towards the autumn of 1940, with the catastrophes of Norway and Greece, the defeats in North Africa, the threat of England's invasion – the Battle of Britain not yet fought and won – the Nazi grip on Poland, and Krakow in particular, tightened to a stranglehold. Karol found he could no longer sustain his student-style casual job as store messenger, which had given him freedom of movement and plenty of time to himself. He needed a more permanent job to protect him from arrest or deportation. He had seen too many visible and distressing signs of the humiliation of the great town with which he identified not to be aware of the dangers.

All Polish newspapers had been closed down, and journalists, refusing to work on German publications, became a persecuted breed. Yet secret newspapers gradually came into being, and by the second year of the war forty-three secret publications were in existence. Now no books were published, while the owners of bookshops allowed to remain open had to sign a Gestapo order to withdraw all sales of books in French or English. Everywhere young men and women were in flight from deportation and the lists of wanted Poles grew by the month – in the two provinces of Lodz and Inowroclaw alone by September 1940 it had reached the figure of 20,000. In Nowy Sacz a Pole imprisoned with many others cuts his veins to write on the walls of the prison in blood: 'Poland has not yet perished.'

In Krakow, tramping everywhere in disintegrating footwear repaired by his father, or increasingly in wooden clogs, worn without socks, Karol viewed the visible cultural wounds multiply: ancient monuments and historic buildings gutted, refurbished with new interiors, translated to coarse or profane Teutonic use. The victors smashed up the magnificent monument of King Ladislaus Jagiello, carved by the sculptor Wiwulski, 'presented to the city of Krakow by M. Paderewski [the musician] in 1919 at the 500th anniversary of the great Polish victory over the Knights of the Teutonic Order'. Broken fragments lay for a long time in the yard of the Mining Academy. The equestrian statue of Kosciuszko standing near the entrance to Wawel Castle, the work of Marconi, the Polish sculptor, was also pulverised.

While the Nazis overthrew the noble ghosts of the past, they posted in public places daily lists of those wanted, those about to be shot, and those who had in the last twenty-four hours been put to death. This brutal, up-front accountancy was the opposite of the 'disappearance' tactics of more recent dictators, and carried along with it legalistically worded justifications.

Karol's constant companion was Juliusz Kydrynski. Neither he nor Karol was now safe, but they were shortly favoured by being organised, together with several other high-flying students from the university, for employment in a protected industry that would supply them with the *Ausweiss*, the necessary identity card carrying exemption from forced labour in Germany, or deportation to the camps. Karol himself was suggested to Henryk Kulakowski, the Polish general manager of the Belgian-owned Solvay chemical plant, producing the caustic soda used in making explosives, blasted from calcinated limestone. Kulakowski, retained by the Germans for his expertise, did what he could on the side, in this essential war-effort industry, to keep alive the flame of Polish resistance. Some claimed another Solvay official paid off the Gestapo to close its eyes to the haven given to this collection of the young Polish intelligentsia.

It was hardly a haven. From the quarry in the Krakow suburb of Zakrzowek where Karol began work, limestone blocks, mined and split with dynamite, cut with wire and hammer, in a pit hundreds of feet deep, were loaded on tramcars or in iron carts on a narrow gauge rail to be transported to a factory in another industrial area, Borek Falecki, a few miles south of the quarry.

Karol began by laying rail track between Zakrzowek and Borek Falecki, and acting as brakeman; he wrote to his friends the Kotlarczyks in October, 'I earn very well (relatively speaking, of course) and workers "supplements" are most welcome (these are extra rations to the usual monthly rations of stringy meat, kilos of black bread, marmalade, cigarettes, and a litre of vodka).' 'Most of my colleagues work like this,' he added. And typically: 'And it does us a lot of good.'

Karol complained little, but his day was a tough one: he walked from the flat for forty minutes, an hour perhaps, across fields to the quarry, according to Wojciech Zukrowski, another of the young gang, 'wearing a hat with frayed band, a jacket with bulging pockets, and mended pants covered with limestone dust and stiff from splashed oil'.

The big wooden clogs completed his costume. Work began early, at eight, and lasted to the middle of the afternoon.

The winter of 1940–41 was very harsh, with temperatures constantly at −22°C. Karol and his friend Juliusz, 'the wild man of the theatre', managed warm, short breaks in a hut heated by an iron stove. The professional quarrymen, old hands, were sympathetic to the young contingent working alongside them, while Karol traded his vodka and cigarettes for lard to keep up his strength, and to bring back some succour and strength to his father, whose health was declining. Their former supply of plentiful Polish coal had dried up. But while the old man, alone in the Tyniecka Street flat, chored for his son and struggled in the sub-zero temperatures to keep himself warm, Karol and his friends found survival as quarrymen, although Karol spent much of the time exhausted, chilled to the bone, and rapidly losing weight.

Almost overnight the solitary mystic and romantic playwright vanished. Karol continued relentlessly in his devotional readings and profoundly pious observances. But the change in his writing was from that of a Macaulay or a mystical Walter Scott to the young Wilfred Owen in the First World War trenches. True, there were glimpses in those first two dramas of anger, or realistic bitterness, but now his writing took on a harsh, gritty and very sparse dimension, as if informed by the cold, the space and isolation of the quarry depths, the danger and toil of the activity itself.

Over the next year or two Karol conceived four exceptional poems in which he related natural stone to vaults in building, to the human arteries and heart, to anger, love and of course to Jesus. He called the first three poems, in turn, 'Material', 'Inspiration' and 'Participation'. He realised a rather beautifully balanced image in the second one, which again glorified in, and celebrated, the power and unifying principle of work. This brought love to man's heart and psyche; and, he claimed, man

> matures through work
> which inspires him to difficult good;

also, perhaps more profoundly, he claimed he understood how inspiration did not end with the hands, although it began with them.

It enters the heart and mind, and
down to stone centres it descends through man's heart
and from the heart's centre the history of stones
grows large in the layers of earth.
And in man grows the equilibrium
which love learns through anger.

Through this theme of learning love through anger, Karol suggests how deeply he was affected by his reading in the works of St John of the Cross, to which he had been introduced by Tyranowski, and that in the dark night of the soul, or the blackest of emotional or physical circumstances, he sought and found the *via negativa*, the true energy of love, of hope and compassion.

But if in that winter of 1940 one thing in Karol's life was real and true, it is this: that well balanced although he was, he felt deep anger and conflict, and who was to say, in the absence of more tangible and physical substance, it was not this that fuelled him and kept his vital forces burning?

Anger, outrage, were in conflict with love and compassion; how *did* you cope with man's dreadful inhumanity to man? He ended 'Inspiration' with this matchless observation: to learn from anger, he wrote,

(your speech must not break at the lever's tension:
the fulcrum of anger and love).

He distilled in these poems a very concentrated frame of mind, work started from within, and 'the greatness of work is inside man'. There was no compromise with manipulating emotions, no cheating, no feigning of noble feeling for effect. Love feeds on well-grounded anger, while in triumphant conclusion, the experience of work creates an inner structure of the world: 'Where the greater the anger, the higher the explosion of love.'

This was Wojtyla in the harsh winter of 1940; but in February in the new year he confronted an even worse test – or disaster.

Since Christmas 1940 his father had been bed-ridden and seriously ailing and Karol used to stop by for a late-afternoon dinner at the Kydrynskis' flat, where Juliusz's mother, now known affectionately by

Karol as 'Mama' or 'Grandmama', set aside something for him to carry back and heat up for his father to eat. With Juliusz's sister Maria the two young men left one afternoon for the semi-basement flat or 'catacomb'; on arrival Maria began warming up the food and Karol went along the corridor to attend to his father; moments later he returned saying that his father was dead.

Maria recalls how distraught the discovery made Karol, because he had not been with Karol senior during the day and at the time he died. 'Karol, weeping, embraced me; through his tears he said, "I was not at my mother's death, I was not at my brother's death, I was not at my father's death." ' He then ran out to fetch a priest from the local parish church to administer the last rites.

He was desolated, shocked, and as he told someone in 1994, 'I never felt so alone.' That night Juliusz kept him company while, on his knees praying, Karol watched over the body of his father. February 18 was the date, Karol senior was sixty-two, while the cause of his death was a heart attack. Four days later, on an equally bitter and cold day, Father Figlewicz celebrated the funeral mass in the chapel at the Rakowice Cemetery, where Lieutenant Wojtyla was buried in the Kaczorowska family tomb.

Over the next weeks and months Karol visited the cemetery every day to pray at the grave, while in the middle room of the Kydrynskis' flat to which he moved in order not to be on his own, the family remarked on him lying often on the floor, prostrate in prayer. Mieczyslaw Malinski, who was younger than Karol, and who later left engineering to study alongside him as a seminarian, felt he was so distressed that something awful might happen, but that Tyranowski's Carmelite influence, about which he, Malinski, had been sceptical, helped him to regain his equanimity.

He still kept on hard at his studies, making an effort pacing up and down the flat to learn French vocabulary; he attended mass every day. Staying at the Kydrynskis' deepened his friendship with other families, one in particular, the Szkockis, one of whose daughters, Zofia, invited him to concerts at their home. Zofia's husband was in a prison camp, and again we glimpse a sustaining relationship with a young woman, as Wojtyla permits himself to observe, in *Gift and Mystery*, 'The dark period of the war and the occupation was brightened by the light of the beauty which radiates from music and poetry.'

But the Debniki basement, which had been salvation for father and son, where they had spent together the brief years before he reached the age of twenty-one, was now empty. Orphaned and alone, Karol was his own sole family. His case strikingly resembled that of Jean-Paul Sartre, the founder of existentialism, who wrote, 'I grew older in the darkness, I became a lonely adult without father or mother, almost without a name.'

The national news could hardly get worse. The day before his father died, a Franciscan, Father Maximilian Maria Kolbe, beloved and well known for his magazine *Knight of the Immaculate*, in which he urged Poles to hold to the truth of inner virtue in spite of 'armies of occupation and the hecatombs of concentration camps', had been arrested. He became number 16670 at Auschwitz – as Oswiecim had now become Germanified. Some time later, towards the end of May, they forced Father Kolbe to work building a crematorium. News of this filtered through slowly to the quarry workers; at this time all Auschwitz internees were Catholics, soon to be joined by Russian prisoners of war when in June 1941 Hitler invaded Russia.

In March, thanks to an ethnic German manager, quarry life eased for Karol as he joined Franciszek Labus, an older man in charge of dynamiting the rock. Karol's function was to drill holes and place ammoniac charges and fuses to blast the stone into pieces that could be sent on for processing. This rock-blaster warned Karol that if even a gram of explosive went missing, 'it would be Oswiecim . . . for you'. But he did not need to, for Wojtyla was not by temperament or conviction a resistance dynamiter.

He had joined Unia, the underground organisation whose leader and founder was Jerzy Braun, a philosopher and poet. This was a federation of patriotic organisations, non-political in aim, to foster a future Christian Social programme. Karol took the oath before Stanislaw Bukowski, a prominent Unia figure, who worked by day in Krakow as manager of a big cigarette factory. Some of Karol's friends did become combat members of Unia, but numbered among the ultimately fifteen hundred members in Krakow were non-combatant professors, scientists, and distinguished experts.

Far from the title of his poem 'Mystery of the Art of Work' Karol performed lowly functions among limestone. As he later recalls, Labus 'would occasionally say things like, "Karol, you should be a priest. You have a good voice and will sing well; then you'll be all set . . ."' As for Labus himself, he said later, of his young assistant, 'I was so sorry for him because he wasn't really any good [at the work]. He had such delicate little hands.' In fact Wojtyla, as I can vouch from taking his right hand in mine, had manly, powerful hands, perhaps more accurately described as 'worker's hands'. Hands were crucial. 'Hands are the heart's landscape,' he writes in The Quarry, 'They split sometimes/Like ravines in which an undefined force rolls.'

Others in the quarry, unlike Karol, did not heed the warnings about stealing ammoniac and dynamite sticks: one, his friend Wojciech Zukrowski, had joined the underground army, the AK (Armia Kro-jowa – home army), and he did steal for the guerrilla units. According to him Karol opposed armed struggle against the Germans, for Poles had done all they could in 1939, while 'the rest is in the hands of God – and Providence guides our destinies'.

Such quietism was sorely tested, not least close to hand when, crushed by stone from a misguided blast, a fellow worker died:

> And a stone smashed his temples
> and cut through his heart's chamber.
> They took his body, and walked in a silent line.
> Toil still lingered about him, a sense of wrong.

The anger in Karol still rippled below, turbulent but unseen: should 'his anger', he asks of the dead miner, 'now float into the anger of others?'

> It was maturing in him through its own truth and love.
> Each week or month brings fresh and shocking blows.

The persecution of priests mounted, for they defied the Hitler directive that they should preach only the humblest obedience to their German masters. Everywhere the subjugators beat and humiliated priests; they forced them to labour in public places, supposedly to hold them up to ridicule, although the effect was the opposite.

At Czestochowa, where Karol senior and son had gone on their pilgrimages to the Madonna, the Gestapo stole precious votive offerings from the walls and terrorised worshippers; elsewhere they shot up pictures of the Virgin. Shipped back to Germany, pyxes, monstrances, tableaux, etc., the sacred symbols of the mass looted from the churches of Poland, were presented by Hitler in a 'generous' gesture of the Führer towards the 'friendly' Spanish nation.

Nearer home Karol saw the Gestapo, on 23 May, raid St Stanislaw Kostka, and arrest its thirteen Silesian priests, all of whom were deported and died in Dachau later. In that same church, as Cardinal Wojtyla later recalled that black day, his friend and mentor Jan Tyranowski, rehearsing with the choir, escaped notice.

The church survived with a skeletal staff: as Karol later said of his Debniki parish church, 'Only an old parish priest and the Father Provincial remained.' When the Nazis shut down the Dominican priory school of Krakow's Holy Trinity Basilica, and used the yard as a supply depot young priests would sneak out at night to 'appropriate' food to give away to the town's starving people and fill the bottom third of the shipping canisters with rocks, claiming 'And that's why the Germans lost in Russia!'

In the Reich territory of occupied Poland rich and poor were deported from their homes to make room for the half million resettled ethnic Germans from East Poland, the Baltic states, and other regions. In Krakow they expelled home-owners from the smart streets like Krasinski, Mickiewicz and Slowacki Avenues and the Wawel Castle area, to form a new German quarter, strictly regulating what possessions they could take with them, and at first not providing any alternative housing. They renamed everything and Krakow's revered old central square became Adolf Hitler Platz.

But once again, for Karol, there was some compensation: in the summer of 1941 two happy events were set to transform the life of the isolated and extraordinary young man who had just passed his twenty-first birthday.

7

The Actor Carries the Problem

(1941–42)

Karol persuaded his mentor and friend Mieczyslaw Kotlarczyk, who was now thirty-one, to leave Wadowice with Zosia his wife and two children, and come and settle with him in Krakow, moving into his Tyniecka Street flat, vacant since the death of Karol's father. With this move another fated or providential stage of Karol's 'life or death to all eternity' began.

The move was no easy matter, because Wadowice, where Nazi rule had been harsher than in Krakow (and both Kotlarczyk's brothers had been arrested), lay on the west bank of the Skawa, over the border in the German-controlled Reich territory. In the General Government conditions were easier, for Poles enjoyed higher status and fewer restrictions. This border was guarded and patrolled, so they had to move at night, but even safely arrived in Krakow they had to obtain identity cards, while Kotlarczyk, at pains to hide any visibility as an intellectual, found work as a municipal tram driver.

He was fortunate and arrived at the right moment. The high school in Wadowice where he taught had been shut down, and he knew that like thousands of other men there was little else for him to do but wait to be drafted as slave labour and sent to Germany. Malinski noted him as 'a short man with black hair and bristly face' who spoke in a 'hoarse and dull voice', often in 'a loud whisper'. Equipped with his *Kriegswichtiger Betrieb* – work and identity permit – he was safe for the time being.

Once in Krakow he and Karol, together with Kydrynski, Halina Krolikiewicz, who acted as courier between Krakow and Wadowice, where her family still lived, Danuta Michalowska, his former classmate, Zukrowski from the quarry, and others, held a meeting on 22 August 1941.

At this meeting, in the flat belonging to the Szkockis, whose daughters became part of the group, Kotlarczyk outlined in his burning and passionate style his idea for the Rhapsodic Theatre, so named from the Ancient Greek school of poet-reciters and musicians who, placing the emphasis on words and the rhythms of utterance, performed the epic tales. Karol explained:

> The actor is a rhapsodist. That does not mean he only recites. On the other hand, it does not mean he simply 'acts'. Rather, he carries the problem. I have often pondered the 'place' of the actor in the rhapsodic concept of theatre. He hardly ever re-creates a given character or embodies it on stage. In performing his part, he repeatedly has to change from the first to the third person: he ceases to speak *as* a given character and begins to speak *about* him. The rhapsodic actor does not become a character but carries a problem; he is one of those who carry the problem of the whole performance.

Apart from its experimental nature, the main aspect of the Rhapsodic Theatre was, as Kotlarczyk said, 'its protest against the extermination of the Polish nation's culture on its own soil, a form of underground resistance movement against the Nazi occupation'. However – and this is important – although the group included a member who was an underground literary publisher, as well as the quarry worker who stole dynamite for the AK underground army, and although it gained support from Unia (orientated towards Christian and cultural resistance), it remained throughout a passive movement: Wojtyla never believed under any circumstances in shedding human blood.

Before the inaugural meeting in August they had already begun to mount plays. For their first clandestine performances, for audiences of thirty to forty people assembled illegally according to Nazi law, they concentrated on Slowacki's *King-Spirit* and rehearsed this through September and October 1941. Karol in this first production, in its demonstration of the conflict or struggle for power between God-inspired and power-seeking spirits, played mainly King Boleslaw the Bold, responsible for killing the martyr Archbishop Stanislaus of Krakow, the patron saint of Poland. He also narrated the beginning.

Delivering the text of the king murderer he orchestrated him, as

Halina attests, in his beautiful baritone voice in a repentant, fugitive way, conveying the moral dilemma of killing a good bishop. In subsequent performances he slowed down, emphasised even more the confessional element, warning against 'emptiness of the soul'. Fifty-three years later he corrected a lunch guest who had mentioned him as 'playing the role': no, he affirmed with emphasis, 'I was *reciting.*'

King-Spirit adopted the method which became a hallmark of their style of interspersing individual speeches with passages spoken as a chorus by some or all of the actors; this could happen very quickly, in a line or two, and this ritualised use of carefully edited texts could be very effective.

The Rhapsodic Theatre gave four performances of *King-Spirit*, the first on 1 November 1941, following this with another Slowacki work, *Beniowski*, which explores the adventures of an eighteenth-century Polish-Hungarian nobleman, but with topical digressions on their present-day life and times. Again Karol took the central role. They performed mainly in that flat of the Szkockis while their daughters played musical accompaniment from Chopin. The actors wore black and scenery was minimal.

Conditions changed dramatically again in Poland, for in July of this year Hitler broke the Ribbentrop-Molotov pact with Stalin, and invaded Russia, incorporating under German occupation that third part of Poland, by far the larger slice, which had been taken by Russia in 1939 in their co-ordinated move to eliminate Poland. Almost overnight, Polish prisoners of war, among them some of Karol's friends such as Jerzy Kluger and his lawyer father who had been shipped east and interned in camps, found themselves moved further east to Russia and imprisoned, subsequently 'released' and then trained to fight in a Free Polish division against the Germans under the Polish General Anders, finally transferring to Western fronts. Although the Germans announced one victory after another over the Russians, the reality on the ground was different. The demands on German fighting power grew greater and greater, and one detects, if only very slightly, a lessening of the grip of Nazi control over its Slav colony with Krakow as its new, glorious capital. There were, after all, bigger prizes to the east, so while the curfews, the daily executions, the sudden arrests and deportations went on, movement of the young group from flat to flat in pursuit of safe and secure venues grew a little easier.

Meantime Karol moved to a much easier and safer job, still within the munitions complex. Transferred to the Solvay chemical-processing plant in Borek Falecki, where the tramcars loaded with limestone arrived, he now had a two-hour walk from his home. His main activity at the factory was to carry wooden buckets of lime on a wooden yoke from furnaces up to a water processing 'laundry' where impurities were washed out. He also delivered liquid to be tested in the laboratory. Electing to do night shifts, sometimes double night shifts, in order to have more consecutive free hours, he seized the opportunity this indoor work gave him to pray and reflect.

Often he would stop off now on the journey to or from the plant to attend mass or pray at the old timbered parish church in Podgorze run by Redemptorists, who are a religious congregation founded in 1732 near Amalfi, Italy, by St Alphonsus Liguori, to spread the Gospel to the poor and most abandoned. In the middle of the night he would kneel to pray and his fellow workers would find him on his knees.

One member of the kitchen staff reported to her supervisor, telling her, 'This God-loving boy is an educated boy, very talented, he writes poetry and now he writes about St Theresa . . . He has no mother, and he is very poor. Give him a bigger slice of bread because what he gets at the plant is all he eats.' She did so; the industrial labourers who surrounded him daily treated him mainly with tolerance and humour, conniving in his tireless desire to read and respecting his surreptitious study. Life as a *robotnik* was tough.

> . . . the plant was a true seminary, albeit a secret one . . . At the time I did not realize how important the experience would be for me. Only later . . . did I realize how important . . . Every day I had been with people who did heavy work. I came to know their living situations, their families, their interests, their human worth, and their dignity. They knew that I was a student . . . I never encountered hostility on this account. It did not bother them that I brought books to work.
>
> They would often say [during the night shifts]: 'We'll keep watch; you go and take a break, we'll keep an eye open.'
>
> I was able to observe their deep but quiet religiosity and their great wisdom about life.

Here Karol made his firm connection between intellectual theory, complex thought and the wisdom and common sense of ordinary workers. He retained a lifelong pride that for four years he had shared the hard lot of workers. Visiting an Italian Solvay chemical factory in March 1982, he told workers, 'My time as a worker I consider a gift from God.' He had gained and everywhere took with him 'irreplaceable knowledge' of the world of work.

In July 1941 Rudolph Höss, Commandant of Auschwitz, who was brought up a Christian and nearly became a Catholic priest, arrived in Berlin for a new briefing on the camp's function; according to which

> The Führer has ordered the final solution of the Jewish question and we, the SS, were assigned this mission. The existing liquidation sites in the east cannot cope with the large operations expected in the future. I have therefore chosen Auschwitz for this purpose because of its convenient location in terms of transportation, and, second, because the site can be easily isolated and concealed.

(Höss symbolised that impersonal evil that Wojtyla as pope later was to identify as not only belonging to Nazis; a homebody and animal lover, Höss did not reflect and once 'given an order I had to carry it out'; never 'stooping to torture and beatings', he claimed 'the emotion of hatred is foreign to my nature'.)

Subsequently, according to the most modest estimates, over a million Jews as well as many others were to die at Auschwitz, but for the moment the soul of Poland was transfixed, riveted by the fate of one individual. On an autumn day in 1941, like a messenger's speech in a Greek tragedy after a grisly but foreshadowed and foreordained massacre or murder off-stage, another extraordinary narrative of the universal battle between good and evil seared Karol's awareness.

Weeks earlier in July the guard at Auschwitz reported a prisoner had escaped. No matter that he had not – later they found him drowned in a camp latrine, at least master of his own suicide – for the SS set in motion the usual reprisal procedure: for each escapee they killed ten or fifteen prisoners. Franciszek Gajowniczek, one of these selected at random for lethal injection (Zyklon-B had not yet been installed), cried out in anguish, 'My wife, my children, I shall never see them again!'

Maximilian Kolbe, who in Auschwitz had been assigned to building a crematorium for the new application for over a month now, heard him, came forward and saying he was a Catholic priest made a bid to take the place of the condemned man, who was relocated. This was accepted by the SS as well as by the condemned man. The guards then marched this former popular Catholic publicist, together with the other condemned nine to Block 11, the execution block, notorious to those who brought information in and out of Auschwitz for its inhumanly tiny and cramped cells and torture chambers. The yard had steel plating fixed to its wall to deflect the firing-squad bullets from damaging the brickwork, while the architects of execution had paved the yard with gravel to absorb the blood.

Naked, their filthy uniforms taken to be fitted on new arrivals, the condemned ten crowded together in an underground cell. Without food or water they languished here for two weeks; guards shot or kicked to death those who shouted complaints. When the SS could not hear, Father Kolbe led his fellow condemnees in saying the rosary and singing hymns to 'The Holy Mother of the Unhappy', while another prisoner, a Pole, privileged as janitor and interpreter, witnessed that 'I had the impression of being in a church'. This man, Bruno Burgowiec, reported later (and SS guards at the post-war Nuremberg trials confirmed this) that the camp officers in charge decided that Father Kolbe, and the three still alive out of the nine others, were taking too long to die.

On 14 August 1941, 'the sick cell was needed for new victims. So they brought in the head of the sick quarters, a German, a common criminal called Bock, who gave each in his turn an injection of carbolic acid in his left hand. Father Kolbe with a prayer on his lips gave his arm to the executioner.'

Gajowniczek lasted out his imprisonment, surviving to rejoin his wife and children after the war. News of the substitution and sacrifice spread across Poland like wildfire, exemplifying as it did the union between patriotism and religion. It became, in particular, part of Karol's own personal mythology of martyrdom, and in 1982, a year after his own escape from death, Pope John Paul II canonised Kolbe as the second saint of his pontificate, echoing Christ's words, 'He gave his life for a brother.'

News of the eastern front and the German advances dominated Polish minds through the autumn and winter of 1941–42. Meantime

Karol continued to perform in the coterie theatre, although this was coterie art with a difference, performed in the shadow of death. Setbacks to the Nazi regime, such as the defeat of the Luftwaffe by the RAF, the receding threat of Germany invading England, the Allied advances in North Africa – as heard in the secret BBC broadcasts – gave only glimmers of hope. America had not entered the war. The resurrection of Poland would happen, no doubt, and Roosevelt and Churchill both paid tribute to the stubborn resistance of the Poles: 'Poles, the heroism of your people standing up to cruel oppressors, the courage of your soldiers, sailors and airmen, shall not be forgotten,' said Churchill. 'Your country shall live again.' But when would this happen?

Karol pondered what his role would be in that new Poland, if he survived to see it. At the end of March 1942 the Rhapsodic Theatre put on *Hymn*, a poetry cycle by Jan Kasprowicz, interpreted as a Passion oratorio for Easter. Two months later they followed this with *Wyspianski's Hour*, a condensation or amalgam of this outstanding playwright's work taken from his *Wedding* (an acerbic look at Polish society), his *Acropolis* and his *Study of Hamlet*. The celebrated actor Osterwa attended a performance of this, giving the group his blessing and support.

During this hectic period Karol often went over in his own mind the case for and against becoming an actor, an actor-dramatist or, generally speaking, a man of the theatre. No one doubted he had all the skills, power and accomplishments of a future successful *jeune premier* who would in time become an acting heavyweight. He had exceptional intellectual power and interpretative understanding at his finger tips. He was good-looking, with a good singing voice, and a rich and mellifluous baritone speaking range. He had humour and a highly expressive face which could adapt itself from romantic and tragic parts easily to comedy. He was physically very tough, with enormous stamina.

But while Osterwa praised his acting, Karol was beginning no longer to feel sympathetic towards Osterwa's principles. Karol commented to Kotlarczyk that to Osterwa the theatre was an unfortunate 'atavistic burden . . . we are, if I may say, more primitive'. Later he stated how 'I am more attracted to people with a mysterious interior, a great interior . . . I don't feel any strong bonds.' Even more prophetically, as he told Kotlarczyk, 'I feel some resentment to these predestined celebrities' – by which it seems he reacted against the more visible vanities of the successful actor.

Halina Krolikiewicz retained vivid recall of how good an actor Wojtyla was. This is what Halina said about Karol: 'He scarcely moved a muscle when reciting, but with that voice and his feeling for the words and a way he had of tilting his head slightly so that every eye was on him, I had to keep reminding myself I was in the play.' In every role Lolek was the 'most talented and persuasive' of all the troupe. He submitted himself wholly to the Rhapsodic Theatre 'method', although this was enforced by Kotlarczyk with something of a dictator's power, an occupational disease of theatre directors. Another member of the troupe described how Kotlarczyk could behave 'like a Savonarola' (the Florentine friar who quarrelled with Pope Alexander VI), and he quarrelled with Karol's closest friend at that time, Juliusz Kydrynski, who left the group.

Karol now approached a crucial moment of choice. For the present he had stopped writing plays, but as a subject for a new play there was a character that interested him as a means of exploring his inner being and dilemmas. This was Adam Chmielowski, born in 1846, a one-legged former freedom fighter for Poland, who was captured by the Russians, but escaped and reached Paris, where he studied painting and, on returning to Poland in 1870, exhibited for the first time in Krakow.

Ten years later, by then a successful artist, Chmielowski joined the Jesuit order, suffered a nervous breakdown and left the order. Over the next few years, while a lay Franciscan, he became more and more disillusioned with the social futility of art. Some years later he became a monk, taking the name of Brother Albert, and thereafter founded a movement for the poor and homeless which became famous, while he as its founder died in 1916, 'in an aura of sanctity'. The then Bishop of Krakow, Adam Sapieha, now a mentor of Karol, attended his funeral, giving Karol a direct link with Brother Albert. When he was fourteen Karol heard that Chmielowski's beatification process had been started; in 1938, Poland's president accorded Brother Albert the highest national award – the Grand Ribbon of the Order of Polonia Restituta.

This combination of heroic virtues, artistic talents, priestly vocation and a sense of mission, fascinated Karol. We can see from his play *Our*

God's Brother, which he began thinking about in 1941 and the first draft of which he completed in 1944 (but went on rewriting until 1948), how the voices of the various characters, embodiments of the temptations, doubts and desires which Karol himself underwent, must have made their presence felt upon him. But not in passionate turmoil as in *Job*, or possibly the lost *David*, but rather in the forms of a well-ordered and good-tempered debate, with echoes perhaps – in its heavier overtones of the religious faith – of another drama of the inner life: T.S. Eliot's *Murder in the Cathedral*. In this Thomas à Becket, before his brutal murder, in turn confronts his fearful protectors, the women of Canterbury, his four well-mannered yet intellectually slippery tempters, and his eminently persuasive murderers, the four Norman knights.

Most of the action of *Our God's Brother* takes place in the monk hero's mind. Some of the 'inner theatre' of *Our God's Brother* reveals Karol's own state of mind in the years immediately before he wrote it. Bringing together events and characters from different periods, Karol's first act shows friends and admirers of Adam in his studio who have come to look at his unconventional portrait of Christ. Adam tells his friends, among whom is another artist, an actress, a critic and a theologian, 'Thank you for taking an interest in my work – which has never succeeded fully or found total expression.' Certainly here is the young, struggling Wojtyla, full of insight into himself yet with an engrossing difficulty to resolve. As the theologian comments on the Christ painting, 'It reveals to us the immense tension within the artist. And that has its own force.'

Karol based the character Max on an eminent nineteenth-century Polish artist, and he based other characters on historical figures, but the character Madam Helena is particularly revealing of Wojtyla's circle, moulded as it is on Helena Modrzejewska, Poland's greatest actress, who lived from 1840 to 1909. Buried in Krakow she also (naturally!) was a great Polish patriot, deported from Warsaw by the Russians in 1895 and barred from ever again entering Poland, although of course she did.

Madam Helena remains a shadowy person, unlike some of Karol's female characters in *The Jeweller's Shop*, his later play about love and marriage. This suggests he had as yet not much deep knowledge or awareness of what went on inside women, and could not characterise their interior being.

He does not flesh out his characters, for example as Shakespeare does, following their highly changeable, spontaneous and completely unpredictable switches of emotion or mood – this kind of realism was never his intention. But Madam Helena does have an intriguing and revealing talk with Max, who represents another side of the argument about the artist's calling. She is described in an earlier draft as the 'Lady with the power of catharsis', in which, after talking at length in the rather stilted prose (which Karol's translator says stems from the philosophical comedies of Karol's favourite Cyprian Norwid), she compliments Max, saying 'I marvel at your capacity to enter someone else's train of thought.'

Max replies: 'A simple technique of flexible personality, of mixing with people. And you must know it is the exchangeable man [i.e. the man who can adapt easily] who does it. And he is neither the most profound, or the most interesting. It is the non-exchangeable man [i.e. the integrated, ontologically secure man] who is the most interesting.'

Through Max Karol develops a theory that reflects his own concerns: Max values art because it stimulates him, fulfils him. He is not too concerned about the public reaction to his work, and yet while scorning applause he also yearns for it. It is important for him to draw a line between the exchangeable man, and the 'non-exchangeable man known only to himself'.

In the debate about the nature of the artist (and, by implication, Wojtyla's own preoccupation) Adam comes up with a specific demand to Madam Helena: 'What does it cost you,' he asks, 'to play Ophelia or Lady Macbeth?' She answers, 'In a way it costs me all my life. Yes . . . but it is a curious price, a stranger ransom. Each time I pay it in full; each time I pay it all over again.' Adam answers, significantly if obscurely, 'I cannot buy myself out at that price.' Madam Helena asks what he means: 'From whom? Yourself?'. To which, Adam answers: 'I am not alone.' [*Pause. They concentrate on 'Alone'*]

Karol, probing his own being, puts similar self-analysis into the mouth of the art critic Lucian, whom he based on Lucian Siemienski, professor of literature, poet, critic, a Goethe-like figure and a revolutionary. He points to a clear assertion – Karol's realisation that he could never be an artist like other artists.

Lucian describes how Adam can transform a great many things within himself and then mark the results on canvas. But he is not a typical painter:

Try to understand the difference. Each of you tries to find on canvas the various possible and successive solutions to your lives. Your lives happen, take place, on canvas. That's why you can't see them differently; you are bound to your canvas, subordinated to your palette. With Adam it is different. For him the need for canvas and paint drags way behind his deepest being. He turns to them almost reluctantly, almost scornfully because, after all, he regards them as a means and requires them as such. But that is all. His attitude toward his craft is far more detached. He is far more independent. Basically, he lives within himself, develops and contracts in himself, not on canvas.

Here Karol presents a parable – an analogy – for the true nature of man: the need for canvas and paint drags way behind, so the deeper being will never be satisfied by art.

Towards the end of this first act a stranger appears who tells Adam he is insufficiently aware of his own anger – 'Your other friends,' he says, 'want at any price to reduce your anger to an outburst of artistic genius.' The Stranger believes there is greater social use to which such anger can be put. Adam has already commented that 'Society is like a sick organism. But a sick organism soon spends itself, reaches its limits and fails; society can hide the disease within for a long time. Or rather, it can hide from the disease.' It is anger, which by exploding constructively, can make society aware of the disease.

In the second act Karol brings that unrealised anger to the fore: exploring the side of Adam that is running away from himself (called flippantly by the theologian 'a vocation'). The contentious figures of the first act have disappeared and Karol places us in 'The Vaults of Anger'. It is perhaps the most complex, fascinating expressionistic piece of dramatic writing he ever composed.

In terms of his spiritual development Adam is rejected by the poorhouse, and in his ongoing conflict, or the irresolution of his deep interior anger, he engages in debate with an *alter ego* figure, The Other, who pushes him further and further in the direction of that hidden force or vocation, scorning his artistic side: 'There is a strange contradiction between what you say and think', he observes, and 'You bypass both the lie and the truth. You are a true artist.' Adam is clearly going to free himself from the 'tyranny' of art but also the 'tyranny' of intelligence, for he has found a different image to follow (and here the writer adds a personal note as a stage direction, quite ingenuously it seems: [*I do not know whether it is true Adam burned some of his painting to free himself for Christ in the poor*]).

The limits of drama have been reached in what, for Karol, is unreality. Adam ends the play by integrating his anger in joining the Franciscans and attaining the rank of Brother Superior. As such he concludes:

> Ah well. You know that anger has to erupt, especially if it is great [*He stops*]
>
> And it will last, because it is just.
>
> [*He becomes even more deeply lost in thought. Then he adds one sentence, as if to himself though everyone else listens attentively*]
>
> I know for certain, though, that I have chosen a greater freedom.

A greater freedom! To which Karol added the stage direction: [*This was one of the last days in the life of Brother Superior*]

Indirectly here, then, we glimpse Wojtyla working out his mission of self-realisation. Earlier in the play in a stage direction he has shown more than anything the limits, or boundaries, of his own artistic inclinations and skills, beyond which he is not prepared to go. Significant perhaps, too, is what he left out, which is of a piece with Wojtyla the man. He condensed, transposed in time, or simply omitted some events of Brother Albert's own life – his novitiate with the Jesuits, his nervous breakdown and cure, his activities which other more sensational dramatists would surely have exploited – while as in all Karol's plays none of it unfolds in the action. But for Karol mental illness, or a fear of madness that often haunts figures of towering intellectual temperament such as he was, never seemed to have been much of a personal concern.

The living tissue of Adam's drama is that people and objects unite in him, 'charged with an obstinate force from within, accepted or rejected, won and lost, found and forgotten'. Adam constantly exchanges some part of his old self for some part of a new one, but while gain and progress result from this exchange there is also pain. And in this process 'he is revealed to himself, constantly *astonished* [Karol's italics] at his own fate. It must be so, because thanks to that astonishment he reveals in himself the love that works through him.'

Karol is above all concerned in *Our God's Brother* with Brother Albert – or Adam as he is called in the play – 'overcoming the artist in himself'. To this extent it is a kind of Shavian 'problem play', in which the playwright sets out through the characters to debate and resolve a specific personal or social issue. Karol also deals with another important issue, that of revolution, and the hero's sensitivity to social issues would seem to have been worked into the scheme after the war, when he rewrote his first draft. He made the play's final message and resolution, the necessity of being moulded by love, more general and predictable, but in some of the interchanges between 'Adam' and the antagonists in his soul's development Wojtyla speaks in his own authentic voice.

So the real Adam finds his path: Karol appreciates Brother Albert's lifelong influence over him as particularly important. Crucially he states, 'I found in him a real *spiritual support and example* in leaving behind the world of art, literature and the theatre, and *in making the radical choice of a vocation to the priesthood.*' In *Wstancie Chodzmy!*, his penultimate memoir, he states that in Brother Albert's 'memory, in his heart, he was for me a very strange person. I was spiritually bound to him . . . I saw in him a model which was right for me – his life history helped me to leave behind art and theatre.' *God's Own Brother* marked the most powerful and dramatic moment in his life, his 'conversion' – as significant as that of St Paul on the road to Damascus – from fledgling artist into committed disciple.

8

Hidden Forces Produce
the Strongest Actions

(1942–45)

But to give up the theatre was not by any means the whole story of Karol's decision to become a priest.

Joining Jan Tyranowski's Living Rosary movement (in which each member would say one of the mysteries every day) had led to his deepening of devotion to the Mother of God, during which he became convinced that while he knew Mary led him to Christ he began to realise that Christ leads us to his mother. Reading the 'rather florid and baroque' treatise of *True Devotion to the Blessed Virgin* by the Breton saint Louis de Montfort, he said, also helped him considerably: 'Yes, Mary does bring us closer to Christ; she does lead us to him, provided that we live her mystery in Christ.' He grew so devoted to his copy of this, carrying it with him everywhere, that its cover became stained with lime from the Solvay plant.

Alongside others he knew who secretly aspired to the priesthood he also tackled a set book for would-be seminarians. Sitting by the Solvay plant boiler he struggled for a year with *Ontology* or *Metaphysics* (1926) by Father Kazimierz Wais. 'I actually wept over it,' he said later; '. . . after hacking through this vegetation I came to a clearing, to the discovery of the deep reasons for what until then I had only lived and felt . . . it opened a whole new world to me.'

In mid-December of 1941 sixteen-year-old Maria Kotlarczyk had fled from Wadowice and joined her brother, his wife and Karol in the Tyniecka flat. In August 1942 Karol's aunts, who still lived upstairs, forced her to leave, fearing the Gestapo might, if an unregistered girl was discovered there, wreak reprisal on the family. They moved her on to Kroscienko, where she succeeded in obtaining papers for survival. She recalled, fifty years on, the 'catacomb' apartment in which she stayed as having a theatrical atmosphere, with constant rehearsals going on. She said that no one was afraid.

She escaped what everyone knew came to camp inmates of her age. The Germans infected Polish girls with gas-gangrenous wounds for sulphonamide tests. Using X-rays they sterilised the newly captive Russians *en masse*; at Sachsenhausen they injected hepatitis virus, at Ravensbrück inflammatory liquids into the uterus; phologonomon (infectious) induction, injections of typhus vaccine, experimental bone-transplants, the forced drinking of sea-water . . .

By now the introduction of Zyklon-B, manufactured by Degesch, the vermin-combating division of I.G. Farben, had been substituted for lethal injection and had speeded up the final solution at Auschwitz, now termed by Commandant Höss 'the greatest institution for human annihilation of all time'. Höss had himself, by using Zyklon-B on rats and other vermin in the camp, discovered its exterminating efficiency, which he communicated to Adolf Eichmann. As in a large-scale industrial operation firms submitted competitive tenders for processing the dead, disposing of 2,000 bodies every twelve hours. German Armaments Incorporated designed five furnaces, corpse cellars with gas-proof doors and observation posts, over which they planted lawns; every now and again they installed concrete mushrooms to cover the shafts down which the 'sanitary orderlies' shoved the amethyst crystals of Zyklon-B. The dead and dying clawed each other desperately trying to get out, but most of each consignment of prisoners died in twenty-five minutes in 'one blue clammy, blood-spattered pyramid'.

Of 8,700,000 Jews in Nazi territories in December 1941, an estimated 5,800,000 were to be murdered by early 1945, while by the end of 1941 alone half a million Jews had been shot by special extermination squads in the wake of the German armies advancing into Russia. But not only Jews died. Himmler announced in March 1941 that when Germany invaded Russia they intended to kill thirty million Slavs – not straight away, but slowly reduced by the forced-labour policy till every last ounce of work had been extracted from them on the minimum of rations, and they were fit for no more than extermination in the ovens – an expendable raw material. This second function of Auschwitz is often overlooked: the camp as a new form of human society dedicated to a new form of slavery – 'of human beings continually replenished and expendable'.

In February 1942 Archbishop Prince Sapieha sent news to the Vatican about the concentration camps whose inmates were 'deprived of all human rights, handed over to the cruelty of men who have no feelings of humanity. We live in terror, continually in danger of losing everything if we attempt to escape, thrown into camps from which few emerge alive.'

Sapieha insisted this letter be committed to memory and destroyed by Father Risso Scavizzi, its priest-courier to Rome, and he warned Pius's diplomatic Secretary of State Giovanni Montini (the future Pope Paul VI) that the publication of such information (about Oswiecim-Auschwitz) could give rise to further persecution. In May of the same year, 1942, Pius and Montini heard for the first time of the mass exterminations of Jews in Poland, Germany and the Ukraine from Father Scavizzi and other Knights of Malta chaplains who travelled back and forth from those countries to Rome.

Father Scavizzi reported that when he told Pius, 'I saw him weep like a child.' Pius, through Montini, had subsequently written to Sapieha about the ghettos and Auschwitz. Sapieha stuffed the letter, brought to him by Father Quirino Paganuzzi into the stove, telling Paganuzzi, who had witnessed the gruesome removal of Jews from the Krakow ghetto, 'if I gave publicity to this and it is found in my house, the head of every Pole would not be enough for the reprisals Governor Hans Frank would order . . . It's not just the Jews . . . here they are killing us all . . .' Specifically of the Krakow Jews Sapieha said:

> The worst thing of all is that those unfortunates are left without help, cut off from the whole world. We cannot, we must not say so for fear of shortening their lives. We are living through the tragedy of those unfortunate people and none of us is in a position to help them any more . . . There's no difference between Jews and Poles . . . They have taken away our bread and our freedom . . . but at least we have our lives, and with life there's hope of seeing the end of our Calvary.

Underground Polish culture continued to operate. On 3 October 1942 the Rhapsodic Theatre opened its *Norwid's Hour* in which those themes close to Karol's heart, the meaning and function of art, especially as applied to Poland, were explored through excerpts from *On the Freedom of the Word, Promethidion* and *Chopin's Piano*. Sometime in that same autumn Karol told his fellow actors that he had begun attending the secret seminary and would be leaving the theatre to follow his studies. But although he had made the decision and informed his friends, Karol did not leave the Rhapsodic Theatre straight away. It was not until 1944 that he stopped acting for them; by then he had appeared in all seven wartime productions of the company, for which they had held over a hundred clandestine re-hearsals and given twenty-two performances to their carefully selected audiences. For a group that was essentially non-professional this was a lot of plays and an impressive number of performances. But he had determined upon becoming a monk, perhaps also because this would give him more opportunity for private study and composition than he would have as a regular priest. In his early biography Malinski gives an eye-witness account of Karol's visit to Wawel to communicate his new decision.

> We entered the precincts of the castle, which, being the residence of the Nazi governor general, was guarded by German police. Father Figle-wicz lived in a building opposite the main entrance to the cathedral. We walked up a flight of broad, highly polished wooden stairs and were greeted by a cheerful-looking priest with pleasant manners who gave us tea in a small parlour. He then went off with Karol to another room and they did not come back for some time. I wondered what could be going on – it seemed too long for confession or for an ordinary chat. Eventually, they came back and exchanged a few words of farewell, after which Karol and I set off for home.
>
> 'Why were you there so long?' I asked.
>
> Karol did not seem to hear my question, but simply said:
>
> 'I wanted to tell you that I've decided to become a priest.'
>
> I said nothing, but reflected: 'Just as I thought.'
>
> 'That's what I was talking to him about.'

This account has been disputed – how did they pass the guards? – but Karol has passed no comment. Was it Father Figlewicz, or was it Father Jan Piwowarczyk, the rector of the now virtually defunct seminary, who would be formally responsible for accepting him? What would it mean, joining a seminary stripped of its academic means of philosophical and theological formation? Many of its students had already been shot or sent to Auschwitz. It seemed Karol was about to change one secret life for another, or rather add one on top of another.

His acting friends argued with him and tried to dissuade him. Kotlarczyk in particular tried desperately hard to persuade him to reverse his decision; for Kotlarczyk the theatre was God's instrument to serve Poland and the church. Another biographer reports how his friends organised an all-night debate between Karol and Tadeusz Kudlinski, in which this close acting friend and former Jagiellonian student used every possible biblical and literary persuasion to overthrow his arguments. But Karol had been summoned: 'Kotlarczyk believed that the Living Word and the theatre were my calling, but Lord Jesus believed it was the priesthood, and somehow we agreed on that,' was how the Pope later phrased it.

So he began a new life, rising to take part in the 6.30 mass in the archbishop's private chapel in his palace on Franciszkanska Street. He served at mass with another seminarian, and when the seminary started training in earnest in October 1942, underground professors of the banned Jagiellonian University who had survived also began, secretly all over Krakow, to teach again some 800 students.

The seminary, strictly speaking, was still a faculty of the university and students, perhaps ten or more, were called 'parish secretaries', many coming in from outlying areas. During the day, or in night shifts, Karol still worked at the Solvay plant but he now had an easier routine. In November 1942, during the 400th anniversary of the birth of St John of the Cross, founder of the Carmelites, Karol called on the father provincial of the order, expressing his wish to join, but was gently discouraged with the reason the Germans would not agree for him to leave his vital war work to become a monk. He was told to come back later. Archbishop Sapieha put his seal on this by a more positive admonition for Karol to follow the active rather than contemplative life.

The loudspeakers on the Krakow streets disseminated censored news in German, now mainly of hollow or invented victories over the Soviets. At the Zoscinkis' home one evening in late November the Rhapsodic Theatre played *Pan Tadeusz*, giving Karol the opportunity to repeat his schoolboy success in delivering the epic poem, when, as he began reciting the confession of Father Robak, the priest, the

German voice from the loudspeaker outside drowned his voice with propaganda lies.

Karol did not stop. Tadeusz Kwiatkowski, who later married Halina, recalled how he 'did not alter his tone. He spoke softly, calmly, as if he was not hearing the barking of the loudspeaker.' Karol told Juliusz Osterwa, who said he would have stopped his performance straight away. 'No, we cannot allow oneself to be dominated by the invader.'

The group's final full production in March 1943 was Slowacki's *Samuel Zborowski*, a drama about the sixteenth-century Polish nobleman executed for his rebellious stand. Karol played the title role. His studies had significantly moved on from the philosophy of the previous autumn: he had continued to struggle at length with Kazimierz Wais's dense, contemporary metaphysical work, but he now inclined more to Aristotle and Thomas Aquinas, he told Frossard, and even more specifically to theological rather than philosophical texts. And more and more he came under the influence of one man whose presence in his life dominated the next few years: the Polish-Lithuanian aristocrat archbishop, Prince Adam Stefan Sapieha.

Karol must have asked himself often, how could Sapieha have survived when he so powerfully stood for everything opposed to Nazism, its dictatorial methods, its amorality, its atrocities and, on every level, its inhumanity? Why or how had they not locked him away in a cell, or concentration camp, had him liquidated, or sent him into exile? They could not have worried unduly that his removal or death would inflame Poles to acts of rebellion, or rise as a whole nation, for the Poles, fully crushed as they were, were already in a state of defiant subjugation, and likely to remain so.

There is an anecdote to the effect that Hans Frank, who enjoyed absolute rule in the General Government, sought an invitation to dinner in the Archbishop's Palace, and when this finally came the 'Unbroken Prince', as he was known, and the bumped-up Nazi lackey, himself a prosecuting lawyer, sat at opposite ends of the dinner table while a waiter brought black bread made partly from acorns, jam boiled from sugar and red beets, and ersatz coffee.

Sapieha explained to his alarmed guest that he could not risk a member of his household staff being prosecuted for buying food on the black market, and that this was the full amount the Poles, from their ration books, ate as their entitlement. But while this story of sticking to the rules might be exaggerated, for Polish rations were better – if little better – than this, Sapieha did have a reputation for the controversial gesture which upset conventional expectations, especially those that stemmed from his aristocratic lineage. Some even went so far as to claim that Sapieha's aristocratic mien confronted the enemy with the silence not of compliance but of contempt, as if they were creatures too far below decency to merit recognition.

For instance, at his inauguration as Krakow's bishop in 1912 he had shunned the gentry, who awaited his arrival, by visiting a poorhouse. He fell out with Pope Pius XI, who earlier in life as Apostolic Visitor had felt affronted by Sapieha convening a conference of Polish bishops and refusing to allow him to attend. When Sapieha asked twice in 1939 to retire at the advanced age of seventy-two (having been denied the cardinal's hat which was his due), he was ordered to stay at his post.

A further reason given for his survival was his cunning: he was too clever to let the Germans catch him. What he did behind the scenes extended right across a whole host of proscribed activities: from enabling priests to grant Jews Christian baptismal certificates; from clandestine contacts with the underground army, to interceding with the authorities in all kinds of ways, as well as comforting those betrayed or bereaved; and of course all the time he was preparing for the future of a free Poland by instructing young priests. He smuggled out warnings to allies (which went unheeded). Isolated, cut off from the Vatican, which though supposedly neutral was encircled by Mussolini's Rome – and could well have done with a Sapieha figure in charge – Sapieha stood alone. One devotional writer claims that 'bloodiness alone could not sustain a man in these desperate circumstances. Every night at 9 p.m. the seminarians saw the Prince Archbishop go into his chapel alone, for an hour. It was understood that he was presenting his problem to his Lord, and that he was not to be disturbed.'

Sapieha was indeed remarkable, a gaunt figure of iron will, beak-nosed and with piercing eyes, possessing natural authority and great dignity, according to one of his subordinates in the palace. Without losing power he was never defiant, openly hostile or critical of the oppressors. Therefore, at some level, while retaining his dignity as far as possible, he took his responsibilities to maintain order and the church's hierarchy seriously, thereby earning the approval of the Nazis who anyway, and up to a point, advocated keeping in place existing structures. (As far back as 1940 Gauleiter Frank in his diary assessed that 'to the Polish imagination, the Church is the central point of reference, constantly shining in silence and thereby playing in some way the role of the eternal beacon'.) In secret, apparently so impressed was Frank by the example of the 'Unbroken Prince' that he became tempted to embrace the Catholic faith. But he didn't convert, not anyway for the time being.

A German document recording his audience with Frank on 5 May 1944 states that the Governor had a new policy towards Poles, which he hoped to have ratified in Berlin. It gave Poles better treatment while working in the Reich, full religious rights, and claimed to prepare the way for a 'purified' Catholic Poland obtaining cultural and partly political autonomy (along the lines that had allowed Krakow and Galicia to prosper in the Austro-Hungarian Empire). In return Frank requested Sapieha to denounce Bolshevism and the English, while the 1944 document claimed Sapieha condemned the partisans as murderers, and laid some of the blame on the Jews. Called a staunch defender of Polishness (*Polentum*), the Germans also credited him with an understanding of collaboration (*Zusammenarbeit*).

While he was in no way playing a double game, there must have been some strong indication from which the Germans connected his leadership with the ordered and compliant, yet productive, subjected state of the majority of the Poles. The Poles saw Sapieha as their leader. The Germans needed him to fulfil their own appalling plans and he, while resisting these, supported the Germans in neutral areas which did not indicate approval – such as public order – while continually pressing for reason and reform; for example, for more priests to be trained. Paradoxically, then, the Germans, under the leadership of Hans Frank, needed this Polish leader in charge of their subject Slav population, who gave the Nazis an example of dignity and order, while never flattering or kowtowing to them (similar to that relationship – as depicted by Pierre Boulle, the French author – between Colonel Nicholson and Colonel Saito, his Japanese commandant counterpart in the prison camp during the building of the bridge over the River Kwai).

No one reproached Sapieha; quite the opposite, he was hailed as a heroic Catholic leader; yet as a virtually captive cleric he supported underground movements and gave what personal help he could to victims of Nazi persecution. He had style and a sure touch: all Poles knew where he stood. The Nazis felt instinctive respect for a natural leader. They felt (or Governor Frank felt), they could excuse Sapieha's presence, even his aloof manner, which could be interpreted as defiance, and justify him as an aristocrat of ancient Lithuanian stock. The Poles could love him and worship him as being (although hidden) an underground leader who held power until tyranny was broken and a new order arrived.

The Allies, gathering strength with America fully committed to the cause, ignored pleas to bomb and paralyse the death camps. The Nazi intention of clearing Warsaw of the rest of its Jews in the ghetto provoked, in April 1943, the Warsaw ghetto uprising. While the Jews held out for nearly a month, the Nazis killed half of 60,000 men, women and children. They transported the remainder to Treblinka. At roughly the same time in Krakow Jews were expelled from their ghetto; the Nazis murdered scores in a massacre in Zgoda Square, among them Aszer Anszil Icchak Seltenreich, a rabbi Karol knew from the Wadowice synagogue who had moved to Krakow. None of this information was hidden from the West, but it was mainly ignored: even the so-called Black Books, with minute documentation and graphic photographs of atrocities, published in London from 1941 onwards, together with statements from the Polish government-in-exile, failed to prompt action other than military campaigns. I have one in my hand as I write this. In their indexes they contain comprehensive lists of Poles, Jews and Gentiles alike, murdered, tortured or incarcerated. They print the whole specious legality of Nazi conquest. A particularly sinister aspect of Nazi rule was the methodical thoroughness of its bureaucratic documentation and the conviction of its intellectual arrogance.

Seminarians risked their lives daily by studying theology. A fellow server at the archbishop's morning mass, Jerzy Zachuta, failed to turn up one morning: the Gestapo had arrested him, taken him from his home and, shortly after his name appeared on those lists posted of condemned Poles, shot him. As if, with the complete loss of his family, the daily disappearance of friends and fellow countrymen, the arduous daily round he suffered, this was not enough for Karol, another near tragedy befell him which could have come right out of the book of Job.

On 29 February 1944, after his double-shift and as he wearily made his way in the dark on the road from the Borek plant to his home, Karol was struck down from behind by a *Wehrmacht* truck which vanished without stopping. A woman passing on a tram saw him lying unconscious in the ditch by the roadside, alighted and examined him to see if he was alive. His head had hit the kerbstone and he was covered in blood. The woman, Jozefa Florek, stopped a passing car whose occupant, a German officer, made her fetch muddy water from a ditch to wash away the blood. The compassionate officer, whose name is unknown, commandeered a lumber truck to carry Wojtyla to the Kopernik Street hospital where for nine hours Karol was in a coma. He awoke at last to find his head bandaged for concussion and that he had cuts and an injury to his shoulder.

They kept him in hospital for a fortnight and afterwards he convalesced for more weeks at the Szkockis' where there was a piano and the two daughters to keep him company; he then managed to escape for some time into the countryside, vacationing in July with a local parish priest.

On his return from his convalescence in early August 1944 the city of Krakow buzzed with rumours, lying reports, eye-witness accounts of the great Warsaw uprising. As news of the advancing victorious Red Army which had reached the city's suburbs reached the ears of the long-suffering people, apprehension had already risen with hope for the future. Nearly half of the former inter-war Polish republic was now in Russian hands, so liberty was at hand. But was it to be liberty? There was now something of a potential breakdown in Nazi rule in those parts of the General Government in Krakow still in German hands, and especially in the towns other than the capital.

Warsaw erupted on 1 August 1944 in a well-planned uprising of the 30,000-strong AK army, logistically supported by hundreds of thousands of ordinary citizens. The small Communist underground army, often at odds with the AK, took part in it, but the retreating Germans defeated the Soviets on 4–5 August in a tank battle near Wolomin. In September the Soviets were again advancing and reached the Vistula, then withdrew six miles, breaking off contact perhaps in retribution for that historical defeat of the Soviets in 1920, but mainly so that those opposed to their future domination should have no military muscle. Churchill raged, while Roosevelt neglected to help the Poles in favour of keeping up his 'friendship' with Stalin. This gave the Germans a free hand not only to crush and annihilate every sign or vestige of resistance, but to raze and obliterate the whole inner city. Deeds of heroism were uncountable, while the Russians refused the British and American air forces the use of airfields to supply and reinforce the uprising. Not before two months, however, was the whole city subdued, and three months later when the Russians entered Warsaw, 'they found not a single person still living within the limits of a city that in 1939 had been home to more than a million-and-a-quarter Catholic and Jewish Poles. Except for the two cities hit by atomic bombs, no others in Europe or Asia suffered devastation equal to that of Warsaw, caught between German wrath and Allied perfidy.'

In Krakow repercussions were immediate, as the Germans, in a pre-emptive move to stop any further uprising, rounded up some 8,000 young men and older boys. On 'Black Sunday', 6 August, German trucks descended on the suburbs, while police and military combed the houses. When they raided Tyniecka Street Karol and the Kotlarczyks remained in the 'catacomb'. Zosia begged Karol and her husband to hide in the garden among the shrubbery.

'But my begging was in vain,' she said. 'Karol knelt and began to pray. Finally the Germans broke into our two-storey house. The upstairs apartments had to be opened ... I don't know how it happened, but they didn't enter our quarters in the basement. Karol still knelt in prayer, my husband sat motionless at the table.' How could it not have happened? 'Hidden forces produce the strongest actions,' says the Pope.

Sapieha acted quickly, giving his secret seminarians refuge in the palace. He dispatched Father Kuczkowski, a young priest who came from Wadowice, to collect Karol. The priest obtained the aid of Mrs Szkocka to act both as scout and decoy on the return journey. She walked ahead, watching out for Germans, followed by Kuczkowski in a cassock and Karol, who wore his working clothes and wooden clogs, and carried large notebooks. They crossed the Debnicki bridge, passing through the old town to safety. Malinski, who had been in hiding in his sister's house, also found sanctuary, together with ten other seminarians who were now, as they joked 'under house arrest', and hid there for the next five and a half months. Among Karol's new companions were Staszek Koscielny with his 'chubby face'; Karol Targos with 'stammering voice'; Wladek Majola with his thick glasses; Janek Sidlo with his 'sleek black hair and the military boots he wore under his cassock'.

Karol became a non-person. He simply had to disappear completely. His absence from the plant was quickly noticed, and the Germans sent letters, then searched for him.

At the East German Chemical Works the Polish manager, Henryk Kulakowski, had to be persuaded to take steps to validate that disappearance. Father Figlewicz, sent by Sapieha, put the case, and Kulakowski, who remarked 'I would jump into the fire for the archbishop', took the appropriate steps to list Wojtyla as having left, so that as he himself said later, the authorities 'were unable to find my trail'. In the chaos and breakdown of the ensuing months, to find him could not have been a high priority, for hundreds, even thousands were slipping away from the General Government, and from the west of Poland, to find temporary security behind the Soviet lines while they awaited liberation.

Meantime, should they be raided at the palace, Sapieha gave the seminarians in hiding false identity papers and the disguises of minor orders who sought refuge from the fighting. He now became not only their mentor but their rector, holding classes in his drawing-room, while they slept next to the chapel in a second-floor dormitory. Helped by two other priests Sapieha had a full, demanding daily schedule for his nucleus of new ordinands, and they were even able to include the visits of outside lecturers. Juliusz Osterwa, who had last seen Karol perform in secret, met him again in clerical garb when he visited to tutor them in elocution and sermon delivery. Jan Tyranowski also visited Karol, their last meeting before Tyranowski, who had been seriously ill, died.

November 11, in those last months of declining Nazi rule, saw Karol, at his own request, tonsured in the private chapel – this shaving of the crown of the head (abolished by Pope Paul VI in 1972), performed by Sapieha, symbolised initiation into the clerical state. On 21 December Sapieha conferred on Wojtyla the orders of exorcist (the minor order of casting out evil spirits, also abolished by Paul VI in 1972) and acolyte. The fast-track diocesan acolyte was well on the way to full priesthood. He spent Christmas holidaying in the mountains with another parish priest, so fear of arrest must have receded sufficiently for the seminarians to leave their hiding place.

During the day of 17 January Father Figlewicz celebrated in Wawel Cathedral his last mass of the war. The Germans, now in full retreat, blew up the Debnicki bridge, shattering the glass of the Archbishop's

Palace windows in the blast. The following morning the Russians arrived at the palace: three generals, including Marshal Koniev, commander of the Russian-Ukraine army and much praised by Krakovians for his swift advance which saved the city from pre-planned demolition, alighted from their jeep to thank the archbishop for his resistance to the Nazis. Two days later Marshal Rola-Zy-mierski, who headed the Moscow-controlled Polish Provisional Government of National Unity (at Yalta Britain and the United States had conceded or placed Poland in Stalin's sphere of interest and control), arrived in Krakow. With no democratic resistance left after the crushing of the Warsaw uprising, a new oppression in the name of a different ideology was in the offing.

Karol volunteered to clear up the old seminary buildings where the SS had had its barracks and prison, and where latterly the roof had fallen in and the largely French inmates burnt furniture to warm themselves. There were three latrines heaped with frozen excrement. He rolled up his sleeves, seized a shovel and addressed himself to the Augean task, chopping it up and carting it away. He had to breathe through the mouth to stop vomiting – hardly a symbolic way to celebrate victory and liberty, but not bad for a future successor to St Peter.

In a summary of those years from 1939 to early 1945 he issued the most humble of disclaimers: he claimed that he was spared much of the 'immense and horrible drama'. He could have been arrested any day.

> Sometimes I would ask myself [he said], so many young people of my own age are losing their lives, why not me? Today I know that it was not mere chance. Amid the overwhelming evil of the war, everything in my own personal life was tending towards the good of my vocation. I cannot forget the kindness shown to me in that difficult period by people whom the Lord placed in my path, both the members of my family and my colleagues and friends.

Poland's slide into totalitarian communist rule, at first not complete, supplied a significant degree of liberation for Wojtyla and his fellow seminarians to continue and complete their studies as novice diocesan priests, but it was to present new perils. Once again it was to become clear that not to co-operate with the ruling, despotic authority would be to risk punishment by death or deportation.

For Poland it was yet another great betrayal. Territorially, the redrawn Poland, moved to the west, regained its lost German territories, but now ceded to the USSR over a hundred thousand square miles of what basically had been the former Polish Ukraine. According to some historians this led to the future persecution of Roman Catholics in the USSR – in the Lithuanian and Ukrainian so-called Soviet Socialist Republics.

But it produced one decisive result which would have a profound effect in the future: with the 60,000 square miles the redrawn country gained, and with virtually no significant minorities left, a racially and religiously unified Poland for the first time came into being. This unity made it, or helped to make it, when the moment arrived, culturally strong. In its new submissive resistance to Russia it was to grow over the next four decades strong enough to trigger the most dramatic political reversal of the twentieth century: the collapse of Communist rule in 1989.

9

The Black Hood Went Over His Head

(1945–46)

In 1945 Karol applied once more to become a novice at the Czerna Carmelite monastery, but Sapieha robustly refused him this, pointing out how much diocesan priests were needed. Obedience to his archbishop saved him from that particular romantic aspiration. Alone, and sometimes depressed in that confined atmosphere of the secret seminary, Karol wrote a long poem, titled fittingly *Song of the Hidden God*, in which he again yearned in the Carmelite tradition for mystic isolation in union with God. He published anonymously the poem he wrote in those five months, in instalments in early 1946 in *Glos Karmelu* (*Voice of the Carmelites*), the Carmelite monthly magazine. This was his first published work.

But perhaps it proved enough that he had expressed his hidden self in verse, telling himself to 'endure, endure', in patience and silence, until the hidden God made his appearance. The sun, the return to life, was inexhaustible and 'Death is only the sun's ray/too short on the sundial of hours'.

He also voiced, although muted in these new poems, an underlying feeling of thanks, of gratitude for having been granted survival. Above all, as a young priest-to-be, he wanted to love more and more:

> the Lord taking root in the heart is a flower
> that longs for the warmth of the sun,
> so flood in light from the day's inconceivable depths
> and lean upon my shore.

As he deliberated in one of his favourite sayings later, 'Liberty is the measure by which one is capable of love.' Through his intention to become a priest he was on the way to developing that capacity to its limit. And within that love, the full expression of sexuality, the human involvement with and desire for another being, was seen by him as a limitation to a very different form of love.

G.K. Chesterton notes about St Francis of Assisi something that was also – in what Chesterton calls an 'uncanny way' – happening to Karol Wojtyla: that in his life there had begun to run a sort of double meaning, 'like his shadow thrown upon the wall. All his action had something of the character of an allegory; and it is likely enough that some leaden-witted scientific historian may some day try to prove that he himself was never anything but an allegory.'

For this transition from art to priesthood, or to potential sainthood, Chesterton has the fine and suitable image: 'The great painter boasted that he mixed all his colours with brains, and the great saint may be said to mix all his thoughts with thanks. All goods look better when they look like gifts. In this sense it is certain that the mystical method established a very healthy external relation to everything else.'

Critics of religions, sceptics and 'realists' generally, find difficulty in believing that a heavenly love can be as real as an earthly love, but it says something for the strength of Karol's friends and theatre colleagues that they seemed to understand him fully, although sometimes reluctantly, and that like Chesterton's St Francis, Karol 'was a Lover. He was a lover of God and he was really and truly a lover of men . . . A lover of men is very nearly the opposite of a philanthropist.' And further, that 'His religion was not a thing like a theory but a thing like a love-affair.'

All those who had helped or supported him in the realisation of that love affair – not least the women of Krakow, his fellow actresses, the mothers and grandmothers of his friends, whom he had adopted by calling Mama or Grandmama, those who had fed him, found him clothes, kept him warm, worried over his arrival or return – joyfully participated in his ordination, and the masses and ceremonies of the following days, which might be termed, in the language of the mystical poets, the 'consummation' of that love affair. Now also Wojtyla's life found its own daily celebrant: a fellow priest, Adam Boniecki, who began to list each stage, or each day with its observances, as Boniecki does in his *Kalendarium*, his extraordinary act of devotion to Wojtyla, which follows day by day and records the first fifty-eight years of the Pope's life in exhaustive detail.

In Rome in March 1945, Pius XII had bestowed a cardinal's hat on Sapieha and on his return to Krakow the students who met him carried him and his car from the station to St Mary's Church in the Old Town market square, restored now after the war's end.

'You must first finish that which has been commenced,' Sapieha had told Karol at that earlier time when he applied to train as a monk. Now, after six days of spiritual retreat, alone, Karol received Sapieha's blessing. On 1 November 1946, day of the Feast of All Souls, in the palace with Sapieha officiating, Karol Wojtyla became a priest. Joy and light filled his whole being, a strong contrast with the dank grey day outside. At the very moment when at long last he received the laying-on of hands a strong memory came to mind. This was the image of Jerzy Zachuta, the young fellow seminarian who like him had pursued his religious studies in secret, and who one day disappeared. The day after his disappearance, reading the lists of Poles arrested by the General Government, Karol learned of his friend's fate. He had fallen into enemy hands and was due to be executed. It was towards him, for him, that Karol Wojtyla said his first prayer as a priest.

The impact of his ordination he registers in simple words when he was

> . . . in that [private] chapel during the singing of the Veni, Creator Spiritus and the Litany of the Saints, lying prostrate on the floor with arms outstretched in the form of a cross, awaiting the moment of the imposition of hands . . . There is something very impressive about the prostration of the ordinands, symbolizing as it does their total submission before the majesty of God and their complete openness to the action of the Holy Spirit who will descend upon them and consecrate them.

So it happened that his priesthood had become, as he said, 'marked by the great sacrifice of countless men and women of my generation'.

The following day, the Feast of All Souls, he celebrated his first mass in Wawel Cathedral. On that day priests are allowed three masses, so he said all three for the repose of the souls of his mother, father, and brother. On each card, offered to friends and Maria Wiadrowska, his mother's sister and his godmother, the sole relative who attended, he wrote a verse from Mary's Magnificat (Luke 1: 46–55): 'Fecit mihi magna . . . Krakow Nov. 1 1946 – He has done great things for me . . .'

In the whirl of priestly activities that followed he said masses at his old Debniki parish church, in his birthplace, Wadowice, at the Church of the Presentation of Our Lady in the presence of Father Zacher, his old catechism teacher, and yet another at the cathedral for Unia colleagues from the cultural resistance, who were beginning even now to be persecuted again by the new conquerors. His fellow actors from the Rhapsodic Theatre, Halina and Tadeusz Kwiatkowski, had married and, on 11 November 1946, he baptised Monica, their first child, who cried so much that he got slightly flustered and, ever in a hurry, left without realising he had forgotten his frugal snack in the hallway: two slices of black bread spread with bacon fat.

Halina recalls how Karol, holding her child tenderly in his powerful forearms, as she described it later, released the baptismal droplets on her brow, pronouncing in his rich voice the words, 'Ergo baptiso . . .' She and his other dear friends, she thought, 'had not lost a fellow artist to the priesthood, but had gained a new Lolek' who would be with them and behind them one way or another, giving them renewed spiritual energy. She thought of the main roles they had played together, in particular in Sophocles' *Antigone* when she – in the eponymous role, and he as her brother Haemon – had remained defiant towards Creon the tyrant and suffered death together in resisting Creon's unjust laws. In France that very same play, rewritten by Jean Anouilh with stronger contemporary overtones, had become the masterpiece of resistance drama.

However, when he was invited to an anniversary meeting of the Rhapsodic Theatre, Karol could not attend. He wrote to Kotlarczyk that maybe this was God's design, or at least this is how he himself understood it . . . 'I should be present in your activity, just as a priest should be present in life, should be a hidden driving force. Yes, despite all appearances that is the main duty of the priesthood.'

He had lost all his own family, and was fated never to begin another. Up to that crucial moment of ordination, while he had close friendships and powerful personal loyalties, no greater intimacy in his life can be detected. Andrzej Deskur, a fellow seminarian, who later moved to Rome and became the Pope's confidant, said to the Un-broken Prince that Karol, Sapieha's star pupil, 'has a wonderful sense of humour but it's a hard job to get close to him – he's such a private person'. To this the cardinal prince found answer: he felt that Karol was afraid of becoming too close to anyone for fear he would lose them. In his heart, however, and later saying 'Personally I have never felt lonely', Karol rejected the arguments of those who opposed celibacy on the grounds of loneliness.

It would seem that Governor Hans Frank, former overlord of Krakow, finally shared an unexpected not to say eerie closeness to Sapieha, his former captive prelate. The Allied Commission tried Frank along with leading Nazi war criminals at Nuremberg. On 16 October 1948 Frank, fifth in the queue to the gallows after Joachim von Ribbentrop, Ernst Kaltenbrunner, Alfred Rosenberg, and Field Marshal Wilhelm Keitel, was executed:

> There was a brief lull in the proceedings until Kaltenbrunner was pronounced dead at 1.52 a.m. [Kingsbury Smith, an American journalist, writes the valediction.]
>
> Hans Frank was next in the parade of death. He was the only one of the condemned to enter the chamber with a smile on his countenance.
>
> Although nervous and smiling frequently, this man, who was converted to Roman Catholicism after his arrest, gave the appearance of being relieved at the prospect of atoning for his evil deeds.
>
> He answered to his name quietly and when asked for any last statement, he replied in a low voice that was almost a whisper, 'I am thankful for the kind treatment during my captivity and I ask God to accept me with mercy.'
>
> Frank closed his eyes and swallowed as the black hood went over his head.

Could the Unbroken Prince himself, one wonders, have received Frank before his arrest into the Catholic church?

Part Two

THE HIDDEN BREATH OF
THE SPIRIT WILL UNIFY ALL

O the mind, mind has mountains; cliffs of fall,
Frightful, sheer, no-man-fathomed.

Gerard Manley Hopkins
'No worst, there is none . . .'

Christ told his Apostles . . . that they were the exceptional people; the permanently incongruous and incompatible people.

G.K. Chesterton
St Thomas Aquinas

A Catholic theologian spends many years in discovering a new insight and then just as many years in proving that it is not really new.

Mark Schoof
Dutch Catholic Theology

Living in Little More than a Hut

(1946–48)

Rome is a city where flesh and blood can never
Be sacrificed, or mistaken, for abstractions.

C. Day Lewis
An Italian Visit

Sapieha picked Wojtyla, now twenty-six, to chaperone in Rome a prized new seminary student, Baron Stanislaw Starowieyski; so only as an 'afterthought', claimed Malinski, did Sapieha detail Wojtyla to leave Krakow for two years, to obtain his master's degree followed by a doctorship at the Angelicum Institute (known today as the St Thomas Pontifical University), run by the Dominicans. Whether or not he would have wanted to leave Poland at all, he showed as ever unquestioning obedience to his archbishop's preferences.

The Angelicum devoted itself to following the life and teaching of St Thomas Aquinas, one of the founding fathers of Catholicism. Aquinas believed truth could be grasped through a disciplined reflection on the world. He, said Wojtyla, 'explains how, with the gifts of the Holy Spirit, a person's whole spiritual being becomes responsive to God's light, not only the light of knowledge but the inspiration of love'. Aquinas authoritatively explained the mechanism of transubstantiation whereby the 'Real Presence' – the conviction that the real body and blood of Christ is present – is transmitted into the bread and wine of Holy Communion. This was endorsed by the Council of Trent (1545–63), and remains a central tenet of Catholic faith.

After spending five days in Paris, Karol arrived in Rome on 22 November 1946, and accepted a place at the tiny Belgian college in the

Via del Quirinale, a four-storey building with only very rudimentary conveniences (two of the Pope's present-day biographers note with consternation that there were no showers, but this was hardly unusual for the time), but of classic charm, out of sight from the road behind a wall and surrounded by trees. The students, of mixed nationalities, numbered twenty-four, and Karol, adept already in German and well versed in French, began to learn Italian and English. Conservative as he was, Sapieha was also worldly-wise and steered Karol away from the élitist, private-army mentality of the followers of Ignatius Loyola, the founder of the Society of Jesus, that was to develop fiercely over the next decades. The Dominican attitude had its own drawbacks too, maybe too strongly emphasising intellectualism, but of its inclination to underline traditionalism, and its solid Cartesian logic, there was no doubt. Sapieha must have felt his protégé was in safe hands.

Karol much needed a period of quiet, of consolidation, of reflection; above all to digest the extraordinary upheavals and griefs, apart from the constant danger and excitement, that he had experienced during his twenty-six years. As the environment for this, his base at the Belgian college, in spite of the rudimentary comforts and poor food cooked by Belgian nuns, suited him well.

Writing to Kotlarczyk in Poland, he reported how he would recite the Gospel of St John in Polish aloud by himself, reading that and the other gospels every day, and while he kept the company of Polish friends, he visited many of the varied treasures Rome had to offer. As he wrote to Helena Szkocka, 'The second essential thing – immersing oneself in Rome . . . a chapter that absolutely cannot be described in a few statements. There are so many levels, so many aspects of this subject. One continuously relates to different details of it, and one feels richer all the time.'

The impact of Rome, its presence, stole over him strongly, and then worked from within. It seems significant that when he came to reside there permanently as pontiff, he would refer to Rome as something inner and creative, such as an artist might look for and find: for many days, he said, he had criss-crossed the city, then of one million inhabitants, but that he 'couldn't find the image of that Rome I had brought with me'.

It came to him slowly, 'especially after touring the catacombs – the Rome of the beginnings of Christianity, the Rome of the Apostles, the Rome of Martyrs, the Rome that exists at the beginning of the Church, and, at the same time, of the great culture that we inherit'. As H.V. Morton, the travel writer, said, 'a visit to Rome is not a matter of discovery but of remembrance'.

Following his doctoral programme at the Angelicum Karol embarked for his thesis on the subject of mysticism and St John of the Cross. The Dominican Reginald Garrigou-Lagrange, his director, intent on guiding his student's reconciliation of the speculative, imaginative map of the mystical terrain of the spirit with the more down-to-earth approach of St Thomas Aquinas, found himself covering much ground he had already explored in his monumental works on the interior life of the soul, most recently in his *La synthèse Thomiste*, published in the year of Wojtyla's arrival.

Karol and Garrigou-Lagrange disagreed over the finer points as to whether or not God could be categorised as a 'divine object'. The conclusion of Karol's dissertation, which he wrote in Latin, suggests again that his powerful creative spirit refused to abandon an essentially poetic vision of God's own creation. The intellect was a powerful tool to rationalise and explain faith, but in the end God could not be objectified. We come to know God as we come to know another person, through mutual self-giving, through finding 'God by participation' in shared or interactive exchange. The encounter is of a personal nature, which cannot be grasped intellectually through faith. The drift or tendency of this encounter is very much in the direction of humility, into a position of non-arrogance, yet we can talk with God in interior monologue. Both God and man or woman preserve their unique identity.

'You might make a sketch of St Francis,' wrote Chesterton, but 'you could only make a plan of St Thomas like the plan of a labyrinthine city'. In the plan of growth in Wojtyla's life we can see a more labyrinthine development coming through confrontation and opposition, through a dynamic tension. Chesterton expresses what is true about much of what Wojtyla is beginning to believe as a basis for his thought and action in the future, namely

> that it is a privilege of people who contradict each other in their cosmos to be both right. The Mystic is right in saying that the relation of God and Man is essentially a love-story; the pattern and type of all love-stories. The Dominican rationalist is equally right in saying that the intellect is at home in the top-most heavens; and that the appetite for truth may outlast and even devour all the duller appetites of man.

From a list of Angelicum library books he borrowed, recorded by Boniecki, Karol's reading showed dogged determination – or possibly the influence of outside distraction. He renewed, for instance, the standard textbook (Henry Benedict Markelbach's *Summa Theologiae Moralis*) thirteen times – a total of six months. Seven times he took out an identically titled work by Hieronymus Holdin, the Jesuit whom Sapieha had often described to Karol as his teacher at Innsbruck. For lighter reading, renewable by the month rather than the fortnight, he borrowed several times *La vie intérieure*, by the Belgian Désiré Cardinal Mercier, a 'neo-' or 'transcendental' Thomist (interpreting Aquinas in the light of modern thought), who also sought among other things to reconcile the Anglican and Catholic churches.

Karol demonstrated the ability to draw out and obtain the best from his years of rigorous study in Rome under the aegis of his Dominican director, known as 'Reginald the Rigid', then nearly eighty years of age. His mind blended 'the embodied ideal of the princely priest' (Sapieha) with that of the 'theologically articulate' Garrigou-Lagrange.

This was decidedly not an experience at the cutting or exploratory edge of the new theology, but it brought him round again to excavating the heart of the human person (which Manley Hopkins called the 'inscape') and experiencing, this time intellectually, the central drama of human life: man's encounter with the divine.

Meantime his observation and love of the city continued to grow and deepen. He said in later years that a doctorate in theology could be gained elsewhere, but as his rector in Krakow, Father Karol Kozlowski, had told him, it was more important to 'learn Rome itself'. This consisted not only in contemplating the immeasurable artistic and historic treasures with their many layers of life and death, persecution and celebration, glory and decay, but also in listening to the present, hearing around him the devastating experiences of those who, like himself to a lesser degree, through war had suffered or nearly suffered death and deprivation.

Rome at its liberation applauded Pius's wartime stand or lack of it, at least for the moment until questions began to be asked. At the start of 1944 Rome had been starving, while according to John Conway, an Anglican Ulsterman, 'German troops encircled the tiny Vatican territory on all sides, and a feeling of impotent claustrophobia tinged the panic-filled atmosphere . . . The tunnel under the Gianculum was filled with refugees and beggars'. On 4 June in the same year, by contrast, half a million Romans walked freely to St Peter's Square through transportless streets to shout themselves hoarse with joy. They acclaimed Pius, *Defensor Civitatis* (Defender of the City), as their saviour – 'Viva il Papa!'

But two years later, in 1946, culturally, socially, politically Rome was in a ferment of conflict, while reconstruction of the city was slow and underfunded. On all sides poverty, opportunism, corruption, vice, prostitution were evident, on a scale which must have been unimaginable in its openness to one who had a dark and close experience of death and torture, but had seen little of the ravages of licence or unbridled self-interest.

For example, the explosion of left-wing theatre and film in the neo-realist movement, with works such as Vittorio De Sica's *The Bicycle Thieves*, Roberto Rossellini's *Rome, Open City*, which were assailed by *L'Osservatore Romano*, the Vatican newspaper, must have been all too evident to Karol, who listened to and saw everything going on around him. There must have been much that he questioned, some that even gave him offence, but the pattern of a man who preferred to receive offence than to give it had already strongly formed. Luchino Visconti's impact on post-war Italian theatre during these years points to the immense cultural disruption. Visconti delighted in provoking and horrifying the middle class with his productions, for example, of Sartre's *Huis Clos* (*No Exit*) and Erskine Caldwell's *Tobacco Road*, and his film *The Earth Trembles*, and he embodied the harshest left-wing reaction to the Fascist values that had dominated Italy for over a decade. Fascism celebrated the family and heroic men: to Visconti the family was a nest of hysterical, incestuous criminal vipers, and heroic men were pathetic dwarfs. Even so, Visconti, as a scion of a duke of Milan who possessed the aristocratic love of displeasing, while he joined the Communist Party, nevertheless retained his loyalty to the faith. In his blistering productions

Evasion was impossible; this was a hall of crime and expiation, where the leprous and the possessed tore ferociously at each other in love and hate. The magma of repressed violence erupted to the surface under the pressure exerted by the defeat of Fascism and was conducted along the breaches the war had opened in society's harmonious façade. The cardboard sets of the old order collapsed. On stage and in the

auditorium, Visconti unleashed a storm of violence never before seen in
any theatre.

This was a far cry from Kotlarczyk's Rhapsodic Theatre. Karol, a keen
theatre-goer, attended works written by the existentialist Sartre and
other Marxist, nihilist, or just purely hedonistic writers such as Marcel
Achard or Tennessee Williams. Later, during the deliberations of
Vatican Two, the Council called by Pope John XXIII to reform the
church, he read left-wing periodicals as well as *Wiez* (published in
Warsaw), which seriously engaged in dialogue between Marxist and
Christian points of view. Not only did he embrace that which was
contrary to his faith, as part of the wider experience of being human,
but he also seriously sought a compromise or working relationship
between Christian and Communist beliefs.

Likewise he noticed the difference in the extrovert and forward way
– to take a simple case – many Romans or Italian men treated women.
This was very different from what he had experienced in his native
Poland where 'Polish women are on the pedestal'. Romans had a
reputation summed up by Stendhal in the previous century: 'Nothing
could touch those hard-hearted Romans,' he wrote, 'but a woman's
blood.'

Likewise the glories of Italian religious art to be found in the
Vatican and the innumerable churches all over the city hardly showed
restraint, or even sexual chastity, possessing little of the rarefied
eastern spirit of the icon, or the Madonna of Kalwaria. In the
Renaissance sensuality of Michelangelo, Bernini, Cellini, Raphael,
and especially Caravaggio, Karol could discover little evidence of
'gentle Jesus meek and mild'. He witnessed the abundant pull of the
flesh: Michelangelo's Sistine Chapel image of a naked Adam and Eve
created in God's image stayed with him all his life – while Michelangelo's own life demonstrated some very human foibles. Wojtyla
celebrated the power of the fresco image in his last years:

> God created man in his image,
> In the divine image he created him;
> Male and female he created him
> And though they both were naked
> They felt no shame in the presence of each other.

In the classical museums and ancient sites he frequented as a tourist, he found even franker exposure of the male and female naked form. Such powerful physical expression did not escape him, drawn as he was to a love of the glory that was Rome. How do I deal with all this, he must have asked himself, how do I reconcile this unabashed love of human beings in all their forms and wildest manifestations, with the strict pronouncements of the church on sexual morals, marriage and the celibacy to which I am now, and for ever, committed? He saw evidence on all sides that Renaissance popes like Juliusz II and Leo X, who were patrons of Raphael and Michelangelo, lived as luxuriously as any secular prince.

Rome also introduced Wojtyla to Vatican politics and policies. The Holy See was frozen out of the post-war settlement, as it had been after the First World War in 1919, yet politics and religion in its psyche or mind-set were inextricably entwined. Monsignor Alfredo Ottaviani, a Vatican functionary, trumpeted the continuing church control, claiming that 'You can say whatever you like about the divinity of Christ, but if, in the remotest village of Sicily, you vote Communist, your excommunication will arrive the next day.'

The church denounced, too, existentialism (as represented by Jean-Paul Sartre) and polygenism (denial by the Jesuit Teilhard de Chardin that the whole of humanity was descended from Adam and Eve), as 'errors of belief'. After the terrible war it proclaimed its unity with the sacred vocation of Rome to which three million visitors flocked in 1950 to celebrate the Holy Year.

Karol had arrived in Rome with Stanislaw Starowieyski, whom he kept as his best friend and companion when he travelled Italy to visit Assisi, Perugia, and other places associated with the saint who called himself the Brother of the Sun and Moon.

He met Father Joseph Cardijn, the Belgian priest who founded the Young Christian Worker movement and who came to the Belgian college to talk about the experience of work in the context of belief. The Worker Priest movement had begun in France and the Low Countries over twenty years before. He met and discussed ideas with members of what became known as the New Theology, the Dominicans Marie-Dominique Chenu and Yves Congar, and Jean Danielou and Henry de Lubac, both Jesuits who were to be disciplined and have their teaching suppressed by Pius XII and the Holy Office a few years later.

Karol's first sight of a pope was of Pius XII, the 71-year-old Eugenio

Pacelli. Presiding in St Peter's over the solemn veneration of a newly proclaimed Blessed, he was carried by flunkeys on the *sedia gestatoria* complete with ostrich feathers and escorted by chamberlains. Karol did not approve much of the paraphernalia: the Rhapsodic Theatre played with the minimum of props and scenery, while 'the appearance of the Pope in this floating chair which rolled from side to side amid a storm of photographers' flashes had something moving and frightening about it'. While the Pope recited the solemn prayers Karol reflected on the crisis of the Catholic church in the immediate post-war situation.

Pacelli believed in concentrating all papal power in his own hands and when Cardinal Luigi Maglione, his Secretary of State (the chief political post in the Vatican, combining the duties of prime minister and foreign secretary), died in 1944, he had taken over his duties and responsibilities. Pacelli had never been, as Karol knew, a notable friend of the Poles, or a diehard supporter of Jews even when they were arrested on his own territory by Italian Fascists and Germans. The Italian historian Andrea Riccardi reports, 'Jews were deported from a few hundred metres from the Apostolic Palace.' (But there were other instances when Pius had done all he could to shield Jews and help them escape arrest and deportations.) Riccardi further accused Pius XII of disregarding during the war 'the systematic destruction to which the Polish people, whose ties with the Holy See were profound, were submitted'.

Timidity and silence, muddled ambiguities of statement, a lack of clear-cut direction, an indecisiveness and lack of confidence – these charges were also laid at the Vatican's door. But was Pius *Hitler's Pope*, as the title of John Cornwell's recent book alleged? Right up to the present this has been a hotly argued question, with passionate defence of Pius countering the flimsy if not entirely negligible documentary evidence for the prosecution. While he rarely if ever made personal criticism, Karol must have been aware of the statements Pius made in defence of his ambivalent attitude towards Hitler's Germany: 'You must not forget,' Pius told a journalist on the *Osservatore Romano*, 'dear friend, there are millions of Catholics in the German army. Would you like to place them in the middle of a conflict of conscience?' This resulted in what was known as his 'silence'.

Just before being elected as Pope Paul VI in June 1963 Archbishop

Karol with Emilia, before his first birthday, 1921.

Karol Wojtyla's parents, Emilia and Karol senior, on the day of their wedding, 1904.

Karol senior as an officer in the new Polish army, *c.* 1925.

First communion, May 1929.

Wadowice market square, *c.* 1930.

The goalkeeper:
Karol with the ball.

The choirboy, 1930: Father Figlewicz (*centre*), Karol on his right.

The cadet: Karol (*far left*) at army summer camp, 1938.

Sapieha, the Unbroken Prince, 1950.

The stage lover: Regina (Ginka) Beer and Karol in *Virgins' Vows*, 1938.

Ginka, before fleeing Poland in 1939.

The poet and actor with the 'Slowacki look': Karol Wojtyla, 1939.

Halina Krolikiewicz, Karol's most frequent leading lady.

German soldiers tear down the white eagle of Poland from a police station, 1939.

Governor Hans Frank (*left*) among ruins of Poland's Foreign Office in Warsaw.

Polish women rounded up as slave labour, 1941.

Resisting Poles shot, then hanged
as an example, 1941.

The basement flat in Tyniecka Street, Krakow.

The Solvay factory worker: Karol
Wojtyla, 1942.

The mystic: Jan Tyranowski.

The theatre director: Mieczyslaw Kotlarczyk.

The seminarist: Karol Wojtyla, 1943.

Karol with his aunt and godmother, Mrs Wiadrowska, Poland, 1943.

Karol with students, summer camp, 1952.

Skiing with an improvised pole at
Zakopane in the Tatras, 1952.

Archbishop Wojtyla, 1967.

Cardinal Wojtyla outside Wawel
Cathedral, 1968.

Giovanni Battista Montini (who as the Vatican official had dealt with Poland during the war) defended Pius's wartime record in a letter to the English *Tablet*: the occasion was the savage attack in Ralph Hochhuth's play *The Representative* on Pius's 'calculating political opportunism'. Montini claimed that Pius's

> omitting to take up a position of violent opposition to Hitler in order to save the lives of those millions of Jews slaughtered by the Nazis . . . will be readily understood by anyone who avoids Hochhuth's mistake of trying to assess what could have been effectively and responsibly done *then* [Montini's italics] . . . An attitude of protest and condemnation such as this young man blames the Pope for not having adopted would have been *not only futile but harmful*.

If Pius had behaved as Hochhuth blamed him for not doing, he would have, in Paul's words, 'been guilty of unleashing on the already tormented world still greater calamities'.

On becoming pope, Paul VI commissioned four Jesuit historians, among them Robert Graham, to research and assemble all relevant documentation bearing on Pius's wartime record in order to dispel the notion or representations of the 'Black Legend' of Pius XII. Twelve volumes of material appeared over a period of sixteen years, known in short as *Acts and Documents of the Holy See Relating to the Second World War*, and these 'decisively established the falsehood of Hochhuth's specific allegations'.

The response Wojtyla made to the charges against Pius when in 2000 as pope he was asked, was the abrupt 'Read Father Blet'. Pierre Blet was one of the four historians who had subsequently independently made and in 1999 published a scholarly digest of the original work (*Pius XII and the Second World War*). He called Pius a victim of 'calumny': among many covert actions he had secretly informed the allies of German war moves in 1940; later, he had been in contact with the German generals who plotted to remove Hitler. He quoted Robert Kempter, deputy chief of the Nuremberg war-crimes tribunal, who defended his silence, saying that public denunciation would merely have increased the suffering of those under Nazi control. But there is not much doubt that had the Catholic church stood up more positively to Hitler and the Nazis (as in Poland), there would have been fewer Communists and Marxists in the post-war Western world. Certain countries, such as France, would not have experienced such a dramatic fall in Catholic belief ('de-Christianisation').

During his first days in Rome, Karol met Cardinal Hlond, the Primate of Poland, who lived in exile. Hlond, criticised even by Pius for being weak-spirited in leaving Poland, greeted him cordially, and later, for a few moments, Karol was introduced to Pius XII at a private audience for students of the Belgian College. Pius XII was notably shy and timid on such occasions; no fighter, he had implemented a policy towards the Germans over the Jewish question of 'studied impartiality' – the phrase used by his predecessor Benedict XV during the First World War.

How did Karol view him in 1948? Officially in a respectful way, but privately he observed and understood the otherworldliness of the man; while seeing this, he would first have noted his virtues. The opposite of Cornwell who, 'while exonerating Pius XII of Nazi sympathies, nevertheless entitled his book about him *Hitler's Pope*', an English writer in 2004 commented. The question will never be fully resolved – neither will it go away. General de Gaulle, the French wartime leader and a notable Polonist, when he met Pius in 1944 wrote that he 'judges everything from a point of view that transcends human beings, their enterprises and their quarrels'.

In February 1948, while Karol was still in Rome, Pius wrote to the German bishops, sympathising with the alleged 'injustices' their people suffered in the post-war period, including the resettlement (for many a second time) of twelve million German nationals from east of the Oder and Neisse from that Polish territory incorporated into the Reich, which had been returned to Poland. The new Communist regime in the 'People's Republic' used this as anti-papal propaganda, while Cardinal Wyszynski, the new primate of Poland, together with most Poles, felt outraged.

As refreshment from academic work, Karol visited Holland with Starowieyski, where they stayed for ten days during the holidays: 'We travelled through the land of windmills and tulips,' while in Amsterdam they viewed the masterpieces of Dutch painting. Everywhere the hospitality was so generous that 'I recall we did not spend a cent on lodging or meals'. Also he went to Belgium, where during a summer month he took charge of the Polish Catholic mission among miners at Charleroi and talked to immigrant families. These excursions served to reinforce his bonds and communion, after the example of St

Francis, with ordinary working people. He said (to André Frossard) that St Francis 'did not think himself worthy of ordination and remained a deacon', and, about Brother Albert Chmielowski, the subject of his play, 'his most faithful disciple in my country . . .' in these words of an excellent biographer: ' "He gave his soul". There you are! I ask you, what is a priestly vocation if not an appeal to give one's soul? We priests badly need models to teach us to be demanding towards ourselves.'

Karol's longest stay outside Rome, in July and August 1947, was in France. Father Starowieyski recalls that during two to three weeks in Paris they used the Metro, and that 'the behaviour of the French often left a lot to be desired'. But Karol said to him, 'You know, during these Metro rides one can superbly attend to one's inner life.'

But contemplation apart, here again he engaged non-stop with those around him:

> It was then that I read with great interest [Abbé] Godin's book *France, pays de mission* and that I visited Father Michonneau's suburban parish. I also read Father Boulard's studies and had occasional contacts with the *Mission de France* movement [whose motto was '*témoignage*'], bearing witness to Christ in everyday life. At Marseilles I had a short meeting with the community of Father Loew (a convert from Protestantism, a doctor and worker priest). I took part in a *Semaine sociale*.

He loved hearing confessions in Rome and kept this up every other Sunday in a suburban parish; he maintained his Krakowian practice of kneeling to pray on hard chapel floors, instead of the kneelers provided. Faith and humility alone were not enough – Karol says in his 280-page Latin dissertation, delivered in the early summer of 1948 to the Angelicum – for a psychological union of intellect with God. Faith had to be 'nourished by love and illuminated by the gifts of the Holy Spirit, especially of wisdom and reason'.

He received the highest possible commendation and marks from his teachers, but because it was not printed, according to Angelicum rules, his theology doctorate was withheld. The reason given was that he could not afford to pay for its printing. He was unconcerned. He received his doctorate from the Jagiellonian University later in the year on his return to Poland. A critique of his thesis from one of the

Jagiellonian staff, and recorded in Boniecki, found Karol's analysis of St John's text too dialectic and yet not closely philological enough, claiming that 'he spent too much time making his own arguments'.

On 15 June 1948 he wrote to Helena Szkocka on his departure from Rome that the time had passed with enormous speed. Study, observation, meditation – 'all act like a spur to a horse'.

Karol now had a Polish friend in Rome who was to remain in the Vatican until he became pope. Andrzej Deskur, like Karol, was no ordinary priest: he came from a noble family whose castle had once been the seat of power in Sancygniow, and during the war he and his family had hidden Jews on their estate. Born in 1924, Deskur, with brush-cut, blond hair and a blunt, disconcertingly humorous manner, trained as a lawyer before joining Karol as a fellow seminarian in Krakow. Rome proved ideal for the development of his diplomatic skills, and as their friendship deepened Deskur became Karol's confidant, guide, and source of rich insider information in the corridors of papal power.

Karol arrived back in Tyniecka Street in mid-June, to be greeted by his old friends, in particular Father Mieczyslaw Malinski, and the other Mieczyslaw – Kotlarczyk – of the Rhapsodic Theatre, who still occupied the flat.

Karol did not stay long; a meeting with Sapieha in which the cardinal congratulated his former seminarian on his doctorate thesis, led to another request from Karol to join a closed Carmelite order. Sapieha flatly turned this down. Sapieha then assigned him to a humble post assisting a parish priest in a remote and backward part of Poland.

In April the very palpable prospect of Communism had been defeated in the Italian capital in the general election with the return to government of the pro-America, pro-Vatican Christian Democratic party led by Aldo Moro, but in Poland there had been no such luck. Here the fragile attempts at democracy and power-sharing had broken down, various democratic leaders fled to the West, and Stalin had installed a puppet government. Karol in Rome, at the first report that Stalin had refused American aid to Hungary, saw foreboding signs. The Communists sucked one after another of the eastern republics, which had been guaranteed political autonomy at the Yalta conference, into their totalitarian bloc.

Elsewhere than in Poland national churches suffered much more. Already, in 1946, for collaborating with the Nazis Archbishop Stepinac in Yugoslavia had been committed to life imprisonment. Cardinal Mindszenty, Hungary's primate (who had served prior to the war's end a prison sentence in a Fascist jail), after a rigged confession and trial received life for treason. His defiance of Communism was absolute, and subsequently over a thousand Hungarian nuns, monks and priests were arrested and sentenced. Czechoslovakia hardly fared better: Archbishop Beran, in 1949, together with thousands of his clergy and members of contemplative orders, was arrested and imprisoned.

Poland was a different matter. In this land of dramatic church history a new heroic priest in the same Polish tradition of unbroken prince or *pater patriae* had been in the wings, waiting. He was of an opposite mettle from the temporiser Cardinal Hlond, still primate while Wojtyla had been in Rome, and even from the aristocratic Sapieha, whom he resembled in power and independence.

Nineteen years Karol's senior, Stefan Wyszynski, while holding a doctorate in canon law, embraced some socialist doctrines. During the thirties he had vigorously campaigned in the press and from the pulpit for a more just and equitable society. While condemning Communism and extreme Polish nationalism he had little truck with the main cause, as he saw it, of the great increase of left-wing ideology, namely the unbridled capitalist culture of greed: 'They do not want to believe,' he said, 'that the reason for this growth [of Communism] is not so much Bolshevik propaganda as the lack of work, of bread, and of a roof over one's head.'

Unlike the convinced non-combatant Wojtyla, during the war he served as a mature chaplain in Warsaw and in the forests of northern Poland with the armed patriots of the AK, during which time the Gestapo arrested and held him at least once before letting him go. With the death of Hlond at the end of October Pius appointed Wyszynski, now Bishop of Lublin, as his successor. A practical activist, he began at once to implement plans for the survival of Catholicism in Poland that were at one and the same time both a defiance and an accommodation or compromise. The nation's culture and identity, once again emerging from the ashes, became ready – although to be scrupulously overseen – for revival. Wyszynski reinforced Karol's innate spirit of resistance.

Sapieha's health was now in serious decline, but he engineered two final formative appointments in the life of his protégé. The first was to this poor parish thirty miles east of Krakow. As a Christian foundation Niegowic dated back a thousand years, but what Karol found here consisted of little more than a small wooden church set among birch trees.

Riding on carts, dispensing pretty quickly of his own meagre possessions to the poor, the old, and the needy, Karol began his ministry with a symbolic gesture one day to become universally known: 'It was harvest time,' he recalled. 'I walked through the fields of grain with the crops partly already reaped, and partly still waving in the wind. When I finally reached the territory of the Niegowic parish, I knelt down and kissed the ground. It was a gesture I had learned from St John Vianney.'

This new territory had no running water, electricity or sewerage. Living here became a direct confrontation with ordinary human nature, the life of nature itself, and the seasons. In the mainly peasant community of the Niegowic parish, in his own description 'hilly with argillaceous [clayey] soil', Wojtyla ministered to 5,000 Catholics, played football, sang, acted, walked and rode in carts. Living in a glorified hut with another priest, he taught in the local schools, celebrated mass in a number of the thirteen villages in the parish, organised Living Rosary Circles, put on plays (in one he played the role of a beggar who turns out to be Christ), arranged and rehearsed choirs, and even took students to the theatre in Krakow. When celebrating the parish priest's fiftieth year of ordination, he proposed a new church be built in brick as a present to mark this. This was his first such initiative which came to fruition.

That winter proved hard. Karol told Malinski of a typical pastoral visit when he would leave in his cassock, overcoat, alb and biretta:

> Over beaten path in the snow. But snow will cling to your cassock, then it will thaw out indoors, and freeze again outside, forming a heavy bell round your legs, which gets heavier and heavier . . . By evening, you could hardly drag your legs, but you have to go on, because you know that people wait for you, that they wait all year long for this meeting . . .

Confession became a direct experience, an experience from within because, as he also told Malinski, you can't play at being woodpeckers in the confessional, one pecking on one side of the grille, the other pecking back from the other side. 'You have to establish a dialogue and treat it seriously from the heart.'

In the Catholic view of confession the priest has made a strong and complex relationship with God, and by virtue of this relationship he is able to interpret and focus on the penitent through his own relationship with him or her, which can be creatively helpful in expanding the penitent's life into freedom. Again Karol placed strong emphasis on the inner life, on making contact with the person within – both priest and penitent alike.

11

My Train to Krakow
Isn't until after Midnight

(1949–58)

The Communist control of Poland dawned grey with streaks of bright light, but the grey dawn that promised freedoms unimaginable under Nazi rule soon palled. The spring of 1949 saw Father Wojtyla recalled to Krakow, a posting which became effective from mid-August. Remaining in Poland for the next thirty years, Karol integrated pastoral and academic work without any slackening of tempo in either. The commitment made was both phenomenal and total: a regular sixteen- to eighteen-hour working day.

In Krakow he assumed the post of chaplain at St Florian's, and his days of travelling by cart were over. Blessing marriages, christening children, celebrating mass, organising retreats for students – St Florian's parish was attached to the Jagiellonian University – were but one side of the demanding schedule. In the two years he officiated as auxiliary priest at St Florian's he christened 229 children.

On the other side were the more inward-looking, theoretical or artistic activities. He sustained contact with the Rhapsodic Theatre, attending performances and discussions afterwards, and in 1950 participated in the dedication ceremony for the construction of their new theatre. He counselled and confessed the actors, blessed their marriages, while his flat was still used for rehearsals.

A particular innovation of his were courses run for engaged couples, unheard of at this time, to prepare them for marriage and family life, both under threat in the Communist state. He especially loved and approved of Chesterton's assertion, 'The family is a cell of resistance to oppression', which he believed indicated 'its moral value' and defined 'its proper structure'. He was sometimes late in attending functions, often detained by penitents in the confessional, discussing their private lives or moral issues. The niece of Cardinal Sapieha had two daughters, and as catechist and confessor, Wojtyla was 'never' on time: an 8 p.m. appointment might begin at 10.30 p.m. Once, when he was due to speak after dinner about religious youth in France and Belgium, his audience of invited priests grew seriously offended by his protracted absence. However, when he arrived he charmed and impressed them with his lecture.

So his reputation augmented, and with it his network of friends and helpers until there could not have been a more popular young priest in the whole of Krakow. 'What does it mean to be rooted more deeply, for example, in your children, in your husband?' he would say to those who flocked to hear him.

> It is related to your love for them. The ability to discover their humanity in them, to experience them deeply, to bring them up. To remain objective and sober about fellow human beings, in order to draw them where we are heading. Then those whom I am leading, they, too, will become rooted more deeply in themselves and in their blessings. Love is not bedazzlement, a sugary emotion; sometimes it is even anger – if necessary, opposition. To live more deeply in our professional duties, in the people with whom we live. There are people everywhere, preying on you, they are treacherous. But love prevails. St John of the Cross said: 'Where there is no love – there you should carry it, and there will be love.'

While he continued in name to be vicar of St Florian for ten years, he was relieved of his pastoral duties after only two. Late in 1951 he was told to take two further years off to study for another doctorate. This time it was not on Sapieha's instruction: he had died, aged eighty-five, in July of that year, and tens of thousands had lined the streets as the cortège passed on its way to Wawel Cathedral for his burial mass.

Sapieha provided a lasting example for Karol in future positions he would come to hold, especially that of cardinal in Poland during Communist rule, but even the future one of pope. Sapieha had seen in the long term a pattern or design in Karol's life that he could help to implement. He had been, in Karol's own words, the 'real *pater patriae*', the father of the homeland. He had crucially fulfilled that need of Karol's for a replacement for the father he had lost, at whose grave he still prayed every day.

Sapieha also had a strong hand in influencing his successor, Archbishop Eugeniusz Baziak, to keep Wojtyla focused on professional activities that would nourish and develop the inner man. So while Karol broadened and deepened his philosophical and theological reading for an assistant-professorship examination at the Jagiellonian, he had time to write more poetry and drama.

But he was never to forget, never to abandon, his overall respect and devotion to the female side of man's nature and his own which began with his feelings towards Emilia and had continued, in accordance with 'the mandate of Jesus' to make 'Mary the Mother of God's Grace within me, the Mother of my supernatural interior life'.

'O, the supernatural in man needs a mother, how much indeed! It leads to a new principle of existence, which is beyond nature . . . Didn't St Paul write to his brethren: "My children, to whom I give birth in pain"? This statement is like an outburst of the material self-awareness in the priest.'

Picture him, now, after he has turned thirty. This is the time when other Krakovians began to worship him. As a child in the 1950s in Krakow, Malgorzaga Hruzik Mazurkiewicz, whose house he visited, recalls his tall lanky figure wearing torn clothes. He was an anti-Communist, she said, and his pockets were full of sweets that he gave away to children. Not to be cynical, she says of her fellow Krakovians, 'I sometimes wonder if they believe in the Pope or they believe in God.' A friend of hers, she recounts, says the Pope is like a narcotic: 'I can't stop talking and thinking about him.'

He now wore glasses, 'heavy bi-focals', solid, horn-rimmed, and we see these in photographs of him in Krakow. He signs personal cheques, his autograph shows a very strong hand. Later he is never photographed in glasses, according to Michael Straiton, an ophthalmologist, because his sight has not deteriorated and he finds distance vision unimportant. Later he wears contact lenses, but it is hardly, as some have claimed, a mark of personal vanity. He has never driven a car. Vanity never influenced the clothes he wore: frayed cuffs and collars, ill-fitting second-hand cassocks, cast-off pullovers and trousers. Given a present of something new, he would invariably pass it on.

What salary or expenses he received he would donate to charity. If someone gave him an envelope with money, he passed it on without opening it, to someone who needed it. His hours were long: after discussions and meetings that would last well into the morning, he would rise at five or six to say or attend mass.

In 1941 Karol had warned against the 'red banner and an unreal international humanism . . . that has nothing to do with Poland'. In the drab and grim post-war Communist state the new authorities called Krakow a black, reactionary and 'clerical-landlord' city. But even so they maintained here as elsewhere communication with the people, for they could not but acknowledge the great strength of Polish Catholicism. With Karol's own, by now well-established, habits he posed little direct threat to the *aparatchik* authorities: the essence of his life, in its style and its embrace of a working man's poverty, was 'plus communiste que les communistes'.

The regime at first judged him harmless and paid him little attention, a down-at-heel figure who took equality for all men not just at its face value, but followed the teachings and examples of Brother Albert (and his mentor St Francis) so faithfully that he might to some even have appeared something of a simpleton. This method was one of being open to people whatever their opinion or political conviction: negotiation and selective compromise, these were his methods of operating.

Since he had taken up duties at St Florian's he attended new productions of the Rhapsodic Theatre. Forbidden by the Communists to speak or publicly utter a prayer at the ceremonial laying of the foundation stone in 1950 for their new building, he silently consecrated the building plot. He wrote up the Rhapsodic style in 1952 in an article, using the memorable description that the actor 'carries the problem'; this was in the year before the Rhapsodic Theatre was suppressed in the general stifling of cultural freedom.

The death of Stalin, in March 1953, pushed the higher authorities of the church in Poland once again into extreme crisis. On a visit to the Vatican Primate Wyszynski defended himself and his fellow Polish priests against the accusation that he was 'soft on Communism': the true nature of the mounting persecutions and arrest of senior priests tested his belief that 'martyrdom is always a grace and an honour', but not the present need or demand of Catholic Poland: 'I want my priests at the altar, at the pulpit and in the confessional – not in prison.'

Already in January 1953 a show trial in Krakow of four priests and three laymen on charges of spying for the CIA demonstrated a new vicious attitude, resulting in the death sentence for the head of Wojtyla's much-cherished Women's Living Rosary Circle and two lay workers in the Debniki parish, and life sentences for the rest (the death sentences were not implemented).

Nevertheless while allowing freedom of worship, and the annual great pilgrimages such as Karol's favourite of Czestochowa, government intimidation, apparently to please hardliners both in Poland and in Moscow, and support the East–West hostility now at its highest point with the Korean War, culminated in moves against the figurehead.

In September 1953 Bishop Kaczmarek of Kielce, held in prison on treason and spying charges for two years, was sentenced to twelve years in prison. Three days after this, on 25 September, they arrested Wyszynski, now elevated by Pius XII to cardinal. Baca, his dog, bit one of the plain-clothes policemen. The cardinal tended the wound before being driven away to a Capuchin monastery in north-west Poland and placed under house arrest. Many other restrictions strengthening state control over the church came into force.

Wojtyla, meantime, went on river and mountain holidays, and later in the year a nuclear-physicist friend, who accompanied him on trips in the Gorce Mountains, recalls how easily Wojtyla took to skiing again after his long break since high school, but that as his guest Wojtyla insisted, in spite of no facilities, on celebrating mass every day. He stopped at village churches along the skiing route, or celebrated al fresco, putting on the cassock he carried in the satchel strapped to his back. He used a collapsible chalice and sometimes said mass in a barn with a straw altar, or in peasants' cottages, or on mountainsides with kit-bags and branches fashioned into an altar.

Dressed in lay clothes he would accompany girls on overnight excursions. They called him 'uncle' so as not to identify him as a priest. In 1953 he travelled with a mixed party to the Bieszczady Mountains, where they were so caught by rain that border guards put them up in a kind of attic. They slept, 'The girls on one side and the boys on the other', while it rained solidly for two days. On kayak trips he would rise early to bathe alone and say mass at an altar of two upturned boats with a cross of paddles lashed together.

'A small episode: upon the suggestion that we purchase first class tickets, Father Wojtyla protested, saying: "No, no, we travel with the people!"' Thus it was that trips to the mountains, for varied forms of sport and recreation, became over the next years, and with younger student parties, merged into spiritual retreats. But he noticeably had difficulty in controlling weariness in the evenings. In November 1954 he was awarded the Bronze Badge for Hiking Tourism, signifying he had completed lowland excursions on foot totalling 166 km. He was not close to the epicentre of the church's struggle although he did publish poems and articles in *Tygodnik Powszechny*, under his pseudonym Andrzej Jawien. This was closed down for refusing to publish a eulogy of Stalin.

W.H. Auden in his essay in *The Dyer's Hand* on 'Genius and Apostle' argues that an apostle is an ordinary human messenger like a man who delivers mail: 'He cannot wait for certain divinely inspired moments to deliver his message and, if his audience should ask him to show his credentials, he has none.' But called upon by God directly, he has no choice. Karol, called by those depths of grief and sorrow to which he had already been destined, had no choice but to act as an apostle. Through the very losses he had suffered, through the end-games he had so far lived through, life had defined him as a living witness to God. But more than this.

As Auden goes on, a man of talent, a potential artistic genius, is called to his vocation by a natural gift with which he is already endowed, and these come to be his life, an 'objective test to prove whether his calling is genuine or imaginary'. There is no such test in the life of an apostle: 'Every apostle is a member of a class of one and no psychological background can throw any light on a calling which is initiated by God himself.'

Wojtyla was both genius and apostle: both of Auden's statements were true of him. He can now be seen more and more combining the apostle's calling and the gifts of the genius. But he had, as we have shown, already subordinated the second to the first, yet without, in his case, losing the power of the second – his literary and dramatic skills – as incorporated with, or working alongside the first. As an apostle he had forsaken everything for unhonourable and unimaginable yet ultimate rewards, but as a genius, remarkably, he was enabled to go on developing his gifts. He had some instinctive, precocious knowledge of the path that would lead to that astonishing integration of opposite forces in his mind and personality.

We can see his awareness of the contrasting aspects of the human
personality, in what he tells his students during one retreat:

> Each of us carries two people within the human person. One is who I
> am, the other is who I should be. This is a very deep tenet of the human
> person and its inner life. It is not a deception, it is a reflection of reality.
> He who denies it either lies or . . . is very deficient. This applies
> particularly to the young . . . Human life is not conventional – it is
> turbulent, uneven. Man tipped the original balance and continues to
> live in it restlessly. And it is difficult for him to restore the tipped
> balance. It will not happen without struggle, one has to be prepared for
> it, one must even love it from the start.

Here he expresses the kernel, the essence of what one day he would
become as pope, unquestionably great in that combination of genius
and apostle he would achieve by engaging in the struggle to 'restore
the tipped balance'. Two people within the same person, not to be
denied, but in balance: and his a turbulent life, an unconventional life,
lived in conditions of struggle.

The conscious pursuer of the ethical ideal, the genius as opposed to
apostle side of Wojtyla, was intensely active during these two years in
the production of his dissertation, which earned him his second
doctorate. In particular and crucially in view of how the world during
his long papacy would increasingly become obsessed with sexual
politics, and affected by uninhibited activity leading to a pandemic
of sexually transmitted disease and social breakdown, he turned his
attention to sex and the nature of human love.

To begin with, what was, he asked himself, the significance for
Catholic ethics of Max Scheler, who was an early twentieth-century
Jewish convert to Catholicism? Scheler, a Viennese-born philosopher,
had published in 1912 *Ressentiment*, in which he argued masterfully
that Marx was justified in his criticism of the capitalist sentiment but
wrong in his purely materialist and economic vision of society. Scheler
refused also to give importance to the class struggle, believing it can
only lead to resentment and hatred. *Ressentiment* analysed this
negative and universal condition of man in both its political and
personal contexts, an examination of the disease of contemporary
society in terms of 'Phenomenology' – the school of philosophy based

on the study of physical and spiritual phenomena and of experiences in human existence.

Edmund Husserl, a Czech-born Jew and contemporary of Scheler, is generally regarded as the father of phenomenology (which later provided one of the building blocks for existentialism). *Ressentiment*, first defined as a philosophical concept by Nietzsche, denotes an attitude arising from a cumulative repression of feelings of hatred, revenge, envy and the like. Karol had seen much of this as a child and young adult and reacted strongly against it. In laying *Ressentiment* bare, in what he called his 'philosophy of the open hand', Scheler believed in the unique significance of human emotions, especially that of love, and the importance of saintly or heroic models for developing the moral life. How close it was to Karol's present thinking and future, not to say lifelong, preoccupations may be measured from Scheler's assertions that 'the endless accumulation of pleasurable objects produced by modern civilization tends to benefit <u>nobody</u>', or Scheler's explanation of how the industrialist's false values have come to power: 'Cleverness, quick adaptability, a calculating mind, a desire for "security" and for unhampered communication in all directions . . . They are set above courage, bravery, readiness to sacrifice, daring, high-mindedness, vitality, desire for conquest, indifference to material goods . . . loyalty to one's family.'

Scheler makes a distinction between genuine self-love and

> what is really a peculiar sham form of love, founded on *self-hatred* and *self-flight*. In his *Pensées*, Blaise Pascal has drawn the classic picture of a type of man who is entangled in many worldly activities (games, sports, hunting, also 'business' or unceasing work for the 'community'), and all this merely because he cannot look at himself and continually tries to escape from the vacuum, from his feeling of nothingness.

Scheler's assessment of St Francis in relation to modern art and expression was especially close to Karol's:

> When Francis of Assisi kisses festering wounds and does not even kill the bugs that bite him, but leaves his body to them as a hospitable home, these acts (if seen from the outside) could be signs of perverted instincts and of a perverted valuation. But that is not actually the case. It is not a lack of nausea or a delight in the pus which makes St Francis

act in this way. He has overcome his nausea through a deeper feeling of life and vigor! This attitude is completely different from that of recent modern realism in art and literature, the exposure of social misery, the description of little people, the wallowing in the morbid – a typical *ressentiment* phenomenon. Those people saw something bug-like in everything that lives, whereas Francis sees the holiness of 'life' even in the bug.

The feminine role, too, predisposes to *ressentiment*, which some might say the future pope would only too directly experience. Scheler argues:

> To the extent that women are assigned passive roles, to the extent that they are not expected to act out feelings of hatred and revenge, to the extent that they are, or are supposed to be, the weaker and accepting sex, to that extent women are likely to be more subject to *ressentiment* than men. When women tend to reject certain masculine values which they secretly crave they may be said to be engaging in *ressentiment* behaviour.

His professors at the Department of Theology, Lublin University complimented Wojtyla's critique of Scheler's work on its 'superbly constructed flow of deductions'. But his conclusions were mainly negative. For Karol, Scheler placed too much emphasis on feeling and not enough on conscience: his system did not permit the Catholic to grasp the complete picture. Scheler acknowledged Jesus as being at 'the heart of history', but the evaluation of the inner world of 'the feeling of Jesus Christ' to the status of merely a model without the divine authority to command, fell short of the causality of the whole man, in Wojtyla's judgement, for it is pure and 'ethically untethered' emotion.

But while rejecting Scheler's ethics Wojtyla preserved some of Scheler's sociology for later use. He would make an increasing use of his emphasis on personal intuitions, the phenomenological method, as a tool in reworking his Thomism, with its emphasis on Dominican rationalism and the intellect. He was also able to transform these intuitions from their source in his emotional awareness or consciousness to that of a person in his deliberately willed actions. To summarise this complicated line of reasoning, Wojtyla had now become a Christian existentialist, the essence of the latter being that you become the person you want to be by choice, by 'intentional will'. Ethical or moral norms had become by virtue of the Divine plan or intention 'a revealed given', or precondition, and as such must in his view take precedence over lived experience, or other means or theories, from which values may be derived.

The fact that he became an existentialist (and had read widely in the works of Jean-Paul Sartre, its founder and popular leader) made Wojtyla ostensibly, at least to the Communist leadership in Poland, very tolerable and modernist in outlook.

But unlike Sartre, politically he was a quietist, he was non-confrontational. Jerzy Turowicz, editor of *Tygodnik Powszechny*, a weekly paper founded in 1945 that had published Wojtyla's articles and poems, and of which the Pope remained a lifelong reader, said, 'He is neither on the right nor the left, and he is not even a nationalist.'

Karol was now a qualified Jagiellonian professor with two doctorates. Lublin University, the prime seat of Catholic learning in Poland, engaged him to lecture on 'Act and Experience', and discuss the philosophical ethics not only of Scheler but of Plato, Aristotle, Augustine, Aquinas and Kant. Later he was to lecture on 'Norm and Happiness', exploring with grave reservations David Hume and Jeremy Bentham, the utilitarian English philosophers who advocated the 'greatest happiness of the greatest number'. Combining these demanding academic duties both in Krakow and Lublin, where he conducted courses for women on 'parity of heart' and celibacy, he lectured too on marital ethics (showing 'matrimony' and 'mother' in Polish and Latin came from the same root), love and responsibility, perfectionism – and just about every other aspect of moral and ethical life.

While Wojtyla took no part in politics, he was well aware of the rift between the Polish church and Communist state. Since 1953, when it clashed with the Council of State's edict that priests should take a loyalty oath to the People's Republic – which also had taken upon itself the appointment of bishops and pastors – the Polish church remained in a locked state of intransigence and refusal with its cry, 'We are not allowed to place the things of God on the altar of Caesar.' But for the moment, at least, this conflict was not in the foreground of Karol's life.

*   *   *

In his early thirties, and not in any way prepared to deny his full-blooded nature (and that his commitment to priesthood entailed chastity), he embraced and publicly made sexuality into a major ethical problem. As he told students at a retreat at St Florian's in March 1954:

> Sexual drive is a gift from God. Man may offer this drive to God exclusively through a vow of virginity. He may offer it to another human being with the awareness that he is offering it to a person. It must not be a matter of chance. On the other side there is another human being who must not be hurt, whom one must love. Only a person can love a person. To love means to wish for the other person's good, to offer oneself for the good of the other. When a new life is to come into being as the result of the act of giving oneself, this must be a gift of the person given out of love. In this area one must not separate love from the [sexual] drive. Love is not a fantasy, if it is tied to sexual drive, it guarantees through that drive an extension of love in a new, aroused life of a new person. If we respect the sexual drive within love, we will not violate love, we will not bring love to ruination.

This is an important statement: Wojtyla always acknowledged his own sexual drive, always felt close to it while offering it as a major part of his commitment. It was to make him a credible, indeed original and inspired Christian interpreter of sexual morality. As pope he would bring sex out into the open, and endeavour to reconcile it with Catholicism and the caponised and gelded mentality of a dysfunctional Christian sexual philosophy.

To further this direction of his ambition he was collecting material and writing draft chapters for a book later to be published as *Love and Responsibility*. In December 1956 at Czestochowa he met Dr Wanda Poltawska, who was to help shape his work. A Krakow psychiatrist and a victim of Ravensbrück, where Nazi doctors injected diseased bacilli into her bone marrow, Wanda backed his views on contraception. She argued it was psychologically harmful and led to neurosis, and collected evidence to support this. She also held that the contraceptive attitude led – when the contraception did not work or was forgotten – naturally to abortion. She became a close friend of Karol, and she saw him as an absolutely pure person, able to master his reactions fully. They both believed that self-discipline and exercises in self-denial helped form chastity. Six years after they met she was diagnosed with terminal cancer. Karol wrote at once to Padre Pio, the Capuchin monk stigmatic (whose hands allegedly bled with the wounds of Christ), and asked him to pray for her. Before operating to remove the cancer the doctors took an X-ray and found the growth had gone, an example of Pio's miraculous power, Wojtyla believed, which with other examples would qualify him for sainthood, and lead to his 2001 canonisation.

Superstition is never far below the surface in the Roman Catholic church. It has been alleged that sometime in the 1960s Wojtyla had gone to visit Padre Pio, who also had been gifted with second sight (Graham Greene, a Pio devotee, had once visited him to confess, waited for three whole days in a queue, then, when his chance came, fled). Pio told Wojtyla, who forever remained silent on this matter, 'One day you will be pope. But your pontificate will be short and it will end in bloodshed.'

By 1956 Karol held the chair of ethics at Lublin and his lectures were packed, with students sitting on windowsills, on the floor and lining the walls. He appeared in frayed cassock over olive-green trousers, wearing 'shapeless shoes'. He was popular as a confessor, always available for chats and could be 'touched' for small non-repayable loans. Colleagues would refer friends suffering deep personal and emotional crises to him.

In late 1957 he attempted to travel to Louvain in Belgium, with the hope of visiting France and Switzerland, to further his researches into sexual ethics, but was refused a passport as part of the restrictions on clerics travelling abroad. So instead he kayaked and trekked in the mountains, went on numerous skiing trips, and while on a kayak excursion on the River Drawa he and his party of twelve read together *The Screwtape Letters*, C.S. Lewis's lively dissertation on the omnipresence of Satan – 'Evil,' he told his young audiences who called him 'Uncle', 'is like an avalanche, it starts with something small, and grows incredibly.'

In the aftermath of the abortive Hungarian revolution of 1956 Wladyslaw Gomulka, who, freed from prison had assumed power in October 1956, wished to avert a Hungarian-style uprising and therefore in a pre-emptive move forestall Soviet intervention, forced his government into *rapprochement* with the Catholic church. This came about in an extraordinary way.

In June, demanding better pay and conditions, rioting Polish workers at Poznan clashed with security forces in a three-day battle. Army and police killed fifty-four people and injured 200. In the feeling of outrage that followed, Edward Ochab's government managed to stay in power. Then in October, under General Waclaw Komar, a new commander, Polish armoured divisions prepared to combat the Soviet army should it invade Poland as it had Hungary. Nikita Khrushchev came to Warsaw, rowed with and ranted at the bald, bullet-headed but more moderate Gomulka, but fearing all-out war withdrew advancing Russian units when, only sixty miles from Warsaw, they came upon Komar's tanks drawn up ready and prepared for battle. In this bloodless repeat of the miraculous victory of the Vistula the Russians conceded defeat and in the aftermath of this resistance of Communist liberals and Gomulka – but with continuation of Soviet military bases and Polish membership of the Warsaw Pact agreed – the Polish government set Wyszynski free, and released the other prelates. In a new concordat between church and state Wyszynski went back to Warsaw with the authority to renew co-operation and inaugurate reforms to improve Catholic freedom of worship. It was a great turning-point, and one which would pave the way, in the fate of Wojtyla the Krakow priest-pedagogue, for him to become a source of authority and prominence.

But not for the moment. This was Karol's period of disengagement, and with his researches into sex and marriage he was hardly a Vatican eye-catcher. In a decidedly understated way he would appear, wrote Father Romvald Waldera, at his lectures

> in an outfit not typical for a Krakow professor. Instead of a distinguished black hat he wore a leather cap, his cassock covered with a dark green coat made from a material most likely meant for a blanket. On spring and summer days, in the recreation hall (where the lectures were held), he would throw his trench coat over the back of a chair, a coat, which, as I noted, was of poorer quality than mine.
>
> During the break, he would read his breviary in a corner or go one storey up to the chapel, where he would kneel on the floor despite the great number of kneelers softened by cushions.
>
> He lectured walking back and forth on the podium, and he did not so much lecture as proclaim a complex divine-human lesson. He was able

to repeat particular issues in many versions. He would summarize everything again and then pause, looking at us, certainly wishing to convince himself that we had comprehended what he told us. Thanks to this I was able to record in a thick notebook almost all his lectures.

When he was examining us we had the feeling that he grew tired.

Yet when, after his philosophical forays into Kant, Aristotle, Sartre and Scheler, he would speak to young people, as he did in the Ursuline Sisters Chapel in March 1958, he spoke directly and from the heart:

Contemporary life is disrupted, it has an excess of purposes which draw man in, use him up and leave him sterile . . . This surfeit of goals disperses the completeness and unity of life. Man needs homogeneity, he would feel much better if he had but one goal . . . A surfeit of goals, an overproduction of sensations, we grab at them with our senses. But this one goal, embracing all functions, must be achieved with the mind.

The voice was loud and clear. He might have been discoursing in the twenty-first century. Meantime, in 1958 on the outskirts of Krakow the Communists were transforming their socialist dream into reality. Krakow, although undamaged in the war by either Nazi or Allied bombing, was drab, undercapitalised and underprivileged. It was to continue stagnating under Communism for forty years, and in 1985 was described to me as being like Glasgow in 1946. Materialism was materialism even if consumer goods were thin on the ground.

In Communist eyes Krakow was an élitist, proto-capitalist city, so they simply demolished a lot of it; at the same time, in the suburb of Nowa Huta, centred on the steel industry, they constructed a hideous model workers' town filled with apartment blocks, some of them containing 450 flats, and disparagingly styled 'human filing cabinets'. The intention was to sap energy and material importance from the old town centre: Nowa Huta, with its giant Lenin steelworks, was to be a people's paradise of the future, a symbol of socialist and atheist Poland; the first town ever to be constructed without a church, a churchless dream, a town without spires.

On 10 July 1958, the Secretary of State wrote to Cardinal Wyszynski, informing him of Pius XII's nomination of Revd Karol Wojtyla to bishop, and ordering him to accept the 'Canonical consent' from

Rome. According to Malinski, Archbishop Baziak of Krakow went to the Vatican behind Wyszynksi's back. The primate liked pastors, not academics. He liked people he knew well personally. Wojtyla's ability to concentrate on two things at once also infuriated him.

Karol received this news while kayaking on the Lyna River in the Mazurian Lakes region of northern Poland – 'He was a sportsman, you know,' tartly observed the cardinal twenty years later, and on Wojtyla's subsequent flying visit to accept the nomination, he continued, 'I asked him what he intended to do in the near future . . . [he] replied that he was going to return to the lakes and continue his camp.'

Father Jan Zieja reported plaintively the loss it entailed to academia, 'You educate a man to become assistant professor and "a statesman emerges".' While still in Warsaw this newly nominated bishop paid an unexpected visit, reported Zieja. Towards evening an unknown man dressed as a priest knocked on the gates of the Ursuline Sisters' convent on Wislana Street. He was led into the chapel and left alone.

> When he did not emerge for some time, they looked in on him. He lay prostrate on the ground. The sister stepped back, filled with respect. 'He must have an important matter, perhaps he's a penitent.' After another while, the sister looked into the chapel again. The priest still lay prostrate. But the hour was late. The sister went up to him and shyly asked: 'Perhaps Father would be so kind to come to supper?' – The stranger responded: 'My train to Krakow isn't until after midnight . . . I have much to discuss with the Lord. Do not disturb me.'

Before his ordination ceremony on 28 September 1958 Karol asked for a running commentary of the long and complicated proceedings for the crowds both inside and outside Wawel Cathedral. Baziak, who was to celebrate with the bishops of Opole and Wroclaw, forbade this. Malinski commented on Wojtyla's appearance prior to the start – he stood, with his head, his face, very tight, almost sad. He regretted, perhaps, the absence of close family. Aged thirty-eight he was the youngest Polish priest ever to be consecrated bishop. In spite of the grey wet weather the Wawel Cathedral and the square outside were crowded.

Baziak conducted the consecration, anointing Wojtyla and solemnly bestowing on him the symbols of his new office, the pastoral staff or crosier, the bishop's ring, while he prayed. 'Receive the ring, the symbol of fidelity, in order that, adorned with unshakeable faith, thou mayst keep inviolable the spouse of God, his Holy Church.' As the final symbol of office, Baziak conferred on him the twin-peaked short mitre – Karol insisted on a short mitre instead of a tall majestic one.

At one point during the long ceremony a former Solvay worker shouted, 'Lolek, don't let anything get you down!'

To the end of his life he carried the motto on every letter and document: capital M for Mary beneath a cross, with the dedication from the Breton saint Louis de Montfort, to the Virgin – 'Totus Tuus' ('All Yours'; the motto is masculine, the whole phrase: 'Totus tuus ego sum'). This was sniffily denounced later by the Papal Prefect as being like a commercial advertisement or trademark. Karol had read it first in the Solvay chemical plant.

Just after his ordination, the relentless pressure of activity caught up with him and he fell ill. They tested his blood, gave him a marrow biopsy and diagnosed mononucleosis, a form of anaemia. He commiserated with the doctor who had to saw through his hard bone, and who then told him that after convalescence he would need to take vigorous exercise regularly in summer and winter, a prescription with which he eagerly complied for the rest of his life.

12

Sexual Drive is a Gift from God

(1958–60)

There is a tantalisingly personal glimpse of Wojtyla's life in the fifties in *The Jeweller's Shop* (1960), his final play. Anna is speaking:

> I recall one month particularly,
> and in that month, one evening:
> we were hiking in the mountains,
> a big group of people but very close,
> our friendship was especially strong –
> we understood one another perfectly.
> Andrew was then quite clearly interested in Christine.
> But this did not spoil the pleasure of the ramble for me.
> For I was always as hard as a tree
> that would rather rot than topple.
> If I cried for myself,
> it was not from disappointed love.

'If I cried for myself, / it was not from disappointed love.' It was, the character suggests, from something else. In these years Karol's relationship with the theatre still continued to provide many pointers to the man within.

In 1957, after the relative thaw the year before, in his favourite publication *Tygodnik Powszechny* (itself active again), Karol had written under his pseudonym Andrzej Jawien a plea to support the Rhapsodic Theatre's existence because of its power to transmit thought. But a few years after the Rhapsodic Theatre performed Wyspianski's play *Acropolis*, a very different and more sensational

Polish experimental group took the same play and turned it into something audacious and original, appealing across national boundaries because the word became secondary to the impact of the performance. In the words of Jerzy Grotowski, the innovator from Wroclaw, it was the actor who was pushed to a 'ripening', by a

> complete stripping down, by the laying bare of one's own intimity – all this without the least trace of egotism or self-enjoyment. The actor makes a total gift of himself. This is a technique of the 'trance' and of the integration of all the actor's psychic and bodily powers which emerge from the most intimate layers of his being and his instinct, springing forth in a sort of 'translumination'.

Wyspianski's play is set in Krakow Cathedral on the night of the Resurrection of Christ. Scenes are enacted both from the Old Testament – including Jacob's struggle with the angel – and from the legends of the ancient world; for example, Paris's wooing of Helen. Providing a grotesque, latter-day analogy for the cathedral Grotowski transposed the play into Auschwitz, into the extreme circumstances of the extermination camp. His impeccably trained group, clumping around in heavy wooden *chodacki* (clogs), of the kind Wojtyla wore throughout the occupation, and wearing sackcloth with holes cut in it to reveal flesh, had now a direct impact on the audience with its vivid expressionistic style, not primarily through the word but because each actor engaged 'in a sort of psychic conflict' with the spectator.

This kind of theatrical shock, which delivers the full horror of the shattering circumstances, the terror of obedience to the camp guards, interspersed with dreams of love, of nobility, of life, is in a very different category from the Rhapsodic Theatre: it is messianic, as its leader proclaimed in his seminal book *Towards a Poor Theatre*. It shows, although harnessed to good intentions, the anarchic, perhaps more selfish and certainly secular amorality of exploratory genius, with no restraints imposed on words used or deeds enacted, which Wojtyla, in *Our God's Brother* had firmly left behind.

He expresses this in 'Actor', a short poem written in 1957, identifying himself with the former many parts he played, but definite in his renunciation of those parts.

So many grew around me, through me,
from my self, as it were.
I became a channel, unleashing a force
called man.
Did not the others crowding in, distort
the man that I am?
Being each of them, always imperfect,
myself to myself too near.
He who survives in me, can he ever
look at himself without fear?

Yet in a deep sense he remained a man who was always acting – in the sense defined by the English actor David Burke:

Acting is mostly a twin-track activity. In one track runs the role, demanding thoughts ranging from, say, gentle amusement to towering rage. Then there is the second track that is monitoring the performance: executing the right moves, body language, and voice level; taking note of audience reaction and keeping an eye on fellow actors; coping with emergencies such as a missing prop or a faulty lighting cue. These two tracks run parallel, night by night. If one should go wrong, then it is likely that the other will misbehave too.

No such Grotowskian aspiration towards total theatre inspired Wojtyla in *The Jeweller's Shop*, yet his future life did in its own very personal and unique way become total theatre on a worldwide stage as he played out his role, cast by God, as endgame pope. Through his poetry, plays and philosophical works he dreamed and intellectualised his life before being called upon to live it. But for how much longer would he be able to go on doing this?

A drama of inner development, recounted both in the past and present 'as if reflecting', according to its English translator Boleslaw Taborski, 'a metaphysical perspective', *The Jeweller's Shop* is both a simple and complex work, with a grace and authority worthy of Paul Claudel's plays. As such it represents faithfully Wojtyla's characteristically oblique way of thinking and his simple, lucid way of saying things. Described by the author as a 'meditation on the sacrament of Matrimony, which from time to time is transformed into drama' it unfolds in three parts, recounting events in the married lives of three couples.

In the first, Teresa and Andrew become engaged and get married. Teresa never expected Andrew's proposal. One night, on a hiking holiday by the lakes – 'I shall never forget the small lakes that surprised us . . . like two cisterns of unfathomable sleep' – she hears a strange, undecipherable sound, a premonition, a signal which is both a mystical warning and promise: a disproportion between 'the wish for happiness and a man's potential'. The Jeweller, who never appears, stands for the durability of the sacrament of marriage. 'I had an impression,' says Andrew, 'of being seen and recognised by someone hiding inside the shop window.'

The second act portrays the marriage of Stephen and Anna, exploring in the deteriorating state of mutual unhappiness the 'border line', as Anna calls it, between selfishness and unselfishness. Hurt by Stephen's indifference, his absences drinking, his silence, she goes back to sell her wedding ring to the Jeweller, but leaving the shop meets a mysterious stranger called Adam. Beginning with him, Anna tries to make contact with other men, but without success. She, ultimately, is afraid of love, of its deeper unity, which will unite the couple. Adam tells her that 'the divergence between what lies on the surface and the mystery of love constitutes precisely the source of the drama'. This, says Adam, is one of the greatest dramas of human existence for the surface of love has a current sometimes so stunning that it carries people away and they are happy. But they haven't 'absorbed the whole secret of love . . . in fact they have not yet even touched it'.

In the final part Monica and Christopher, the children of the two previous couples, edge towards uneasy matrimonial union, because love is by its very nature difficult. The point here is that human love as expressed in marriage will not withstand the pressure of reality unless underpinned by a deeper union in the love of Christ.

Wojtyla is here in it too, a compassionate shadow as Adam, who 'represents those who have never married and have no family but have a profound understanding of love and marriage'. There is even a brief touch of description by Anna in part two, which suggests Karol: 'so manly and grave./Thought dominated, and a tinge of pain'. How like me you are, he tells her, you and your husband, 'you are both like me'.

Adam listens and identifies. So does Wojtyla. The play is a distillation of years spent in the confessional, listening to the problems of ordinary people, or in seminars and retreats, arguing and debating with singles or couples.

The Jeweller's Shop, first published in *Znak*, the Krakow monthly for intellectuals, signed again with the name of Andrzej Jawien, was later adapted for radio in various countries and even later (1990) made into a feature film starring Burt Lancaster as the Jeweller (who in the text never appears); in France Jean-Louis Barrault said, in a preface to the published version in 1979, that it 'emanates a profound poetry'. Paul Scofield, the English actor to whom I sent a copy in 2003, considered it a 'revelation . . . astonishing in its utter simplicity and its knowledge and understanding of the secular world. To possess such understanding when living a life of such authority is a protean gift – almost schizophrenic – and to be an artist in addition to such religious devotion must be the rarest example.' When Karol sent the typescript to Kotlarczyk for his consideration, he mentioned in his letter that it was in the 'rhapsodic style . . . more conducive to meditation than to drama'. Kotlarczyk never directed it. When Wojtyla became pope it attracted more attention and exposure than it might otherwise have done, yet its quality remains undeniable.

Wojtyla had written his thesis on St John of the Cross, who may be deemed the most mystical and calm of the Catholic saints, and what impresses us now about Wojtyla the bishop is the unusual calm which he brings to any crisis. As bishop a definite spiritual security, a measured tranquillity, enters his life that he is never to lose, while at its very centre as he stands firm in his defence of freedom of conscience resides a quite unique, even mysterious, self-possession.

The attitude might be summed up by his observation that 'even Communist bureaucrats were created by God', and that residing inside them too, somewhere, was a conscience. Perhaps he remembered also Hans Frank at Nuremberg, and that his own life had once been saved by a German officer. Archbishop Baziak, who had ordered Wojtyla to complete his third doctorate thesis, had, as successor to Prince Sapieha as mentor and director, considered it to his new bishop's advantage that he was not too close to the more militant Wyszynski. As well as the primate, eight bishops and nearly a thousand priests had been put in prison. But Wojtyla now taught at Lublin, which was the only Catholic and non-Marxist university behind the Iron Curtain. This was his alibi, his 'cover' if you like, for he was not considered dangerous.

Ironically as someone who never kept personal money, never

banked in the High Street, held no bonds or securities, he was a paragon of Communist virtue. Malinski, his fellow seminarian from wartime years, deciding to give him a name-day present of a razor, determined upon throwing away the old one first, as he was sure Karol would otherwise have given away the new one. Malinski said that when you saw him walking along the street you would easily mistake him for a *clochard* (tramp), a nobody – and I would add, even a Beckettian character, for as with Beckett's characters no one could possibly envy him. Malinski said that 'his extraordinariness wasn't worn lightly – it wasn't worn at all'.

From 1956 onwards, through the Cuban missile crisis and at many intermediate stages up to the showdown in 1990 and the end of totalitarian rule, the seeds of the defeat of European Communism were sown. Even at this early date, as Wojtyla is reported to have told Archbishop, later Cardinal, Henryk Gulbinowicz, he thought the whole Russian empire (including the Soviet Union) was 'a house of cards', and that once the population could be inspired to face up to 'the big bluff' the whole edifice would come tumbling down. Yet liberals in the West continued to believe Polish Catholicism was medieval, backward, icon-worshipping and rabble-rousing, harking back to the time when faith was based upon ignorance and collective hypnosis. The West looks down, wrote Frossard, with a self-satisfied superiority on the 'benighted inhabitants . . . of that obscure country who have not the opportunity to benefit from the latest trends in today's religious thought, those influential currents that spring from doubt'.

For years Wojtyla had been integrating his reading and experience into a major creative work, and testing its contents by handing out chapters for comment by students and colleagues. The JNKUL, the Learned Society of the Catholic University of Lublin, published *Love and Responsibility* in 1960, the same year as *The Jeweller's Shop*. In it Wojtyla explores what he calls 'the history of a confrontation' of doctrine with life – but a very different one from that of his cardinal superior with the Polish People's Republic. Wojtyla argues in the preface to a later edition that the book 'is open to every echo of experience . . . we have in mind all those things which do not always show themselves directly as part of the content of experience, but are none the less a component, a hidden dimension of it'.

Not concealing his pride he speaks of 'the quite extraordinary vitality of the book . . . Great books have a great though not always an easy lot. Their destiny is great because even their misadventures reveal what they might have been expected or perhaps were intended to disguise: their true greatness.' He also claims that lack of personal experience is 'no handicap' to pronouncing on love between men and women, and conjugal life, 'because they [i.e. he] possess a great deal of experience at second hand, derived from pastoral work', emphasising that the book is 'the result of an incessant confrontation of doctrine with life'.

'Man . . . a complex, "many-layered" being,' he affirms in now-familiar style, 'manifests himself in many different dynamisms, each with its own specific interior ends.' The gist or theme is that it is not only morally reprehensible to subordinate another person to the quest for one's own pleasure, but it is also reprehensible to strive on another's behalf for a good which takes no account of the nature of that person. If with the first contention he was riding into battle with the hedonistic self, the second seemed aimed at the secular but socialist 'nanny' state.

While he was sitting round the campfire with his students reading aloud *The Screwtape Letters*, many such statements as to how evil worked with great intellectual and emotional subtlety must have made their mark. In C.S. Lewis's satire on evil, Screwtape, the senior devil, instructs his nephew Wormwood how to beat the Enemy (God) in the battle to win over a young Christian to their side. 'One of our great allies at present is the Church itself,' Screwtape instructs Wormwood: to corrupt and tempt his patient, 'Make his mind flit to and fro between an expression like "the body of Christ" and the actual faces in the next pew.' More seriously,

> The whole philosophy of Hell rests on recognition of the axiom that one thing is not another thing, and, specially, that one self is not another self. My good is my good and your good is yours . . . The Enemy's [i.e. God's] philosophy . . . aims at a contradiction. Things are to be many, yet somehow also one. The good of one self is to be the good of another. This impossibility He calls *love* . . .

In *The Screwtape Letters* we find the essential Wojtyla theme, 'All great moralists are sent by the Enemy not to inform men but to remind them, to restate the primeval moral platitudes against our continual concealment of them.'

To overthrow these in the central realm of marriage and sex, Screwtape advises Wormwood that they have to produce 'a general misdirection of what may be called sexual "taste" . . . Working through the small circle of popular artists, dressmakers, actresses and advertisers . . . the aim is to guide each sex away from those members of the other with whom spiritually helpful, happy and fertile marriages are most likely.' *Love and Responsibility* amplifies these witty reflections.

'The realm of the spirit is affected by sexual differences,' Wojtyla stated firmly, and 'virtue can only come from spiritual strength', i.e. from a relationship with God, not from a person's own ego. The dividing line between selfishness and unselfishness is very fine, he says at another point; and as with himself the book's unity and integrity came from its clarity and awareness of the difference between psychology and ethics, and its ability to reconcile and enrich one with the other – always provided in the final reckoning that it was the spiritual that determined and had the final authority.

Wojtyla defined psychology as the means by which the specific mechanism of the will operates. He confined himself to an in-depth examination of married love, not sexual or relationship differences, or abnormalities, seducers' 'displays of tenderness', or the coquette playing on the senses, and so on. Although he never married he still saw married love as a metaphor for all human love. He was acutely aware of the damaging effects of poor sex education, lack of training in the correct attitudes (he goes so far – which will raise politically correct eyebrows – as to list adolescent masturbation as one of a 'variety of aberrations').

Of coitus interruptus, much practised in Latin countries, he states that while the male often supposes he is doing this to protect the woman, he is denying her orgasm and upsetting her nervous equilibrium: an instance of a good intention leading to an unsatisfactory outcome. He dismisses objections 'of an allegedly hygienic and medical nature made against chastity and sexual self-control', e.g. the fashionable 'a young man must have sexual relief'.

Birth control, even at the beginning of the permissive 1960s, was the big issue. He presents the opposition's case for birth control (most persuasively propounded by Thomas Malthus, the 'Anglican clergyman' – although Wojtyla neglects to say he was a professor of political economy): the limitation of births, argued Malthus, is an economic necessity. Wojtyla agrees that 'Sexual intercourse gives men and women so much pleasure, so much intense enjoyment . . .' that this leads to the use of contraceptive methods, 'by their very nature harmful to health . . . causing temporary barrenness . . . chemical means . . . in their very nature cellular poisons . . . to kill genital cells'. The rubber or metallic means cause 'local injuries in the woman's reproductive tract' – and more importantly 'interfere with the spontaneity of the sexual act, which is something women find intolerable'. (Wojtyla dislikes the textbook sex notion of the woman rolling the condom on to the penis, of reducing sex to a kind of glorified infant care.)

To support his argument he quoted Mahatma Gandhi (the spiritual authority for a billion Hindus):

> to say that the sexual act is an instinctive activity, like sleep, or the appeasement of hunger, is the height of ignorance. The existence of the world depends upon the reproductive act, and since the world is God's domain, and a reflection of his power, this act must be subject to controls [which must come from within man], the purpose of which is the continuation of life on earth.

'Gandhi confesses,' adds Wojtyla, 'that twice in his life he had succumbed to propaganda in favour of artificial contraceptives. He had, however, come to rely on one's own internal impulses, to control oneself. Let us add that this is the only solution of the problem of birth control at a level worthy of human persons.' There could never be negotiation over this judgement. The best contraceptive was the twenty-four days in each menstrual cycle when the woman is not going to conceive. How can you be sure, argue the sceptics, which days those are? Wojtyla would answer, 'You cannot expect certainty as a right. Human life is not like that.'

Even fifty years ago, when he gathered material for his book, Wojtyla never denied sexual libido, the enjoyment resulting from use; quite the reverse he elevated or proposed it into a proper context or situation, which in terms of Catholic sexual morality was revolutionary. He put the woman first. There were places in the woman's body 'which conduct sexual stimulus with especial ease – the so-called erogenous zones, which are considerably more numerous in women than in men'. He detailed how the curve of arousal in woman as opposed to a man rises more slowly and that the

> man must take this difference between male and female reactions into account, not for hedonistic but for altruistic reasons. There exists a rhythm *dictated by nature itself* [my italics] which both spouses must discover so that climax may be reached by the man and by the woman, and as far as possible occur in both simultaneously. The subjective happiness which they then share has the clear characteristic of the enjoyment which we have called 'frui' [Latin root of fruit, 'frui' – to enjoy], the joy which forms the harmony between one's own actions and the objective order of nature.

As for the man, he especially must closely observe the reactions of the woman; if he didn't, 'There is a danger her experience of it will be qualitatively inferior, will not involve her fully as a person.' If sexual arousal was not followed by detumescence, 'which in the woman is closely connected with orgasm', this could lead to hostility, and in the word made so potent by Scheler, resentment – possibly growing out of all proportion to the cause and leading to marital collapse.

'Resentment', Wojtyla claimed in a passage which again showed his provocative and original turn of thought, arose from an erroneous and distorted sense of values, and betrayed a lack of objectivity in judgement and evaluation that had its origin in weakness of will. He believed it possessed 'the distinctive characteristics of the cardinal sin called sloth', and arose from the fact 'that the good is difficult'. It was 'a feature of the subjective mentality: pleasure takes the place of superior values'.

This unceasing dynamic is shown in those two attitudes towards resentment. The one, unresolved, of the woman who cannot reach orgasm in sex, leading to lifelong resentment and marriage break-up. The second, how resentment must be overcome or sublimated in any relationship of true value, expressing love and respect for the person or if that person is God, then God. Here the drama of his early play about Job was once again enacted. The first came from direct experience, listening to and observing how people think and feel, the second from inner response, from responsibility, a quality which was based on response. The dichotomy is important and brings us back to Wojtyla's acceptance of man's divided nature.

Long before the emergence of political correctness Wojtyla grappled with 'faulty views' on sex. Prominent among these was seventeenth-century British puritanism with its extreme but popular belief (at least among male puritans) that women were basically the work of the devil, and sexual relations licit only for procreation. Reaction to such puritanism led directly to nineteenth-century utilitarianism and the J.S. Mill and Benthamite philosophies summed up by the notion that the righteousness of action is determined by 'the greatest happiness of the greatest number' principle. Watching human sex life as represented on British television many might take issue with Wojtyla's belief that 'the sex life of animals is on the natural and instinctive level, that of man on the personal level', but Wojtyla seriously claimed that utilitarianism 'introduces into their relationship [i.e. of man and woman] a paradoxical pattern: each of the persons is concerned with gratifying his or her own egoism, but at the same time consents to serve someone else's egoism'. The result was that both persons sank to the level of tools. 'If I treat someone else as a means and a tool in relation to myself I cannot help regarding myself in the same light. We have here something which is pleasure, or the maximisation of pleasure, which will always stand in the way of love.'

Freud, too, had in Wojtyla's view a reductive narrow vision, for to 'interpret all the phenomena of human life from earliest infancy onward as manifestations of the sexual urge' was to depict man 'only as a subject, not as an object, one of the objects of the objective world'. Libido means in Latin 'enjoyment resulting from use'; emphasising the pleasure principle in sex, Wojtyla maintained, Freud ignored the sexual urge which is to create new life, to imitate the work of the Creator. So, claiming the sexual urge is 'libidinistic', directed solely towards pleasure, Freud – like the utilitarian philosophers – ignored the 'inner self' of man, removing from man his responsibility as to how that sexual urge should be used. This responsibility 'is the fundamental, the vital component in the sexual morality of man'.

Ahead of his time Wojtyla identified an approach which, as cultural hostility towards Christianity grew, was to become a new secular dogma – the present-day tendency towards situationism or situational ethics, which may be summed up as 'I think according to my situation' – e.g. poor, in ill-health, a woman, etc . . . and which he compares to existentialism, and might be crudely summarised as evaluation on the basis of context. This proclaims the 'primacy of experience over virtue', causing a rejection of duty in the name of freedom. It was from France, from the influence of Sartre, the novelists François Mauriac and Graham Greene (a novelist heavily influenced by France and French Catholicism), that situational ethics had come to hold so strong a position in modern thought. It is, Sartre apart (and Sartre calls the Jesuits the spiritual leaders of the Communists in *L'Être et le néant*), Catholic-grounded in a deep sense – only too familiar in Greene's novels of failure, of 'sin mysticism'. But it was through advertising, i.e. every situation can be materially addressed by the use of a commercial product, that situationism gained worldwide influence.

It gave Wojtyla satisfaction, in his passage on situationism, to bridge the gap between the two disciplines of psychology and ethics. This is the key to the success of *Love and Responsibility*, for, as Wojtyla wrote, '*There is no possibility of psychological completeness in love unless ethical completeness is achieved.*' This expression of the importance of man and woman as sexual partners was to remain central to his thinking when he became pope, so much so that he elaborated and published during his papacy further meditations on the same themes, beginning with *The Theology of Marriage and Celibacy* (1986) and ending with *The Theology of the Body: Human Love in the Divine Plan* (1997). While in between, over a five-year period at his Wednesday general audiences, he delivered written addresses based on ideas originally expounded in *Love and Responsibility*.

The views on sexuality, in particular female sexuality, provoked much 'situational' derision. For example, Clare Short, before she became a British cabinet minister, in 1993 said, 'The pope's a silly old fool. You have these men, these priests, who, if they are to be believed, have never had sex in their lives, and they're telling the rest of the world how to have sex. It's tragic.'

The reader less dismissive than Clare Short might justly ask a number of questions. First, how does Wojtyla actually know that, as he states in Chapter III, part II, sensuality is more strong and importunate in men, that it is fickle, that the tendency to conceal sexual values is more pronounced in girls and women who are in turn 'less aware of sensuality and of its natural orientation in men, because in them emotion is usually stronger than sensuality, and sensuality tends to be latent in men'? How can he be presumptuous enough to proclaim that 'the experience of shame is a natural reflection of the essential nature of the person', and moreover that

> A woman wants to be loved so that she can show love. A man wants to be loved so that he can be loved. In either case sexual modesty is not a flight from love, but on the contrary the opening of a way towards it. *The spontaneous need to conceal mere sexual values bound up with the person is the natural way to the discovery of the value of the person as such* [my italics].

We have explored above a possibility that prior to his commitment to the priesthood, or during his late school years or the early years of German occupation, Karol may have experienced a love or passion for a woman leading to an expression of sexual feelings, even consummation of desire, which left an indelible influence. The second, undisputed answer would be his accessibility and openness to the pain of others. 'Confession,' he told Malinski, 'is the acme of our activity as priests, and it is here that we encounter human beings in the path of our personalities.' At all levels and in all circumstances of life, not only in the confessional, people bared before him their innermost being.

Wojtyla had in his early twenties witnessed his mentor Sapieha, unremitting in his refusal to grant annulments, hearing suppliants on bended knee voice their marital grievances and incompatibilities; during four years as a labouring man he had heard the constant banter and sexual ribaldry of labourers and how they would, in a male environment, discuss women and wives (he continued to hold re-unions with his former Solvay co-workers once a year); also he had read widely in current sociology and sexology, especially the works of French existentialists – one example was Simone de Beauvoir's *The Second Sex*, in which she argued that women had unjustly and for too long been subjugated to male domination.

Even further back he could observe that he was intimate with his father's view of his deceased wife; he mixed for three years with actors, insurgents on the run, refugees in flight, those who were about to die, all of whom had, or reflected on to him, their own preoccupations, desires and practices. So he could, while with them, and with his mimetic powers, disguise himself to all extents and purposes as 'one of them' in his avuncular role with students of both sexes, both on holiday and in the university.

One student had tape-recorded his talk about the women in the New Testament – the woman at the well, Mary Magdalene the prostitute, Martha and the Virgin Mother – and Jesus's impact on them. This is what he said: 'Women must develop what I would call a spiritual instinct for self-preservation, and a certain method of defending their own personalities. The path to this is in interior independence.' This was based on self-knowledge, while Jesus's power was to liberate them to be themselves. Women, he continued, can never find personal fulfilment through a man: 'With Christ, women are independent and, so to speak, do not need men; when they get married, this independence means that they are persons and not objects.'

Karol had the confessional as his source of knowledge: here he saw into the hearts, souls, and sexual habits and fears, of his penitents. His recall was astonishing, and in propounding sexual ethics he had found a subject which both drew the best out of him, and gave a new breadth to modern Catholic thought on sex, freeing it from guilt and sinfulness and the grim attitude that it is permissible only and exclusively with a view to conception.

An attempt at an even fuller explanation of man, the culmination of Wojtyla's creative philosophical ambition, was yet to come. Appropriately enough, this was to be called, in its definitive version, published in English in 1979 after Wojtyla became pope, *The Acting Person*.

13

The Tangle of Bushes and Shoots

(1960–65)

During the five years between his consecration as bishop in 1958 and his selection as Metropolitan Archbishop of Krakow following the death of Baziak in 1963, Karol kept a low political profile. He demonstrated how, to adapt a statement of his from *Love and Responsibility*, 'making allies of potential foes is perhaps an even more decisive characteristic of self-mastery'. The puppet regime's belief that Cardinal Wyszynski and he were at odds (based on the sceptical cardinal's disapproval of his selection as archbishop) meant that Wojtyla was the churchman more favoured by the Communists.

The Polish primate had the outlook primarily of a patriot who now believed at all costs that Polish Catholicism had to compromise with the state to survive, while Wojtyla looked more to international Catholicism and the future. Wyszynski wanted, some claimed, not trusting intellectuals or figures who dabbled in theatre or poetry, but a yes-man. Wyszynski conveyed none of his differences openly to Wojtyla, who was most likely aware of them, but he tried hard to keep Wojtyla's name off the list of candidates. But Wojtyla's camouflage of quietism and apolitical distance provoked the No. 2 Communist leader, Zenon Kliszko, into pressuring the cardinal to nominate him. Wojtyla was also a popular choice, but it was bizarre, to say the least, that out of Communist sponsorship and the leadership's misreading of both Wojtyla's character and the teachings of Christ, Karol should have been set on the path to Rome. Now he was archbishop he would be there to promote the basic right of the interior person to pray and practise his faith according to his conscience. 'Today,' he said in one of his first sermons, 'our work is made more difficult; our hands are tied; doors are not opened to us; we must storm heaven violently to gain it for ourselves and for the souls entrusted to our care.'

Although he spoke only of storming heaven and not party head-quarters, and of 'kneeling before the great cause of God', this did not presage well for the future, and Kliszko was, according to Stanislaw Stomma, a moderate Catholic deputy in Poland's puppet parliament, 'disappointed and annoyed'.

Secret police files opened after the collapse of Communism in Poland reveal that the UB, the secret police, assessed Wyszynski as rabidly anti-Communist, a traditionalist with a chip on his shoulder who had been stigmatised by being born into a family of menial church servants. He had a vested interest in feuds with the state, as they promoted the power of the church, while his 'shallow, emotional and devotional Catholi-cism' was identified as the same as that of the ignorant Catholic masses which provided the strength of the church.

Wojtyla, on the other hand, is lauded as being an intellectual, one who had contacts with leftist youth and had worked in a Krakow chemical plant 'which possessed considerable traditions of worker movements . . . He rose in the Church hierarchy not to an anti-Communist stance but thanks to intellectual values (his works on Catholic morality and ethics, such as *Love and Responsibility*, have been translated in many languages).'

From their point of view admirable, politics was in this secret analysis 'his weaker suit; he is over-intellectualized . . . lacks organis-ing and leadership qualities, and this is his weakness in the rivalry with Wyszynski'. His secular lifestyle warranted their support of Wojtyla, and because of Wyszynski's resentment over his elevation, they 'should act positively on matters of prestige that would improve Wojtyla's self-esteem', demonstrating, 'our ill-will towards Wyszynski at every opportunity, but not in a way that would force Wojtyla to show solidarity with Wyszynski'.

The facts hardly supported this report – apart, that is, from Karol's humility, his continuation of a life of poverty and indifference to material trappings – for, now he was ensconced in episcopal surround-ings and had, albeit frugally, all his daily needs met, he was hardly an exponent of Marxist-Leninisim. One suspects even that the report may be a piece of clandestine subversion in favour of Wojtyla. As if to confirm how much the authorities misjudged him, in September 1962,

having resigned from teaching theology at the Jagiellonian he intervened with the regime over their order to requisition the seminary
building at Manifestu Lipcowego Street and turn it into a secular
teaching college. In an action unprecedented for a Polish prelate he
visited party headquarters to stop this move and effected a compromise: the 'Pedagogical' college would use an upper floor of the
building, the seminary keep the rest.

Wojtyla's aspirations towards international Catholicism and the
future were now to be boosted by his involvement with a church
event of profound and lasting significance. Pius XII had nominated
Karol as auxiliary bishop of Krakow on 4 July 1958, when he was
thirty-eight, the youngest bishop in Poland. Only three months later,
on 9 October, Pius had died in Rome, having reigned as pope for
nineteen and a half years. The new pope, Angelo Roncalli, John XXIII,
campaigned at once to promote Christian unity, and removed mention
of 'perfidious Jews' from the liturgy.

   Those very same Communist authorities who tried so hard and with
considerable success to smear Pius XII and the papacy, starting in
1946 when Kremlin propagandists began the legend of the monster
pope later taken up and expanded by others, had refused to allow
Wojtyla to travel abroad on several occasions. For fourteen years he
had worked as a dedicated pastor, priest and bishop, but at the end of
1962, for the first time since he was a student, he was back in Rome
for the Second Vatican Council, called by John XXIII. Here, staying at
the Polish College, he met the English archbishops Heenan and
Worlock, the latter calling him in his secret diary 'a young Pole with
an immensely strong face'.

   The Second Vatican Council (1962–5) marked Wojtyla's entry on
to the international stage and the emergence of the Polish episcopate,
or body of bishops, as a force in World Catholicism.

   Pope John XXIII initiated the Council, the calling of which he put
down to a sudden inspiration of the Holy Spirit. His objective was to
be a new Pentecost, a way to regenerate the church, bringing all
aspects of it up to date and paving the way for reuniting the riven east
and west churches of Christianity. Wojtyla told Malinski that John
XXIII, when asked 'How many people work in the Vatican?' replied,
'Probably about half.'

   John was almost eighty-two when he opened the Council in St

Peter's on 11 October 1962, and closed the first session on 8
December. Wojtyla, a member of the preparatory commission, attended all four sessions of the Council.

In 1959 he had proposed topics to be covered; appropriately for
him: 'an opportunity for priests to have a close relationship with all
areas of life in the world, including sports and the theatre'. But
revitalisation of the liturgy in view of the consumer society, and more
theoretical ethics based on 'personalism' (putting individual wants
first) were also on his list.

Again travel, the expansion of horizons, came at an opportune
moment, providing new stimulus for the inner man, finding expression
in verse, in his play *The Radiation of Fatherhood*. He actively served
in commissions and on committees, acting as chief spokesman for the
Polish bishops. But in these early years of the Council, the formative
inward influence, through his receptivity, remained uppermost. He
admitted to André Frossard that the Council 'helped me, so to speak,
to synthesize my personal faith'.

It couldn't have been easy. Malinski commented that alongside
normal rational debate was a 'mysterious underground campaign of
gossip and slander (against Pope John and other reforming bishops),
conducted by unknown forces . . .' It took the form of whispering, of
anonymous leaflets and even of ostensibly serious articles which were
in fact 'full of malice and brutality – a ruthless battle with the sole aim
of compromising, ridiculing and destroying the adversary, whoever he
might be'. In spite of this Wojtyla made his mark.

Participation affected him: later in *Crossing the Threshold of Hope*
(1994) he recalled that among the 2,400 prelates, his seat, in the young
generation of bishops 'was right next to the entrance of St Peter's
Basilica. From the third session on – after I was appointed Archbishop
of Krakow – I was moved closer to the altar.' His emotions on being
back in Rome were potent: '. . . it takes great effort to carry the boat,'
he wrote in a poem, but we shouldn't fear change.

By the end of the third session, in 1964, John XXIII had died and
been replaced by Paul VI (Giovanni Battista Montini), the Vatican
insider and experienced diplomat, whose election was both rapid and
predictable. In October 1963, Karol had attended the second session,
staying on in December to visit, with a dozen other Polish bishops, the
Holy Land for the first time in his life. Its impact was described at
enthusiastic length to his priests back in Krakow. They spent many

hours by Lake Gennesaret, stopping at the point where the River Jordan flowed out of the lake, where the banks were covered with trees and dense vegetation, so different from 'the stony and desert-like Judea'. They were 'struck by the beauty of the landscape, gently rolling, with mountain ranges stretching in different directions'. They looked at Galilee, the native land of Our Lord, mainly from Mount Tabor. 'We went up the mountain in the evening, and after nightfall, and in the morning before sunrise, and again and again, in order to look at this land, the land sanctified once and for all by the presence of the Son of God.'

Back home Nowa Huta provided the main battleground for church–state confrontation. The socialist dream, a Nowa Huta bare of places of worship, was short-lived, for when on 27 April 1960 the cross was forcibly removed from the lot designated for the construction of a new church the local people rioted. The church and state were heading towards new confrontation and the apolitical scholarly bishop found himself at its centre. The construction of the church became for the next fifteen years a *cause célèbre*. At the end of 1963, on Christmas night on the open field of the chosen site, Wojtyla celebrated midnight mass for a large crowd: his phrase for it was 'a new cave in Bethlehem'. The following morning, in the Wawel Cathedral, he made a direct and emotional appeal to a packed congregation, fuelled by new urgency from his travels:

> throughout the whole year people participate in Mass standing under the open sky. On feast days they must stand in the sleet and rain. The Midnight Mass in Nowa Huta which I just said was celebrated in a great freeze. Several thousand people participated . . . What a closeness between this and what I had seen in Bethlehem: a humble grotto open to the elements.

Wojtyla had already had one audience, on 30 November 1963, with the new pope who – now installed for five months – was to reign for the next fourteen years. Paul was about to depart for Bombay. They reminisced about Sapieha, while the Pope, said Wojtyla, 'seemed pleased that I had been a worker for several years at the Solvay Plant'. Karol commented afterwards on how the position of pope affected Montini: 'The style with which he initiated [his papacy] is costing him quite a bit . . . This is a man of great depth . . . He senses the contemporary world with all its problems and he sometimes carries that world.' It was taking its toll: from up close his face was 'fatigued with love. He is tired.'

Paul was slight, with a balding head and prominent nose. His large, clear grey-blue eyes under their black bushy brows, reflected an intense and sensitive mind, often, it seemed, criticising its own reflections. He almost darted from place to place, but his manner with people was guarded and gentle. He emerged as a pope who could be both painfully indecisive and, once he had made up his mind, doggedly authoritarian. But the native hue of his resolution, as Hamlet noted of himself, was often 'sicklied over with the pale cast of thought'.

Strikingly observant as Wojtyla was, he had noticed this at their first audience. Like Dr Johnson's ideal biographer he picked up the small detail that encapsulated the man. Wojtyla presented Paul with albums from the coronation of Our Lady of Ludmierz. This moved Paul, and Wojtyla in his account, continued, 'He looked through everything to the end . . . I tried to somehow prevent him from doing that, because it seemed to me that it wasn't necessary to peruse all these pictures so scrupulously, but he looked at them . . . and it wasn't only a formality.'

Wojtyla had grasped the nature of the man who was, more than anyone else, to prepare his own way to become pope. Earlier, as Archbishop Montini of Milan, Paul had defined that intensity he brought to his vocation:

> We need to live at this high temperature. Why? Because the priesthood is a great reality that fills those who live it fully with great joy, that becomes burdensome only when the temperature falls and tepidity sets in. Why should that be? Because we have renounced so much . . . we have forgone many, so many legitimate and sacred things in order to be in the *agone*, in the contest, to be athletes of the spirit.

Montini, by contrast, felt 'earthed' in the comfortable integrity of Wojtyla's high intellect and bold simple trust (and lack of guilt). The Pope loved and understood Poland as a friend of long acquaintance and deep knowledge. After that first audience Wojtyla's meetings with Paul VI became increasingly frequent. On 7 December 1965 at the final session of the Council Wojtyla made his eighth and most significant speech during the debate on religious freedom. 'Do as you would be done unto' was the gist of this, namely, following the precepts of his former rector of the Jagiellonian, Pavel Wlodkowic, who had spoken in typical Polish fashion against the policy of the Teutonic Knights in forcing pagan Lithuanians to convert to Catholicism. The church had to concede to others the liberties of thought, speech and action it demanded for itself. Wojtyla's chapter 'Marriage and the Family', based on *Love and Responsibility*, was included in the final Council document *Gaudium et Spes*.

With its sweeping liturgical changes the priest at mass no longer acted as mediator between God and the congregation, but now became 'president of the assembly' or even 'gameshow presenter'. It predicated a church that would listen, with a new style of bishop such as Archbishop Winning of Glasgow who would plead for trust and openness, and repudiate repressive authority. The Council became a controversial turning-point in the partial attuning of the church to the modern age. But conservatives quickly realised that even to appear to be 'consulting' would raise hopes or fears of change. 'Do not consult if you want a quiet life' or 'They have robbed us of our liturgy' were commonly voiced sentiments.

After the Council Karol actively implemented its decisions, in Rome as well as in Poland, attending four out of the five general episcopal synods it set up; at the 1971 synod he was to be elected a member of the steering committee. According to Cardinal Benelli, later Archbishop of Florence, 'If there was one man who believed in the Second Vatican Council and had a firm will to carry it out, it was Cardinal Wojtyla.'

'You know,' Karol later confessed, 'I wrote many parts of books and poems during the sessions of the Council.' Even so, and with the ever-increasing external demands and commitments of the church and the faithful, in May 1964 he published, again pseudonymously, in the journal *Znak*, the short prose poem 'Reflections on Fatherhood', expanded later into *The Radiation of Fatherhood*, which, although in dramatic form, is more of a dialogue than a play, and realised again his concept of 'inner theatre'. This was the last time he explored thematically in a narrative form, mainly through two characters, Adam and Monica, father and daughter, his favourite preoccupations of childhood, fatherhood, motherhood – and loneliness.

MONICA: Father, father, I am here! We have come back from the mountains.

It is lovely. The tents drying in the sun.
Resin drips down the bark, tall grass, a path runs across
hardly, hardly trodden in the grass. A man can hide
and muse. Discover the depths of other beings and his own –
discover, reach. Reach with what is in me that which is in You.

Adam's first line prefaces a dramatic meditation which is as complex as Wojtyla's mind and soul. There is darkness in it: 'For many years I have lived like a man exiled from my deeper personality yet condemned to probe it –' And that moment, like a flash, now carried a further resonance of his function as a priest: 'When I wanted to tear out of myself the meaning of the word "father".'

Adam goes on that, through his name, 'I must encounter every man . . . I have a difficult name.' A priest interpreter, Father Jozef Tischner, claims in a programme note for a performance that the ultimate sense of *The Radiation of Fatherhood* is that fatherhood creates a man, and enables him to understand himself. But there is a further dimension which is by now quite familiar:

the tangle of bushes and shoots through which one
forces one's way
while gathering raspberries or blackberries.
Our way takes us there.
But it is not enough to look from the outside.
You must enter
You know the thicket that is *in me*.

Given his capacity for inner, mystical meditation he astonishes us with his powers of activity. The outer man ceaselessly engaged in action, yet the inner person continued to feel that the 'thicket', the complexity – the tangle of thoughts and feelings – was in him, and that he needed them. In his forties Wojtyla was still searching, still relentlessly enquired at a philosophical and theological level into eschatological destiny (the science of the four last things: death, judgment, heaven, hell). During the whole of the decade until publication in 1969 he determined in spite of the claims upon his time to collect material for a further philosophical masterwork, or – some have perhaps more accurately described its combination of many themes and motifs – an unfinished symphony of ideas.

14

Was this Goodbye to the Inner Man?

(1965–77)

Wojtyla felt the Second Council was a great gift to the church and back in Poland he began to take many practical measures to implement its teachings. Wyszynski felt differently. On a visit to Rome, speaking fluent Italian, the cardinal in effect told the Pope that to implement Vatican Two would be disastrous, because in Poland everything that happens in the church had to be assessed 'from the standpoint of our experience' – suggesting, perhaps, that Wyszynski himself was tainted with situationism. Bluntly put, Wyszynski did not think the church was in need of reform. Ecumenism was irrelevant in the clerical and hierarchical Poland where priests strictly adhered to dress and enjoyed sacred status. The psychology of faith was serene and confident but saved from smugness because 'tested in the crucible of persecution'; moreover Wyszynski believed in explosive confrontations with the Communist authorities, not passive coexistence. He hated the Kiss of Peace in the new mass, and as densely crowded processions and pilgrimages were the bedrock of Polish piety, he lamented the lack of Mariology (lore relating to the Virgin Mary) and the neglect of enthusiasm for popular devotions. Vatican Two, he might in his own terms justly have claimed, was aimed at the defeatist and declining church in Western Europe and at capitalising on the liberal surge of faith in America and its guilt-ridden affluence. In Poland Catholicism had residual self-confidence, there were seventy bishops, a superabundance of priests and, generally speaking, religious freedom.

Paul hoped to visit Poland for the May 1966 millennium celebrations and to promote the Council's deliberations. He resented the idea that Poland could be understood only by a Pole. But Gomulka cancelled his much-cherished plan. So the deliberations of the Council were not formally aired in Poland until in 1972 Wojtyla published his *Sources of Renewal*.

During these 1966 celebrations Communist demonstrators blocked the entrance of the car carrying Wojtyla and the icon of the Black Madonna from Czestochowa to the diocese of Wadowice. Wojtyla attempted to remonstrate, but the party mob shouted him down. The procession, in spite of this, with the empty picture frame and lighted candle, moved forward.

Paul took his revenge on Gomulka, if popes may be said to do this. He appointed Wojtyla cardinal on 29 May 1967. In Paul's mind this redressed the balance with Wyszynski, for by now he was familiar with Wojtyla, but the nomination greatly surprised Poland. Cardinals have to retire from governing at the age of seventy-five, although as lifelong members of the College of Cardinals they can vote to elect a pope until the age of eighty. At the age of forty-seven Wojtyla had twenty-eight years ahead of him until retirement age in which to exercise and expand his influence, which was by now greater than that of the primate.

He still took no concern for his appearance, away from church formality, in the eyes of the world. Even his chauffeur would complain. When Wojtyla travelled to Rome to receive his cardinal's hat Father Pieronek, his secretary, had to borrow 200 dollars from the Polish College to buy his new robes.

On 28 June 1967 Paul VI invested Wojtyla and twenty-six other new cardinals, including another Pole, John Krol of Philadelphia, in the magnificent Sistine Chapel ceremony. Next afternoon, bathed in light from the setting sun, the Pope and the cardinals celebrated solemn mass in St Peter's Square.

Paul gave an audience for Wojtyla, for Polish pilgrims and the entire Polish community in Rome. 'This gift is not for me,' said the new cardinal on his return home, 'but for the entire Church of Christ in Poland, and particularly for the Church of Krakow.' At Ludzmierz, a month later, a young girl greeted Wojtyla and recited a poem 'whose final words express the expectation that he would now become pope. This aroused general amusement. The cardinal did not laugh – he bent down with dignity and kissed the little girl on the forehead.' He thought – as some of his friends and colleagues had already told him that he would make an excellent pope – that a Pole could never be elected. 'I can go no higher,' he said.

In June 1967, Cardinal Wojtyla remained living in the Archbishop's palace where he had hidden in 1944. He did now have a staff of nuns who cooked and ran the palace, but otherwise little had changed. Cardinal Emmett Carter, of Toronto, went to stay with Wojtyla.

> It was one of the most embarrassing things I ever did: he insisted on giving me his room. Then I wanted for something and I went all over the old palace. I couldn't find him; but I couldn't find another bed, either. I don't know where he slept. I asked him in the morning, but he brushed it aside. I was relieved to see him looking rested – I'd been awake thinking about him – as I'm quite sure the place didn't have another bed. I had a good look.

The following year Wojtyla installed a copy of the Black Madonna of Czestochowa in Krakow for a lengthy visit that included his own presence at 120 ceremonies and celebration of fifty-three solemn liturgies. Meantime the battle for the church at Nowa Huta continued. There, at Easter in 1967, he made an emotional appeal at the Resurrection Mass: 'Many a time since those days, people have "decreed" the death of Christ . . . many a time, they have announced the death of God, saying: "there is no God", but they did not realise that then man and his intellect must fall into nonsense.'

Still there was no church. Grudgingly, and unexpectedly – but as a gesture towards Wojtyla – the authorities gave way and later in 1967 granted permission for the construction. After a further delay of two years Wojtyla could proclaim with pride, 'Today, everyone is looking at Nowa Huta . . . They look with the eyes of the soul, with the eyes of faith, the eyes of hope and love . . . A moment ago I placed a cornerstone into the foundation . . .'

Paul VI had blessed personally a stone from St Peter's but it was not until 1977, ten years after a pickaxe wielded by Karol removed the first earth, that the church was finished. Its completion, in the unusual physical form of an ark, became something of an international event and a triumph over harassment, planning difficulties, and deliberate obstruction. This was a high point of Wojtyla's influence and presence in his native land, as with his rich baritone voice (later described by the

English actor Alec Guinness as one of the finest speaking voices he had ever heard), he swelled the hearts of the suburban crowd and visitors from bordering states as well as France, Belgium, Holland, England, Canada, the US, Finland and Italy.

> This is not a city of people who belong to no one. Of people, to whom one may do whatever one wants, who may be manipulated according to the laws or rules of production and consumption. This city is a city of the children of God . . . This temple was necessary so that this could be expressed, that it could be emphasized . . .

He paid tribute to those who 'began to build it with their suffering. We pay them the highest respect . . . Was it not possible – is it still not possible – to take any other path as we continue to struggle to build other houses of God which are so necessary in Poland?'

The hard work and wide travelling took its toll. Recovering from a spell of anaemia caused by overwork, he exercised vigorously, lived the outdoor life, reading books, singing, and playing the guitar. In one incident, a New Hampshire woman broke her leg on a ski holiday in Poland. She was serenaded down by a group of fellow skiers, learning later the guitarist was Bishop Wojtyla, who often in retreats took his guitar along and sang late into the night with fellow priests. In another incident, Wojtyla, now cardinal, skiing on a mountain and unwittingly crossing the Czech border was stopped and asked to show his papers by a slow-witted Czech policeman who then exclaimed, 'A skiing cardinal – do you think I'm off my head!' Wojtyla had to accompany him to the border police post to convince them he was who he said he was.

He was not going to change his style: he would never hurry, seeming to have all the time in the world, while Father Pieronek recalls that, on skiing trips with him and Father Stanislaw Dziwisz, who was a champion skier and now his chaplain, 'You could say anything you wanted to . . . argue, quarrel a bit, but, in the end, you found yourself accepting the thoughts he was propounding.' Perhaps he was setting a precedent.

Running his Archdiocese of Krakow like a seminar he had both trusted his subordinates and accepted criticism. Father Andrzej Bardecki, without knowing Wojtyla was the author, one day bitingly and even rudely criticised a document Wojtyla had prepared. Wojtyla

called him in and said, 'You're right. It's not good. But I think you
ought to know, Andrzej, that I was the author of the draft – I did it
when I was very tired.'

He showed great skill at defusing arguments: silently but calmly,
imposing his authority. One day a junior member of his staff insisted
he took some action; he repeatedly refused, and when his antagonist
got very angry he took off his pectoral cross and held it out: 'Here, you
rule.'

Wojtyla drafted *Humanae Vitae*, Paul's encyclical of July 1968, the
result of years of intensive thought on the subjects of abortion and
artificial means of contraception – use of the latter had become
widespread since the introduction of the pill. Much of Wojtyla's
exposition from *Love and Responsibility*, and especially the intellectual rigour with which he demolished the case for artificial birth
control, stiffened Paul's resolve to reject the findings of his own
commission, a small majority of which favoured it. According to
Paul Johnson this gave the encyclical an

> original and positive content which a simple reiteration of traditional
> Catholic teaching would have lacked. Most Catholics, having learnt
> that the Pope's verdict had gone against artificial contraception, did not
> trouble to read any further, and in the immense and noisy controversy
> which followed, some of the central arguments in the encyclical went
> almost unexamined. The rage and incomprehension which greeted
> *Humanae Vitae* helped to form a defensive bond between the pope
> and the young cardinal.

Humanae Vitae stopped not only Pope Paul's flow of encyclicals but
also the forward-moving clock of welcome – or unwelcome, depend-
ing on where one stood – change. Paul wanted both to stem the
undermining of papal authority resulting from the Council, and at the
same time to resolve or find the solution to the moral dilemma
presented by contraception. A member of Paul's commission, an
obstetrician, stated roundly, 'I cannot believe that salvation is based
on contraception by temperature and damnation is based on rubber.'

Cardinal Heenan, the British primate, interrogated by David Frost
on television as to what he would reply to a couple wanting to practise
birth control conscientiously, replied without hesitation, but in confused syntax: 'God bless you. If they're following their conscience,

then in the sight of God, which is all that matters – the priest, the bishop, the Pope doesn't matter compared with God – if every person is really dealing with Almighty God.'

Wojtyla had attended and occasionally reviewed productions right through until the second closure of the Rhapsodic Theatre in 1966 when he saw Wyspianski's *Acropolis*. On 22 August 1965 he had said mass in Wawel Cathedral to celebrate the theatre's twenty-fifth anniversary. Ironically enough Wojtyla's blessing, proclaimed from the pulpit, sounded the death knell, for the authorities liquidated it in the following year, prompting the now red-hatted Wojtyla to write to Kotlarczyk that the closure proved there was no ideological freedom in Krakow. He then challenged the authorities, stressing his own wartime involvement in it, and the service for Polish culture it had performed, and asked for the decision to be reversed; but no one replied.

While Wojtyla campaigned against the closure, or 'liquidation', of the Rhapsodic Theatre, a Warsaw performance of a favourite play, *The Forefather's Eve*, by Mickiewicz, which is anti-Russian and fiercely patriotic, provoked student riots and savage government intervention. In August 1968 Gomulka aided the crushing by Russia and her allies of the Prague Marxist-liberal experiment by sending Polish troops to Czechoslovakia. Not long after, in December 1970, tanks fired on Gdansk port workers who were rioting against poor conditions and pre-Christmas price wars, and killed forty-eight.

'The measure of the tragedy of the recent days is the fact of Polish blood spilled by Poles,' Wojtyla responded from the pulpit in the new year. In a mistaken measure to whip up popular support, Gomulka, once the liberal but now the Moscow hardliner, fired Jews from government and teaching jobs, and preached anti-Semitism. Jews, although only 30,000 now remained from the huge pre-war total of more than three million, for the most part left, to be followed by Gomulka and associates being dismissed from government. The replacement was the moderate Edward Gierek, who had once worked as a coalminer in France and Belgium. A convenient means of scapegoating between warring Communist factions, the animosity towards Jews continued.

Wojtyla, petitioning for new churches, demanded new freedoms for worship and now gained in the eyes of the authorities the reputation of an inflexible defender of the church, although he preferred negotiation and compromise. He praised the Italian atheist Communist Pier Paolo Pasolini:

> Not so long ago, the Gospel according to St Matthew was filmed in Rome. The author of the film was a great Italian director, an atheist. The creator of the film showed in his work this gaze of a mother at her husband, at his heart, when he was full of apprehension and later when thanks to the Holy Spirit, he understood the mystery which had taken place in Her. This film perfectly renders the gaze of Mary at her husband's soul.

He could be very forthright: 'Sometimes it takes a greater hero to refuse a destructive drink, than to stand with a bayonet eye to the enemy.'

In this decade of intense activity, and now he was cardinal with an ever-rising public profile, Wojtyla began to travel more, and in 1969 made his first visit to the United States. On this he remained himself. He never went local, never tried to be extrovert or hearty, and he did not change his style of dress or thoughtful manner. Someone said about him, 'This will never do.' Photographs of him in his cardinal's cassock no longer convey the bespectacled strained visage of the intellectual trying to balance his academic career with that of the pilgrim priest. He looks and embodies the Sapieha ideal of the Cardinal Prince – expansive 'with wide wings', tough, powerful, the true leader of a Polish people. He shared this role with Wyszynski, and never wavered in his loyalty to his primate. Asked once what percentage of the cardinals in Poland skied, he answered, 'Forty per cent.' His interviewer queried, 'But, your Eminence, there only two Polish cardinals.' 'In Poland,' answered Wojtyla, 'Wyszynski counts for sixty per cent.'

At the same time as all this went on he still nurtured the inner questioning spirit, impelled by a lifelong and burning desire to understand 'man' exhaustively. He went on thinking, taking notes, drafting and redrafting chapters for the book that would eventually be published as *Osoba I Czyn* (literally translated, 'Person and Act'). Man, in the widest possible sense, is the object of his inquiry, and having defined his vision of human love and responsibility in sex and marriage, he now started from the premise that while contemporary science had extended beyond all possible or foreseeable imagination the boundaries of knowledge and the practical applications of that knowledge, this had not helped us to deepen our understanding of man as a person. 'Having conquered so many secrets of nature,' he writes near the beginning of *Osoba I Czyn*, 'the conqueror must have his own mysteries ceaselessly unravelled anew.'

With a taste for paradox that he himself embodies Wojtyla proclaims a second motivation. We take man for granted, he writes, so the study of him is neglected: 'He risks becoming too ordinary for himself . . . It was . . . to oppose the temptation of falling into the rut of habit that this study was conceived.' As Cardinal Heenan once remarked to Cormac Murphy-O'Connor, a successor of his, given a choice between reading a book or visiting a hospital, he would always visit the hospital. But for Wojtyla there would be no choice. He would do both.

The first edition of *Osoba I Czyn*, this new work, was published in Polish in Krakow in 1969, but not until 1979 did an English edition appear, much revised and developed, although still by general consensus a dense and wordy exegesis. In late 1972 Anna-Teresa Tymieniecka, a 'phenomenologist' philosopher who lectured in New York and was married to a Harvard economics professor, read the Polish edition and wrote full of admiration for Wojtyla, 'a kindred spirit', inviting him to a conference in Montreal. Declining this, Wojtyla asked her to visit him in Krakow, and here he told her that her response surprised him 'because when my book was discussed in Lublin it was completely torn to shreds. I lost all confidence in it.' An attractive and slender strawberry-blonde, Polish-born aristocrat, she and Wojtyla began a friendship that lasted for years. Anna-Teresa became self-appointed adviser and editor of the English version; it was an unusually intense relationship, again as with Wanda Poltawska, as George Hunston Williams, another New York philosopher who first met Wojtyla through Anna-Teresa and her husband, believes, this attachment was based on a highly charged 'erotic energy, though not acted upon'. Many have held Eros is the basis of philosophy, but Williams went further: 'I don't think he understood what she's coping with in his presence . . . magnet pulls steel particles. He doesn't know that.' Anna-Teresa when questioned dismissed such nonsense by calling herself 'an old-fashioned Polish lady' who considered that 'sexuality is not a matter for conversation of any sort'!

When she revised the book with him this led to 'long-winded

arguments', as she said, over a phrase or a word. She spent, according
to some, hundreds of hours with him, which gave rise to Communist
undercover agents claiming he spent time with a woman (i.e. had a
relationship, presumably sexual). But then, and later when he was
pope, journalists scoured the earth, looking for women who had been
his lover, wife or companion: 'They found none because there were
none.' The question of sexuality apart, Anna-Teresa could be quite
forthright in her view of Karol: he was, she said, 'multi-faceted . . .
extremely colourful'; he loved contradiction, and was 'by no means as
humble as he appears. Nor is he modest.' Anna-Teresa championed
this dense and difficult work, and in return Wojtyla gave her 'all rights
of translation in all languages'. She dramatically titled the English
version *The Acting Person*, which in a curious way, although the
content touches little on this, emphasizes Wojtyla's continuing affinity
with the actor.

   In both versions there are seven chapters and an introduction. The
first is on consciousness, the second on human dynamism. Then
follow, as the portrait of the existential man builds in complexity,
but slowly: chapters on the structure of the person in self-determination ('man can only govern himself if his self-possession is proper to
the person'); on fulfilment in self-determination; on the integration of
the body (taking Wojtyla back to his favourite Thomist explanations
of its importance). The penultimate chapter attempts to pull it all
together so this covers the integration of the person, soul, body and
feelings ('The feeling of one's body is a necessary condition for
experiencing the integral subjectivity of man'), while the last, called
'Inter-subjectivity by participation', which gives in its wording a
flavour of the theoretical density, still has a simple starting point.
Namely, that we cannot live in isolation: 'Man acts together with
others.'

   What does it mean to be good? What is the good of good? What
makes up authentic human action? What makes authentic language?
These questions Wojtyla asked continually of himself, of society (but
he did not take Polish Marxism seriously for it had no 'intellectual
content but only an institutional content', according to a commentator
in 1957), of his books and mentors, and no doubt of God himself. His
'internal dynamism', a typical phrase from *The Acting Person* ('he
feels what determines his own ego and his dynamism'), remained
colossal. So, often dense and complicated in expression, *The Acting*

Person shows him at one with his beliefs, his personalistic philosophy, at one and not afraid of his body (or of sex), not alarmed by the subconscious (confessions of nightmares, of temptations, were part of his communication with God and his priestly colleagues, keenly aware as he was of responsibilities, faithful to commitments). *The Acting Person* was the nearest he could come to giving a complete answer.

Rocco Buttiglione (the philosopher in 2004 denied the post as Commissioner for Freedom, Security and Justice in the new European Union because of his Catholic faith – even though he explained it would not affect the performance of his public duties) became an ardent advocate and defender of *The Acting Person*. He said it represented the pinnacle of Wojtyla's achievement as a pastorally engaged intellectual, and also reflected, as a former theatrical expert, his view of human life as structurally dramatic. At the centre of Wojtyla's championing of the human person as subject rather than object, Buttiglione suggested there was a 'hidden theological tendency'. There was also an expression of Wojtyla's commitment to 'solidarity', defined as the attitude by which individual freedom is deployed to serve the community, and which allowed 'man to find the fulfilment of himself in complementing others'. Such was the notion of 'solidarity' first expounded by Wojtyla, and seven years later, embodied in the Polish workers' movement of the same name, it would change the history of the twentieth century.

The Acting Person had its critics. Even professional philosophers who read it twice, found it hard to understand. A leading English Catholic philosopher, Michael Dummett of Oxford, concluded that by following the phenomenological speculativeness of late Husserl and Scheler in method, it 'proceeded by pronouncement' rather than by argument, that it was sparing of examples, failed to state rival positions and give the reasons why they were unacceptable, and that it was unnecessarily obscure. But this, summed up Dummett, did not mean it was mistaken.

The American Anglican Huntston Williams considered that basic criticisms came down to its language: it was 'neither a rounded anthropology nor a developed ethics of action'; that it mingled, without due care to discriminate between, the intersecting vocabularies of two philosophical languages, Thomist and phenomenological, and that it could have benefited from more examples. He felt quite indignant about this. 'Not only does Wojtyla fail to provide *exempla*, but from a phenomenological point of view, he also fails to achieve what other phenomenologists have done, that is, carefully to observe the "given" data unveil what the conditions are for this given.' Huntston Williams goes on, 'If he could have only remembered he once wept in the boiler room of the Solvay chemical works during the Occupation trying to master Father Wais on metaphysics or how he much later so despaired of understanding the *Formalismus* of Scheler that he first translated it into Polish to get a grip of it!'

Wojtyla's Krakow priests joked with the cardinal that if one of them ended up in Purgatory, reading *The Acting Person* from cover to cover, it would earn him his freedom: this extracted from him the nearest thing to a belly laugh. Nevertheless *The Acting Person* as a personal credo represents culmination of his inward development. He expresses – and is to continue to express in the future – defiance at that dictate of Hitler to Hans Frank on 2 October 1939 that had struck right at his heart: 'Priests will preach what we want them to preach and if any priest acts differently, we will make short work of him: the task of a priest is to keep the Poles quiet, stupid and dull-witted.' Not only did Karol's own stored-up anger, given flesh by the word – like Alexander Solzhenitsyn's, who also became the living symbol of an oppressed and enslaved nation – find expression in its assertion of the value of the human person; but he was still spurred on by the early loss of his beloved family to integrate the rich and different aspects of his personality.

While he tirelessly probed the complexity with words, at the centre of this man there was the mystic, someone asserting that complexity remained inexpressible and even simple, like Teilhard de Chardin saying 'the incommunicable part of us is the pasture of God'. He saw himself as an enabler. 'I am a giver, I touch forces which expand the mind', as he wrote in a poem. With no gap between private convictions and public image, the transparency and depth is dangerous, provocative:

> The world is charged with hidden energies
> and boldly I call them by name.
> No flat words; though ready to leap
> they don't hurtle like mountain water on stones
> or flash past like trees from sight . . .

The mystic in Wojtyla had remained active but from now on the outer man, formed in the crucible of the inner man's suffering, anger and unceasing fidelity to love, had to dominate. The self-styled warrior for truth was destined to stride out on a universal stage. As well as developing the inner person to the greatest extent, he drew up his battle lines:

> Many are the evils which threaten man on this earth. There is the evil which touches mostly the body, the evil which paralyses our physical powers. There is the evil that comes from the elements of nature: fires, cataclysms, floods. We hear much about them: hurricanes, collapsed mines. We read about them all the time. And quite rightly Christ tells us to pray to the Father: 'Deliver us from evil', from every evil. And quite rightly we sing in our supplications: 'From wind, hunger, fire, war . . .' from every evil. But especially dangerous is the evil that comes from man.

It would not be long before he found that final evil directed against himself.

15

Death, the Place of Greatest Concentration

(1978)

The two versions, *Person and Act* and *The Acting Person*, were bookends to Wojtyla's years 1969–78, the decade before he became pope; before the real drama of his extraordinary life was due to begin.

In 1969 Karol had discovered, on his first ever trip to America and Canada, the institution of the cocktail party, surprised that guests stood about holding glasses in their hands – unlike the Polish practice of downing vodka in one gulp. If he didn't like cocktail parties, he developed a taste for press conferences.

In 1971, in another resounding echo of Poland's wartime martyrdom, Karol attended St Peter's for the mass of beatification for Father Maximilian Kolbe. Before Paul VI's celebration, Karol, at a press conference, pointed out the Franciscan not only saved one man out of those ten condemned in reprisal, he also showed the other nine how to die. Fifteen hundred Poles attended, together with Franciszek Gajowniczek, whom Kolbe saved from execution, and the two cardinals Krol of Philadelphia and Wyszynski.

Others voiced reservations about Kolbe's saintliness, reminded his admirers that as a priest he had founded and directed *Maly Dziennik*, the most anti-Semitic of any church-affiliated daily paper, and that through this the Polish church and by extension churches elsewhere fanned racial hatred and played into the hands of the Nazis. Even after Gomulka's dismissal, Gierek's more moderate administration refused to acknowledge most victims murdered in Auschwitz were Jews.

In February 1973 Karol flew to Australia, New Zealand, New

Guinea and the Philippines. As the first Polish cardinal ever to visit the Antipodes he drew vast crowds in Adelaide, Perth, Sydney and Brisbane; notably in Melbourne, in great heat and humidity, he celebrated mass on the cricket ground. The languages of the mass were Italian, Polish, Dutch, French, Croatian and Maltese, while the prayers of the faithful were heard in Chinese, German, Syrian, Arabic, Lithuanian, Latvian, Czech, Russian, Slovak, Slovene, Ukrainian, Hungarian, Irish, Spanish and Portuguese.

In 1976 he was back again in the States, attending the Eucharistic Congress in Philadelphia (but also stopping off at Boston, Detroit, Chicago, Los Angeles and San Francisco). He found, not surprisingly perhaps, the Americans rootless in their absence of tradition, and 'condemned to some kind of conformism'.

By now he was firmly Paul VI's favourite, and as a mark of this the Pope had asked Wojtyla to conduct the Curia Lenten retreat in February 1976 held behind closed doors at the Vatican's St Matilda's chapel. Wojtyla had little time to prepare his 'meditations', which puzzled – indeed daunted – the Curia but were applauded by Paul, prey as he was to increasing pessimism about life, the church, and the limits of his own power to influence the world to become a better place. Wojtyla's addresses during this retreat were published as *Sign of Contradiction*, and they are austere, also pessimistic, very conscious of the power of evil, and decidedly different from the upbeat ideas of *Gaudium et Spes (Joy and Hope*, 1965), and Vatican Two's seminal *Pastoral Constitution on the Church in the Modern World* (1965), to which he had significantly contributed.

Was Wojtyla playing to the gallery, or the papal throne, or was he suffering a malaise frequent to those in their mid-fifties who have reached a ceiling, apparently, of worldly achievement? According to Peter Hebblethwaite, Paul's biographer, Paul had listened wonderingly as the 56-year-old Polish cardinal spoke of God's infinite majesty and 'the call to experience it in absolute quiet like Trappists in their monastery, like Bedouins in the desert and even like Buddhists'. Wojtyla quoted St John of the Cross:

> To attain to this which you know not,
> you must pass through that which you know not.
> To attain to that which you possess not,
> you must pass through that which you possess not.

> To attain to that which you are not
> you must pass through that which you are not

and then conveyed his best wishes to the Pope, now seriously ailing with arthritis, who during the retreat had reached his eightieth birthday. Didn't Erasmus, asked the Pope's doctor, say that arthritis was the illness of those destined for longevity?

Wojtyla backed up his birthday greeting with the Polish phrase, '*Sto lat*', which Paul knew meant 'May you live to be a hundred!', the equivalent of 'For he's a jolly good fellow'. Paul's face then fell, but Karol gently rebuked him, 'One should never set limits to divine providence.' Didn't he mean, Hebblethwaite claimed, Paul may have asked himself, 'One cannot set limits to God's *mercy*?' But the twenty-two austere sermons of the Curia Lenten retreat offered a fresh and sparkling set of insights into central religious issues. Wojtyla had spiced his reinterpretations 'with references to the Marxist theory of alienation, French structuralism and even the works of Hans Küng. The performance might have seemed merely brilliant and adroit, had it not also given the impression of heartfelt gravitas.'

Paul had continued to perform great service to the church in Poland, which he still hoped to visit in 1976, but which Moscow again forbade, showing a misguided approach that would benefit Wojtyla. In December 1977 Gierek, on his own request, had come to Rome to seek a truce with the Catholic church, and so avoid more clashes. In spite of Gierek's hollow protestations on behalf of family life and education Paul had the measure of his 'new' policies – living space for only two children per family, abortion on demand – and remaining the astute diplomat gave Gierek no concessions or backing.

Wojtyla saw Paul many times in private audience; probably, in the mid-seventies, more than any other cardinal. But Paul, who still wore a penitential hair shirt and thorns against his flesh during the Lenten retreat, was visibly in decline. Nearly three months after Wojtyla consulted with Paul for the last time, on the evening of 6 August 1978, Paul died from a heart attack.

This happened while Wojtyla was on holiday near Rome. From the strain of his punishing itinerary he had been sick for two weeks in April 1977, and had a bad attack of flu in February. In his Corpus Christi sermon in 1978 in Krakow before he left for Rome, ultimately to become pope, he once again summed up Poland's difficult and glorious past, a past that has 'wrung tears from whole generations, a past in which generations were shackled and bled'.

On 11 August, Bishop Deskur met Wojtyla at the airport and drove him straight to the Basilica, where Paul's body lay in state. Immediately afterwards he recalled his meetings with Paul for a Vatican Radio broadcast; then he described his feelings on seeing him dead.

> I knelt, I prayed and I looked into that face which I had seen so many times in our conversations. Eyes which had been so alive, are now closed. He rests in the centre of the Basilica in front of the altar of St Peter . . . I no longer speak with him, I can no longer speak with him about any of those matters of which we had spoken in the past. He is in another dimension. He looks at a different Face. Death remains the place of greatest concentration in the state of which I have seen him on this earth.

Popes, on the whole, have the skill and foresight to manage their own deaths. Paul VI certainly did. Although the arch-enemy of Catholicism Jean-Paul Sartre had observed that 'while we are preparing our speech from the gallows we may catch a cold and die on the way', Paul died neatly on the feast day of the Transfiguration, reminding Christians that among the mundanities the Risen Christ is present.

He had asked that no photographs should be taken of his mortal remains, and requested no embalmment, and to the massive crowds who approached twelve abreast to view his body in St Peter's, his decomposing remains were a sobering sight. The throng recited the rosary, but held in check the usual rapturous outpourings of grief. To one onlooker Paul's face was already brown, the ear almost black; the mouth gaped open. On the other side of his body, out of sight of the crowds, two fans revolved in a vain attempt to keep the air fresh.

The holy will was a deed of gratitude for all the gifts he had received: 'I must leave this wonderful and turbulent world, I thank you Lord,' he wrote, unaffected by the stress and gloom that had filled many of his working hours as pope. He had, as a temperamentally timid man, become, as one commentator wrote, 'courageous out of virtue'. He was a marked contrast to his predecessor Pius, the autocratic monarch who was secretive and with a mysterious, what some have described as 'angelic', private life. (Graham Greene wrote in the Jesuit magazine *The Month* of the canaries Pius kept as pets: 'They walk over the table pecking at his butter, and his favourite takes crumbs from between his fingers and perches on the white shoulder.' The Black Pope, general of the Jesuits, told *The Month*'s editor off for trivialising the papacy.)

Like Pius, Paul had been unable to project his personality through the media and photographic exposure into the world, and perhaps more for this than for any other reason his attempt to open up a dialogue with the modern world had failed.

Karol remained in Rome for the funeral mass on 12 August. With a first meeting of fifteen cardinals who were in Rome, the conclave of cardinals to elect the new pope had already begun to gather the day after Paul died. Paul had left one fierce legacy to his successor, imposing the most stringent conditions in a draconian document entitled 'Romano Pontifici Eligendo'. Paul decreed, before reaching eighty, that cardinals over eighty should not be included in the conclave, and recommended diocesan bishops and Curial cardinals should retire at seventy-five.

This prompted one 89-year-old, Cardinal Alfredo Ottaviani, a baker's son, to question why, if eighty-year-old cardinals were incapable of electing a pope, should a pope of more than eighty years be allowed still to exercise his office? Another cleric called the restriction 'a sort of moral euthanasia', while Archbishop Marcel Lefebvre, the hard-core conservative Frenchman from Lille who refused to accept Vatican Two, declared he would 'refuse in advance a pope who was elected by a conclave which excluded the over-eighties'.

Paul hoped the conclave would have 'the character of a sacred retreat. No pact, agreement, promise or other commitment of whatever kind which could oblige them to give or not to give their vote to a certain person or persons' was allowed, although the cardinals could exchange views. They had to swear many oaths, under pain of excommunication, notably the No. 49 commandment: 'We likewise promise, bind ourselves and swear that whichever of us by divine disposition is elected Roman Pontiff will not cease to affirm, defend and if necessary vindicate integrally and strenuously the spiritual and temporal rights and the liberty of the Holy See.'

Wearing red cassocks, white surplices, the red mozzetta shoulder cape and birettas, 111 cardinals formed the conclave that assembled in the Pauline Chapel on 25 August 1978; from here they proceeded to the Sistine Chapel, where they listened again to Paul's final rules, in particular those on secrecy, and swore their oaths. The conclave could have happened a thousand years before except that, in a directive that brought it up to date, 'Technical instruments, of whatever kind, for recording, reproduction and transmission of voices or images were forbidden on penalty of immediate expulsion.'

They expected it might take a long time to elect the next pope, while accommodation or cells were cast for by lot – some in poky little offices with unplugged and dead telephones, others in forty-foot-high Renaissance reception salons. They slept on 'a simple infirmary bed borrowed from the College of Propaganda Fidei; [with] a red-shaded lamp by the bed which was too faint to read by; a wash-basin, soap (made by Donge of Paris) and Kleenex; a bucket for slops; a writing-table with note-paper and an ashtray, a prie-dieu'. Cardinal Siri of Genoa, a leading conservative, said 'It is like being buried alive', but the cautious, gentle Cardinal Hume of Westminster commented, 'Many people criticize the way a conclave is arranged, but it came to me that all these arrangements were symbolic – there was nothing between the cardinals and God. That seemed to me to be right.'

So, curbed in gloomy surroundings, this college of princes of the church – one of them destined to be dragged supposedly unwilling to the pontifical throne – making its choice did not constitute the main 'protagonist' or driving force behind the election – or so pronounced Bishop Tonini of Ravenna: 'The real protagonist is the other, whose presence and involvement transform the event completely and make it a community act of the Church.' By this Tonini meant the Holy Spirit, and he quoted St Augustine to prove his point that the cardinals only designate their choice as pope, they do not give him power: 'Christ has reserved power to himself: to us he has given the ministry of service.'

But Hume hardly echoed this in a sermon he preached before the conclave in San Silvestro Church saying that 'rarely does God inter-vene in human affairs with that immediacy which would make momentous and grave decisions so much clearer . . . It is through human instruments, then, that the divine purpose is worked out and achieved.' He might have added that human instruments are often fallible, but didn't.

Of the 111 cardinals, three were appointed by Pius, eight by John XXIII. Voting was strictly secret, and, to win, the new pope needed two-thirds of the vote plus one; this usually entailed several ballots to identify the main choices. The other 100 had never before taken part in an election. Twenty-seven cardinals were Italian, twenty-nine from other European countries, eleven North Americans, nineteen Latin Americans, thirteen from Asia and Oceania, and twelve from Africa.

The average age was sixty-six. Paul had not forbidden 'exchange of views concerning the election among the cardinals', but no one could have foreseen the presence of thousands of television and press journalists, as well as thousands of Catholic activists for change of all kinds who buzzed unceasingly on all sides round this highly secret and protected hive.

Wojtyla, attuned as he was to all the pressures and manifestations around him of dissent – and with an eye both for character and anecdote, although guarded in his expression of both – must have studied closely all the job descriptions of pope that were bandied about (e.g. 'a man of holiness, a man of hope, a man of joy . . . who can smile'). Later, in 2003, an English archbishop would tell me that 'there had been no pope in history who knows his bishops better' and this, we assume, was even more true of Wojtyla with regard to his fellow cardinals.

Ladbroke's of London had been offering odds on the contenders, prompting Tonini to declare, 'This is unworthy of the tact of the English!' (He certainly had a rose-tinted, *circa* 1950 view of English restraint.) From the start the extreme traditionalists such as Siri of Genoa, who was an intransigent enemy of Vatican Two, would have seemed not to stand a chance, for they had the weight of propaganda against them: liberal theologians of all kinds who demanded wider representation for the choice of pope, or the abandonment of the papal prerogative, or the reversal of Paul's ruling on birth control and many other so-called 'reforms', held sway in the media world. But this did not affect the cardinals who, in the first ballot, in spite of some of them advocating a non-Italian pope, voted four Italians, Siri, Albino Luciani of Venice, Sergio Pignedoli of Milan, and Sebastiano Baggio, a Curia cardinal, ahead of the rest. Wojtyla, to his surprise and consternation, according to a confidant of Cardinal Siri, received four votes in his first ballot, König of Vienna eight.

In the next ballot the right-wing cardinals switched to Luciani of Venice, who had himself been advocating a Third World pope. By the end of the first day, on the fourth ballot, in a surprisingly rapid result Luciani received not only the required majority of two-thirds plus one, but a near unanimous endorsement. The six-foot-four Frenchman Cardinal Villot, the Secretary of State, who acted as *Camerlengo* or chamberlain, and who was, during the *sede vacante* or interregnum, the official keeper of the keys of Peter (he was mocked for not finding the fisherman's ring with its pontifical seal until four days after Paul's death), asked whether he would accept election. Luciani answered tactlessly but from the heart, 'May God forgive you for what you have done!' excusing this later as a 'school memory', a quotation from St Bernard of Clarivaux, who in 1145 reproached the cardinals for electing an unworldly Cistercian who took the name Eugene III. It had, said Luciani, suddenly 'popped into my head'.

Wojtyla knew Luciani as a simple and unworldly man. On his election he took the name John Paul I, to show by professing to combine the good qualities and influence of John XXIII and Paul VI that he was the successor of both. A good omen for Karol, who responded to signs and symbols, was that John Paul entered his papacy on the day of Our Lady of Jasna Gora. On 27 August, in the evening, he celebrated mass in the Sistine Chapel with the new pope; the next day he had a brief audience with him.

Like others Wojtyla must have been only too aware of the Pope's frailty, which had its appealing side. This shows in a photograph taken of Wojtyla with John Paul I: the Pole appears chunky, down to earth, dynamic, while Luciani is bespectacled, ethereal, remote, his white hat at an odd tilt on the back of his head. Popular choice although he was (chosen, some claim, to block the ambition of the traditionalists), the popularity was all on the surface, for few seemed to know Luciani from the inside. Outwardly he gave the papacy an image of humility to the poor, the downtrodden, the disadvantaged everywhere: as patriarch of Venice he had discarded the procession of magnificent gondolas to mark his inauguration; as pope he refused a coronation, using 'I' in his addresses instead of the regal 'we'. As a small man (only five foot five inches in height) John Paul's dispensing with papal trappings was not perhaps the best way for him to proceed, as no one could see him (at first he stopped using, as had Paul, Pius's *sedia gestatoria*, but then had to re-instal it in order to be seen by the crowds). He allowed himself to be invested only with the pallium, a Roman secular and pagan shoulder-band.

His first speech, which he stayed up all night to prepare, or at least to rehearse, struck Wojtyla as a routine and lacklustre affair, and later it became known it was not his own work, but written by Cardinal Benelli and others in the Curia. He may have shown admirable traits of a minimalist towards display, confirmed by *Humilitas* – his papal motto, retained from his times as bishop – but his mind seemed ordinary, and indicated a main desire to play safe. For example, he had never once addressed the Second Vatican Council, while the crowds had hardly flocked to worship in San Marco's, Venice – a few hundred, mostly tourists, had been about the sum of his pastoral drawing power. Explaining this, he said:

> When I preach in St Mark's, I have a hundred, a hundred and forty, at most two hundred listeners. Half of them are tourists who don't understand Italian, and the other half are wonderful people but they are . . . well, getting on in age. Then the editor of *Messagero di San Antonio* said to me, 'Write for us, and your audience will increase a thousandfold.' He convinced me.

So Luciani had begun writing *Illustrissimi*, which were letters to authors such as Goethe, Christopher Marlowe, G.K. Chesterton, but also to the fictitious Mr Pickwick and Mickey Mouse, using the one addressed as a peg on which to hang a moral or religious point; in a letter to Trilussa, the Roman poet, for instance, he, like Wojtyla, considered literature part of the preparation for faith – itself not 'a stroll through pleasant gardens [but a journey] sometimes difficult, often dramatic, and always mysterious'.

Luciani was the first pope from a purely working-class background. His sincerity and openness were transparent. His mother, in an age of illiterates, was a scrivener, but worked in domestic service too; his father was an emigrant bricklayer or electrician who found jobs most of the year in Germany and Switzerland, returning home for winter. Edouardo Luciani, his businessman brother, known as 'maestro Berto', just after his election said, 'It's difficult to be pope – but it's even more difficult to be the pope's brother. I can't get any work done with all these journalists pestering me from morning till night. I would like to send them all to the devil, but what would my brother the pope say? He's landed me in a right mess.'

Radiant, simple, universal in appeal – or dangerously naïve, and out of touch with reality? – John Paul I impressed the unworldly. When he appeared in front of his first St Peter's crowd of 200,000, again with skullcap askew, his hair at the front emerged in an unruly quiff. Hume found it disarming, 'It is always a bit of a winner if you can have your skullcap slightly asquif [sic] – it suggests a degree of incompetence which is not threatening.' Hume was a great admirer: 'Seldom have I had such an experience of the presence of God . . . I am not one for whom the dictates of the Holy Spirit are self-evident. I'm slightly hard-boiled on that . . . But for me he was God's candidate.'

But the photograph with Wojtyla registered how lonely and isolated a figure in the Vatican John Paul became almost from the start.

Back in Poland Wojtyla fought on against the 'blind dogma', as Paul had called it, that 'degrades and makes human life sad'. Communism, it seemed, was irreversible. He presided over a national pilgrimage of miners in Upper Silesia: 'Long live the cardinal, long live our bishops' shouted the 100,000 worker pilgrims. Wojtyla, dressed in crimson, attended by Cardinal Baum from Washington D.C., addressed the crowd and demanded the government open new factories and (now thirty years later) ensure the reconstruction of churches destroyed in the war: 'A family without Sunday is a family without a father, and a wife without a husband.'

He made a trip to Germany in September 1978 with a delegation of Polish bishops. This was the culmination of a process begun in November 1965, when he and the bishops sent a letter asking for reconciliation to the German episcopate. This letter expressed understanding of the suffering experienced by the Germans, ending with the words, 'We forgive you and ask your forgiveness.'

When the text of this had become known the Communist Party began a ferocious campaign against the bishops with the motto 'We will not forget and we will not forgive'. The workers at the Solvay plant joined the campaign with a letter to the cardinal, stating, 'There is nothing the Germans have to forgive us, since the direct guilt for the outbreak of the Second World War and its bestial course fall exclusively on German imperialism and fascism, and its successor, the German Federal Republic.' The letter also rebuked Wojtyla, 'astonished' and 'indignant' at his participation: 'your actions, Rev. Archbishop . . . were not like those of a good citizen at all.'

Wojtyla, in a response 'to this grave public accusation against me', reminded the workers he was once a labourer in the Solvay plant: 'the best school of life and the best preparation for my present tasks'. The workers, he said, had not studied fully the exchange of letters between the German and Polish bishops. If they had, they would have seen the Polish bishops had sent 'a long and emphatic compilation of wrongs' that the Germans fully accepted and that they had asked first God, then 'us', to forgive the guilt of their nation. Following this, 'our request of forgiveness maintains its proportions, in accordance with the Gospel. Never has it been so in the relations between people, especially over such a long period of time, that people would not have something to forgive for which to ask mutual forgiveness.'

Secondly, he responded 'as an individual who has been wronged. Wronged, because I was accused and defamed publicly, without any attempt to look honestly at the facts and the essential motives'. He reminded them that when he worked in the Solvay plant, what united them 'first and foremost was a respect for the human being, for conscience, individuality, and social dignity'.

The workers remained adamant, publishing a rebuttal, but the process of reconciliation continued, and during his 1978 German visit Wojtyla delivered two discourses at Fulda, and a third in Cologne. The two churches were now, he said, 'reinforced in truth and in love' and their meeting together had helped to 'heal the wounds of the past, both ancient and more recent'. Unknown to him, these moves, together with his very active participation in the synods in Rome, where he impressed the German-speaking cardinals, were, without any intention on his part, to make him popular.

On 16 September, back at Roczyny in Poland, on a beautiful sunny day in sight of the Carpathians he had so loved since childhood, Wojtyla preached how the papacy was a great cross as well as a great office. John Paul I, he said, has taken up the 'cross of contemporary man . . . of all the tensions and dangers which arise from various injustices'.

It was a cross John Paul was ill-fitted to carry. 'In the walled enclosure of the conclave the psychodrama of Christian alienation is played out,' said a former Benedictine prior in disapproval of the conclave election. Substitute the word 'Vatican' for 'conclave' and you have a strong indication of what happened during John Paul's first weeks. He had no close family in attendance, no lifelong or even recent household or entourage to support him.

Aged sixty-five, his medical history had never been properly scrutinised in an effort to maintain his welfare and good health, while it emerged only in a general audience later that he had been in hospital eight times and had had four operations. According to one account of John Paul's papacy Archbishop Marcinkus of Chicago is quoted as saying he had come 'from a small ageing diocese . . . then all of a sudden he's thrown into this place and he doesn't even know where the offices are. He doesn't know what the Secretary of State does.'

In brief, the immediate pressure on the new pope quickly became impossible to carry. 'There comes a time,' observed Hume, 'when all the clapping stops, when the pope ceases to be news, and that is when the truth dawns.' For John Paul this fatal moment came quickly. He was soon viewed as a 'worn and etiolated' figure in the palace and Vatican gardens, wrestling with problems that clearly were too great. In a Spartan routine he rose at five, retired at nine, eating 'like a canary' (in Italian slang). The Orthodox Metropolitan Nikodem of Leningrad (now St Petersburg) called on him, and collapsed and died in his study. To be pope when such things happened, John Paul told the chamberlain, Secretary of State Villot, was *une charge très lourde*.

On Thursday 28 September he retired to bed and while reading Thomas à Kempis's *Imitation of Christ*, with the light still on, at about 11 p.m. he died. He was not found until next morning when Father John Magee, his English-language secretary, came to wake him. The cause of death was a massive heart attack, although later several conspiracy theories that he had been murdered were formulated or fabricated only to be discounted, sometimes by the same person; but the vision of hope and peace through example had been cruelly dashed to pieces.

Wojtyla heard the news when eating breakfast next to the kitchens in the episcopal palace. Jozef Mucha, his chauffeur, told him, and according to Dziwisz he blanched and froze in mid-gesture, retiring to his chapel, where he remained on his own for the next few hours.

As John Paul's body lay in state in St Peter's, where Romans mourned him in droves, the grief was profound. The body already seemed smaller than one remembered him, while the face had a greyish pallor, 'his red shoes showed hardly any sign of wear'. Black umbrellas and meagre diplomatic representation dominated his funeral, during which the cardinals, seated on green plastic chairs in St Peter's Square, received a heavy dowsing. Wojtyla travelled to Rome to be among them, and they numbered ninety-five. Two days before he left for home he had this to say at a special mass:

I still have him before my eyes, I see his face, as he rises and turns toward the approaching cardinal-kamerling [chamberlain]. To the question – do you accept? – he responds: I accept. And then immediately his name: John Paul. And then a great joy: first, the joy of the College of Cardinals . . . then the joy of Rome that same evening: Habemus Papam! And the next day the joy of the Romans, of the pilgrims, of the visitors: spontaneous, indescribable joy! And the joy of John Paul himself, who was a joyous man, he smiled easily, he opened himself easily to people, he was simple and humble. And he won everyone over by this.

Wojtyla now stayed on till the beginning of the conclave fixed for 14 October. He had to rationalise the death, make sense of it in terms of the divine plan. He meditated again on John Paul's life, accepting the thirty-three days of his pontificate had been 'sufficient. Love has a different reckoning, obeys different laws . . . the laws of time are suspended . . . love can be fulfilled in a short time. Sometimes in one action – one action suffices.'

He did not speculate or pass judgement on what that action might or could have been. More crudely Archbishop MacKinlay told one ghoulish investigator who probed for causes other than natural or medical for the death of John Paul, 'They called him the *smiling* Pope.' He paused again, 'But let me tell you something . . . That was a very *nervous* smile.'

Wojtyla might well have been apprehensive before the second conclave assembled. The night before, Archbishop König, Wojtyla's close advocate and a candidate who had himself received the largest non-Italian vote in the previous ballot (eight), told the London *Times* correspondent that perhaps the time had come to elect a non-Italian. At seventy-three, liberal-minded and astute, König thought himself too old, but he had, one might well infer, set the ball rolling. He is reported to have encountered Wyszynski just before the conclave began and asked him whom he favoured, to receive the reply 'No one.' König suggested Poland should put forward a candidate, to which the primate answered, 'My goodness, you feel *I* should go to Rome. That would be a triumph for the communists.' König countered that there was someone else, to which Wyszynski replied, without mentioning Wojtyla, 'No, he's too young, he's unknown, he could never be pope . . .'

But in spite of the rumoured canvassing on his behalf by supporters, chief among them Bishop Deskur, Karol was sure he would not be elected. 'Don't bother to take my photograph,' he told a *Time* magazine journalist, 'I won't be elected.' He had booked to fly directly back to Poland without waiting for the 'coronation' ceremony.

However, Wojtyla had received four votes in the August conclave, which had much surprised him. Wilton Wynn, another, long-experienced *Time* correspondent, reported that 'the votes for Wojtyla apparently had come from the German-speaking bloc of cardinals led by the Austrian Franz König. It was the first time in his life Wojtyla had faced the realistic possibility that he might become pope and that looming possibility threw him into a panic.'

By the October conclave he was very much his own man again, radiating his usual calm. The prevailing mood was sober, sombre, realistic. But, the day before it began, Deskur, Karol's closest Polish friend in the Vatican, suffered a severe stroke and was rushed to the Gemelli Hospital, where he lay unconscious. Wojtyla visited him, celebrated mass at 7.15 a.m. the following morning, called on Deskur again in the afternoon an hour before the 'Veni Creator', beginning of the conclave. Wojtyla apparently fortified himself, or sought distraction, by taking with him for reading matter, into this first meeting of the conclave, an unidentified Marxist philosophical journal. His thoughts would seem to have been far away from becoming pope. He certainly had no desire to leave his beloved Krakow.

The day after the death of John Paul I Karol had written a poem called 'Stanislaw', reaffirming the church's bond with Poland through the figure of the martyr Bishop Stanislaw, his predecessor at Wawel. Stanislaw was, by the sword of King Boleslaw, 'baptised' in blood so that Poland might go 'many times through the baptisms of other trials'. This might have seemed like a prophetic adieu to Krakow – it was accompanied by other omens such as his pen breaking while he wrote it – but at the time it was no such thing, merely a preparation for what he and Wyszynski were planning for the ninth centenary in 1979 of Stanislaw's martyrdom.

Karol's inner emotions prior to the conclave were turbulent, as witnessed by Marek Skwarnicki, the Krakow poet, literary critic and editorial board member of *Tygodnik Powszechny*, which published Wojtyla's poetry. Skwarnicki says he asked the Pope later whether he had not finished 'Stanislaw' in the Vatican but 'I obtained no answer . . . We don't know if he stopped writing . . . he ceased to reveal his poetry when he became a pope.'

Skwarnicki thought election as pope would prove an emotional earthquake for him and, lunching on 5 October with Wojtyla and Jerzy Turowicz, an influential Polish editor, heard Wojtyla describe how on the day John Paul's death was announced he had been visiting the mountains when a violent storm erupted. In his account he became carried away by emotion, then stopped, feeling he might have gone too far. When his secretary Father Dziwisz entered to signal Karol's next appointment Wojtyla strongly embraced his two visitors – so fiercely that the two men left the room both physically and emotionally shaken. Just after Karol had gone Dziwisz told them, 'Pray for Cardinal Wojtyla; pray for his return to Krakow.'

But all this sounds too easy in retrospect. 'Stanislaw' remains:

> The hidden breath of the Spirit will unify all –
> the severed words and sword, the smashed skull
> and the hands dripping with blood – and it says:
> go into the future together, nothing shall separate you.
> I want to describe my Church in which, for centuries,
> the word and the blood go side by side,
> united by the hidden breath
> of the Spirit.

Wojtyla again visited Deskur, fearing he might die without regaining consciousness, then his car, driven by a Polish monk, brought him back to the Sistine Chapel. He had drawn cell No. 91 by lot, where the windows, as for everyone, had been nailed up to sever communication with the world outside. His seat in the chapel was in the second raised row on the left-hand side – behind König. And here began a high drama which became the order of the following two days.

Each cardinal, facing the two rows opposite him across the Sistine Chapel's central aisle under the aegis, behind the altar on the north wall, of Michelangelo's *The Last Judgment*, contemplated the choice of their future leader, who would, however bad or good he proved, become a world figure. Each cardinal had, on a desk in front of him, a pencil and pad on which to write the name of his preferred candidate, which he did – unsigned to preserve anonymity – then drop his folded paper in an urn. Three cardinals watched three other cardinals unfold the papers, then read the names out so they knew who was in the running, who was out, who was ahead, who behind.

But the favourite, now since John Paul's death considered a foregone conclusion, was Giuseppe Siri of Genoa. Old as he was his sagacity had been widely appreciated for he had warned against leaving everything up to Providence or the workings of the Holy

Spirit. By now the commendations for the swiftly departed pope were sadly growing thinner and less regretful than immediately following his death; that of Cardinal Timothy Manning of Los Angeles for example, who said, 'He made his statement and then dropped off the stage.' Siri pulled together the general vagueness of what John Paul appeared to offer in a sermon on 5 October:

> With his style so close to the Gospel, it can be said that Pope John Paul I opened an era. He opened it and then quietly went away. In all simplicity he spoke on the firmness of Catholic doctrine, on ecclesiastical discipline, on spirituality which is the basis of the human existence. He affirmed that there is a hierarchy in these things – first the grace which comes from God and then the logic that we must never abandon – and then he was silent. The people understood and loved him.

Siri put his weight behind those three imperatives, Catholic doctrine, ecclesiastical discipline, and the 'primacy of the spiritual'. But would it be enough to secure his election? The Lebanon had just erupted in civil war, with rockets and bombardments of the Maronite Christians, while in Italy the Red Brigades murdered two men, and the case of Aldo Moro, the kidnapped president of the Social Democrats, at whose funeral Paul VI had unexpectedly presided (as well as writing an appeal to the Red Brigades), suggested the need for a pope with more worldly skills than John Paul.

Rome appeared to have become a city of murder and murky intrigue. Moro's will, promising he would have broken with the Christian Democrats whose compromise alliance with the Communists he had engineered, provoked uncertainty and gloom over whether or not he had been tortured before his murder. Corrado Balducci, a Vatican demonologist, a specialist in his knowledge of demons, predicted, 'During the next pontificate there will be a great cataclysm, which could take the form of a third world war.'

But Siri had thought Vatican Two was 'the greatest disaster in recent [i.e. of the last 500 years] ecclesiastical history'. He didn't like women in trousers – or evening masses – and he had been described in the influential journal *The Inner Elite* as 'the arch-conservative's arch-conservative'. In secular terms Siri committed a solecism just before the conclave: he insulted a journalist. Asked about his dislike of evening masses, 'I don't know how you could ask such a stupid question,' he told a *Gazzetta del Popolo* interviewer. 'If you really want an answer you will have to sit there and shut up for three hours.' He then denied he had given the interview, but the *Gazzetta* breached the rules and published this lapse of his prized serenity on Saturday 14 October, just before he and his peers became incommunicado. Also the influential König (his name means king but he was more a kingmaker) did not support Siri: asked if Siri would restore the coronation ceremony if elected, König answered, 'No, he would have a simple, humble ceremony in St Peter's Square; but then, afterwards in private, he would have a marvellous coronation with all his friends present and incense billowing all over the place.'

The main rival to Siri was Giovanni Benelli of Florence, who had been the architect of John Paul I's election. Benelli was clever and sophisticated, with a chess-playing mind, altogether a consummate schemer and seasoned administrator. He had written Luciani's inaugural speech. He was, as the conclave began, clearly the second favourite. Richard Dowden, the editor of the English *Catholic Herald*, shook his hand, noting 'the vigorous grip, the calloused hands and the unresponsive eyes'. The crowd cheered Wyszinski, the heroic Pole, symbol of the Church of Silence, as he walked down St Peter's aisle, but he didn't stand a chance. Cardinal Hume was championed by the London *Times*, which said in a leader that Paul VI and Benelli had not been able to control the runaway church of the 1970s. The loyal English *Guardian* was sure that Hume would be elected: 'One name was on everyone's lips.' But this was far from the truth.

The first day of voting, Saturday 14 October, resulted in stalemate. An Italian pope was expected as inevitable. Grim and gloomy as the mood was, no one even brought up the name of Wojtyla. Cardinal Joseph Malula said later, 'I never once heard the name of Wojtyla mentioned.' But it was also noted that for the first time in history the Italians, numbering twenty-seven out of 111 cardinals, could not by themselves determine the outcome; as Karol had said, Paul VI had enlarged the college 'to place greater emphasis on the Church's presence in the contemporary world and the missionary character of the Church'. Four times black smoke from humid hay belching up a pipe and out of a sixth window of the Sistine Chapel signified failure. Benelli had apparently peaked at around 70 votes. Failing to reach the necessary 75, he had been cancelled out by the forty cardinals who opposed his managerial style – 'a manager of God Inc. more than a man of God'. A Benelli papacy would have meant, one Curialist claimed, 'twenty years of dictatorship', although a speedy turnover of documents. That evening, König later told Wilton Wynn, 'We ate supper together, but there was very little discussion. In the cool breeze of the courtyard of San Damaso, we took our evening stroll in silence. There was a strange tension among us. To this day I have no human explanation for the choice on the following day.'

There was, according to Cardinal Casariego of Guatemala, a lot of whispering going on in the Sistine Chapel. In the midst of all this he thought he heard the name 'Bottiglia' ('Wojtyla' mispronounced) – and he wanted to know who 'Bottiglia' (Italian for bottle) was, but was silenced by Siri and others because Wojtyla sat near by. According to Benny Lai, who reported the John Paul I ballots in the book *The Secrets of the Vatican*, Siri received 59 votes on the third ballot, Benelli a few more than 40. But on the next day, Monday 16, according to a French journalist, by the seventh ballot Siri's followers had abandoned him while Benelli received only 38 votes. What swung the vote to the unknown contender? We do know, from what Wojtyla himself said later, that in a conversation, probably taking place between the sixth and seventh ballots on Monday, Wyszynski told him, 'If they elect you, I beg you do not refuse.' So by this ballot he must have been aware of the eventuality.

So why and how did the turning-point arrive when 'Bottiglia' gathered a significant number of supporters? The Dominican Cardinal Luigi Ciappi said it came after lunch on that second afternoon: 'a decisive change of mind took place in the room next to the dining room, where they served an appetizer and later coffee. The atmosphere there was always more joyful and relaxed, and it was then that the supporters of Cardinal Wojtyla persuaded the other members of the Sacred College.'

But there had been three more black smoke signals on that second day, two in the morning, one in the afternoon. The result was on a knife-edge as the swing towards Wojtyla had failed to be decisive. It was the Italians who held back, and as a bloc vote they could not be edged out. The tension became enormous.

Then Cardinal Sebastiano Baggio, the Curial Prefect for the Congregation of Bishops, cast his vote in favour of Wojtyla and the necessary number of Italians followed suit. König said, 'When the number of votes for him approached one half [of what was needed] he [Wojtyla] cast away his pencil and sat up straight. He was red in the face. Then he was holding his head in his hands . . . My impression was that he was completely confused.' He had the requisite number.

The decisive eighth ballot, on which Wojtyla was elected pope by 94 votes out of 111, ended at approximately 5.20 in the afternoon of Monday 16 October. The powder mix to add to the hay for the appropriate signal was fed into the iron stove in the corner of the chapel. At 6.18 white smoke rose into the still October air as the teller, Cardinal Tisserant, announced to the excited cardinals that Karol Wojtyla, cardinal of Krakow, had been elected pontiff. Villot approached Wojtyla, asking in Latin, 'Do you accept the election?' to which Wojtyla replied, 'With obedience in faith to Christ, my Lord, and with trust in the Mother of Christ and of the Church, in spite of the great difficulties, I accept.' The cardinals applauded.

For the moment he was smitten, seated alone at a table, according to Krol, his head in his hands, his body slumped as he took stock of the situation. 'I felt desperately sad for the man,' Hume said. 'But someone has to carry this tremendous burden, and be confined in this small space.'

So here he was. Aged fifty-eight, five foot ten and a half inches tall, with the build of an athlete, a broad smiling face, Slav cheekbones, blue eyes, pink cheeks like a child, he was led out of the chapel by the Sistine functionary to the left and under *The Last Judgment* to be invested in papal white. The flight to Krakow was cancelled by his secretary Dziwisz, who set off to Piazza Remario, where Wojtyla had stayed, to collect his minimal luggage of a battered suitcase, and bring it to the Apostolic Palace. Refusing to sit, the new pope – who in accordance with the practice of his predecessor took his name John Paul – received his brother cardinals standing, embracing each warmly. When Casariego came up to him the Pope said affably, 'Now you know who "Bottiglia" is.' They next sang the Te Deum, then the Pope left the chapel and, proceeding through the halls of St Peter's, mounted to the central balcony, the Loggia, to address the darkened square overflowing with a crowd that was both curious and then surprised, even unbelieving at this unexpected outcome. The great actor was at one with the great self-regulator as he waited to deliver the address he had committed to memory while the ceremonies were performed. The Swiss Guards marched into the piazza, the papal flag was unfurled, the great cross on the façade of Michelangelo's basilica suddenly illuminated. Cardinal Felici announced the traditional words, 'Habemus Papam!' – but with a most untraditional follow-up . . . 'Cardinalem Wojtyla . . . Ioannem Paulum Secundum!' After the initial cheer the crowd grew eerily silent.

This remarkable example of courage and imagination on the part of the cardinals in choosing Wojtyla came about first from König's initiative to choose a non-Italian; second, from Wojtyla's networking with the younger cardinals, in particular Joseph Ratzinger of Munich; then, given Luciani's sudden death, his own relative youthfulness and robust health was an important factor; the influence of the American cardinals, some of whom had visited Poland for the consecration of the Nowa Huta church, especially Chicago's Cardinal Krol of Polish origin, also played a significant part.

Wojtyla's track record of attendance at all four sessions of Vatican Two and his very active participation at five meetings of the Synod between 1967 and 1977 were an important asset: he was so eminently an all-rounder. But the most significant reason for his election was his mastery of language, and the importance he attached to the word. In him the word was made flesh: through his widely published and known books the cardinals had read him. They had a sense of, and familiarity with, the man, a nearness to the inner person which they felt confirmed by his presence. So, overall, Wojtyla's election was a triumph of his power of communication.

John Paul made his great debut – at once breaking protocol that the new pope should give only a brief blessing in Latin – and retired into the caves of the Vatican. Clearly he was anxious, first of all, to win the good favour of the people of Rome, and he felt this strongly, together with his own apprehension on embarking on a permanent exile from Poland. He had scribbled, immediately upon election, an address which he delivered in Italian, which now had the further virtue of appearing improvised and spontaneous. And of course he spoke in the easy natural style of a born actor, a happy smile on his face, taking his time, pausing and repeating phrases, which were applauded. He confessed he was afraid to accept the nomination, which he undoubt-edly was, although in keeping with his deepest instincts it was for 'the Other' he was afraid, not for himself, but for the Roman people. '*Carissimi fratelli e sorelle*', he began,

May Jesus Christ be praised! Dearest brothers and sisters, we are all still grieved after the death of our most beloved Pope John Paul I. And now the most eminent cardinals have called a new Bishop of Rome. They have called him from a distant country, distant but always so close through communion in the Christian faith and tradition. I was afraid to accept this nomination, but I did it in the spirit of obedience to our Lord Jesus Christ and of total confidence in his Mother, the most holy Madonna.

A Vatican official tried to shush him up, a token of things to come: 'Basta,' said the official, horrified at this departure from the usual protocol: using 'I' and the vernacular Italian!

I do not know whether I can explain myself well in your . . . *our* Italian language. If I make a mistake, you will correct me. And so I present myself to you all to confess our common faith, our hope, our confidence in the Mother of Christ and of the Church, and also to start anew on this road of history and of the Church, with the help of God and with the help of men.

Vicar of Jesus Christ on Earth, as he had now been elected, successor of the Prince of the Apostles, the *Pontifex Maximus* of the universal church, the Patriarch of the West, Primate of all Italy, Sovereign and absolute ruler of the Vatican State and City – it was to the title of Archbishop and Metropolitan of Rome that he related most immediately. While he won over his first crowd, who showed their delight, especially when he asked them to correct his mistakes, his fear remained.

He understood only too well what people were going to expect of him, in what was now the hugely expanded and amplified 'marriage' of himself as priest and successor of Jesus to his 'bride' the Roman Catholic church. As we know from *Love and Responsibility* and *The Jeweller's Shop*, marriage, being a commitment and choice of the will to love, was the central element or sacrament in man's destiny in relation to God and his life beyond the grave, yet, at a human level, it was also the arena for the 'interplay between love and fear'. As Teresa in *The Jeweller's Shop* says, 'There is no hope without fear and there is no fear without hope.'

And now Wojtyla was in Rome. Boniecki, his dutiful chronicler and priest, records on page 837 of his remarkable *Kalendarium*: 'last entry in the "Chronicle of Bishop's Activities" of the Metropolitan Archbishop of Krakow, dispatched to Krakow from Rome, entered after the election:

' "About 5.15 pm – John Paul II".'

Part Three

THE POPE OF
THIS DISTRACTED GLOBE

Truth doesn't drip oil into wounds to stop the burning pain,
or sit you on a donkey to be led through the streets;
Truth must be hurtful, must hide.

Karol Wojtyla
'Gospel'

McGregor reeled off a miniature lexicon . . . 'Ecumenical resurgence. Social renewal. Gender equality. Biblical computeracy. Social facilitators. Catechetical facilitators. Liturgical facilitators. Programmatic pastoral development. Task forces. Ministry Teams. Problem solving. Communal healing. Inculturation. Horizontal prayer. Outcome Based Education. Virtual Reality. Collaborative Ministry. Concept of giftedness. Strategic Planning. That's the digital vocabulary of faith in America now, my young friend . . .'

Malachi Martin
Windswept House

16

Peter, You Are the Floor

(1978)

'I say, Gertrude, have you heard the news?'
'What news?'
'About the new Pope! He's a *Pole*!'
'What's that? The new Pope?'
'Listen, Moses says the new Pope is *Polish*!'
'It's not possible!'
'Quick, quick, tell the Count!'
'Where's the Count? The new Pope is a POLE!'
'Count, Count, listen, the new Pope –'
'Hooray, the new Pope is Polish!'
'How absolutely marvellous! Count, have you heard?'
'Hooray for the Count, the Count for Pope!'
'A toast to the Count!'
'Oh, just look at his face!'
'Hooray for Poland, hooray for the Count!'
'Three cheers –'
'*For he's a jolly good fellow, for he's a jolly good fellow . . .*'

Iris Murdoch
Nuns and Soldiers

The Polish bishops were quick to seize on the heroic role played by the Polish church in Wojtyla's election. In their statement calling the Pope 'servant of the servants' they claimed it not only as an achievement of the Holy Spirit, but also of Holy Mary, the Mother of the Church, and Our Lady of Jasna Gora, and a reward for the entire Polish people 'for their faith and the vitality of their religion'. On a personal level this was echoed by eighty-year-old Helena Szczepanska, who had known Karol as a baby and watched over his pram in the coutyard: such a link turned her into a television celebrity. 'This is our reward,' she said, 'for so many sufferings, deportations, massacres, all the indescribable torments of the twentieth century. We have been rewarded for not having lost hope.'

But what would their masters make of it? The day after the election the Italian *La Stampa* declared in an editorial, 'The soviets would rather see Solzhenitsyn made secretary-general of the UN, than a Pole become pope.'

The world press stampeded, careering off in all directions, but in the main on a rampage of adulatory frenzy. For Catholics the overriding feeling was summed up by Dr Tomas O'Fiaich, Archbishop of Armagh and Primate of All Ireland, who said that the grief caused by the sudden death of John Paul I had been turned into joy. Derek Worlock of Liverpool was overjoyed, saying, 'He is certainly no mere academic. He has a particularly warm heart, and in relaxation can be a most joyful companion, leaning back at the end of the day to sing his Polish folk songs with a nostalgia matched by vigour.' More generally, the feeling was expressed that his appointment was crucial and highly imaginative in one particular direction, namely he had 'taken on' the Communist Polish government so many times. It was only recently, 'towards the tail-end of last year he accused the Polish press . . . of distorting the truth about student demonstrations against the government . . . A pope to put the fear of God in the persecutors.'

Back in the homeland, in Warsaw, Kazimierz Kakol, Polish Minister for Church Affairs, whose motto was 'If we can't suppress the Church, at least we can do all we can to limit its influence', had just prior to the announcement of the result been discussing the conclave with foreign journalists. He hoped the new pope would continue the *Ostpolitik* of Paul, namely *rapprochement* with Communist states, although this was condemned as soft in many areas of the church. 'Now if they elect a Polish pope,' the minister joked, 'I'll buy you all champagne!' This is what he had to do only ten minutes later, to his own stupefaction, and subsequently he felt very uneasy, as did his colleagues who on the one hand felt national pride, on the other deep fear and dismay. Henryk Jablonski, Chairman of the Council of State, and First Secretary Edward Gierek, the virtual dictator of Poland, issued warm statements, giving with one hand, taking away with another (no photograph of the Pope wider than one column, no headline wider than two). But out in the streets it was different: symbols came into their own.

Students tore yellow and white cloth into strips to make Vatican streamers, and draped Polish flags in red and white across the statue of poet-hero Mickiewicz, restored in the market square and in front of their cardinal's former residence.

The telephone exchanges seized up as frenzied exiles rang relatives in Krakow. For days they could not get through. Long-term atheists were as choked with emotion as young students, who so roared with joy at the unbelievable news that the walls began to shake in their halls of residence. All night long Krakovians swayed and seethed in the crowded streets, 'making emotional impromptu speeches, singing religious and patriotic songs (often one and the same), reverting again and again to what often seems like the alternative national anthem – *"Sto lat, sto lat, niech zyje zyje nam"*.'

But if there was a delirium of joy there was also, for this deeply emotional and religious people, a downside. Krakow had not only lost a favourite son, but its father confessor, its unbroken prince who under the capacious wing of his protection had given the city a very special mission in the world. This was now over.

'There is sure to be great rejoicing in your country today,' a friendly cardinal in Rome said to Wyszynski. 'Yes,' he agreed, 'but there will be none in the heart of Wojtyla.' Eager for news of Krakow the Pope rang the Archbishop's Palace. Ten colleagues received his call. He asked them, 'What are you all doing?' 'We are in tears,' they answered. 'Then come to Rome, and we'll shed tears together.'

'We feel great pride, a great joy, but also a great sadness, because we love him and he has gone from us . . . We must give him up now.' These were the general sentiments. When would he come back, they asked in silence.

Karol Wojtyla came to the papacy with formidable intellectual pre-paration for the post, with an unbelievable range of experience in determined resistance. He had been schooled in tougher trials of life than almost anyone else in the Vatican, except for his close friend Archbishop Andrzej Deskur. Having changed into modest clerical dress and hardly distinguishable from an ordinary priest, one of his first actions on his very first day was to take the papal limousine to visit Deskur. 'He taught me how to be pope,' he said as he entered his room in hospital; many years later, recovered although physically impaired, Deskur, now a cardinal, summed up Wojtyla's formation: 'Everything the Holy Father endured in his life, prepared him for what he had to be. Just as an arrow is made ready for the shot from the bow, God prepares the proper people, He prepares his arrows.' This integrity of service gave Wojtyla a legitimate and strong pride in himself but always within limits.

On that first full day as pope, Wojtyla celebrated mass with the other cardinals and in his address, delivered in Latin, his characteristic voice was heard for the first time, as he leant forwards, head to one side in a listening pose (as if while speaking he wanted to hear how he was being received). He expounded long-familiar ideas: the church was on a pilgrim journey; the norms and directives of the Vatican Council – 'what was "implicit" should be made explicit in the light of experiments that followed'; collegiality should be a prime aim. To support this he invented a striking symbol of collegiality, abolishing the traditional blessing the Pope gave the cardinals, he asked them all to bless each other and to bless him. He wanted to achieve as a goal the abolition of what he called 'the drama of division among Christians'.

On this first day, too, as an indicator of what was to come he summoned Polish friends in Rome to meet him a week later in the Paul VI auditorium for an informal gathering he called 'Farewell to the Motherland'. His concern over his status as pope 'from a far country' continued over the next few weeks, indicator of his settling-in to his new nationality as a Roman. He wrote to Giulio Andreotti, the Italian prime minister, who recorded in his diary that he received a beautiful letter from the Pope, expressing a desire for close and deep union between the Polish people and Rome. He stated how he himself felt 'profoundly Roman and is desirous of serving in the best possible way the beloved people of Rome, and from Rome, all Italy, which is included in a special way in the duties of the successor of Peter'. How should he present himself to the Romans when he came from so far away? The figure of St Peter again came into his mind in a Sunday Angelus message: 'And this is what I thought: Nearly two thousand years ago your ancestors accepted a newcomer; so you, too, will welcome another now. You will welcome John Paul II, as you once welcomed Peter of Galilee.'

In Assisi he repeated that he was not born in Italy and therefore felt more than ever the need of a 'spiritual birth' there. He stressed, as if it was a mitigating circumstance, that he was not there of his own free will. He prayed to St Francis for spiritual citizenship. 'The Lord has elected me. In the Lord's name, I beg you, therefore, welcome me!'

In spite of the doubts as he took command of the Roman stage, as absolute ruler of the most theatrical state in the world, his instinct for the right, impressive gesture showed how little he had lost of his earlier acting skills. Above all he had the gift of great timing, which meant he knew how to be still, how to pause for effect. He put one in mind of those earlier Polish epics that had become part of his lifeblood. Beginning on 22 October at his inauguration mass he spent nearly an hour greeting the cardinals, helping the older ones to their feet, and with those who did not kiss his ring he faithfully kept his right hand behind his back.

His preferred gesture was a double-armed bear hug to show both affection and courtesy. In the London *Times* Peter Nichols wrote that they might 'with no great stretch of the imagination have been transformed into Knights awaiting a kiss from King Arthur before setting off on another legendary adventure'. Clearly he enjoyed his involvement in the drama of mass, and with ceremony, establishing his own style and his pace.

Yet what of the 55,000 square yards of building crammed into 108 acres over which he had been elected to rule absolutely? St Peter's Square, a sixth of the total area, can hold, as it often did during his reign, 300,000 people. Apart from its architectural and artistic treasures – the colonnaded Bernini masterpiece, the Basilica itself, the *Sancta Sanctum* behind with its attendant museums and papal palaces – the tiny Vatican state boasts a heliport, a postal centre, a railway station, a telephone exchange, a newspaper and communication offices, a residential complex for visitors, an academy of sciences, papal hives and vegetable gardens for his table, further colleges, halls and palaces, including tapestry-restoration workshops, and of course barracks for the Pope's security force of Swiss Guards. The Vatican employs 2,300 people, including 300 women and 800 priests or members of religious orders. The Vatican income is in the region of $160 million (small by comparison with any major business), and this comes mainly from museums, rents on real estate, an Italian state 'dowry' conferred in 1929, and worldwide plate collections in the churches. The US contributes most, followed by the Germans, then the Italians. (The Vatican annually attracts some six million visitors.) Expenditure is mainly on the payroll – nearly half – the Vatican Radio and the *Osservatore Romano* newspaper, the maintenance of diplomatic links; and general upkeep.

From this city the Pope, sovereign by divine not elective right (i.e. God has directed the cardinals, who are the Holy Spirit's tool, and not the other way about) and therefore drawing his power from God himself, has three parallel structures to guide and control. The first of these is the city itself, relic of temporal power which once was great, but now a guarantee of the Pope's independence from the influence of any nation to use his power. Second is the Vatican state, which accredits ambassadors and appoints and regulates nuncios in some 120 countries in the world (at differing levels of diplomatic representations). Third, the universal Catholic church, whose first and overriding concern is to proclaim and to spread the faith, primarily by the means of the various congregations – those for the bishops (over 4,000), for clerics, and the monastics.

He is helped in this by the various congregations and pontifical councils; among them is the Congregation for the Propagation of the Faith, whose powerful and influential prefect is known as the Red Pope. This keeps watch over missionary churches, especially in Africa. Finally, heading what might be called the executive wing is the Secretariat of State, headed by its Secretary, whose position can be considered similar to that of head of government as well as foreign minister. Overall this administrative body, which implements papal power and will, is known as the Curia. The religious orders are distinct from this, for example, the Jesuits have their general, known as the Black Pope and, while answerable to the Pope, the orders have their own constitutions.

Now, there are two sides to the executive power of every pope who rules the Catholic church: as Cardinal Murphy-O'Connor points out, the priest or bishop must 'identify with pope qua pope whatever he is like – he's got to keep it all together'. In his apostolic authority he is responsible for the continuation of the church, he is the apostolic link with Peter and 'as such links past and present'.

But there is also the question of how the Pope behaves as a human being, in perilous or difficult times; and this is a very different matter.

So what would happen to the inner man Karol Wojtyla now he was

pope? Would he become extinguished, like some of his recent predecessors? The Vatican, we must remember, is first and foremost a
tomb. The authenticated remains of Peter are there, under the floor. As
reported by Matthew:

> Then Simon Peter spoke up. 'You are the Christ,' he said, 'the son of the
> living God.' Jesus replied, 'Simon, son of Jonah, you are a happy man!
> Because it was not flesh and blood that revealed this to you but my
> father in heaven.
>
> 'So now I say to you: you are Peter and on this rock I will build my
> Church. And the gates of the underworld can never hold out against it. I
> will give you the keys of the Kingdom of Heaven: whatever you bind on
> earth shall be considered bound in heaven: whatever you loose on earth
> shall be considered loosed in heaven.'

This had led to Peter's crucifixion, in AD 67. And he chose as a sign of
humility towards Christ to be nailed upside down. He was buried
eighteen feet below St Peter's high altar, and in 1968 his reliquaries,
confirmed by Paul VI, were placed in the niche where they can be
viewed in the crypt. The extraordinary monument to this burial stone
marking the death of Peter was crowned in the mid sixteenth century
by Michelangelo, who was appointed by Pope Paul III, and as Victor
Hugo wrote, 'superimposed the Pantheon on the Parthenon and
created St Peter's'. His basilica with its colossal size – 430 feet high
by 613 feet long – nevertheless had something about it very germane
to this new pope, which he must have acknowledged. Unlike many of
the monstrous eruptions of modern city planning, in the balance and
harmony of its proportions it possesses a human scale.

At the opposite end of the enormous and potentially submerging
responsibility Wojtyla now assumed was the venal side of Vatican life,
its sinister, not to say its Satanic shadow, which so many anti-papal
commentators have demonised. A place pullulating with insane ambition:

> The Vatican is a court, a palace of gossipy eunuchs. The whole place
> floats on a sea of brilliant bitchery. To get on here you need a sponsor,
> you have to suck up to somebody. [Pasquale] Macchi [Paul VI's
> secretary] and [Monsignor] Marcinkus were the ultimate sponsors
> in the seventies. The only reason they keep Marcinkus on is . . . while

he's in office he'll keep his mouth shut. He knows too much. Paul VI was gullible and made a lot of big mistakes: Marcinkus is still protecting him. And he's protecting this one, too. Who knows what money Wojtyla's shunted through to Solidarity and all sorts of apocalyptic eastern schemes . . .

Of course, the great prize would be to become a Prince of the Church. Then you get a big apartment and you can have your 'cousin' or an 'aunt' looking after you. That's a tiny minority . . .

Among Vatican officials are the 'flashers', they're just for the show, the dressing up, the vanity; then there are the 'lazy blighters', completely demoralized and doing the minimum and merely hanging on; then you have some leaders who are really good men, who are effective and good priests; finally you get leaders who have become twisted and weird with a way of life they can't cope with. The first two sorts are the devil's victory, I always say. I always think of Cardinal Newman's comment: in Rome the view is clear from the top of the hill; down below is full of malaria and swamps.

These thoughts, which sound like a prose account of Milton's hell, come from John Cornwell's *A Thief in the Night*, placed in the mouth of an anonymous 'Monsignor Sottovoce'. Many accounts of the papacy sensationalise an extreme corruption that is mainly fictional. Mystery and centralised control excite a desire to demystify and destroy. The reality is duller and more moderate than supposed. Nearer the mark was the dynamic and congenial Deskur, confined to his wheelchair, who told Jerzy Kluger when he instructed him to shut the door behind him: 'You know what the Vatican is like – everyone spying on everyone. You can't imagine. Only Dante could describe it. I'd shut it myself but it takes me so much effort to get into that infuriating wheelchair.'

But for the more extreme aspects of this imprisonment Wojtyla, as in most things, seemed to be well prepared. First of all he did not exactly go or come 'into exile' on his move to Rome, but like a champion boxer or an international opera star he brought his entourage, his staff, along with him. He had learned well from the example of his two predecessors the truth of the French proverb '*Dieu l'aide qui s'aide*' ('God helps him who helps himself').

Before he left Krakow his housekeeper for eighteen years summed him up, 'I never saw him angry – always working, at mealtimes, at breakfast. Told him off – not to read; he smiled, put book away.' To Sister Jadwiga, in charge of his secretariat, he had always given his notes on his return from visitations. 'He never fussed or got angry,' she said. This comment reveals a Karol not much changed from the Solvay plant worker queuing for his meagre rations – and being given an extra helping. The pattern was hardly to alter. The difference was that he ate more. He now preferred, instead of a continental breakfast, to start the day on a robust helping of ham and sausage. His favourite beer, Zywiec, came direct from Poland.

As soon as he could he brought to Rome his Krakow staff of five nuns. Sister Germane cooked, alternating Italian and French dishes; Sister Fernand shopped; Sister Eufrosyna took dictation in French, English and German as well as Polish; Sister Mathilda took care of his wardrobe; overall in charge was Sister Tobiana.

Surprisingly, in terms of living space, he was now living on a smaller scale than in Krakow. He flung open his apartment windows, horrifying Vatican staff who sneered at his 'Polish air-conditioning'. Since his tenure as cardinal in Krakow his appearance had assumed a massive voluminous power as if, like Thomas More's bird-god, he had spread his protective wings over the faithful. He disregarded the 'done thing', striding vigorously in his heavy walk to greet Poles.

When meeting 1,500 journalists for his first press conference he gave frank, undercutting and disconcerting replies. He would do what he could, 'provided *they* will let me' (he meant the Vatican officials). He said life in the Vatican was 'tolerable'. He told Jerzy Turowicz in a more or less public aside, 'Well, they're putting me through the mill today, and no mistake.' He seriously underlined the responsibilities of journalists as a whole: 'It is so hard to discern events and convey them to others. In the first place they are nearly always complicated. It suffices to overlook a single aspect, to ignore it or belittle it intentionally, or alternatively to exaggerate, and the whole picture of reality or prediction of the future is falsified.' Of freedom of speech he said, 'Consider yourselves happy that you enjoy it.' He spurned the siesta, which didn't endear him to Vatican servants, preferring a two-mile hike in the gardens. He gave 'healthy nightmares to protocol slaves until they either fade[d] away or adjust[ed] themselves'.

Rising at 5.30 he worked an eighteen-hour day. Exercise, quick shower, prayer and meditation, and mass at 7 a.m. began his day. Breakfast at 8. He worked in his office until 11, then the morning meetings, audiences, etc., 1.45 lunch, then worked alone again till 6.30; Holy See administration till 8 p.m., and after dinner preparation reading for next morning; compline, final meditation and private prayer; then bed at 11.30 p.m. He still had Dziwisz who had spent thirteen years in his service. Messenger, adviser and privileged confidant, Dziwisz had also the task of ensuring the notoriously unpunctual pope arrived on time for meetings. When he moved about Wojtyla still had his four briefcases, two stuffed with papers, the other two with books.

He did concede to a neater, cleaner appearance from that of the Krakow period. During one garden outing he met a gardener, extending a hand in greeting. Abashed, the gardener looked down at his own grimy hands, but the Pope seized both, pressing them against his spotless white cassock: 'I know they're dirty, but I don't do my own washing,' he said.

When a week into his papacy he gave the audience for Poles in the Paul VI auditorium, he greeted Jerzy Kluger, now settled in Rome with his Irish wife and their family, and called him to a private meeting backstage. He embraced his old friend and while Kluger bent on one knee to kiss his ring, John Paul gripped him firmly by the elbow and yanked him upright. 'You must never bend your knee to me. Stand straight as you always have.'

But here began the mythologising process (to be swiftly followed by the demythologising process). People heard, remembered, felt that one day he would be pope. At once the former actor became formidably photogenic, which presupposes on his part a kind of complicity. 'The photograph is a mirror,' wrote Roland Barthes (in terms of a politician's electoral appeal, but it applies as well to a churchman), 'what we are asked to read is the familiar, the known.' As pope Wojtyla was a natural advertisement for prayer and holiness, not because he was putting anything on but because everything in his face and manner could be seen so clearly – at the same time the viewer of the photograph was 'exposed and heroized', in other words a strong transference on to the viewer took place. From a photograph of the Pope what came over was exactly the same as meeting him face to face, but did not in any way diminish wanting to see him in the flesh, to be in his presence.

This is the point at which the inner man apparently vanishes – or does he? He now has, for sure, reached his ultimate destination, one towards which he had never consciously aimed. He cannot go higher. He occupies the chair of St Peter. But what about the heights, the exalted position? 'So many colonnades,' he had written sixteen years before in a poem about the Basilica, 'it is the floor that guides . . . and joins the spaces within us.'

And now he wrote to Felicja Wiadrowska, the daughter of Maria Anna Wiadrowska, the only living member of his immediate family, who was on his mother's side:

> Dear Luisa, God has decreed that I remain in Rome. It is indeed an extraordinary edict of Divine Providence. These days I think a lot of my parents and of Mundek, but I also think of your mother and father, who were always so good to me. I remember also our dearly departed Janina and Adam [Felicja's siblings], and our dearly departed Rudolfina, Anna and Robert. I commend their souls to God. They were all very good to me. I also pray for the soul of our dearly departed Stephania, my father's sister.
>
> Now you are the only one of my closest family . . .
>
> John Paul II
Vatican City, 27 October 1978

17

He's Cleaned up His Plate

(1979)

I have expressed a desire to go to China, because sometimes the pope should use bold words . . . It is also necessary to speak courageously. Words are as true a witness as actions.

John Paul II

In terms of *The Guinness Book of Records*, over the next twenty-seven years (by 2005 illness had severely restricted movement) John Paul II broke all the records. First, he was the youngest pope for 140 years, the first non-Italian for four and a half centuries, the first Pole ever. He told André Frossard a *barzelletta* or *jeu d'esprit*: 'The pope was praying and he asked God: "Lord, will Poland regain her freedom and independence some day?" "Yes," said God, "but not in your lifetime." Then the pope asked: "Lord, after I'm gone, will there be another Polish pope?" "Not in my lifetime," said God.'

As Bishop of Rome, Wojtyla has made 146 trips inside Italy and visited 301 Roman parishes; as pope, 104 outside, visiting nearly a thousand localities in 129 countries, in which generally speaking he met every head of state. He travelled over a million and a quarter kilometres, equivalent to thirty-one circuits of the earth or three and a half round trips to the moon. He delivered well over 3,000 discourses . . .

And on and on. The record is stupendous. But what about Jesus of Nazareth? How many discourses did he deliver? How many trips abroad? How many hands of heads of state did he shake? There you have the huge and perfect paradox of the Catholic faith in the modern age. The Pope, following this original Messiah in imitative admiration did not for a moment claim he was the Messiah. He was only the witness. He did it out of love for the other. As he said over and over again, 'Liberty is the measure of how much love we are capable of giving,' and giving so much love, he gained strength and liberty by the embrace he gave. But there was nothing egocentric about it, for, as he quotes Christ in St John, 'I say nothing on my own authority but speak thus as my Father taught me. This commandment holds for all the apostles as well; I am profoundly convinced of it.'

He saw his first duty as that to conserve. On the dressing table in his sparsely furnished Vatican bedroom he had two framed photographs, one of his parents taken just after their marriage, the other of his second father, Sapieha. In a drawer he kept his brother Mundek's stethoscope.

The travelling pope was born in January 1979, with audiences in multiples of millions all around the world. A journalist's sketch, replete with names and numbers, captures the essence of the new Wojtyla.

On Thursday, 25 January, 1979, the special jet airliner of Alitalia carrying John Paul II took off at eight in the morning. The yellow and white flags of the Vatican flew over the airport. The crew of six Italian pilots was under the command of Giorgio Coacci, with 130,000 flying hours to his credit. The aircraft was divided into sections A, B and C. The first was reserved for the Pope, the second was occupied by 25 persons of his immediate entourage, among them the Deputy Secretary of State, Archbishop Casaroli [soon to be nominated Secretary of State]; the secretary of the Vatican Council for Public Affairs Cardinal Sebastiano Baggio; the Chairman of the Conference of the Episcopate in Pueblo, Monsignor Martin; the prefect of the papal household, Monsignor Marcinkus; the trip's organizer, Monsignor Noel; the papal Chief of Protocol, Monsignor Juliusz Paetz; the private secretary of the Pope, Father Dziwisz; his personal physician, Dr Mieczyslaw Wislocki; Monsignor Joseph Kowalczyk from the Vatican State Department; two Swiss guards; the head of the Vatican security service and his deputy; the official Vatican photographer, Felici; and the Ambassador of the Dominican Republic to the Holy See.

In section C were 140 other people, among them 72 newspaper and electronic media correspondents and cameramen.

A few minutes after take-off the curtain of section A opened and John Paul II appeared. His conversation with the press lasted an hour and twenty minutes. He endeavoured to reply to questions in the language of the person he addressed. Asked by an American journalist whether he liked his work after the first three months on the throne of Peter, he replied: 'Do I like it? This is my duty. But I must say that in carrying it out I am helped by divine grace. Also by the support of many people. There is a great deal of it. I should like to hope that Americans will also grant me such support. I like to work. When I work I am happy. It is my good fortune that I can concentrate all my strength on carrying out the duties of my office.'

His first choice, significantly, was to visit Third World countries in Latin America, during which in Puebla, Mexico, he addressed a general conference of Latin-American bishops. The voyages were of very short duration – the longest ten days, on average three to four days and often literally flying visits.

The Curia tried to apply the brakes to John Paul's wanderlust, while even senior church officials publicly criticised it. But a common misunderstanding is that John Paul was the first pope to travel. He was asked why he behaved from the start as if he had so little time to gather good folk together before the apocalyptic storm broke, and he defended himself as not being the first: his predecessors especially Paul VI had started this practice. He justified his intention to accept most invitations: 'The more difficult the life of men, of families, of communities and of the world becomes, the more necessary it is for them to become aware of the presence of the Good Shepherd.' He felt it was an imperative.

A year later, on his first trip to Africa in May 1980 he raised the question again, saying how he read in newspapers that he should not travel, and this time he claimed he must not be thought of 'exclusively as the successor of Peter, but also as the heir of St Paul who, as we well know, never stood still; he was always travelling'.

In the anti-clerical land of Mexico, where the Masonic lodges still harboured hatred of the church, and where the persecuting spirit, as shown in Greene's *The Power and the Glory* with its relentless pursuit of the whisky priest by the police, persisted among the authorities, over the time he spent there some twenty million people (according to

Mexican police estimates) turned out to see him. They counted the crowd assembled at Puebla as between eight and ten million, but it was probably half this. Here he affirmed a stance which was to become an important and lasting principle of his papacy – much ignored in the West – that of support for the poor of the world, 'the immense multitude of the rural world', against the exploitative and 'unlawful' rich who used popular religiosity to selfish ends.

Moved as he was by a message from Mexican native Latin-Americans bluntly expressing their suffering and sorrow, he spoke in texts rewritten from their original drafts when he addressed over half a million Indians in Oaxaca on the 'cause of humble people, of the poor' whose culture, whose traditions he and the church loved, yet who were so often 'abandoned at an ignoble level of life and sometimes harshly treated and exploited'.

The church teaches the legitimate right to private property, but defends no less clearly that there is always a social mortgage on all private property, in order that goods may serve the general purpose that God gave them. And if the common good requires it, there should be no hesitation even at expropriation, carried out in the due form. It was 'necessary to carry out bold changes' to be rid of the barriers of exploitation, of 'intolerable selfishness, necessary to undertake urgent reforms'. To this end he told the leaders, the powerful classes, to listen 'to the cry of the destitute . . . It is not just, it is not human, it is not Christian, to continue with certain situations that are clearly unjust.'

This was a radical Christian message, reaching all the way back to his play *Our God's Brother*, in which Brother Albert advocates 'creative . . . fast anger', the anger that 'must' explode.

When John Paul's airliner took off for his return from Mexico City he observed a very strange phenomenon. Over the surface of the metropolis of thirteen million people the entire, vast cityscape twinkled with thousands of flashes of light. On board the plane they thought at first it was the reflections in house windows, but over the address system the pilot told them it was the city Mexicans holding mirrors to reflect the sun's rays in the direction of the climbing airliner. When the jet banked the Pope had 'an excellent view of the myriad small flashes signalling a parting greeting', with 'the edges of that scintillating carpet . . . marked by the rough outlines of mountains and extinct volcanoes'.

*   *   *

On 2 June the Pope's white Boeing 727, *Città di Bergamo*, touched down at Olcecie airport. Warsaw was so transformed with flowers, flags and bunting that it looked more like Rome than the bleak, dowdy capital of a Communist state. The church in Poland had never been stronger, with an estimated 90 per cent of the thirty-five million Poles baptised Catholics, and at least 75 per cent practising believers. At the airport Cardinal Wyszynski, the Polish primate, welcomed Karol. Instead of the wooden clogs of his wartime years Wojtyla wore neat, maroon-coloured, soft leather slippers and, folding his arms during the welcoming speech from Wyszynski and government functionary President Jablonski, revealed a glittering stainless-steel wrist watch.

Three million people assembled in Warsaw to honour their countryman now vicar of Christ, and during the nine-day tour there were many outstanding, emotionally and spiritually moving, moments. Having already delayed the visit from May, when John Paul had originally intended it to coincide with the 900th anniversary celebrations of the death of St Stanislaw, and having imposed a host of restrictions on press and television coverage, and an alcohol ban, the government did what it could to contain and belittle the impact.

It failed. Wojtyla now reached his full stature and maturity as papal head of the Polish church. Previously he had always willingly stood in the shadow of Primate Wyszynski, whom now he generously acknowledged, standing next to him, saying, 'Without your faith, this Polish pope would not be on the chair of Peter.' He passed on to his successor in Krakow, Archbishop Franciszek Macharski, the pectoral cross once belonging to Sapieha which he had been given, joking, 'I'm giving it to you because it's a little worn.'

At once began the Pope's 'skilful technique of making apparently innocuous, indeed quite acceptable, observations which could nevertheless be read as criticism by anyone so disposed'. In his reply to the welcome, he emphasised for all time this link between Poland's popular piety in history and the present: 'May the Virgin Mother of God open wide to you this her kingdom, devoted without reservation to the successor of St Peter upon the see of the bishops of Rome.' With the Communist President Jablonski standing by impassively, it at once put an end to the long-term effect on Poland of the humiliating setback suffered in 1920 by the Lenin hierarchy, when Lenin seethed and swore after this gigantic defeat at the Vistula that they would keep 'shifting from a defensive strategy over and over again until we finish them off for good'.

Wojtyla quoted the sixeenth-century pastor Piotr Skarga, the impact of whose life he had explored in *Jeremiah*, the play he wrote in his twenties: 'This old oak tree has grown as it has, and not been knocked down by any wind, since its root is in Christ.'

The most remarkable effect of this highly theatrical homecoming with its forty public appearances was the complete bonding of the Polish people with John Paul. The crowd would immediately surround him [in one report] 'as in an embrace, and they would not let him go. They followed him on the road; they waited for him at every crossing; they greeted him in every town and village'. In the warm late-spring-time weather, Poland overflowed with flowers and every house, every wayside cross and shrine, was decorated, the streets he passed were strewn with blossoms, and people tossed flowers from windows as he rode by. This embrace reached its fullest intensity when he stood before the crowds.

In Warsaw's Victory Square, before a thirty-foot-long oak cross draped with a blood-red stole to signify the Resurrection, he celebrated mass for 300,000 people. In Gniezno, the ancient primatial see where over a thousand years before, Prince Lech, leader of the Christian tribe of Polans, saw a white eagle building its nest and followed this with his first castle and Poland's coat of arms (the name Gniezno is derived from the Polish for 'nest'), a vast throng again assembled in a 93-degree heatwave. The sweltering weather surprised him. 'It was so hot in Rome I thought I'd come to Poland where it would be cooler. You see, even a pope can be wrong!'

His repertory seemed boundless. Soldiers' songs, boy scouts' songs, Ukrainian ditties and traditional old favourites such as 'The Red Bell' (which he sang almost solo) followed the formal occasions. Before starting a new song he would look around and anxiously ask, 'Do you still remember this one?' Sing-songs stretched far into the evening, amidst jokes, anecdotes and good cheer.

John Paul spent three nights and two days visiting the shrine of Jasna Gora, bastion of Poland's spiritual survival. The ancient monastery on the hill overlooking Czestochowa became his temporary retreat. 'One has only to place one's ear close to that holy site to hear a nation's heart beating in its mother's bosom.' He held closed sessions of the Polish hierarchy, and yet again to rapturous receptions from different assemblies – nuns, priests, students, factory workers, the sick and disabled – extolled the virtues of Poland, and the icon of its Black Madonna shrine. One observer in the crowd told me how the people shouted over and over again, 'Come closer to us . . .' 'I'm coming closer to you,' he shouted back, and did. There was a sudden change as he began quietly to pray, 'like a man talking to his mother. A million people were eavesdropping on an intimate moment.'

'Mary leads the way to the Kingdom of Christ victorious . . . I am a man of faith,' he declared, 'and I learnt to be one here.' He had wanted to visit the miners in Silesia, but this was refused by the Communists. Instead he said mass for them at the monastery and they flocked there in their hundreds of thousands: miners, technicians, engineers, mine managers. 'The miners wore the *czaka*, the ceremonial plumed hats, and their wives were decked in the vivid Silesian peasant dress with brilliant scarlet bandanas on their hair.' The government witnessed the humiliating spectacle of a quarter of a million miners singing 'Christ has conquered, Christ is King, Christ commands our lives' at the top of their voices.

'The Second Coming is the only event that would top the homecoming of God's Vicar on Earth,' wrote Jerzy Saunders from Cincinnati after the Pope's first visit to Poland. In Krakow John Paul expressed his homesickness: 'I have discovered in Rome it is not easy to leave Krakow behind. My heart has not ceased to be united with you, with this city, with this "Polish Rome".' He lodged in his old room in the episcopal palace, left untouched since he departed: simple bed and table, on the wall a replica of the Jasna Gora Madonna. Once again the old butler, Franciszek, there since the war, waited on him – and wept with joy at his homecoming.

This was now his base and every night a dialogue struck up between him and the city's youth who besieged his residence, sometimes clinging to the roofs of surrounding houses to get a better view: there were bantering, songs, chanting late into the night, and scuffles with plain-clothes police who beat up a priest who tossed him a bouquet. Students unfurled a Polish flag which not only revealed the usual white eagle but now had the crown restored on the eagle's head. The crowned eagle was the symbol of Polish resistance.

Wojtyla journeyed to Wadowice, his birthplace, greeted a crowd of 15,000 in the square and on the soccer field, and said mass in St

Mary's, walls painted a delicate beige for the occasion, scrolls and mouldings white, just across the street from where he had lived: 'Every detail,' he affirmed, 'brings back memories of youth.' Every window displayed a joyful face, a banner, or a tribute – a portrait of the Pope, candles, blue-and-white or yellow-and-white, Black Madonnas of Jasna Gora. He named all the Beskidy mountain peaks visible on the horizon. He lunched with Monsignor Zacher, his old teacher, now in charge of the parish.

In the afternoon he boarded the white helicopter and flew to Oswiecim, the site of the former Auschwitz-Birkenau death factory. No pope before him had walked through the main gate under the wrought-iron lettering *Arbeit macht frei* – 'Work liberates'. In the underground cell where Maximilian Kolbe had died he bent and kissed the stone floor. He placed flowers, then knelt in silence at the wall of death, the site of innumerable executions. He said mass for 200 priests and four bishops, former inmates of concentration camps, survivors of the 2,647 clergy whom the Nazis had killed during the occupation. With bent head and in sombre mood, in a voice now grown noticeably hoarse as he delivered his homily, he recalled for the rest of the million who attended (and this time without any Communist restrictions) that six million Poles, a fifth of the nation, had perished. It was, he said, another painful reckoning with the conscience of mankind; and it was necessary to think with fear 'how far hatred can go . . . how far cruelty can go'.

'Oswiecim is a *testimony of war*,' he pronounced, 'and war brings a disproportionate growth of hatred, destruction and cruelty. It cannot be denied that war also manifests new capabilities, but it is the reckoning of the losses that prevails.' In spite of the displays of human courage, heroism and patriotism, 'That reckoning prevails more and more, since each day sees an increase in the destructive capacity of the weapons invented by modern technology.' He added that 'Not only those who directly bring about wars are responsible for them, but also those who fail to do all they can to prevent them.'

As he ended the sermon hundreds wept, and a black line of smoke from a distant factory appeared lazily on the horizon; a woman, a former inmate, said, 'Every time I see a bird flying here I am reminded of the dead. Birds were the only living things which could touch the camp fence wires without being electrocuted.'

Next morning, in a return to festive mode but in torrential rain with a voice even more hoarse and tired, he celebrated mass in Nowy Targ, the doorway to the Tatra Mountains, in an airfield of six square kilometres filled to overflowing with a crowd dressed in all the colours of the rainbow. Whole parishes came from across the adjoining Slovak and Hungarian borders, as well as the local *gorals* (mountain men) in embroidered jackets and white felt trousers, and women in striped skirts. Thousands of Czech Catholics were barred from attendance by frontier guards: 'Do not forget your Czech brothers,' those who got through appealed to him, tears on almost every face. John Paul emphasised his own personal connection with the million-strong audience, telling them he would forget nothing. In his homily before the field altar of rough lumber he stressed the family and man's right to work, and his right to the land. Friendly but loaded with double meaning his visit was almost ignored by the local television station, whose lead story featured a pig farm.

Back in Krakow after more worship at Wawel Cathedral and at Skalka an evening crowd showered him with flowers and again sang 'Sto lat, Sto lat'. He had trouble getting heard. 'How can the Pope live to be a hundred when you shout him down?' he asked. 'Will you let me speak?' When silence was restored, Karol Wojtyla said simply, 'I love you all.'

Groups of Krakow youths came to the front and offered small gifts or messages. 'Holy Father,' one student said, 'you are outside Poland, but our hearts are with you,' while another added, 'You are the church's hope and mine.' After they had sung hymns and folk songs, the Pope declared he would not deliver his prepared address. He teased them: 'I will not speak today. I lost my voice and the text I had written is not appropriate to the occasion.' So instead he started, 'But I can improvise in Polish, if I have to!' – and they laughed. He reminisced about the Tatra Mountains. 'When I was told that I was to be a bishop, I asked the Father Primate whether I still could go climbing in the Tatras. He said I could. But now, when I am Bishop of Rome, it might be harder.'

'Then stay with us,' the students shouted back.

'Ah, you're wise now, but it's too late. Where were you on 16 October?' Wojtyla asked. 'You were not there to defend me. Just like the Poles, to close the barn door when the horse has bolted!' Laughter swept the crowd, and Wojtyla kept on chatting, interspersing jokes and admonitions, until 10.30 p.m. when after the long day he looked very tired.

At this point a group of young men lifted a twelve-foot cross high above their heads and suddenly at least 10,000 boys and girls raised up smaller crosses that they had concealed. The forest of crosses faced Wojtyla. 'It was a shattering, eerie scene,' wrote one who witnessed it, 'as the street lights cast shadows on the youthful faces and the crosses held above them.'

Karol stood in silence and after a time said, 'It's late, my friends. Let's go home quietly.'

A guitar band played a song of farewell. He boarded the papal limousine, which moved slowly towards the centre of Krakow. The Pope's hand covered his eyes and his tears.

That same night, so the rumour ran, while Krakow slept, Pope Wojtyla, in plain black cassock with the anonymity that was once a prized possession, roamed the streets alone. With that phenomenal memory of his, he wandered from site to site, recalling his past.

Next day, having met and talked to the students and professors of Krakow's Theological Faculty he was whisked by helicopter to Mogila Abbey, just outside Nowa Huta (he was forbidden to celebrate mass in the new church he had been instrumental in creating, and which had been financed by Polish Americans).

'Why can't the Holy Father visit our church?' cried the people of this city whose parish of 100,000 practising Catholics was now Europe's largest. Father Jozef Gorzelany, former underground-army soldier and inmate of Auschwitz who had been imprisoned during the building of the church for 'violation of the building code', answered tersely, 'They are afraid.'

So outside the thirteenth-century abbey near by Wojtyla gave 200,000 people, including many workers from the vast steel mills and their families, a history lesson about the relic of the Lord's cross lodged there that was the goal of pilgrimages. He proceeded to say how he had raised the new cross at Nowa Huta – having not only dug the first spadeful of earth in the construction but also, two years before as cardinal, consecrated the church.

Given that the Communist state philosophy insisted on Sunday work, he made a radical pitch against Marxist materialism: 'Christ will never approve that man be considered, or that man consider himself, *merely as a means of production* . . . This must be remembered both by the worker and the employer, by the work system as well as by the system of remuneration; it must be remembered by the state, the nation, the Church.'

At his last mass on Sunday morning, on Krakow's common, as the giant bell Zygmunt tolled mournfully from Wawel Hill, two million joined with him in prayer. The bone relics of St Stanislaus, brought from the cathedral, stood on the altar; he spoke of Stanislaus's martyrdom and exhorted the Polish people to be strong. When he held the relics in his hand the crowd erupted in cheers. Seven hundred priests distributed communion. He affixed papal crowns to the picture of Our Lady of Makowiec. They sang 'Oh Lord who has guarded Poland for centuries', and the delegations of parishes, dioceses, workers, students and others moved in procession before him, many bearing symbolic small gifts. Deeply moved he spoke of his feelings: 'Before leaving, let me look again at this Krakow, where every stone and brick is dear to me.'

During the last afternoon he made a private visit to the family tomb in Rakowice Cemetery where his father, mother and brother were buried in Emilia's saddler family grave. At the airport on leaving Wojtyla thanked the security men responsible for his safety, then, on impulse, embraced Jablonski. In return the Communist president bent and kissed John Paul's hands.

> He came at Pentecost [a Pole from Poznan summed up], and it was as though the Holy Spirit had descended on the nation . . . Thousands of people went to confession, people who hadn't been for twenty years or more. They . . . were convinced that they could function now without the Party and the oppressive regime . . . they had been called upon to show themselves once more to the world as a Christian nation.

So here was the beginning of another endgame. In July 1979 one Casimir M. Malik wrote a letter to *Newsweek*: 'The first week of June 1979,' he said, 'will go down in history as the beginning of the end of Communism throughout the world. I believe that the mortal blow has been struck by the visit to Poland of . . . John Paul II.'

But Wojtyla would never have agreed. He would have countered, 'There's a divinity that shapes our ends.' Later he would disclaim responsibility for any political change. His pilgrimage in June 1979 to Poland serves as a pattern, a symbolic shape, for the remaining 102 foreign trips.

Always at the centre of the inner man there remained the genius: an original creativity. That it hadn't disappeared now Karol was pope was only too evident in his inspired two-day visit to Ireland on the way to the US in September of his first full papal year. But there was a different genius, too – in a sense of character disposition – at work in some of the personal detail. When he had travelled to Mexico, for instance, in the front of the cabin Alitalia made a bed for him using the same sheets Paul VI had used on his many trips; these were silk, but Wojtyla asked for cotton instead. 'He prefers a humbler style,' said his entourage, but the Pope demurred, pointing out that silk sheets stuck to his body.

The Aer Lingus jumbo bringing him into Dublin tipped alarmingly to port over the Irish Sea when the journalists on board swarmed too eagerly to one side to greet his appearance before them. Air hostesses took it in turns to peep through the green tweed curtain. The one who had brought him an Irish breakfast of four sausages, four rashers of bacon, a length of white pudding and a length of black pudding, burst through the curtain to blurt out to her colleagues, with eyes shining, 'He's cleaned up his plate!'

Prior to touchdown the Irish newspapers printed the life history of everyone expected to come within a hundred feet of him. They identified the colour of the blanket on his Aer Lingus bed, even the first stretch of Irish turf that he would sight. In contrast to his reception in Poland, seventy-six prisoners were freed from gaol, while the whole prison population was granted extra television viewing of His Holiness. But in the North the Reverend Ian Paisley railed against the coming of 'that Antichrist, that man of sin and perdition', while in the month before he arrived the Provisional IRA killed eighteen British soldiers in an ambush at Warrenpoint in County Down and blew up Lord Mountbatten on his yacht, killing him and some of his family. The two papal planners of the visit were the nuncio in Dublin, Archbishop Gaetano Alibrandi, 'whose diplomatic self-command would give way to a Sicilian vindictiveness when he spoke of the Protestants in the North', and Cardinal Tomas O'Fiaich, Archbishop of Armagh and Primate of All Ireland, a zealous anti-British nationalist.

Security was tight, jealously supervised by Monsignor Paul Marcinkus, the likeable but tough Chicagoan priest, mentioned by 'Monsignor Sottovoce' as the 'gorilla'. Marcinkus, officially head of the internal Vatican Bank, accompanied the Pope on foreign visits as his chief bodyguard. The English *Sunday Mirror* reported that the six-foot-four-inch Marcinkus, spotting 'a sinister figure who was getting too close to the Pope', administered 'a swift knee to the parts that Catholic priests should not reach'. The 'sinister figure' turned out to be a member of the Irish Secret Service.

A third of Ireland's three-million-plus inhabitants were under fifteen and nearly half under twenty-five. Proportionately he was seen by more Irish on this first visit than subsequently in any other country. One million two hundred thousand Irish turned up in the sunlit 'Fifteen Acres' of Phoenix Park for mass with the pontiff who, the wind rustling his silver hair, and multiplying in echo his voice from surrounding loudspeakers, linked his presence to that of the ninth- and tenth-century Irish missionaries: not only St Patrick much earlier, who was 'confirmed in the faith by Pope Leo the Great, but those who had spread all over Europe founding great sees and monasteries in Germany, France, Italy, Belgium, Switzerland'.

In his text, prepared in Castel Gandolfo during the summer break, he played on the theme of Irish persecution, which he identified with Poland's submission to foreign domination and those new slaveries of modern life that had replaced Oliver Cromwell and the penal code: the new persecutions from which Ireland was not 'immune' were 'the influence of ideologies and trends which present-day civilisation and progress carry with them. The very capability of mass media to bring the whole world into your homes produces a new kind of confrontation with values and trends that up until now have been alien to Irish society.'

He listed the false pretences of the pervading materialism, self-indulgence and consumerism, 'when a human identity is often defined by what one owns. Prosperity and affluence . . . a full freedom in all the areas of human behaviour, and new models of morality' were 'being imposed in the name of would-be freedom'. When he turned to terrorism, in his usual manner indirectly but clearly targeting an evil, he said: 'When the moral fibre of a nation is weakened, when the sense of personal responsibility is diminished, then the door is open for the justification of injustices, for violence in all its forms.'

So was he claiming a connection, hinting that consumerism prepared the way for the IRA? At Drogheda, that first afternoon, thirty miles from the Northern border and the scene of Cromwell's horrific massacre (the nearest he could safely travel to the primate's see, which O'Fiaich had first proposed he visit), John Paul preached in the presence of St Oliver Plunkett's venerated head, severed in 1681 from his body by the British at Tyburn, where he was hanged, drawn and quartered.

But strictly impartially he refused to identify the strife in the North as a religious war between Catholics and Protestants, for, as he acknowledged gratefully, the Anglican primate had also invited him to the North. In dramatic words reminiscent of Sean O'Casey's famous denunciation in Act III of *Juno and the Paycock* he addressed those engaged in violence: 'I appeal to you, in language of passionate pleading. On my knees I beg you to turn away from the paths of violence and to return to the ways of peace . . . violence only delays the day of justice. Violence destroys the work of justice.' ('Sacred Heart o' Jesus, take away our hearts o'stone, and give us hearts o'flesh! Take away this murdherin' hate, an' give us Thine own eternal love!')

In gentle but patriarchal tones he warned them that they were in danger of losing everything, themselves and the land they loved. He called on the young to reject the invitation of the terrorists. He called on parents to teach their children how to love and forgive. He called on those with political authority and challenged them to 'show there is a peaceful, political way to justice'. He reminded them that he was under no illusions: 'The ideology and the methods of violence have become an international problem of the utmost gravity.'

Hoping to deflate the impact, a Provisional spokesman later remarked that when he spoke these words the Pope was not in fact on his knees but standing at the microphone, eyes fixed on the unfamiliar English – 'pleading' came over as 'displaying'. Indeed, there was much carping at his English by the literary-minded Irish. When at a Dublin monastery the mainly journalist company sang 'For he's a jolly good fellow!' he took a long pause before replying, 'It was very pleased of me hearing that I am greeted as a good fellow.'

'He hasn't the English that good, you know,' a faithful soul proclaimed at Knock. Yet he could always rise above this shortcoming as he did before 300,000 young people at Ballybrit Racecourse in Galway when, at the end of his sermon, he spoke his best-remembered sentence: 'Young people of Ireland, I love you.' They erupted into twelve minutes of sustained cheering.

Slow and equal emphasis on each word of 'I love you' may have been the technical reason, but as with the 'On my knees I beg you to turn away from the paths of violence' it was the utter transparent conviction, the truth without words, that carried weight – and this in spite of him not being on his knees. He could gather up his whole biography into one telling gesture.

Ironically perhaps, as the once-leading actor of the Rhapsodic Theatre, the best effects were non-verbal. He clasped young heads to him as confidently as if he were the real father; pursed his lips to retain self-control as the crowds cheered; or he'd scrutinise a young woman giving an address as if striving to discover what it was like to be her. In Derry he hugged a boy blinded by a British army rubber bullet – showing beyond argument, beyond his often stern message, that his interest in human lives was universal. As the rumbustious Bishop Eamonn Casey of Galway, his chief minder or host at these events, observed, 'They saw him as a man who lives the values beyond the words.'

Casey noted how John Paul bathed in the adulation and wanted more '*bain de foule*'. The Pope thumped Casey on the chest with his clenched fist and declared, 'You are the strong one!' and Casey twice had to restrain his charge physically, saying, 'Holy Father, I'm in charge here.' 'I again put my hands on his shoulders and turned him towards the helicopter. He just looked at me and went inside. Like a bold child, he knows exactly when he's been bold.'

> To a tiny village in the plains of Mayo, one of the most desolate parts of Connaught, when it seemed that everyone else was leaving for Australia or Boston or New York, the mother of Jesus came. And, being the proper lady that she was, in a land that held women and marriage and the priesthood in high regard, she brought with her her husband, St Joseph, and St John the Evangelist garbed as a prelate. And they also remained silent. Appropriately enough they came in the rain.

These were simple, even naïve words, from a man who had written three doctoral theses and other works of extreme philosophical complexity. On Thursday, 21 August 1879, early in the evening, a group of villagers in Knock, an obscure little town in County Mayo in the West of Ireland, had seen a strange light on the gable wall of the village church. This signalled the Marian apparition that, authenticated later by a church commission, turned Knock into a holy place of pilgrimage and source of miracle cures. In making this the goal of his Irish visit John Paul was asserting, apart from its moral code, the much-neglected spiritual and non-realistic qualities and powers of the Catholic church. Many no longer believed in these.

His presence here was his implicit denunciation of – as well as his expression of regret about – the death of so many outward signs of spirituality. He felt that God's immanence in places, landscapes – as witnessed by visible signs – needed reassertion. The miracles, the Knock visitation, the Black Virgin, Fatima, were important because they brought home to ordinary people the actuality, the reality, the presence of God.

18

Other Points of the Compass

(1979–80)

Satan, notes the American biblical scholar Elaine Pagels in *The Origin of Satan*, defines negatively what we think of as human. Not only does Satan embody conventional evil but he is a reflection of how we perceive ourselves and those we call others. She emphasises how, as well as the one who opposes, obstructs or acts as adversary (the Greek '*diabolos*' means literally someone who throws something across one's path), Satan is not the distant enemy but the intimate enemy, for just as we may recognise the divine within every person there is the other, the dehumanising factor.

Pagels points out that throughout Christian history church fathers believed Christians should think and speak the very same things. Tertullian, for instance, pointed out that the Greek word translated 'heresy' (*hairesis*) literally means 'choice'; thus a 'heretic' is 'one who makes a choice'. Tertullian specifies heretics in a way that perhaps is particularly relevant to how John Paul, in his radical approach to Christian faith, was now to confront Catholics in the First World, and especially in the United States, the richest country in the world.

> Wherever they have hit upon any novelty [quoting Tertullian, Pagels writes], they immediately call their presumption a 'spiritual gift', since they value not unity but diversity . . . Consequently, most often they are in a divided state themselves, being ready to say – and indeed, quite sincerely – of certain points in their belief, 'This is not so,' and 'I take this in a different sense,' and 'I do not accept that.'

Tertullian might have been writing a spiritual profile of America, the land of choice, diversity, novelty – but also 'often in a divided state'. With his resistance to consumer values, and his independent character, Wojtyla did not expect to be popular.

Invited to lecture at Harvard by Anna-Teresa Tymieniecka, who was making her English translation of *The Acting Person*, he declined, as he preferred to stay instead with the priests in Boston or New York. Scheduled to attend a reception of Cardinal Humberto Madeiros of Boston he was happily delayed rafting in Vermont and when he finally got out, reported Anna-Teresa, Dziwisz had no dry trousers for him. When he finally spoke at Harvard the usual stipend for speeches was handed to Dziwisz instead of Wojtyla – 'He can't handle money,' the local bishop told Harvard. He was coached and rehearsed in his English, which was still rather rough but improving. Anna-Teresa and her husband, Henryk Houthakker, Harvard professor and former presidential adviser, warned him to tone down the combative speeches he had prepared.

Tymieniecka said, 'They would have offended many people,' but when her husband tried a second time to convince Karol that capitalism had merit the Pope 'was not very receptive'. Toned down it may have been, but the thrust of his message remained strong. Freedom was his theme, but not what most Americans assumed was freedom. For instance in his Philadelphia homily on 3 October 1979 he said:

> Christ himself linked freedom with the knowledge of truth. 'You will know the truth and the truth will set you free.'
>
> Freedom can . . . never be construed without relation to the truth as revealed by Jesus Christ, and proposed by his Church, nor can it be seen as a pretext for moral anarchy, for every moral order must remain linked to truth. Saint Peter, in his first letter, says: 'Love as free men, but do not use your freedom for malice.'
>
> This is especially relevant when one considers the domain of human sexuality.

Since becoming pope John Paul had not approved a single petition asking for release from the vow of priesthood. (Paul VI used to approve 2,000 annually.) In Philadelphia he declared, 'Priesthood's for ever,' to emphasise which, he repeated in Latin, '*Tu est sacerdos in aeturnum.*' Earlier that day, in Battery Park on the edge of Manhattan, with Ellis Island and the Statue of Liberty in full view, and with Wall Street starkly in front he 'tolled', like the Liberty Bell, the resounding historical symbols, while he underlined in his address that it was the Liberty Bell that had announced two centuries ago 'the pursuit of the common good in society and for the national independence'.

If freedom were to come into conflict with God it became once again the 'primordial temptation' of Adam and Eve. And that temptation he felt was particularly evident here. In affirming the doctrinal and disciplinary adhesive force of the church, he determined to concede nothing to the national atmosphere of hero-worship; so, on 2 October, the second day of his visit, he had addressed the full Assembly of the United Nations in New York; after a standing ovation that lasted seven minutes he spoke for over an hour in fluent, accented English, defending the right to life as fundamental. 'There is no other right that so closely affects the very existence of the person! The right to life means the right to be born and then continue to live until one's natural end: "As long as I live, I have the right to live." ' So human rights, he went on, should not be subjugated to 'political interest' which 'dishonours the noble and difficult mission' of the UN service. For twenty-five minutes while he denounced disproportionately high standards of living, he received no applause.

He blacklisted, everywhere he went, the flesh and the devil of consumer self-gratification; to much of what he said the liberal communities of his hosts found themselves in varying degrees of opposition. In particular he excoriated materialism, both in nations and in individuals. Sexual intercourse outside marriage, divorce, contraception and abortion were also prime targets for his severe tongue – but given authority by his calm and assured delivery, and backed by appeals to the Holy Spirit, recalling the life-giving message passed on to him by Wojtyla senior. But now in his public persona as pontiff he presented an image very different from that of the Krakow pastor who would spend hours in the confessional talking through a parishioner's doubts or conflicts over these very issues on which his public office called upon him to make very definite pronouncements. Out on the open battlefield of good versus evil he had to rally the forces of resistance, and while he was a man as well as pope, in the latter role he could not afford to express the doubts he might feel as the naked man prostrate before his maker in his seven hours of daily prayer.

Americans cluster round superlatives and cheer them. If he didn't apply them to his hosts, they applied them to him. In spite of his often rigorous message this trip became the grand celebrity tour of the epoch. Everywhere John Paul went he was mobbed, and people did not much bother about what he said ('We know all that'), but were there to be seen by others, and to be able to say they had been there. President Jimmy Carter invited John Paul to a White House reception that was more crowded than any in history. The punters said that the Pope's popularity, at least temporarily, was such that had he run for president he would have been voted in by a landslide. In Grant Park, Chicago, where over a million people assembled for mass, and where 27,000 pots of yellow and white chrysanthemums adorned the altar, he addressed that same 'diversity' outlined by Tertullian, speaking to the whole nation as one person:

> Your ancestors came from many different countries across the oceans to meet here with the people of different communities that were already established here . . .
>
> You brought with you a different culture and you contributed your own distinctive richness to the whole; you had different skills and you put them to work, complementing each other, to create industry, agriculture and business; each group carried with it different human values and with them shared the others for the enrichment of your nation. *E pluribus unum*: you became a new entity, a new people, the true nature of which cannot be adequately explained as a mere putting together of various communities.

Some argued that this was over-optimistic; John Paul should, they said, have addressed himself more to satisfying that diversity of cultural origins, advocating that the variousness of human weakness in aspiration should be met with an equal variety of treatment.

The most visible disagreement was over the ordination of women: in Washington, Sister Mary Theresa Kane, a leader of American nuns, stood up to greet the Pope. She was dressed – inappropriately in Wojtyla's eyes – in a tailored brown suit, with a jewelled cross on the lapel. With the usual civilities of the 'privileged moment' shared with the Pope, she introduced him to his audience of nuns. She then delivered, in a soft but steady tone, some at first seemingly innocuous words, urging him to be 'mindful of the intense suffering and pain which is part of the life of many women in these United States'; she called upon him to 'listen with compassion and to hear the call of women, who comprise half of humankind'. Their intense suffering and pain contrasted with 'the powerful messages of our Church addressing the [need for] dignity and reverence of all persons'. From this she progressed to plead (illogically, for what had it to do with 'intense suffering and pain'?) that the church 'must respond by providing the possibility of women as persons being included in all ministries of our Church'. She ended, 'I urge you, Your Holiness, to be open to and to respond to the voices coming from the women of this country, whose desire is for serving in and through the Church as fully participating members' – then knelt and kissed the fisherman's ring. He laid his hand on her head in blessing.

It was a public performance to equal one of his own. John Paul had to feign or give the impression that he had not heard or fully understood (or so the bishops near him thought). But perhaps he was more cunning. He had listened and had heard what she said, but needed time to disentangle the emotion from what sense it might contain. He never pretended to have an instant answer to anything. He countered with a few soothing generalities about how Mary had not been present at the Last Supper, but had mourned at the foot of the cross 'in order to consummate her contribution to the act of salvation'. But it started him thinking: later he would address this question more fully. He remembered no doubt the Mariavite schismatic church in Poland during his youth when the Archbishop of Utrecht ordained nuns as priests and abolished confession and the use of holy water.

Afterwards Sister Kane disingenuously maintained that she had not wanted to be dramatic – her intervention gained huge publicity – but she believed in 'the dialogue approach'. But Claire Randall, an official of the US National Council of Churches of Christ, claimed that the Pope was saying 'God cannot use women in the way He can use men.'

The interior Wojtyla was exacting. As an athlete of the spirit he conserved the church but had no care for conserving himself. Cardinal Carberry of St Louis noted when the Pope first arrived from Ireland, in spite of the Aer Lingus bed, that his face had been ashen with fatigue: 'He himself is to blame, you know. He's very much his own man. He sees a programme and adds things to it, at once.' In Philadelphia 'his own man', Cardinal Kroll remonstrated, refused the hours set aside for rest to become 'totally enveloped in prayer'. As he was flown between farming communities in Iowa, the clattering blades of the helicopter weren't enough to keep him awake. He remarked in Chicago that there was a Polish saying that he who rose early, received God's blessing, 'But perhaps he who gets up early in the morning wants to sleep all day!'

There would be no letting up and he would take his mission to the ends of the earth to fulfil the Vatican Two conception of a pilgrim church in community with the people of God. Above all he was engaging with the world, holding a dialogue. Hence he would insist on suddenly changing his mind and, while having intended to go to bed, would surge out to address the ever-attendant crowds, which did not help. Hands to shake, or the sight of an audience, gave him a shot of adrenaline. In Chicago, when people pushed forward on him and his entourage, the Vatican guards manhandled some of the crowd who were climbing over the shoulders of those in front. John Paul rounded on the guards in real fury (speaking Italian). Competitive pressures between rival cities and the religious tour managers vying for publicity and the best crowd ratings in the press also took their toll. He crooned a goodnight 'Alleluia' in Chicago, where thousands of Polish-Americans sang '*Sto lat*'; in Washington kids regaled him with football rousers: 'Rock 'em up, stack 'em up, bust 'em in two – Holy Father, we're for you!' Outside St Patrick's Cathedral the great showman gave a flower to a girl without saying a word: 'It was,' she said, 'just like it was him and me.'

His first American visit extended his congregation by many millions, and now he was commonly hailed as 'a pope for all the people' and an authentic world leader. Although he had been pope for only twelve months, a journalist in *Le Monde* commented that he had written and said enough to occupy an entire pontificate. When he left, one security man who had been with him all the time said, 'Come back again, but not before 1983 – we're all very tired!' Vatican officials joined in the laughter.

John Paul's grasp of symbolism on the national and religious scale had been evident in the first three of the four 1979 visits, one to the South (Mexico), one to the West (Ireland and USA) and one to the North (Poland). Siddhartha Gautama, the founder of Buddhism, as soon as he could walk took symbolic steps to the four points of the compass. This 'young' pope had now challenged three aspects of the different conditions of his faith – hunger in the South; Communist tyranny in the North; and consumerism in the West. But the fourth point of the compass, the East, would prove to be really tricky, not to say dangerous. His late November visit to Turkey proved, conclusively, after the triumphalist progress through the States, that he had some grander design throughout the world for Christian unity, namely healing the schism of Orthodoxy: as he said about this intended trip on his way back to Rome, 'We are in another dimension.'

In Turkey the government shut him down, surrounding him with armed guards and tanks, not allowing him to say a single word in public. He was not even able to deliver his carefully rehearsed words 'Greetings, soldiers' in Turkish when he arrived at Ankara airport, and sadly pocketed his prepared notes (he managed to kiss the ground). Arriving in a country that had three political murders a day (in neighbouring Tehran fifty American hostages were being held by government-backed mullahs) he was mindful that members of the Greek Orthodox formed but a run-down minority in the powerful predominance of Muslim culture.

It was this minority he determined in particular to honour. He began his dialogue with Orthodox prelates by telling Patriarch Dimitrios in French, 'This meeting is a divine gift.' Later he addressed them in Patriarch Greek – 'How well it is for brothers to live together.' On his three-day visit he wanted to set in motion a near-impossible aim: the realignment of the Roman, European church with the Moscow and Constantinople Orthodox churches. But it would prove to be, both in the short and long term, out of reach.

He also stretched out a welcoming and accommodating hand to Islam, with which he believed Christianity shared moral values; both religions also believed in monotheism which could stand against atheism and materialism: 'I wonder, if it is not urgent, precisely today when Christians and Muslims have entered a new period of history, to recognize and develop the spiritual bonds that unite us, in order to preserve and promote together for the benefit of all men, "peace, liberty, social justice and moral values".' He went out of his way to emphasise the shared, similar values of Islam and Christianity:

> For the Muslim, the universe is destined to be subject to man as the representative of God; the Bible affirms that God ordered man to subdue the earth, but also to 'till it and keep it' . . . The Christian keeps

to the solemn commandment: 'You shall have no other gods before me.' On his side, the Muslim will always say: 'God is the greatest.'

On the first day John Paul had set foot in Turkey, a Turkish-born terrorist, Ali Agça, twenty-three years old, had threatened to kill the Pope. The Istanbul daily *Milliyet* printed the letter with this threat on its front page. Agça was a terrorist on trial for the murder of the paper's editor; three days before, he had escaped from Istanbul's high security Kartel-Maltepe prison.

This reasoning was perverse: 'The Russian and American imperialists fear that Turkey will organize a new power in the Middle East along with brotherly Islamic countries.' They were therefore sending to Turkey in this delicate moment 'a spiritual leader and commander of Crusades, John Paul II. If this untimely visit is not cancelled, I will without doubt kill the pope-chief. This is the sole motive for my escape from prison.'

Born in Malatya Hekinham, 300 miles east of Ankara in 1958, Agça had lost his father, a miner, when he was barely eight, and had, from a fatherless background and suffering an unidentified illness that, according to his mother, made him 'nervous and aggressive', gone to Ankara University to study literature, then to Istanbul University to study economics.

If we did not know his birth was natural we might think he had been spawned from the pages of Dostoevsky's *The Devils* in his incompatible mixture of extreme left- and right-wing theories, and his embrace, in Istanbul, of terrorism. There was also his susceptibility, like litmus paper, to soak up conspiratorial colouring. Nine months before Wojtyla's visit he had assassinated Abdi Ipekci, editor of the respected left-of-centre daily. Informed on by a young man whom he later allegedly killed, he was arrested in a notorious right-wing café in Istanbul in June 1979. He confessed and claimed he had killed Ipekci in league with the neo-Fascist National Action Party of 'Grey Wolves'. His trial had begun in October 1979, and on the night of 25 November, three days before the Pope's visit, with the case unresolved he was 'sprung', i.e. released, from prison by fourteen military sympathisers. In hiding, three days later, he sent his letter to *Milliyet*, in which he also said that killing the Pope would even the score for the 1979 attack on Mecca's Grand Mosque by Islamic radicals 'carried out by the United States and Israel'. John Paul heard about this and shrugged it off good-humouredly with a blessing.

Returning to Rome his first thought was to communicate with his predecessor:

Rome was dark when we landed. The Holy Father was back home. Still in his white travelling coat, he went straight to the tomb of Saint Peter, to bring him the message of his brother from the east and perhaps also to seek support from one who, together with his brother Andrew, undertook the task now carried on by his successor John Paul II.

19

Opening the Ways of the Spirit

(1980–81)

As active, as combative as he was, John Paul found himself at once facing voices of dissent and signs of contradiction, especially in the older Catholic countries. In his new homeland the setbacks to his vision began even before he was pope. A few months before he was elected, Italy legalised abortion: 600 abortions a day or over 200,000 a year were now being performed. While on a visit to Siena in September 1980 he inveighed heavily against this 'great disgrace . . . great sorrow'. Every child had 'the right to life', he castigated his listeners. It provoked hostility from Socialists and radicals, while the Socialist leader Bettino Craxi condemned him as a 'foreigner who does not understand the Italian constitution' (by this he meant the political constitution, not any other).

It was true that as diocesan Bishop of Rome in his second homeland, John Paul found himself in a paradoxical situation. Compared to Poland where the supply of priests was plentiful (20,000: 6,000 more than after the Second World War, with 5,000 in seminaries), in Italy there was dire scarcity. He learned of the serious local problems of Rome and Italy at a three-hour meeting in the Palace of St John Lateran in February 1980 when he had already systematically set about visiting all 292 Roman parishes.

For a population of over three million, Rome had barely more than a thousand pastoral priests; in a society of *dolce vita* values and a falling birthrate, ordinations of new priests were almost non-existent, while in spite of the plethora of historic churches in the centre of the city, over seventy outlying parishes had no church. Baptisms, church managers, attendance were all in decline. The reason was simple: Italy had reached such a degree of secularisation in the modern climate of liberalism, science and technology, that it had become divorced from the centralised papacy. Italians paid lip service to papal authority but ignored it in the daily conduct of their lives, while the Vatican City, self-perpetuating both in size and its administrative ties to the world's billion Catholics (and a magnet to untold hordes of foreign visitors and pilgrims), existed in cultural isolation from the rest of Italy.

But above all Rome suffered the same concentration of social problems that were endemic to the age: insecurity about jobs; fears about housing, health and education; population movement and racial harassment of minorities; lack of communication in families living in high-rise blocks; professional crime, especially in the world of drugs and sex; mindless violence and political terrorism. When John Paul listened to the statistics of decline he looked very pessimistic.

The papacy itself was also to blame, having shown a lack of strategy and an indifference to Italy as a whole. John Paul saw all this clearly and planned to redress the balance between the spiritual and the material: he would make over the next years nearly 150 trips inside Italy. Just after his US visit he told the poor and underprivileged Neapolitans at the Marian shrine of Pompeii that nothing mattered except opening the ways of the Holy Spirit (meaning justice and charity), while all the rest (referring to the US visit) was 'merely a display that could be reckoned superficial'. In this unprosperous area this message went down extremely well. And then he went (April 1980) to the rich industrial north with its many thousands of Communist factory workers, and told a 700,000-strong crowd in Turin that unrestricted capitalism with its inhuman work rhythms, its disruption of family ties, and its bewildering effect on the young, was no better than Communism, which, by declaring God dead, made orphans of everyone.

'There is on the one hand the rationalist, scientistic, Enlightenment approach of the secular so-called "liberalism" of Western nations, which carries with it the radical denial of Christianity; and on the other hand the ideology and praxis of atheistic "Marxism", whose materialistic principles are taken to their most extreme consequences in various forms of contemporary terrorism.' In delivering this text he cut the last clause. This gave the effect to his audience that he was more of a Marxist than a liberal, which was true. But deeper than this, his strategy was to make Italy something it never was before, and something that arguably would never work, but which expressed his own core belief. This was that while disengaging himself from the 'Italian factor' of previous popes, i.e. judging international questions from an Italian standpoint, he sought to realise a vision of something more on the chivalric, romantic lines of Poland: namely a land more devoted to its religious symbols, its shrines to Mary, its saints like Benedict and Francis, or Catherine of Siena, and the Holy Turin Shroud. Spirituality, he indicated, was more important than the Christian Democrat Party. Once again, setting aside the ecclesiastical career structure, he upset Vatican protocol and appointed Father Carlo Martini, a 53-year-old Jesuit, as Archbishop of Milan: Martini became both popular and influential, and later was a favourite to succeed him as pope until he suffered heart problems.

In spite of discords and divisions the Roman and Italian people came to trust and value John Paul as their own diocesan bishop. His spontaneity and enthusiasm for this demanding role would continue, as well as his 'gratitude to my Roman diocesans, who have accepted this Pope from Poland as a son of their own country. The charisma of universality must be well anchored in the soul of this people.' Fifteen years on from his election, he told the people in his parish of the Most Precious Blood in Rome, 'Thanks be to God for this journey, for so many visits, for so many meetings . . . In this way, even with a short visit I am able to be Bishop of Rome, at least to some extent.'

France was a much harder proposition. On his first visit there in 1980 (the first of eight), which was barely more than a weekend, he could do little to change the stereotypical and cynical view of the church held by most French people. At first they could not get over the fact that he was Polish, in other words came from a backward and inferior nation, and a favourite butt of xenophobic humour. Much of the media was outspokenly rude. A satirical cartoon showed the Pope presenting Marianne, symbol of France, (the traditional 'eldest daughter of the church') with the words, 'Let me introduce my eldest daughter', while on the other side was a little black girl, symbol of the backward Third World. Page one of a spoof edition of *Libération*, the left-wing newspaper, was taken up entirely with a photo of John Paul with the caption: 'This paper has been impregnated with the odour of sanctity: sniff it for yourself.'

He attempted to revive the model of the Curé d'Ars or the young pastor in *Diary of a Country Priest*, but when he went to the working-class Paris suburb of St Denis to proclaim the virtues of work, family and nation, these met with stony resistance. As opposed to the revolutionary slogan of Liberty, Equality and Fraternity, his own very Polish morality (which in the face of an atheist Communist dictatorship went down well) adumbrated the collaborationist Pétainist regime of wartime years whose motto was Religion, *Patrie* and Family. The weather did not help (freezing and wet for the end of May), so the crowds were 'small' (for example, 700,000 as opposed to the million expected). Two receptions with intellectuals and government dignitaries were unexceptional and chaotic: in the Elysée Palace gardens scudding rain drove everyone indoors ('Ladies lost their shoes in the rhododendron bushes'; 'Mitterand was there, but looked rather glum'). The other, a pontifical breakfast organised at John Paul's specific request to meet intellectuals and writers, was described by the left-wing press such as *Libération* as 'Somewhat too much of the right'.

His spontaneity and gift for repartee did, however, prevail when he met 50,000 young people crammed in the Parc des Princes stadium (with 35,000 standing outside). He was introduced by Cardinal Martin to answer questions as 'God's sportsman' (by then he must have felt like God's goalkeeper). Twenty-one questions were put to him: among which, Why did he meet with the young in every country he visited? Why did he meet heads of state? What can young people do to prevent a third world war? Why is there evil in the world? Why doesn't the church recognise the immense resource it has in the enthusiasm of youth? How can you be so certain about the Catholic faith?

The improvised flavour of his replies had just the right element of *chic*: he felt at home with this kind of occasion, and for the French who watched on television it became something of a social event – with the sound turned down. Vincent Nichols, now Archbishop of Birmingham, who was in Paris, told me he met two young people who were full of admiration and excitement over the Pope. 'You live together and are not married?' cautiously enquired the young cleric. Their answer: 'What's that got to do with it?' On the whole the French felt they were far too sophisticated for a Polish pope, although one Catholic intellectual did compare him to de Gaulle: 'They say that the intellectuals, the newspapers, the politicians, the leftists and the rightists were all against de Gaulle. The only ones

that were for him were the voters.' The same applied to John Paul:
'The only ones that were for him were the faithful.' They were a
diminishing band.

The next of his European trials came in November, when he visited the
land of Luther, now the Federal Republic of Germany. *Der Spiegel*,
with its Protestant readership, ran a cover picture of John Paul flying
in on a broomstick like a witch. Statistically *Der Spiegel* 'proved' that
the majority of Germans did not want the Pope to visit, while the
twenty-million-mark cost was condemned as outrageous (the Vatican
never footed the bill for papal visits, although when abroad the Pope
always ate and slept 'in his own home' – with the papal nuncio or in
the local bishop's palace, or with a religious order). He never accepted
official hospitality from the host state. Prosperous and with the
barbarities of the first half-century well behind them the Germans
felt, like the French, they were a sophisticated and mature people.
Why should this reactionary pontiff want to invade their land with his
old-fashioned ideas?

He reversed expectations. Television covered the trip live, up to
eight hours a day, sometimes with two long masses, and ratings were
the highest ever recorded. In Cologne, confronting scholars and
scientists in front of the cameras, he both questioned and asserted
the value and independence of scientific research; in Munich he faced
artists and writers, pointing out that the human person is the content
of art; addressing families in Cologne, he insisted that family planning
must be guided by the parents' conscience. 'There is no such thing as a
trial life or a trial death. Nor can one have a trial love.' Likewise he
addressed the old with, as one commentator wrote, 'profound, inner
truths of human life'. Popes are not noted for their sense of humour,
but this pope had one – even for the Germans. Applause broke out in
Cologne after a sparkling exposition crowned with a quotation from
St Paul. He said: 'I thank you on St Paul's behalf.' They were quite
surprised, even shocked by his human dimension: as one observer
wrote:

> The Pope's face: the face of a man immersed in prayer. The face of
> someone who is not officiating or celebrating, but is genuinely ab-
> sorbed, concentrating on prayer. A man wholly oblivious of the
> cameras following him, acting naturally without pretence, but earnest

in prayer. That face turned around the German nation. People who had expected to see a dignitary saw instead a mystic. They could not take their eyes away from that face alive with faith.

In these early travels he made, and while well aware that all eyes were forever on a travelling pope, he became sharpened to the reality not only that he had to address a wide spectrum of different views, but that he would gain personal strength from the embrace he gave to the church worldwide. Not to be strongly authoritarian in doctrine – and decisive in the limited means of action at his disposal – would make him seem weak and indecisive, as Paul VI had been. In any balancing act, there were bound to be victims and casualties. But it was from his travels that he extensively broadened his view of the world and its societies, and gained authority in the eyes of those leaders and governments he was increasingly able to influence in the 1980s and 1990s. With his responses much later to the 9/11 terrorist attack, to the two Iraqi wars, to the Arab–Israeli conflict, to the expanded European Union, and as a result of his increased number of canonisa-tions his worldwide influence grew into the twenty-first century, and with it his power to shape the hearts and minds of a universal congregation. In fact he expanded, in his many travels, the world's view of itself; but far from splitting or fragmenting into different perspectives or views for different situations (like the spin politicians of the Western democracies), he set a standard of submitting all people, problems and nations to the same universal yardstick: the magisterium of the Catholic church and the teaching as laid down in the Bible. To do so actively and positively, and all the time rephrasing, redrafting his documents freshly with a view to this end, was no mean achievement.

But he was an apostle, not an interpreter of consensus. One member of the Roman Curia said that he blessed crowds and prayed, but he did not govern; another remarked that 'He is always travelling in spirit; even when he is here in Rome he is always thinking of his next journey.' Both critics missed the point of the travels, namely that by his magnetic power combined with vision he was enabling more people than ever before to be comforted by religious faith; and by bringing the Christian faith to the foreground of mankind's attention in a way that had never happened before in history, he was holding the mirror up to nature, showing the world that millions did still care.

So, to each foreign visit (going back to his youth of writing plays, and later of structuring his acting roles), he brought a carefully proposed theme and a climax, chosen and appropriate for the country he was visiting, to make them relevant and accessible gifts to the people of that country. But he actively sought out difference and grasped the explosive issues. From his early days, also, he had always been determined that peaceful not violent means should be used to overthrow unjust or odious situations. This stood behind his attitude to the Marxian analysis and legitimation of violence that liberation theology advocated. After Mexico he crystallised his views on the polarised new position expounded by Gustavo Gutierrez, a Peruvian theologian, and the practical commitment of local churches to support the struggles of the oppressed. To severe criticism from extremes of both right and left John Paul objected to the politicisation of the church.

When it could help he made his own dynamic interventions. In 1983 officials advised him not to go to Nicaragua because the Marxist Sandinista regime was fighting American-backed Contra rebels. 'I have to go, I have to help the church,' he told Cardinal Tucci. In Managua Cathedral, hecklers interrupted his sermon: 'Silence!' he roared at them. When he visited San Salvador the rebels were Marx-ists, and in spite of the military regime, and in spite of his refusal wholeheartedly to endorse liberation theology, he prayed at the tomb of this regime's reputed victim, Archbishop Romero, murdered in 1980. He found the San Salvador cathedral closed and nobody in the square: the 'authorised' (that is, the military men), Tucci told me, had 'sterilised the whole district'. Wojtyla told him, 'If they are waiting for me I will go in. Please go inside and find the key.' Emotionally, as can be seen from the photograph of him praying at the tomb of Romero, there was no doubt where he stood, but for the sake of church unity, and his opposition to the violence it could well lead to, he would refuse to make him a martyr-saint.

The Pope reportedly told Professor Fineschi that during his visit to Santiago in 1987 he advised General Pinochet of Chile to resign. He had stood up to the dictator of thirteen years' standing. 'Why is the Church always talking about democracy?' Pinochet asked him. 'One method of government is as good as another.' John Paul answered, 'No, the people have a right to their liberties, even if they make mistakes in exercising them.'

In the broad picture there was invariably interwoven some personal preference, as when in February 1981 he visited the Philippines and Japan, where he spoke to and impressed a mainly non-Christian audience: here he visited the monastic house (in Nagasaki) Maximilian Kolbe founded in 1930. If the Pope had had the time and energy, Kolbe would have been a good subject for a new play. But there was plenty of theatre in the public arena. In Tokyo as Japanese girls in Polish costume danced before him Wilton Wynn witnessed two of them approach the Pope, asking him to join in. 'The pope looked surprised, seemed to hesitate and then, with a shrug of the shoulders and a broad grin, took one of the little things by the hand and walked into their circle.' But Wynn, a few hours earlier, had happened upon a rehearsal of this self-same episode with the same little girl, and a stand-in priest. Everything was theatrically staged – even the spontaneous gesture.

The theme for Japan was destruction caused by war. In Hiroshima, with the skeleton of a gutted building starkly erect in the background as a reminder of the tragic event, he spoke from the spot over which the world's first nuclear bomb had exploded. He spoke in Japanese, the pronunciation of which with European phonetics he had rehearsed carefully: 'War is an act of man. War destroys human lives. War is death . . . Lord, hear me! It is the voice of the mothers who have lost their children. It is the voice of the children who have lost their mothers and fathers . . . Never again Hiroshima! Never again Oswiecim!' Fired up by the simultaneous crisis in his homeland of Solidarity's confrontation with Communism, which never left his mind, he was at his most emotional.

'I could see people crying,' pronounced the rector of Rome's Gregorian University, who was with John Paul. He lectured a convention of scientists on their international responsibilities and the power they wielded which could be decisive for the future of humanity. Emphasising the peaceful value to which scientific progress could be put, he outlined temptations that only too frequently marked its application. The first was to pursue technological development for its own sake, 'as if it were a matter of an independent reality in between nature and a reality that is properly human, imposing on man the inevitable realization of his ever new possibilities, as if one should always do what is technically possible'. The second temptation was that of subjecting technological development to economic usefulness for profit or non-stop economic expansion, thus creating advantages for some while leaving others in poverty. But thirdly there was the most dangerous temptation of all: to subject technological development 'to the pursuit or maintenance of power, as it happens when it is used for military purposes'.

So he was by turns, on these four or five trips a year that continued to the end of his reign, congenial and benign, admonitory and sometimes even threatening. Behind closed doors he would call the local bishops to order, insisting on unity. And as in the clandestine Krakovian meetings of the Rhapsodic Theatre, his words and actions underlined the value of culture as a means of resisting evil. Through his culture man had, Wojtyla said in his often abstract way of putting over the message, more access to 'being'. Wealth and possessions were important only to the extent to which man, through his 'having', could at the same time 'be' more fully as a man, 'become more fully a man in all the dimensions of his existence, in everything that characterizes his humanity'. 'Yes!' he pronounced. 'The future of man depends on culture! In truth, our future, our very survival, are linked to the image that we shall make of man.'

20

Be Sober, Be Watchful

(1981)

Be sober, Be watchful. Your adversary the devil prowls around like a roaring lion, seeking someone to devour.

John Paul II quoting 1 Peter, 12 May 1981

At precisely 5.17 p.m. in St Peter's Square, on 13 May 1981, John Paul had just handed Sara Bartol, aged two, whom he had been holding, back to her mother. An admiring Polish lady thought to herself, 'How young he looks! How handsome he is!' Only nine feet away the gunman, aiming at John Paul's body rather than his head, fired some four or more times, the noise sounding, as witness after witness said, like the 'popping of firecrackers'. An alarmed American female voice cried out, 'Who dares shoot pigeons in the presence of the Pope?'

A Swiss Guard, Alöis Esterman, recruited only the year before, leapt forward to shield the Pope with his body. (Later he too, when promoted to command the Swiss Guard in May 1998, together with his wife was attacked and murdered by a rival jealous guard who reckoned he had been unjustly overlooked for the promotion.) The pigeons had risen in a single cloud and now the white popemobile sped through the Arch of Bells, where John Paul, one of his hands wounded, with no sign of blood or wound from his critically injured abdomen on his gleaming white cassock, aided by 'Monsignor Stanislaw' (Dziwisz), into whose arms he had collapsed as the bullets struck, was carried into an ambulance.

I had the feeling that the whole of St Peter's Square was slowly sinking with us [reported an onlooker], that everything was falling into the void – the open space, the crowd, all the statues on the colonnade, whose baroque gestures seemed to indicate fright and disapproval . . . The faces of the shocked guards were bloodless. One of them near me had a face the colour of chalk under his black hair and I wondered if he was going to faint. No. He was weeping.

The normally taciturn Dziwisz commented that John Paul was moved again when they found the first ambulance had no oxygen.

The Holy Father was not looking at us. His eyes were closed, he was in great pain and he kept repeating short exclamatory prayers. If I remember correctly, it was mainly: 'Mary, my mother! Mary, my mother!' Dr Buzzonetti and a male nurse, Brother Camillo, were with me in the ambulance. It went very fast, without any police escort. Even the siren stopped working after a few hundred yards. The journey [to the Gemelli Hospital], which normally takes half an hour, took eight minutes and that in Roman traffic!

I didn't know if the Holy Father was still fully conscious. He was in intense pain and from time to time repeated a prayer. It is not true that he said, 'Why me?' or formulated any reproach. Nothing like that. He uttered no word of despair or resentment; simply words of profound prayer springing from great suffering.

Later, the Holy Father told me that he had remained conscious until we reached the hospital, that it was only there that he had lost consciousness.

So extreme unction had to be given. I administered the sacrament in the operating theatre, just before the operation. But the Holy Father was no longer conscious.

Several months earlier, similar to advance warnings given by French secret-service personnel of a terrorist attack prior to that on the World Trade Center in 2001, Count Alexandre de Marenches, the then head of French intelligence, informed the Vatican that an attempt would be made on the Pope's life. He sent two emissaries, one a general to give the details, the other a high-ranking official to observe protocol and make introductions. But, as he wisely observed, 'The very basis of evaluating intelligence is that we should never make judgements

according to our late-twentieth-century Judaeo-Christian sensibil-
ities.' His warnings were ignored. He also told President Giscard
d'Estaing, who, it was later reported, failed to inform the Italian
government (responsible, ultimately, for Vatican security, with the
Swiss Guard). How specific the details were remains a secret, but
Giscard d'Estaing, keen at the time to cultivate his own special accord
with President Leonid Brezhnev of the Soviet Union, either disbelieved
the information – he tended to ignore bearers of bad tidings – or
expressly forbade it to be passed on. But was Ağça acting alone? Many
vivid theories for and against this contention subsequently blossomed
into circulation (according to one, the inebriated Brezhnev suggested
to KGB chief Andropov that the Soviet world would be well rid of this
turbulent priest).

Whatever the truth of these, this haunted and wide-eyed young
man, on the run for nearly two years and with further suspected
murders to his name, visited Italy three times, before, on 10 May
1981, he found a room in the Pensione Isa, a nondescript *pensione*
fifteen minutes' walk from St Peter's Square. But was this individual of
both extreme right- and left-wing prejudices being used by a greater
power in a conspiracy to kill? Was he a dumbed-down version to fit
these times of the romantic anarchist: those Wojtyla's fellow Pole
Joseph Conrad called 'unwholesome-looking little moral agents of
destruction'. Or a version of what John-Paul Sartre more grandly
dubbed 'a pointless passion' (a phrase John Paul used in his lectures at
Lublin to indicate the very opposite of what he and the church stood
for). Again, if we were writing a novel we could find this antagonist
had, like a character in epic drama, something symbolic or dynastic
about him. As Lance Morrow expressed it, 'The terrorist assassin's
goal is always drama and publicity; his chief professional concern is
(to put it grotesquely) one of casting.' He went on to produce an image
strikingly apposite to the successor of St Peter: 'The terrorist seizes
what most people value most and crucifies it upside down; he aims
to produce a paralysis of foreboding.' It would seem he matched
Wojtyla's own love of symbolism in the degree of evil, and the extent
to which he was prepared to go.

The photograph of the attempt subsequently published worldwide
supplied a more visible and graphic image of the back and side view of
an unsuspecting John Paul standing on the right side of St Peter's
Square in his 'popemobile' – the high, clear-topped vehicle for max-

imum visibility which replaced the sedan chair in 1979 – and blessing a crowd of 15,000 pilgrims and visitors. They were cheering and enjoying his presence in the late-afternoon sun. On the left of picture a clenched right fist points a Browning pistol at the Pope. This was truly a new dimension of outrage.

At the Gemelli Hospital, stunned shock and panic succeeded each other. The Pope's blood pressure had fallen desperately low, his pulse was almost gone. First he was taken to the tenth floor, where a special room was always prepared for him, but then he was whizzed down to the operating theatre on the ninth floor. Here, Professor Francesco Crucitti, assisted by Professor Corrado Manni, the anaesthetist, with heart specialist Manzoni, house surgeon Breda and a Vatican doctor, were preparing to operate. Crucitti, a world-famous surgeon, had a hair-raising journey to the Gemelli. Two miles away when he heard the news from a nun who was listening to the radio, he drove recklessly through rush-hour traffic, rather haphazardly supported by police motorcyclists. 'Quick, quick!' a nun shouted at him when he reached the ninth floor. In his own account, assistants and nuns threw themselves at him to tear off his jacket and trousers and put on his theatre gown, scattering all round him everything in his pockets – keys, small change, wallet.

> I ran to scrub my hands while someone fastened my gown and someone else put my feet into my boots. During this time a doctor called to me from the theatre: 'Blood pressure is 80, 70, still falling.' When I went in, anaesthesia had begun, the Pope was unconscious and I had my scalpel in my hand. The emergency team had already made the necessary preparations and I had only one thought: to open up without losing a second.
>
> So I made the incision.

The nine-millimetre bullet is a brutal projectile, but missing the central aorta by only a few millimetres, and not touching the spine or any other potentially fatal point, the bullet had followed an unlikely trajectory. 'One hand fired the gun, and another one guided the bullet,' said the Pope later.

> I saw blood everywhere [Crucitti went on]. There were some six pints in the abdomen. We sucked it out, staunched it, sponged it up by every

possible means until we could see the sources of the haemorrhage. I was then able to proceed to stopping the flow of blood. Once the patient had stopped losing blood and the transfusion had been set up, his blood pressure rose again. At that stage we could continue more calmly.

So I explored the abdomen and saw the series of wounds. There were multiple lesions of the small intestine and colon. Some were due to direct wounds – cuts or perforations on the trajectory of the bullet – others to blast . . . in the last part of the colon, I found a terrible laceration caused by the direct passage of the projectile.

No vital organ, such as the aorta or the iliac artery, had been touched, nor had the ureter. The bullet had gone through the sacrum after entering by the front wall of the abdomen. The sacral vein system, which was bleeding copiously, posed a difficult problem: we had to use sterile wax to stop the haemorrhage. But the essential organs, damage to which would have caused death, had only been grazed and the nerve centres next to them had not apparently suffered. Frankly, it was surprising. However, since the patient was anaesthetized, we could not tell if he had escaped damage to the nerves.

Under Crucitti's cool direction the operation lasted just under five hours but they kept him in the theatre longer to be on the safe side. 'At first it was agonizing,' said Crucitti later. 'Then it gradually became clear that . . . he just might survive. I drank some water, and smoked a cigarette.'

When John Paul came round next day, though scarcely conscious, his first words were: 'Have I said compline?' He thought it was still the previous day. It was already midday and too late.

> Earth felt the wound, and Nature from her seat,
> Sighing through all her works, gave signs of woe
> That all was lost,

wrote John Milton of that original Fall of Man when Eve first bit into the forbidden fruit. As the Pope lay between life and death it was a reminder to many Catholics that Original Sin was a cornerstone of their belief, and that they shared the guilt of this crime as well as the grief. In Poland half the telegrams sent on Wednesday night were get-well messages to John Paul; in Wawel Cathedral, at a special mass for recovery Wyszynski, now seventy-nine and dying of cancer, in a cracked voice relayed by a tape-recording, said: 'I am afflicted by various ailments, but they are nothing compared with the sufferings inflicted on the head of the church.' Brazilians, remembering from his visit the previous year, his charisma, his heart, prayed to him as 'John of God'; a parishioner in a *favela* of Rio de Janeiro where as a donation to the church he had taken off and left his gold cardinal's ring, called him 'the best man on earth'. 'The world has gone mad,' cried out a sobbing woman in Madrid.

Equally the shock caused grief among world leaders. Chancellor Helmut Schmidt of West Germany said, 'I feel I've been hit in the abdomen myself.' President Reagan, badly wounded and recovering from the attempt on his life in March, vowed to pray for him. Giscard d'Estaing, having narrowly avoided in the previous month a Corsican bomb, expressed in a message to the Vatican 'profound emotion', while even Brezhnev cabled the Pope that he was 'profoundly indignant at the criminal attempt on your life'. Indira Gandhi, Indian premier, was 'too shocked for words. What can I say?'

England's primate, Cardinal Hume, identified the sacred content of this criminal act, its mimesis or imitation of the Gospel story, calling it the twentieth century's 'most succinct text on the metaphysics of terrorism'. 'The Pope is now,' he said in Westminster Cathedral, 'at one with the countless victims of violence of our day. He, like them, has now followed in the footsteps of a master who was himself so cruelly and callously tortured and killed. He, like his Master, refuses to condemn, is ready to forgive.' Here was the drama of Catholic faith at its height. There was, as the atheist and iconoclast Bernard Shaw wrote about the murder of Gandhi by a Hindu nationalist in 1948, a dark side to any too visible presence of goodness. 'It shows how dangerous it is to be good,' said Shaw.

Two women had also been hit by Agça's bullets: Anne Odre, an American tourist, had been spared by the bullet that first hit her, passing through the Pope's abdomen and then sacrum: her throat was injured, but not seriously; the bullet that broke John Paul's index finger, then grazed his right arm, also struck Rose Hall, another American tourist, fracturing her left arm. Both women were treated in a hospital near St Peter's Square.

After firing the shots Agça had been caught trying to escape, first by a Franciscan nun, and then, having thrown the gun under a trailer lorry on the edge of St Peter's Square, he had been wrestled to the ground by a six-foot-four security guard, then headlocked. When they interrogated him, the Italian investigators could not uncover more than that he was an ordinary, once 'lucid and intelligent' terrorist, for years on the run from police. As to why he committed the crime, whether he had associates, and whether, more seriously, there had been a co-ordinated plot to kill the Pope, he gave highly implausible and contradictory explanations. Both before and after his trial he confessed variously that he had acted alone, that Turkish and Bulgarian friends or associates had aided him, or supported him with money or with his plans to escape. In a note found in his *pensione* room, he proclaimed grandly that 'I have killed the pope' – and subsequently he linked the reason to the Polish Solidarity movement, founded in September 1980, and Lech Walesa – also a target for assassination by him.

Coded traffic between the Bulgarian embassy in Rome and the Sofia headquarters of the Durzhavna Sigurnost, the Bulgarian secret service had increased in the early months of 1981 to such an extent that the US National Security Agency subsequently investigated it in search of proof that Bulgaria had hired Agça and were to pay him $400,000. The Italian investigators supported this idea. But in the first two weeks of May the messages had ceased. While it came to be believed in some quarters that Bulgarian authorities may have conspired with or taken up Agça's hatred and desire to harm the Pope, right-wing Turkish groups were also, at least for a while, possibly implicated.

American security chiefs and agencies found nothing to pin the assassination attempt on Moscow, believing that neither Brezhnev nor KGB head Andropov would have ordered the death of John Paul – quite the reverse, as it would have compounded Russia's already serious difficulties with Poland and sparked off further unrest. As revealed in 1992 documents released by the post-Soviet government, a top-secret cable from Rome reported the wounding of the Pope 'by an unknown assailant. The crime was perpetrated while the pope was driving through a crowd of the faithful in an open automobile . . . Early reports connect this attempt . . . with the complex political situation in the country [Poland]'. But neither this cable nor anything else gave substance to the many allegations of a Communist plot that would follow. It seemed unlikely that, had Agça been hired, he would have publicly proclaimed his intention beforehand. Yet as Robert Gates, director of the CIA, summed up in 1996, 'The question of whether the

Soviets were involved in or knew about the assassination attempt remains unanswered and one of the great remaining secrets of the cold war.'

Little of this concerns our 'inner man'. He considered the event from a spiritual perspective. Material explanations stop at material factors, hitting buffers of fact and circumstance. No official Vatican report on the assassination attempt exists and clearly, on John Paul's request, no attempt was made to investigate. The Vatican Press Office brusquely stated on 5 September 1981: 'The Holy See has never expressed any hypothesis regarding any organization or country that may have ordered the attack on the Pope.'

In 1984 the Italian state charged three Bulgarians and five Turks with conspiracy, but in the trial nearly two years later the Rome court acquitted the accused for lack of evidence, although under one rather sensible Italian law concluded not to declare them innocent. Ağca, brought from prison into court as a prosecution witness, claimed he was Jesus Christ. Thirteen years later, now regularly interviewed on anniversaries of the crime, he still maintained to a *France-Soir* reporter that he was the 'material and spiritual reincarnation of Christ'.

After his operation and after five days in intensive care, John Paul stayed for a few weeks in the tenth-floor Gemelli apartment, where a nun who chose to remain anonymous attended with energetic devotion to his recuperation. He was so undemanding, she reported, never asking for anything, while in his view, people took too much trouble over him. She had on the first day approached him with some apprehension. The Pope! 'The next day it was all over; I was in command of myself again.' One day when he didn't want to leave his bed, she said to him, 'Most Holy Father, you *must* get up to regain strength.' He laughed and said, 'Well, well, sister has got over her shyness!'

His bed, on castors, was not very big (to facilitate movement in the hospital).

> He found the bed a bit short, but he got used to it. He put up with everything. He was a very easy patient. And so simple! Who would have thought it was the Pope, if there hadn't been so many people around him! One day he left his room and when he could see no one in the corridor we heard him saying: 'There you are, they've gone, they've all abandoned me.'

He told the nun: 'The whole world has a right to expect much from the Pope, so the Pope can never pray enough.'

'No, I didn't imagine him differently, perhaps because I saw him here when he came to visit his friend Monsignor Deskur before going into the conclave.'

The worldwide vigil praying for Karol's recovery lasted from Wednesday 13 to Sunday 17 May when a tape-recorded message was relayed from the Gemelli to the crowd in St Peter's: 'Pray for the brother who shot me and whom I have sincerely pardoned.' The rich voice was noticeably thin and weakened: 'United to Christ, priest and victim, I offer my sufferings for the church and for the world.'

But there was even worse to come. As Cardinal Hume once observed, 'The real cross we have to bear is the one we haven't chosen, the one which sits uncomfortably on our shoulders.' Impatiently John Paul insisted on being released and by 6 June, the Feast of the Pentecost, he appeared in St Peter's Square to greet a delegation from the Greek Orthodox Councils of Constantinople [Istanbul] and Ephesus, places he had visited in 1979.

The blood transfusion during the loss of three and a half litres of his rare blood group brought a new peril. Donors had come from all parts of Italy: 'I remember,' said one doctor, 'seeing the head of the Rome Fire Brigade arrive with a number of flasks.' Urgency had meant extensive tests on donated blood were waived aside. One pint had been infected with a cytomegalovirus, a blood-poisoning agent. So now, as a result, he 'came down with a very high fever that brutally jolted him by sweating as if it were midsummer, to shivering as if he were in his shirtsleeves. He was dying by inches every day.'

At first, thinking it was a predictable post-operational infection, the doctors gave him antibiotics, but these did no good. Then tireless researchers working against the clock discovered the contaminant. There was no medical cure, only vitamins and a strong constitution. They had to wait. But it took Karol seventy-seven days to recover from this, for the cytomegalovirus 'can persist in an organism a long time and be reactivated'. But, as the same doctor commented, 'As soon as the fever gave him a respite, he started work again. We would see him go past with files under his arm and we learned later that he revised and corrected the encyclical *Laborem Exercens*.'

Coming round from this second trial, Karol insisted to his doctors, who wanted to delay the reversal operation of the colostomy performed in May until later, that they go ahead at once in spite of a palpable risk of reinfection.

He intervened, telling the surgeon Crucitti,

> Don't forget that although you may be the doctors I am the patient, and that I am entitled to explain to you my problems as a sick man, especially this one: I should not like to return to the Vatican until I am completely cured. I don't know what you think, but personally I feel very well, even supposing that the analyses indicate the contrary. I feel quite strong enough to undergo a fresh operation.

Crucitti noted that this was a 'useful reminder' for the doctor to use the individual's knowledge of himself, and not to act as 'a sort of oracle sending down his decisions from on high'.

Professor Sanna, another leading specialist, gave a similar account of this 'session of the Sanhedrin' (the Jerusalem supreme council in biblical times) at which John Paul convinced his saviours. 'He was tenacious. He used to say, jokingly, "What did the Sanhedrin say today? What did the Sanhedrin decide on my behalf?"' Speaking for more than half an hour he explained that a patient was all too likely to lose his subjectivity or sense of himself, and had to fight constantly to regain it and become again 'the subject of his illness' instead of simply remaining 'the object of treatment'.

And so the poet philosopher playwright, returning to the themes of *Love and Responsibility*, showed he was still intact, reminding his carers that this problem of turning the individual into an object is paramount in the world, and one of its most intractable, both practical and philosophical, difficulties.

His new operation was fixed for 5 August, the feast of Our Lady of the Snows, so that, if all went well, he could be back at St Peter's on 15 August, the feast of the Assumption. The liturgical calendar overcame the medical one. Sanna, like all his colleagues, was struck by the Holy Father's reprimand, which Professor Tresalti summarised rather nicely: 'All my life I have defended the rights of man. Today I myself am "man"!'

The relationship between the surgeon Crucitti and the Pope developed from purely professional contact into one between two ordinary men. 'A journalist claimed that we had broken professional secrecy, and someone even wrote that "we spoke of the Pope as if he were a man"! Certainly. The Pope is not a pure symbol; he is a real figure who has a direct and fraternal contact with the world.' Sandro Pertini, Italy's president and one of Karol's first visitors, told Crucitti, as did the Pope, that he smoked too much. In conversing about the crime, Wojtyla left Crucitti with the impression that he had pondered in vain about the significance of this incomprehensible act . . . 'Did the Turk act on his own account, or was he only a tool? That is one question which he asked himself. If he found the answer, he did not impart it to me.'

Pertini and John Paul also became cordial friends, while later Pertini's home was the only presidential residence the Pope ever visited. In the winter of 1984 after being dropped off by helicopter on the Adamello glacier in the Dolomites, they were photographed walking together on a slippery slope, covered in snow, but with the secular head of state holding on to the Pope's elbow with all his might. Surrounded by security guards and monitors the Pope skied three pistes. Pertini said, 'You ski like a swallow!'

He convalesced in Castel Gandolfo. Here André Frossard with his wife visited him, finding him with sunken cheeks, very thin (Crucitti had told him for a man of his age he was too heavy and henceforth he forwent a substantial evening meal), and – in the fashion of convalescent popes – wearing 'a white cassock without a mantelletta'. Frossard wondered how he could wear such a woolly thick garment in such heat. Wojtyla, fed now with vegetable and fruit cocktails and frugal dishes, took a glass of wine in to his guests. He told the Frenchman how significant it was that 13 May was the anniversary of the Virgin Mary's first apparition at Fatima, and that on the first anniversary of his assassination attempt, in the following year he would make a pilgrimage to Fatima to thank the Madonna for his safe deliverance.

By 4 October he was back in the Vatican, celebrating mass in St Peter's Square. Now the voice again was strong and clear, the step as assured as before. He repudiated all attempts made to hedge him in with protection. He did not like the bullet-proof glass bubble on top of the popemobile which separated him from the source of energy. After the liturgy he stepped out into the crowd as before, and if he felt any fear he did not show it. The mass was televised worldwide and the clear message he sent out was that there would be no change. Three days later he gave his first papal audience in the square since the attack. Officials had wanted to hold it in one of the halls but John Paul insisted he would use the popemobile and so he did, circling it just as he had on 13 May. While he shook hands and held babies, he was not quite so unprotected now, for, to his annoyance, not only was the popemobile fitted with bullet-proof windows, but the assembled crowd had to pass through metal-detectors.

So again, in another symbolic theatrical gesture, he 'repossessed' the square, at the same time exorcising or removing the shadow that had been cast over it. Subsequently he would refer to the event with irony, or even jocosely, but would not allow himself to be questioned. Before his third visit to France in October 1986, when warned of Nostradamus's prophecies about the Pope's death at the confluence of two rivers by Cardinal Decourtray, who thinking of the confluence of the Saône and the Rhône wanted to discourage him from travelling to Lyons, he reacted, 'I assure you, Your Eminence, there is no place more dangerous than St Peter's Square!'

Karol took spiritual advantage of the assassination attempt. As with earlier experiences, the death of those he loved, and the near-fatal accident when he was knocked down by a lorry, it provided an opportunity through suffering for renewal and spiritual growth. He never once complained of pain, and did not once consider suffering it dehumanising or demeaning, but rather like St Paul he rejoiced in it: 'Now I rejoice in my suffering for your sake, and in my flesh I complete what is lacking in Christ's afflictions for the sake of his body, that is the Church.' John Paul expressed a similar gratitude for what he called his 'great divine trial'; he compared himself to St Peter confined and condemned to death who was released by an angel of the Lord sent to rescue him from the hand of Herod. He had had this 'vivid presentiment that I would be saved'.

On 12 May 1982, John Paul made that promised visit to Fatima. 'As soon as I recovered consciousness after the attack in St Peter's Square my thoughts turned instinctively to this shrine', he told the pilgrims, 'and I wanted to express here my gratitude to our heavenly mother for having saved my life . . . In this coincidence I recognize a divine call – though in the designs of Providence there are no mere coincidences.'

The following day, still in Fatima, he consecrated the world to the Immaculate Heart of Mary.

The visit to Fatima was clearly a very personal pilgrimage. During the years 1978–82 he took many initiatives to integrate Marian elements into his own and the church's spiritual practices 'to unite one to the Mother of God in ever new ways'. Thus in October 1978 he had begun reciting the rosary on Vatican Radio, on every first Saturday of the month; in December 1981 he introduced in the Blessed Sacrament Chapel of St Peter's, perpetual adoration of Mary; for Christmas 1981 he ordered a huge crib inside St Peter's, and in the following year an outside crib next to the Christmas tree in the square; he placed a plaque of the Madonna to look down from the Apostolic Palace on the crowds in St Peter's Square. He wanted, often with passion and spontaneity, to spread her influence as widely and deeply as possible. As Hilaire Belloc wrote to G.K. Chesterton, 'She never fails us. She has never failed me in any demand.' John Paul would have agreed.

In 1984 he presented the Fatima shrine with the bullet that had nearly killed him. It was set in the crown of the Virgin's statue at Fatima, alongside 313 pearls and 2,679 other precious stones.

The distance that had always existed between him and others had been confirmed, too, in this failed attempt on his life. He had now experienced 'suffering's refined jealousy, which isolates you from your friends and puts a tiny but unbridgeable gap between you and the compassion that reaches out to you'. He could, as never before, join his own suffering directly with love. As he told André Frossard, when he was young 'sick people used to intimidate me', and he had shied away from looking at people in pain.

Job, his play written forty-four years before, contained the nucleus of the thoughts that Karol now developed on the theme of suffering in his Apostolic Letter *Salvifici Doloris: On the Christian Meaning of Human Suffering* (11 February 1984). In this he pronounced his last words on the meaning of Job's suffering:

> If the Lord consents to test Job with suffering, he does it *to demonstrate the latter's righteousness*.
>
> The Book of Job is not the last word on this subject in Revelation. In a certain way it is a foretelling of the Passion of Christ . . .
>
> Love is also the fullest source of the answer to the question of the

meaning of suffering. This answer has been given by God to man in the
Cross of Jesus Christ.

From now on he and his papacy would be in a different dimension, a
different order of being. Attempts on his life would be made again – as
soon as the following year when in Portugal a Spanish-born priest, a
supporter of Lefebvre (Archbishop of Lille, the ultra-traditionalist
who refused the reforms of Vatican Two), attacked him with a knife,
but was quickly seized by Vatican guards. But of more consequence
was the 'divine reality'. He had recorded a comment on a theatrical
production of *The Divine Comedy*, performed by Kotlarczyk's Rhapsodic Theatre in 1964, that Dante's work was a 'vision of concrete and
historical reality . . . through the eschatological reality given to him as
an object of faith (hell, purgatory, heaven). Reaching even further it
means seeing human reality through divine reality, hence the title *The
Divine Comedy* . . . It is the history of his creative search and, above
all, the history of his love.' This was how he saw his own life and he
might as well have been speaking of himself. Cheerfully, even ebul-
liently, when he arrived for his convalescence he told the crowd that
greeted him at Castel Gandolfo that in his absence their hymn-singing
had got better. Then he solemnly broke the news: 'And now Act Two
begins.'

21

Siege or Sanctuary?

(1981–82)

I am not offended when labelled a conservative. The pope is not here to make changes but to conserve what he has received into his charge.

Act Two's tightening of the dramatic knot may be said to begin with the appointment of Cardinal Joseph Ratzinger as Prefect of the Congregation for the Doctrine of the Faith (formerly the Holy Office, formerly the Inquisition) in November 1981. With this John Paul set the pattern for dealing with dissidents, or essential disagreements within the Catholic church, over matters of the Faith. Difficult cases would essentially be resolved by the Congregation, while he would meet regularly and at length with Ratzinger when they would hold frank and free discussions. While the Congregation would exercise authority in his name, only in the final instance would he himself pronounce, or impose a visible stamp on any one problem or issue. As in other areas of his papacy, this established a style or *modus operandi* early on.

But again it was Wojtyla's personal way of dealing with wide-ranging, even cosmic issues. In the crucible of those early years as a seminarist and philosophy student in Krakow and Paris, and later as a professor and young bishop, when he argued and disputed every possible theological and existential problem, he had undergone the necessary experience to exercise such authority confidently. As he had done with Garrigou-Lagrange and Max Scheler, and with his endless students in lecture halls and on skiing trips, he would read or listen to the exposition of views, present in his own time their cases to God and to Mary, test them in his own dimension of learning, and either then or later talk them through with the correspondents and come to a decision, or express a judgement.

But now he had much less time. A month-long synod had been held in the autumn of 1980 on 'The Role of the Family in the Modern World' in which all kinds of high-minded sentiments were expressed by those attending, such as that of Archbishop John Quinn (of San Francisco), quoting Pope Leo XIII, 'The Church has nothing to fear from the truth.' Cardinal O'Fiaich, Primate of All Ireland, called attention to 'reticent' husbands not being 'sensitive enough to the differences in sexuality between male and female', while Archbishop Worlock of Liverpool dealt with marital breakdown and wanted a sacramental welcome extended to the divorced and remarried. Cardinal Hume spoke of those for whom the 'natural methods of birth control do not seem to be the only solution; some very good and conscientious Catholics just cannot accept that the use of artificial means of contraception in some circumstances is *intrinsice inhonestum*'.

John Paul took notes as often as he could be present, writing vigorously and lunching every day with synod members. His presence, one cardinal told him, helped all those involved. 'Why?' the Pope asked, surprised. 'I didn't say anything.' 'Precisely,' his interlocutor replied. 'You could have intervened. You could have pulled a face or shown disapproval. You did nothing of the kind. You left the Synod free.' Yet at the conclusion in his summing-up, held in the Sistine Chapel, according to one critic he 'rounded on them'. He did not need advice on the family, for he was an acknowledged expert, and he reaffirmed the doctrines of *Humanae Vitae*. Theologians could help the magisterium, was his plain meaning, but their task was to bring out 'the biblical foundation and so-called "personalistic" reasons for the doctrines. There could be no question of keeping the law merely as an ideal to be achieved in the future.'

It was assumed, then, by his adversaries (and the pattern quickly established of 'cold-shower endings' to consultations) that John Paul simply squashed opposition – or had no desire to share the experience of others. In human terms Karol Wojtyla was not like this: yet he had a higher function of keeping the church together, and to this end all his initiatives could be seen as an effort to seek solutions in advance for every tension that became manifest. He would offer complete concentration and thought to a subject, but could not afford to become involved in lengthy discussion. His guardian and watchdog Dziwisz would be forever urging him on to his next appointment. With such volume of business to attend to – and few will dispute the sheer scale of the Pope's capacity for his superhuman task – he needed to find the right balance, 'serve by ruling and rule by serving'. He would have been foolish indeed not to have used the supreme advantage of his position. Christ 'served increasingly, but in the spirit of serving God he was able to expel the money dangers from the temple'.

Cardinal Ratzinger, John Paul's watchdog of orthodoxy and sound doctrine, whom he had befriended earlier, became from the start a particular target for liberals within the church. Although his opinions were sometimes at variance with John Paul's (over the 1986 World Day of Peace he said, 'This cannot be the model,' prompting the Pope to comment back, 'It's his personal opinion!'), he became in 1981 John Paul's closest theological confidant and lieutenant. Ratzinger said wryly that the restrictive side of his job was to help the Pope with the necessary 'Nos' – 'This pope's natural inclination is to say "Yes".' This important observation is often overlooked. Later John Paul confesses, 'Maybe I should have been more assertive. I think this is partly a matter of my temperament.'

As doctrinal tsar, the legendary *Panzer-Kardinal* – as he came to be called – was fifty-four, seven years younger than John Paul, a white-haired German theologian and scripture scholar whose choice con-firmed John Paul's ability both to delegate, and to appoint first-class minds to senior positions. Ratzinger is described in Cornwell's *The Pope in Winter* as 'small, compact, handsome with silken silver hair', but also with 'a cruel mouth and bedroom eyes'; moreover, he reneged on his earlier progressive ideas on dissenting theologians and on remarried Catholics whose earlier marriage had not been annulled.

But the liberal's article of faith that any former progressive leader who, given office, at once becomes intoxicated with power and therefore a reactionary, was in this case incorrect. Neither John Paul nor Ratzinger became more conservative or reactionary as they aged, while Ratzinger remained as consistent in his urbanity and intelligence as the Pope – as his biographer John Allen observed, he remained 'gracious and mild, not one for empire-building'. While he was the architect of controversial aspects of John Paul's pontificate – the crackdown on liberation theology in Latin America, the crusades against gay marriage amd feminism, putting a brake on the theology of religious pluralism (Buddhism, he said, is an auto-erotic spirituality that 'seeks transcendence without imposing concrete religious obligations') – Ratzinger also acted as a strong moderating force, when he opposed, for example, a formal declaration of infallibility for the teaching on birth control.

Early in John Paul's papacy, theologians in particular came into conflict with the Congregation. Hans Küng, priest and professor of theology, author of *On Being a Christian*, had been an attractive intellectual figure for Wojtyla during the Second Vatican Council. A German colleague of Ratzinger's, handsome and articulate, he became the 'first example of a new phenomenon in Catholic life – the dissenting theologian as an international media star'. He crossed swords with the Catholic hierarchy primarily over papal infallibility in the making of doctrinal decisions, which he did not hold to be true. In 1979 the Congregation deprived Küng of his licence to teach Catholic theology because it believed that he undermined that doctrine of papal infallibility pronounced by Vatican One in 1870. This withdrawal of his mandate to teach triggered worldwide outrage in which the Vatican was condemned for restricting academic freedom.

Wojtyla did not relent. Not only theologians must be strictly subordinate to the magisterium, he said, intervening personally, but – dealing directly with Küng's doctrinal difference over infallibility – stated, 'We must be very worried when this gift of Christ is cast into doubt,' continuing, in a letter to the German bishops on 22 May 1980, about infallibility's importance: 'When this essential basis of faith is weakened or destroyed, the most elementary truths of our faith begin to collapse.' But Küng was neither excommunicated, nor deprived of his functions as a priest. He continued to teach and, while maintaining his standing as a charismatic dissident in the eyes of some, over the years his influence diminished. Church unity was the first priority: as Ratzinger said, 'Under this pope it was possible to believe that the house of God is solid and that we can live in this house.'

Another *cause célèbre* for critics of John Paul II was the work provocatively titled *Jesus, an Experiment in Christology* (more tamely, in its literally translated Dutch title: *Jesus, the Story of a Living Person*) by Eduard Schillebeeckx, a Flemish Dominican. This modernist approach to the life of Jesus stated that the Gospels should not be taken literally, and questioned the Resurrection. This was also condemned, while Schillebeeckx's licence to teach was withdrawn. In another similar case, John Paul, on his visit to the South American subcontinent in July 1980, told Brazilian bishops about a Brazilian Franciscan's book that raised problems over Jesus' knowledge of his impending death: 'The theologian knows, by a supernatural instinct, that it belongs to the bishop to watch over his theological activity for the sake of the faith of the people of God.'

In his first encyclical, *Redemptor Hominis* (*The Redeemer of Man*, 1979), John Paul had asserted joyfully that man had been redeemed through Christ, 'redeemed in spirit and in body'. This dictated not only what every human being should do, but also a pope's obligation to oppose everything that was to do with 'having' rather than 'being'. In view of this – and this is where he differed from those many critics and dissidents who opposed him over the next quarter of a century – he saw the church and its rules and procedures as following all this rather than preceding it. 'The Church is the necessary instrument instituted by Christ', writes Charles Moore, 'not the purpose of the whole thing. That is the only reason for its disciplines.'

In their regular and informal meetings over the next twenty-five years when Ratzinger remained the Pope's chief intellectual contact, the Pope's style of discussion, said Ratzinger, was 'provocative', while he approached intellectual matters as a real philosopher – 'touched in the heart by the fundamental questions of what is our life'. The important thing was that as a philosopher he had 'arrived' at ortho-dox Catholic Christian belief. And so, having arrived at such affirma-tion, it was reasonable in his coherent but provocative testing of those who disagreed with him that while he should listen to what they had to say, he should ultimately exercise authority over those who wished for any change that in his eyes could in any way destabilise the church or cause conflict among the faithful. Both he and Ratzinger came to the conclusion that only a church with a strong central authority and rock-solid doctrinal verities could resist a hostile state or culture, and as those cultures became as they did increasingly hostile and intolerant towards direction from above and towards conservative morality, so it was even more important to stand firm. Dissenters such as Küng and Bernhard Häring saw this obedience as blind, the resistance as a 'siege mentality', but it had been reached after a lifetime of experience and the severest forms of testing.

Wojtyla was not a reformer, and it would be foolish to judge him on the basis of innovation; like an actor he had accepted the 'given' constituents of his role, and he would interpret them faithfully. And to that interpretation he brought his own original gifts. On visits to a hospital he held up sufferers as images among us of Christ, and this image applied equally to those tortured in prison camps. 'Christ,' he said, 'calls upon everyone who suffers to collaborate with Him in the salvation of the world. Because of this, pain and sorrow are not endured alone or in vain.' He said, more fully to the sick at Czestochowa:

> It is through this mystery [of the Redemption] that every cross placed on someone's shoulders acquires a dignity that is inconceivable and becomes a *sign* for the person who carries it, and also for others. 'In my flesh I complete what is lacking in Christ's afflictions' . . . Wherever you may be – I beg you to make use of the *cross* that has become part of you *for salvation*.

This personal approach created new terms, new circumstances, new modes of expression, to make the traditional teaching dramatic and accessible. The vivid way he could conceive the Mysteries and bring the immediacy of the Passion into the hearts of those who listened to him easily outweighed the influence of the dissenters, although they went on nursing their hurt susceptibilities.

Häring, for instance, summoned to the Vatican to explain his view on contraception, said in much-quoted words, 'Hitler's courts were certainly more dangerous, but they were not an offence to my honour.' But for the majority of priests, bishops and theologians Wojtyla had set himself up as a new ideal of the Christian person, sovereign, inner-directed and inwardly free, happy for the gift of life and all its wonders – even if the body is crushed or sickened. As the priests and bishops said of him, 'He has shown us a new way to do the old things more deeply.'

Archbishop Lefebvre had a more vociferous and active following than the rather bookish and formalistic supporters of Küng and Schillebeeckx. Lefebvre, at odds with the Vatican since 1976, when he was suspended but continued to celebrate mass with 8,000 faithful in Lille, denounced John Paul's 'flirtation' with Protestantism when the Pope went to a prayer meeting in the evangelical Lutheran Church of Rome. Lefebvre accused John Paul of being 'infected by Humanism' and, far from the liberal critics, blamed the Pope for 'collectivising' the decision-making process, and not taking sole responsibility. In other

words, this time John Paul was too modern. Lefebvre went further in
June 1988 at Econe (Switzerland), where he had exiled himself, and
consecrated four bishops before thousands of his supporters. This led,
reluctantly decreed by the Pope after extensive attempts at dialogue
and reconciliation, to his excommunication. Lefebvre, still intransigent in his hostility to Vatican Two, died unreconciled at the age of
eighty-six in 1991.

A later, highly bizarre case of dissidence demonstrated yet another
side of the Pope's personal power of intervention. Emmanuel Milingo,
a 71-year-old Zambian archbishop, famous for his mass healing and
exorcism liturgies, in 2001 married Maria Sung, a Korean Moonie, in
a mass ceremony in New York. Ratzinger's Congregation threatened
excommunication unless Milingo renounced his bride, while the
Moonies planned a well-financed Catholic church in Africa, autonomous from Rome, with Milingo heading the hierarchy. However a
'dulcet-voiced' Milingo admirer, a woman, persuaded him to go to
Rome to seek reconciliation with John Paul, which he did, believing
the Pope 'would be waiting for us with open arms'.

Milingo first saw Dziwisz, who told him: 'Remember you are an
archbishop. You are an apostle . . . You cannot be happy outside the
Catholic Church.' The Pope then confronted the excited archbishop,
who was passionate to 'wipe out the lies which people have told about
me'.

> The Pope did not discuss anything with me, did not accuse me of
> anything. I greeted him, he asked me to sit down and then said to me
> solemnly: 'In the name of Jesus Christ, come back to the Catholic
> Church.' That was it. He said nothing more. Then I spoke to him, I
> don't remember what I said: he stayed silent, did not react to my words.
> Finally he added: 'Speak to Bishop Bertone. He will tell you what you
> have to do.'
>
> Milingo kissed his feet. 'It was a spontaneous gesture. I had caused
> the Pope to suffer, I had tormented him. I had to ask forgiveness now
> with a gesture.'

The prodigal son had returned to his father.

Archbishop Agostino Casaroli, a leading Vatican expert on Eastern
Europe, the successor to Villot as Secretary of State, was another
astute appointment John Paul had made in 1979, while Casaroli's

right-hand man, Archbishop Achille Silvestrini – effectively the Vatican's foreign secretary – also proved an outstanding diplomat in expanding the Vatican's unprecedented influence in world affairs (both were made cardinals). Cardinal Roger Etchegaray became the papal special envoy, in effect troubleshooter, prominent in John Paul's efforts to avert, in 2003, the Anglo-American invasion of Iraq. These few appointments apart, John Paul stuck with the Curia of Paul VI, making only minimal changes. He did not reform the government of the church. His increasingly centralised rule, it was claimed, engendered a Roman bureaucracy that was 'infested with careerism', notably detailed in a 1999 exposé, *Via col vento in Vaticano* (*Gone with the wind in the Vatican*), written by four Vatican insiders, including a 72-year-old retired bishop.

Wojtyla never believed he 'owned' this house of God. He had no sense of the church as property and he eschewed ownership ('being' was always more important than 'having'). He had once called the Archbishop's Palace in Krakow a 'cage' from which he needed to escape, and – unlike the landowner mentality of many churchmen and those who belong to institutions – he never did, in a psychological sense, 'somatise' (feel it was his own body) with the Catholic church. In all the millions of words he wrote and spoke he rarely identified personally with church structures. For him it remained the living bride rather than bricks and mortar. He felt no need to formulate any structural innovations, and was convinced there was no imperative to reform. The inner Wojtyla stated in effect, 'I never stepped out of line when I was a professor of ethics and maintained, while examining the work of others, my obedience to traditional church authority, so why shouldn't others?' He practised literal fidelity and remained true to it, so why should he not require and expect it of others? All his efforts were directed towards renewal of the missionary spirit. The drama of our lives lay not in the facts of salvation, but in the means by which it could be achieved. His mission was to conserve and not to reform:

> Peter, you are the floor, that
> Others may walk over
> You not knowing where they go.

He was the floor. Like the papacy and the church itself, he would always be there.

22

The Ravelled Sleeve of Christianity

(1982)

We may irritate Rome, but we also fascinate Rome too – at some moments a diabolical Doppelgänger or counterfeit or rival Catholicism, at other moments 70 million believers whom it would be so good to reconcile in one communion and fellowship with the See of Peter and Paul.

Archbishop Robert Runcie 1995

The gap between what is thought and expected of me, and what I know myself to be, is considerable and frightening . . . It is good to feel small, for I know that whatever I achieve will be God's achievement, not mine.

Cardinal Basil Hume
Times interview, 1999

England, Scotland and Wales, the year of the Pope's visit, had just over 0.2 per cent of the world's practising Catholics. Even so, Britain had had a disproportionately strong influence on the Catholic faith.

Before the English Reformation in 1533, England was like present-day Poland a land dedicated to the Virgin Mary, with numerous shrines to her and to native saints such as Thomas à Becket. There was a deeply rooted Catholic tradition in architecture, music and literature, and an openness to intimations of a supernatural purpose, a latitude of mind, in the development of a civilised national identity. In Europe continued the tradition that the Catholic church was 'by divine will, central to the unfolding story of the continent from Roman times'. When the English break with Rome was confirmed by Elizabeth I, and the Settlement of 1559 welded church and state into one entity, membership of the

Church of England became a test of patriotic loyalty. In 1570 Pope Pius X declared the Queen a heretic with no right to her realm, which isolated Catholics in England more, and from then on Catholics were branded as traitors, forbidden to hold public office or meet for worship. Only when in 1801 William Pitt brought Ireland under direct Westminster control (and mindful of the five million Irish Catholics) did the law begin to relax until in 1829 the Catholic Emancipation Act struck off the remaining fetters. While many were patriotic and exemplary citizens, Catholics in English society had grown used to living apart from the mainstream; by the mid-century the Catholic population was three-quarters of a million but still regarded by the rest with deep suspicion: a minority, it was generally believed, who thought everyone was out of step except themselves. However, by 1850, the date of the restoration of the Catholic hierarchy in England and Wales with the appointment of the first Archbishop of Westminster (called by *The Times* 'one of the grossest acts of folly and impertinence which the court of Rome has ventured to commit since the crown and people of England threw off its yoke'), there began a re-flowering of British Catholic culture. This could claim, in the Westminster palaces and the churches designed by Augustus Pugin and Edwin Lutyens, significant national achievements. The music of Edward Elgar, Lennox Berkeley and James Macmillan, the literature of the earlier Cardinal Newman, Gerard Manley Hopkins, G.K. Chesterton and Hilaire Belloc – and subsequently Graham Greene, Evelyn Waugh, J.R.R. Tolkien – had been of an influence often unequalled anywhere in the world. In philosophy, medicine, and science, too, Catholics had been influential. In politics Catholics made substantial headway and are now heavily represented in the country's leadership.

But while punitive laws were lifted, anti-popery remained a virulent cultural tradition. Popes were supected of every vice, especially sexual ones. John Donne wrote in the first paragraph of *Ignatius His Conclave*, his satire on the founder of the Jesuit order, Ignatius Loyola: 'Dost thou seek after the Author? It is in vain; for he is harder to be found than the parents of Popes were in the old times [i.e. they were bastards].' Donne said of Ignatius that he didn't solicit the 'minions' of the popes but in his 'witty lust' strove to 'equal the licentiousness of Sodomites . . . and so made the maker of God, a Priest subject to his lust . . . that his Venus might be the more monstrous, he would have her in a Mitre'.

Equation of Catholicism with sodomy persisted to the twenty-first century, with the widespread assumption that the rule of celibacy inevitably led to homosexuality. There was anti-popery even at the end of the millennium in 1999 with displays of 'Scottish orangeism', when 20,000 Protestants marched into the predominantly Catholic Coatbridge in Lanarkshire, blowing flutes and beating Lambeg drums to the tune of the 'The Men of Harlech' (the crowd's chorus: 'Fuck the pope and the Virgin Mary'). Women writers, too, expressed strong feelings in the anti-Marian, anti-popery tradition. Marina Warner, who made a lengthy socio-anthropological dissection of the Virgin, wrote, 'the foundations of the ethic of sexual chastity [were laid] in fear and loathing of the female body's functions'. She considered that John Paul lamented abortion because of exterminated Poles 'who were failed by the Catholic Church during the Nazi era'. Joan Smith wrote that 'Christ's birth, far from elevating the status of the female sex, is simply further proof that Christianity was conceived in sexual disgust and loathing of women.'

It would not have been far from Wojtyla's mind that Britain had originally entered the Second World War on Poland's side, while 'perfidious Albion' had, outmanoeuvred at Yalta, abandoned his Catholic homeland to the atheistic Soviets. In Britain traditionalist Catholics had not welcomed the alliance with Stalin. Uncle Peregrine – of recusant stock – in Waugh's *Sword of Honour* trilogy, reacts in horror 'The Bolshevists are advancing again . . . if one believes the papers we are actually *helping* the Bolshevists.' This same breed of Catholics did not react well to the Second Vatican Council, while even more moderate Catholics felt alienated. There had been a considerable diminution of influence and practice among British Catholics since the early 1960s when Catholicism was at its zenith, but in recent years attendance at mass had stabilised and even increased.

Wojtyla knew how influenced the Council had been by recognisably Protestant ideas as they had come into circulation through Cardinal Newman. Described by the Pope as the 'father' of Vatican Two, which above all shaped his thinking and practice, Newman's theological outlook had been, in manner and attitudes, not shaped by the 'post-tridentine, syllogistic mode of thinking prevalent in the Catholic church since the 16th century' (that is, it did not proceed from a premiss and from general propositions arrive at particulars). As such it was quite Anglican. As Clifford Longley points out in his biography of

Derek Worlock, this was neglected because 'Newman in his Catholic years was regarded by the English public above all as a notorious controversialist who had betrayed the Church of England for Rome'.

Archbishop Kevin McDonald of Southwark, who for eight years had worked in the Vatican Council for Christian Unity, told me that 'the general feeling in Rome was that "England is a bit of a one-off"'. The religious history of England had been so different because it was 'not a confessional church', and it was difficult for the more philosophic Latin mind to grasp the English 'pragmatic approach' in its many different forms – to understand, for example, the discreet Christianity of Pepys ('ignored', he said, according to Claire Tomalin's 2003 biography), or how William Blake's peculiar theology fitted into the structures of faith.

Ann Widdecombe, an ex-Conservative minister and Catholic convert was of the opinion that 'England doesn't like certainty – doesn't like the setting of moral boundaries; we have an attitude of everyone has to get what he wants, we act as our own arbiters about everything.' MacDonald had echoed this when he had further observed that the Pope has 'great sympathy and outreach and a sense of responsibility to other faiths', but that 'his vision doesn't fit into our journalistic way of thinking'.

Wojtyla also knew England as the home of Shakespeare, the author especially of *Hamlet*, a play that he had studied deeply and written about extensively in his theatre days, and which of course he knew as a work crucial to the ethical, sexual and philosophical study of mankind. The play scene, he wrote, voices a 'truth about the great ethical power of the theatre' and in it Shakespeare makes 'a clear confession of his faith in that power'. Moreover, under Hamlet's words exhorting the theatre's mission 'to hold the mirror up to nature', he says, the 'Rhapsodic Theatre puts its collective signature'.

Hamlet was the Renaissance man *par excellence*; with his religious, Catholic conscience he was in conflict with the new scepticism of Francis Bacon and Montaigne, both of whom made popular a questioning humanism based on empiricism and scientific observation. Also Wojtyla had as a philosopher examined critically the English Enlightenment and the nineteenth-century Benthamite philosophers, so in a much more searching and cautious attitude of mind than some of his earlier papal visits he looked forward and prepared himself.

*   *   *

On 11 March 1982, Dr Robert Runcie, Archbishop of Canterbury, on a visit to Liverpool had just started to preach in St Nicholas's Church when Protestant demonstrators, who smuggled placards into the church, began to shout 'Judas' and 'Traitor', jeer and catcall. The reason was that Runcie had been extending a warm welcome to John Paul II, due to visit in a few weeks' time, and had began to talk about the relationship between the papacy and England, saying it was Pope Gregory in the sixth century who had sent St Augustine to Canterbury.

Violence was in the air. The jeering and catcalls grew louder till Runcie abandoned his theme, picked up a Bible and said he would read from it. He chose the Beatitudes from the Sermon on the Mount, but further boos and hisses cut him short. He then tried to lead the congregation in the Lord's Prayer, but even this was raucously interrupted. 'Christian discussion had become impossible.' The placard-bearers and jeerers won.

Although most moderate Anglicans were on his side, the following month much more reasoned opposition to the Pope's visit weighed in, with Enoch Powell, the right-wing Conservative politician, writing to Runcie that he feared the 'royal supremacy and the authority of Parliament' might be compromised. The Revd Ian Paisley in Northern Ireland thundered against the 'Anti-Christ' pope, while the Free Church of Scotland complained about the 'incompatible' claims of the See of Rome. Runcie's successor as Bishop of St Albans wrote in his parish magazine *Home Words* that 'the Englishman was too canny to let . . . a few days of papal exposure . . . sweep Anglicans unthinkingly into the arms of Rome'. Ironically enough, St Albans abbey had supplied the Catholic church with its only English pope, Nicholas Brakespeare, Pope Hadrian VI, 1154–59.

Runcie had first met John Paul one morning in May 1980 at the papal nuncio's house during the Pope's visit to Zaire. Here Runcie felt the Pope was 'sizing' him up. The Pope said he regretted his lack of understanding of much that went on in Western theology, and in Western attitudes, when he had spent all his ministry in an atheistic country, Poland. Runcie was impressed by him 'as a man of spiritual quality surrounded by this enormous staff and retinue – I was terribly envious of that!'

A subsequent chance meeting, when Runcie was flying out to Nairobi, and the Pope flying back to Rome, was, for Runcie, an amazing drama. He'd done with me. But his plane was delayed by two and a half hours, and my plane had been advanced, so we were both at the airport . . . It was a small airport, and there didn't seem any possibility of keeping us separate. I distinctly remember that I was in a telephone box, and [Terry] Waite was getting a sandwich – we were all hiding round a corner lest we ran into the papal party.

Then we actually *did* meet them, face to face! You could see it registering on the Pope's face – 'I thought I'd done with this lot' – because he'd already had a hell of a day. And we had to explain. And it was then that I realised he didn't understand at all.

Runcie's original idea for the British visit had been for him and Cardinal Hume jointly to invite the Pope. But before he could do this Hume had, with Derek Worlock, been at Castel Gandolfo, where Hume had, 'rather on the spur of the moment', asked the Pope to come to Britain. John Paul accepted on the spot. According to Worlock's biographer there had even been prior, more complicated moves. In a long process that dated from the *Humanae Vitae* crisis in 1968, Worlock and Hume had in 1980 produced, as a result of the National Pastoral Congress in Liverpool, a document called *The Easter People*, the most controversial section of which frankly stated the English Catholic bishops' cautiously liberal views on marriage, contraception and divorce. They had been in Rome to present the Pope with his personal copy for the forthcoming synod on the family, but when Hume handed it across, deliberately opened at the page on birth control, and drew it to the Pope's attention, 'The Pope merely waved it to one side. It was an unfavourable omen. Yet the bishops' document was hardly radical. It declared unhesitatingly that "The encyclical *Humanae Vitae* is the authentic teaching of the Church".'

Worlock distanced himself from Hume's gesture in his account of the handing-over of their document, calling the Pope 'the symbol of unity: To him we said: "Here is our Church in England and Wales. Now, will you come to visit us?"'

Towards the time of the visit tension continued to mount. The Anglican bishops David Sheppard, and Hugh Sebag-Montefiore of Birmingham, voiced concerns; the first over John Paul's ultra-conservative stance on 'human relations and sexuality', and Schillebeeckx and Küng; Sebag-Montefiore feared that he might have to be present at a 'papal allocution in which there was wholesale condemnation of abortion, contraception, remarriage, or the marriage of the clergy'. Runcie wanted to organise a 'dream meeting of reconciliation' and wrote to Hume, suggesting an intimate meeting 'of the dozen or so Christian leaders of real account in the British Isles', at Leeds Castle, 'a place of great natural beauty . . . for a confidential meeting which would permit substantial conversation, over a dinner of Papal proportions . . .'

What did he mean by 'a dinner of Papal proportions'? Hume, for his part, was happy with this idea (which subsequently came to nothing), but voiced his mistaken suspicion that Queen Elizabeth was 'rather cool' about the visit. He worried that the Pope assisting 'at an Anglican Eucharist' might cause 'deep division among English Roman Catholics, who would feel that his presence could carry an implicit public recognition that an Anglican Eucharist is neither heretical nor schismatic'.

Runcie then sent Professor Henry Chadwick, a theologian from Cambridge, as a personal envoy to a pope who clearly relished the chance of a serious theological discussion:

> I explicitly mentioned that we had Protestants opposed to the Holy Father's visit [Chadwick reported back]. The Pope . . . asked me in what kind of honour Anglicans held the saints. I replied that we dedicated our churches to them and decorated them with likenesses of the saints in stained glass and in statues and other representations; that we celebrated the saints in our Calendar; that the Blessed Virgin Mary was celebrated in this way; that there were Anglicans for whom the honour of the Blessed Virgin was very important in their spiritual and devotional life, and others for whom this was not the case. I mentioned Walsingham [there are two shrines there of the Virgin, one Anglican].

A visit to Walsingham, because it was 'so tiny a place', would prove a 'logistic impossibility'. Pope John Paul accepted this judgement with obvious regret.

While the Pope impressed Chadwick with his warmth and enthusiasm, Chadwick found the Curia was intractable. He formed the impression that to the top administrators of the Roman Catholic church Anglicans had come to seem a bore. The Curia felt either that they would 'take them for a ride in a fast car and end up by publicly urging inter-communion in terms they are bound to reject', or that they would by ordaining women to the priesthood without prior ecumenical consultation 'trample on their corns in hobnailed boots'. The Anglican 'apparent insensitivity on this issue' astonished them, and confirmed their suspicions that 'we are at heart simply Liberal Protestants'. Finally, said Chadwick, 'The Holy Father frankly confessed to me that he could not at present imagine what kind of unity we could have with one another.'

Pastor John Glass of Glasgow, a notorious scourge of Romanism, agitated against the Pope visiting Scotland; loyalist paramilitaries threatened to wreak havoc with bombs and guns if he celebrated mass at Bellahouston Park. Mrs Thatcher, the Prime Minister, also a Methodist, did not to want the Pope to come (in 1980 she chaired a small committee considering the implications of Prince Charles marrying a Catholic. One member of this committee had been struck by the 'extreme anti-Catholicism which emerged from the Prime Minister's approach').

These manifestations of dissent apart, with some traditionalist British Catholics putting pressure on the Pope to cancel the visit to Canterbury, what did the Pope feel? Was he apprehensive about coming to Britain? The answer was yes: according to Frossard his advisers warned him that it was a terrible idea. 'The English are cold; all that fog makes them only more so; their education makes them snobbish; they will be polite but stand-offish.' But it says much for John Paul's heroic, Herculean ability to rise and embrace all these potential sources of gloom and pessimism, as well as taxing his physical and mental resources to the utmost – he was at the same time preoccupied with his country's state of undeclared war with Russia, – that he could, once again, apply his particular genius to unravelling a complex situation of danger, and turn it to good.

Suddenly the arrival of the Falklands War in April 1982 swept away ill omens and doubts. It became simply an issue of 'Would he come at all?' He very nearly did not.

With Margaret Thatcher's resolve to recapture the Falkland Islands, the British Catholics, led by the saintly but sometimes over-cautious Hume, appeared to have panicked, knowing only too well the dilemma in which Rome now found itself: John Paul, in coming to England would be setting foot in a Protestant democracy at war with a Latin-American Catholic dictatorship. Moreover, this robustly pacifist pope was well known to be anti-colonial, pro-Third World.

The Pope had directed the Vatican to advise publicly that the trip should be cancelled unless there was a ceasefire. This led to 'mutters at Lambeth about the pope being under the control of Argentinian fascists'. Hume and Cardinal Gordon Gray of Scotland flew out to Rome to implore him not to cancel the visit. ('We must make sure that the final decision as to whether he comes should not be left in the hands of the pope,' Worlock badgered Hume). To ease pressure on him the British government tactfully offered to withdraw any official participation of theirs in the event.

John Paul had defused in 1979 a conflict between Chile (Britain's unofficial ally) and Argentina, and he now asked the British cardinals and three Argentinian cardinals to celebrate with him in St Peter's Basilica a solemn 'reconciliation mass'. During this ceremony, he declared in his homily, 'Peace is an obligation, peace is a duty because all the inhabitants of the earth, wherever they were born, whatever the language in which they learned to express their thoughts and feelings, whatever the credo, political or religious, on which they base their lives, still belong to the one family of the human race.' The difficulties may seem insurmountable, he went on, but they could not prove so in reality. And here John Paul intervened to produce his master-stroke. At the end of this mass he announced that he would go to both Britain and Argentina. The British and Argentinian prelates had to pledge themselves to peace and reconciliation.

Next he sent identical messages to Margaret Thatcher and President Leopoldo Galtieri. But still neither would give way over the fighting. The Pope kept everyone guessing. Finally, only a few days before he flew to Britain, he confirmed that he would go, insisting that his visit should have, as well as a dominantly pastoral nature, a theological theme. Perhaps the nearness of the sound of clashing swords, in Yeats's phrase, prompted a peaceful celebration of the seven sacraments and the avoidance of any lectures on doctrine or politics; he made clear his desire to meet again Queen Elizabeth II, who in October 1980 had called on him in Rome, adding her weight to the invitation.

John Paul touched down at Gatwick at 8 a.m. on Friday 28 May, proceeded straight to mass at Westminster Cathedral (where he baptised four people), and then to a private meeting with the Queen at Buckingham Palace. Runcie eloquently underlined the bond and sympathy that the Pope and the Queen felt in one another's presence: the duty and awareness both carried had a symbolic importance that it was the prime duty of their personalities and faith to uphold in the world. They weren't, in the deepest sense, private persons.

The Queen, Runcie told Humphrey Carpenter, was a person of formal personal piety, which she shared with Prince Charles. Runcie did not 'fully understand her, but that's part of her secret': she would seem, sometimes, to forget she was head of his church, while 'At moments of either high drama or pressure on me, like the papal visit . . . she always went out of her way to encourage – it may have been indirectly, by an invitation to do something; it may have been by a chance word.'

When he met the Queen, John Paul, with his geniality and calm, made her feel at ease. Both managed, as Runcie said of the Queen, 'to combine the mystique and informality which sprang from her own deep sense of vocation'. But while she often made Runcie feel uncomfortable because 'her shyness makes it hard to relax in her presence' and because she created 'a feeling of uncertainty', John Paul registered no such misgivings. They were filmed together walking along the corridors of the palace. Vincent Nichols, there as an official commentator, observed that the Pope showed a remarkable understanding and affinity with the Queen. 'Here was an immediate rapport between two people who understood the cost of duty.'

In his six-day visit John Paul called at Birmingham, Manchester, where he ordained a fair number of priests, and Coventry, where a young nun, Sister Joanna, later to become abbess of the Benedictine Stanbrook Abbey, remembered how young and vigorous he looked when he arrived at the airport: 'His sheer energy and that feeling of being with people of God made it like a great big birthday party.' The Stanbrook nuns had left at 3.30 a.m. and arrived in Coventry at 5 to await his arrival. The Pope stepped out of his plane at 10. People were there from all over the world. Sister Joanna was lost in wonder: 'He's amazing . . . a lot of his energy is prayer life.'

The highlight of the trip was the Canterbury encounter with Runcie, who met him from his helicopter on a school playing field. The Pope was conspicuously amazed at the sunshine, and as they approached gazed in wonder at the splendour of the cathedral. Runcie and the

Pope drove into Canterbury, which the Pope compared to Krakow. Entering the cathedral, a moving moment for both with its 'enormous explosion of welcome and praise which drowned the choir', Runcie noticed the Pope did not bless anyone in the crowd but expected him to do the blessing. Then 'The two men knelt together in silence'. At the end of the shared service, 'As the Pope approached former Primates Lord Coggan and Lord Ramsey there was a glance of recognition when he spotted them. He kissed Lord Coggan first, and then moved on to Lord Ramsey, both men seeming to give each other a great bear hug, and the crowd spontaneously reacted by applauding.'

Finally, primate and pope prayed side by side just near the spot where Becket was murdered.

In Liverpool the Pope visited both the Anglican and Catholic cathedrals. Along the route of his British Leyland lorry decked out as a popemobile, anti-papal Paisleyites waved placards on which was painted: ANYONE BLESSED BY THE POPE IS CONDEMNED TO HELL. The Pope turned towards one, and with a mischievous twinkle in his eye gave the Paisleyites a blessing.

From Liverpool to Wembley Park, where he celebrated mass, with his remarkable presence and flair for gesture and human contact, the tide of ordinary humanity turned in his favour, and the crowds, including thousands of young people, flocked to see him. This did not appeal to all. On the Sunday of the visit, the controller of BBC Television, according to Vincent Nichols, stamped his foot, petulantly declaring, 'I will not have two papal masses on the same day on British TV!'

John Paul flew to Edinburgh (embracing the moderator of the Church of Scotland in front of John Knox's statue) and Glasgow, and finally Wales, where in Cardiff, after expressing surprise that it was not raining, and after celebrating mass, he said goodbye in Welsh and left for Rome. Everywhere he went he met the Polish communities in exile.

After the Canterbury service, Runcie had persuaded the Pope to take a short rest: 'In Canterbury a Pope obeys,' John Paul quipped. While he was resting in the deanery, Prince Charles, in the absence of being formally invited, stole in on him rather unexpectedly, coming face to face with a somewhat mystified leader of the world's billion Catholics.

According to Runcie, Charles behaved awkwardly. Overwhelmed, he sat silently in the Pope's presence, while John Paul, too polite to rouse or admonish him as he would a friend, pondered on the nature of this royal prince. There was no rapport, which Runcie later ascribed to the Pope's poor briefing.

> It was a slightly awkward conversation [Runcie observed with tactful understatement]. It didn't really gel . . . The pope was trying to work out how he fitted in – whether he'd come, as the representative of the royal family, to keep an eye on me [Runcie]! And Prince Charles [was] feeling that it was going to be quite a big step to get on to sort of Laurens van der Post territory.

'There is no hiding,' Vincent Nichols said to me of the Pope. 'If you're looked at, you know you're seen.' In view of Runcie making the connection with van der Post, and van der Post's hypocritical professions of faith (subsequently unmasked by a biographer), perhaps John Paul might have thought that here, too, was a prince of sensitive, unresolved contradictions. The Pope gave Charles the small but customary gift of a rosary. The unscheduled meeting, proving to be a damp squib, left John Paul bemused.

Prince Charles remained in awe of the papal visitor. Later on a visit to Rome he was forbidden by his mother to attend papal mass. In 1995 the Duke of Kent sent the Queen a Christmas card of his newly converted Catholic wife being received by the Pope. It shocked the Queen Mother to whom, according to a palace source, sending a picture of the Pope was 'worse than sending a picture of the devil'. The Princess of Wales again allegedly considered conversion.

Shockingly – for that age anyway – in the same year a royal servant revealed that Charles had a photograph of Mrs Camilla Parker Bowles, his mistress, beside his bed. Even more striking, perhaps, the media failed to give attention to another object on the bedside table, the rosary given to Charles by John Paul during his 1982 visit to Canterbury, which lay beside Camilla's picture. Thirty years before, evidence that a future supreme governor of the Church of England could treasure such a gift from a Roman pope could well have triggered the residual suspicion of popes; a hundred years before it might have provoked something far worse: 'Protestants do not count beads.'

With the Canterbury Cathedral ecumenical service duplicated all over the world, Runcie professed himself pleased with the visit, although he complained that John Paul 'did not appreciate moral ambiguities which arise from living in a free society, and the further responsibility that God puts in our hands'. (One can almost imagine Screwtape writing this to his nephew as a means to entrap the Christian in sin – at all costs get him to 'appreciate the moral ambiguities which arise from living in a free society', etc . . .)

The forecasts for the English visit had been dire but the Pope had paid no attention.

> One might have said [wrote the sceptical Frossard] that England had been repopulated overnight by Neapolitans. The Pope walked with short, dignified steps and drew precise, tiny crosses in the air when he gave people his blessing. Amid the unexpected warmth of the huge mobs of cheering Anglo-Saxons, he was the only one acting like a Brit. His pilgrimages knit up, thread by thread, the ravelled sleeve of Christianity that in the past had a tendency to come apart at the seams.

Visiting England, Wojtyla said, had been one of his favourite journeys, although overshadowed by a war that he did not hold back in denouncing. 'Today the scale and horror of modern warfare – whether nuclear or not – makes it totally unacceptable as a means of settling differences between nations.' On the plane back to Rome, when a reporter asked about St Augustine's theory that under certain circumstances war could be justified he answered that the whole notion of a just war might have been rendered obsolete by technology. But he liked the fact that the British, like the Irish and the Polish, were eccentric and had a sense of humour.

Most of the British, even after the Pope's visit, still maintained they believed in God without ever doing much about it – like going to church. Even the atheist Richard Dawkins (author of *The Selfish Gene*) could not assert the value of science over religion without invoking the authority of religious images and imagery (in *A Devil's Chaplain*, 2003), and he admitted the Pope was one of his heroes. Like Samuel Beckett's character Hamm in *Endgame*, the very blasphemous often asserted what they vehemently denied: '[God] The bastard! He doesn't exist!' Cardinal Murphy-O'Connor told me that it was Wojtyla's policy to leave the British to themselves: 'He thinks we're a balanced church.'

With John Paul's good fortune for being in the right place at the

The two Polish
cardinals
(Wyszynski, *left*) visit
Germany, 1978.

The protégé: Wojtyla with
Pope Paul VI.

With Pope John Paul I in 1978.

The new Pope
John Paul II
embraces
Cardinal
Wyszynski:
'Without you and
your faith there
would be no
Polish pope.'

God's athlete: the cover of
L'Europeo, 1979.

Papal kiss for a young girl, France, 1986.

To Dublin by Alitalia: inside the Pope's plane, 1979.

Praying at the Auschwitz Death Wall, 1979.

Kissing the ground as he arrives on French soil, 1980.

Knock, Eire: an estimated half million await the Pope, 1979.

The assassination attempt, St Peter's Square, 13 May 1981: Agça's Browning pistol circled left.

The wounded John Paul II is transported to the Gemelli Hospital.

The Pope meets Ali Agça, his would-be assassin, 1983.

Kneeling in Rakowice Cemetery at his mother and father's grave.

Contemplating the tapestry of the Christian Auschwitz martyr, Maximilian Kolbe, Poland, 1983.

With General Jaruzelski, 1987.

The Pope greets Lech Walesa, 1989, just before Solidarity is elected to power.

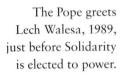

The lone skier, Italian Alps, 1984.

John Paul II embraces Aids sufferer Brendon Rourke, aged four, San Francisco, 1987.

With Prince Charles and
Archbishop Runcie in
Canterbury, 1982.

With the Dalai Lama in the Pope's Vatican
library, 1990.

With Mother Teresa in Albania,
1993.

Queen Elizabeth II received in Rome, 2000.

With President Clinton,
St Louis, 1999.

The inauguration of the restored Sistine Chapel on
the eve of the Millennium.

right time the 1982 visit, and the visit to Argentina eight days later, coincided with the end of the Falklands War and the defeat of Argentina. He spent more time getting there and back in the air than on its native soil. On his arrival his plane taxied to the wrong spot, forcing bishops dashing across the tarmac to clutch their cassocks 'like', as one reporter said, 'characters from a Fellini film'.

His thirty-hour stay with its peace pageant in Plaza España, Buenos Aires, with 120 Latin-American bishops and 1,700 priests, was more in the nature of consoling the wounded pride of the vanquished – on 12 June, his last full day, the final victims of the war fell – than suing for peace. He then set out from Rome to Geneva almost immediately for an international labour conference. Between mid-February and mid-June 1982, four months, he had visited eight countries on three continents, completely happy, noted one commentator in 'his element of quasi-perpetual motion'.

23

What Do They Think I Said Next?

(1983)

> The limits of my language are the limits of my world.
> Wittgenstein

In 1983, Karol Wojtyla practised what others so often preach without doing anything about it. Acting as the 'visibility [meaning man] of the invisible [meaning God]', he set off to forgive his enemy, the man who had tried to kill him.

Just after Christmas John Paul visited the Rebibbia Prison on the north bank of the Tiber, where Ali Agça was serving his life sentence. Six months before, Emanuela Orlandi, a fifteen-year-old girl, had been kidnapped from her family home in Rome. Her father was a Vatican worker. Unconfirmed reports say that a demand was telephoned to Casaroli that the girl would only be returned safe if the Pope intervened with President Pertini to release Agça from prison.

Next day Agça gave a television interview (surely connected with the kidnapping) in which he stated – presumably with the fear he would not survive in freedom, or more simply in his own paranoid version – that the Virgin of Fatima, who saved the Pope, would take her revenge on him if he were set at large. He felt he very much wanted to stay in prison. Asked about Emanuela, he answered, 'She was kidnapped for my freedom. But it wasn't an intelligent action, and it failed.'

John Paul was saved from making an agonising decision, although it is more than likely he would have asked Pertini to pardon Agça, and Pertini would have said no. Twenty years later no one knows what happened to the hapless, innocent Emanuela, but the case has not been closed.

Stubble on his face, his black hair tightly cropped, Ali Agça invited his distinguished visitor into his cell with a deep bow saying, with a shade of irony, 'This is my home.' Those who watched through the cell grille heard no more as Agça took the hand John Paul offered, bent over and kissed it, then lay his forehead against the back of the Pope's hand (an Islamic gesture). He led John Paul to the back of his small cell and the two men sat down closely together, neither moving more than a fraction of an inch. The Pope lightly tapped Agça's knee with his right hand as if to say 'Now let's talk', and for the thirty minutes they were left alone the Pope held on to Agça's arm as he bent over and whispered into his ear in what was construed as a symbolic gesture of forgiveness: Agça was hidden behind the profile of the Pope, so no one could see those 'shifty eyes with a weird glint'. They spoke in Italian, which Agça had learned in prison. Skilled lip-readers claimed they caught or interpreted some of what the Pope said, and that his first question was: 'Who wanted me dead?'

When Frossard relayed this to the Pope on his visit to Castel Gandolfo, he shrugged. Frossard judged 'that couldn't have been right'.

'What do they think I said next?' the Pope asked Frossard.

'Next, they say you asked, "Who sent you?"'

'No shrug this time. So they were wrong on the first question but right on the second. The Pope neither confirmed nor denied it, and I could learn nothing more. There was only silence.'

When others asked the Pope, he told them: 'What we spoke about is a secret between us. I spoke to him as I would to a brother whom I have pardoned and who enjoys my trust.' Later, in a private audience the Pope received Murzeyen Aga, Agça's mother.

In June 1984, a year after the Pope's Rebibbia visit the sensational trial of Sergei Antonov, the Bulgarian airline official and two other Bulgarians and five Turks charged with funding Agça, booking his *pensione* room, planning his best firing position in St Peter's Square, and organising his getaway, began in Rome. The indictment, drawn up from thirty volumes of depositions (25,000 pages), ran to 1,243 pages. The outcome, after twenty-two months, was acquittal for a now-debilitated and 'psychologically disturbed' accused, and the others charged, on the grounds of 'lack of proof'.

The papal nuncio in Sofia told the press in November 1992 that John Paul 'certainly knows the whole truth though I believe he is not anxious to throw light on that entire background. John Paul II is convinced his life was saved miraculously.' Two years later Joachim Navarro-Valls, the Vatican press secretary, said that Agça had reversed his earlier position and now believed, having served a long enough sentence, that he should be set free. Agça, bearded and moustached, in one of his regular annual interviews, pronounced in May of 1992 that it was 'pointless to keep speculating and looking for secret plans and plots. The truth is that on that day not even I knew why I shot . . . I might have done it to make history'.

In bringing to an end, or concluding, this particular endgame I have little doubt that as ever Wojtyla, the inner man, in his talk with the 'grey wolf' as the press nicknamed him, must have reflected his own earlier concerns with language and how everything began with the word that was made flesh. The Old Testament character Ham, son of Noah, seeing his father naked, is symbolically blinded by what he has seen; his subsequent behaviour is to attempt to deny or undo God's commandment to be fruitful, multiply and replenish the earth. Wasn't there in Agça's errant assumption that he had to administer justice himself, that sometimes he was Jesus of the Messiah, something of this too?

Maybe one question Karol asked his attacker was why Agça had not achieved his aim. By any reckoning, visiting Agça was an extraordinary thing to do, perhaps the most extraordinary and revealing moment of the Pope's whole life – of the very essence of that life – because it became, all at once and at the same instant, a public media event, a symbolic act of drama, a personal encounter, and a deeply private if not secret event for which the Pope had undergone long and painstaking preparation in his imitation of Christ.

24

Now for the Polish Endgame

(1983–90)

It is God who has won in Eastern Europe!
John Paul II

Over the part played by any one individual as a shaping force in historical change, and the extent to which those forces are inevitable or predestined, and find or select the right human agents to implement them, there will be debate to the end of time. Tolstoy, in *War and Peace*, dealing with similarly epic characters in a period of international war and political turmoil, holds to the view that 'the activity of these people interested me only as an illustration of the law of predetermination which in my opinion guides history, and of that psychological law which compels a man who commits actions under the greatest compulsion, to supply in his imagination a whole series of retrospective reflections to prove his freedom to himself'.

At Wojtyla's election Alexander Solzhenitsyn told an Italian journalist that 'The election of Pope Wojtyla is the only good thing that has happened to humanity in the twentieth century.' The 1980s, both before and after the failed attempt to kill him, were Wojtyla's main period as an uncontested, so-called world leader holding centre-stage in the main political upheaval of the age, the collapse of the Soviet Union.

Was this a deliberate move on his part, a seizure of opportunities to take the initiative in this monumental endgame? The case can be made, and has been many times, for his heroic intervention and control of events, using Vatican intelligence, the intermediaries of priests and the use of a personal network. A number of critical moments in this progress towards Polish freedom do suggest Wojtyla wielded a commanding influence, and to adapt the adage 'How many divisions has the Pope?' he appeared to have had more divisions than the Polish and Russian armies combined.

The 1956 turning-point in the Polish state–church relationship, with Gomulka's creation of a *modus vivendi* with Wyszynski (both released from prison at the same time), had brought with it not only the release of imprisoned clergy but freedom to publish Catholic views, the permission to repair churches, and even, if a permit was granted, to build new ones. In the 1960s the Polish church, under strict Communist supervision, was set to expand in a manner unprecedented in any European country. In spite of Khrushchev's boast to the West 'We will bury you', Soviet tanks or Stalinist Poles could not defeat more than a thousand years of Christianity in Poland, nor eradicate the two centuries during which it had been, and continued to be, the sole source and basis of national values. Gomulka tried to hold propaganda meetings of the Communist faithful: the crowds reached a quarter of a million; but Wyszynski called into being rallies twice that size. From now on the church was to demand mass on television, a daily genuinely Catholic newspaper and uncensored access to media. The Catholic majority, an estimated thirty million who attended 14,000 churches, wanted religious education, job equality with Communist Party members, legal recognition. But carefully – and Wojtyla was to become master of this – paying lip service to so-called socialism and allowing Gomulka and his successors to appease the Moscow puppet-masters, the church trod the narrow road between confrontation and capitulation brilliantly.

If Poland's leader Edward Gierek should give the new pope in 1978 permission to visit Poland in 1979, had written the *Telegraph* correspondent John Miller at the time, 'it could prove to be one of the great decisions of East European bloc politicians'. General Wojciech Jaruzelski, the defence minister (about whom Polish wits asked, 'Do you know why Jaruzelski always wears protective glasses?' 'No.' 'Because he's trying to weld Poland to the Soviet Union'), was highly apprehensive about the effect of Wojtyla's election.

Like all the other Polish leaders of the day, Jaruzelski confessed he had 'conflicting emotions'. He felt satisfaction and pride at having a Pole on the throne of Peter and hoped it would help the 'international standing of our country'. But he was also worried that the election of Wojtyla would increase the influence of the Roman Catholic church, 'making it a yet more problematic partner'.

With hindsight he discovered that concern was unfounded. 'Successive contacts have shown me that not only does the Pope have a very clear understanding of what is happening in Poland, but he sees it in relation to what is happening in the rest of the world.' So John Paul saw the faults of the system that prevailed in Poland, but was 'also critical of the state of affairs elsewhere, in the capitalist world for a start'. Zbigniew Brzezinski, President Carter's adviser on Eastern Europe, also confirmed how political the Pope's thinking was. While the Pope told him that meeting with Carter had made him feel 'two religious leaders were consulting together', Brzezinski's view was very different, finding Wojtyla 'a man of extraordinary vision and political intelligence', especially his understanding that 'Western man does crave a sense of direction which is firmly and clearly defined'.

On Wojtyla's first visit as pope he had criticised the country's rulers only implicitly, as if by his warmth and appreciation he was encouraging Communism to put on a human face. (A token example was the genuine surprise he caused by spontaneously thanking government security guards.) When the Pope left again for Rome Jaruzelski stood by President Jablonski's side. 'It was moving to see Wojtyla and Jablonski embracing, with tears on their cheeks, but in our situation things can't change all that quickly or easily,' commented a middle-aged Varsovian. Shown a front-page picture of the embrace, a waitress in a Krakow restaurant could not believe her eyes. 'Heavens,' she said, 'times *are* changing.'

There was truth in both reactions. To some extreme anti-Communist campaigners and many Catholics, the Pope's stance looked threatening, like an unholy alliance between two authoritarian systems of thought – Christian Catholicism and atheistic Marxist-Leninism. But the relationship between Catholicism and Communism in Poland could not remain static.

The central question [as Mieczyslaw Rakowski, later Poland's last Communist prime minister, wrote] was whether the two were to advance on a collision course, or whether the pope had succeeded in starting a process of parallel progress towards a society in which commonsense co-operation made built-in ideological conflict tolerable to live with. If that happened, the eventual impact on Eastern Europe and on Marxist attitudes in general could be of immense importance.

These hopes were dashed on 14 August 1980 when workers at the Lenin shipyard in Gdansk locked the gates behind them and declared an 'occupational strike'. They were unhappy that Anna Walentynowicz, a crane operator, had been transferred to another job because of her activism, and demanded her reinstatement. And they had found a leader, a devout Catholic father of six who preached religion as much as labour freedom: Lech Walesa, thirty-seven years of age, a former shipyard electrician, who had already been arrested frequently for demanding a free trade-union movement. In accordance with the Polish observance of symbols, he wore on his coat lapel the image of the Black Madonna of Czestochowa. Bizarre as it must seem to the secular leaders of unions in Western countries, one of the first things the workers did upon striking was to erect on the gates and fences of the Lenin shipyard huge portraits of the Pope and the Madonna, and yellow-and-white Vatican flags. (Some supporters of Solidarity also had close links with the Warsaw rising of 1944: 'They saw themselves as true heirs of the Home Army.')

Every day the strikers flooded in to worship at masses held in the shipyards' courtyard. One sizeable poster proclaimed, 'The Madonna is on strike', while workers elsewhere in Poland stopped work in sympathy. How different could you get from thirteen years earlier in Paris when students and workers similarly brought their country to a standstill with slogans such as 'Don't come back, God, the world is crumbling round you' and 'The more I make revolution, the more I make love'. God had made a comeback, or as Walesa expressed it, the church 'survives under totalitarian regimes because a supernatural ideal sustains its existence'. The ideal of the followers of Daniel Cohn-Bendit, the 1968 French leader, was far from supernatural.

Although the Soviets – its crisis managers including not only President Brezhnev but Gromyko as foreign minister and Politburo chiefs Chernenko and Gorbachev – put immense pressure on Gierek to crack down on Solidarity and the nationwide strike with force, Gierek chose negotiation with the workers and the church. He sought to meet Wyszynski and secure the help of the church, in return pledging 'I shall not allow the use of force against the workers on the coast.'

In August at Czestochowa the sermon Wyszynski had delivered, calling for 'national and civic maturity' and warning strikers about long-term effects, was interpreted as telling the workers to end the strike on the regime's terms. The primate insisted this was not the case, that Polish television had twisted his meaning when he only meant 'pilgrims' should resume work after the annual ceremony. But in Castel Gandolfo, where Wojtyla was on holiday, a communiqué on the sermon allegedly drove him to react angrily and, in front of two visiting Polish priests, to exclaim, anger etched in his face, 'Oh, this old man . . . This old man!' – with the clear implication the primate had become out of touch with events. However, the union had won concessions and Walesa signed the 31 August Gdansk protocol with a large felt tip pen on which John Paul's image was prominently displayed.

In the time-honoured practice of papal asceticism and neutrality popes had to renounce any bias of nationality. Pius XII had even gone to the extent in his homilies and addresses of calling Italy 'Your Italy'. John Paul had similarly to keep his distance while each crisis-stage of the Polish 'High Noon' or endgame exploded, creating new fears, doubts and possibilities.

On Sunday 7 December 1980 at 11.30 p.m. Brzezinski telephoned the main Vatican number and asked to speak to the Pope ('I do not know if the Pope had ever been phoned from the US'). Dziwisz summoned the Pope, who within forty-five seconds was on the line. Brzezinski told him that East German, Czech and Russian tanks and columns (eighteen divisions in all) drawn up along the East German and Russian borders, and a powerful northern group of Soviet troops stationed in Poland, were poised to invade and intervene.

While President Carter, Giscard d'Estaing, Helmut Schmidt and Indira Gandhi pleaded with Brezhnev on hotline teleprinters to call off the invasion, one report claimed that the Pope wrote a personal letter in French, dated 16 December, to the Soviet leader, threatening that if the Soviets invaded Poland, 'he would relinquish the throne of St Peter and return to stand at the barricades with his fellow Poles'. Brezhnev delayed while Jaruzelski, in Moscow, convinced the Kremlin to cancel immediate plans, claiming he could deal with the crisis through political measures and, if necessary, martial law. (At this time too, the Pope had plenty more on his mind, for religious war between Christians and Muslims raged in the Lebanon, while Iran and Iraq were locked in murderous genocidal conflict.)

The next event of consequence had happened in the Vatican, when on 19 January 1981 the Pope met Lech Walesa, his wife Danuta and a thirteen-strong Solidarity team, which included the shipyard celebrant, Father Jankowski, and the crane operator whose removal from Gdansk had sparked off the strike. Also present was Tadeusz Mazowiecki, a Catholic intellectual and old friend of John Paul who later became Poland's first premier of a freely elected government. The Pope's stance was one of support for the expression of freedom and the long-suppressed rights of the Polish workers. Nothing new or unduly inflammatory here, but his position as a vessel or repository of spiritual power – and this power had also a high content of political muscle – served to underpin the aspirations of the Polish people. Like de Gaulle in the Second World War he had become the expatriate rallying point for an occupied or foreign-dominated nation, and he used this prestige shrewdly, never overstepping the mark. Everyone knew he stood for the rights of the Polish workers, but in public his statements radiated calm and caution. For example, 'There does not exist and there should not exist any contradiction between an autonomous social initiative such as Solidarity and the structure of a system that pertains to labour.'

In 1979 in Poland he had told the thousands of journalists who covered his triumphant progress, 'You have brought the whole world to Poland.' Now the whole world looked to the Pope as fear of Russian intervention again increased by the hour. Anticipating this, in March 1981 the Pope sent a telegram to Wyszynski: 'The Polish people have an inalienable right to solve their problems by themselves, by their own power.' He wrote again privately to Brezhnev, reminding him of the Helsinki human-rights charter to which Russia had been a signatory. The astute pressure he applied became an enabling, rather than confrontational, force, for above all his desire was to avoid bloodshed. To this end Walesa was persuaded to make a tactical withdrawal, with the seriously ill Wyszynski kneeling in tears before a reluctant Walesa in order to make him call off the threatened general strike: Walesa called it 'emotional blackmail'.

Wyszynski died on 28 May 1981. In Poland the world stood still, unresolved but daily more fraught with danger until December. Mikhail Gorbachev, not yet in power but later the fourth elected general secretary in three years, perceived in a cautious way what had been happening.

Poland was in a grave crisis, he said, through weakness and indecision on the part of the Polish leadership. But more serious than this, 'The imposition of a socio-political model alien to Poland – albeit greatly altered and partially adapted to national conditions – had run into opposition . . . At first the discontent was of a passive nature and found an outlet in jokes about the authorities.' As the years passed, the crisis had worsened more while, to top it all, the country recklessly amassed a colossal hard-currency debt to the West. Gorbachev recognised that 'Poland was essentially the first to enter the stage that could be called the general crisis of socialism.'

The Soviet leadership feverishly sought a solution between what were to them two equally unacceptable positions: the acceptance of chaos in Poland and the ensuing break-up of the entire socialist camp; or armed intervention by the same forces as before – 'all these could be put in motion' said Gorbachev: 'In this situation, Wojciech Jaruzelski, who had replaced S. Kania as First Secretary of the PUWP Central Committee in October 1981 . . . decided on what he considered the lesser evil.'

On 12 December at 11.57 p.m., 3.4 million telephones went dead and with roadblocks set up in every town, columns of Polish tanks entered Warsaw: martial law had been imposed, crushing Solidarity, with opposition leaders and labour militants imprisoned *en masse*. John Paul commented privately over the indefensible arrest of more than 10,000 people that the country was now a 'vast concentration camp', while at Christmas he lit a candle in his Vatican flat window to show his solidarity with 'suffering nations'.

Gorbachev confirmed that the clampdown had been administrative rather than military. Indeed only nine people were killed compared with the Gdansk uprising in 1970 when forty-eight died. These were miners who clashed with troops in the Wujek coal mine, but to the Poles, with the detention within twenty-four hours of 10,554 opposition leaders, labour activists, actors, artists and intellectuals, it was all too familiar a scenario. They called it a 'state of war'. John Paul did not delay but wrote immediately to Jaruzelski, who ostensibly had taken this action, appearing in uniform on television against Poland's red and white flag, with the Polish eagle in the middle, announcing the dramatic move in his hard, dry voice. From then on John Paul increasingly conferred with Cardinal Jozef Glemp, the new Polish primate, a church lawyer and administrator who at thirteen years of age, during the Nazi terror, had done heavy labour in the fields. On Wyszynski's death, he had appointed Glemp and together with him and Cardinal Macharski, his influential successor in Krakow, they positioned the church carefully in its dealings with the government.

In the evolution from 'state of war' to a negotiated peace Jaruzelski now became the key figure. He was, in his own retrospective words, convinced that he had made the pre-emptive move to rescue Poland from Soviet intervention, and claimed credit for 'saving' his country.

But Anatoly Gribkov, at the time a joint chief of staff of the Warsaw Pact countries, subsequently maintained Jaruzelski asked Russia to intervene militarily and, when it refused, this upset Jaruzelski, who then accused his Soviet comrades of betraying an old friendship. Jaruzelski, in this comedy of errors in which each side accused the other of having got hold of the wrong end of the stick, insisted on an entirely different version of events, claiming that this 'was the reassurance I sought not the reply I feared'.

Whatever the truth of the situation, Polish people by now seemed to be treating martial law with a cavalier, humorous contempt, making endless jokes about the regime. Far from being enforced in Soviet fashion, the nightly curfew met with disorganised tolerance, the casual, laid-back approach the Polish shared with southern Europeans. Jerzy Kisielewski tells of an incident when, returning home after a day working on his newspaper, he

> got into a taxi and the driver, without so much as looking at my face, went on listening to the radio as he drove.
>
> I started to listen too, rather abstractedly. I noticed something wrong, then realised what it was. The driver was tuned into Radio Free Europe, owned by the American government and transmitted from Monaco. Absolutely forbidden officially. The driver had no idea who I was, I could easily have been a plain-clothes policeman. But he wasn't worried. Everyone knew that the risks – terrible in theory – were negligible in practice.

Others claimed that intellectuals deliberately invited arrest to boost their anti-Jaruzelski credentials. An arrest on the orders of the armed forces would be challenged by the police who, from having been a 'revolutionary militia' were now simply the professional guardians of law and order, and bitter rivals of the army. From his palace of Pankow in East Berlin, Erich Honecker, the extreme hardline leader of East Germany, who spent ten years in a Nazi prison, protested,

'Our Polish comrades are not doing enough to repress criminals. If they need assistance from us, we are willing to lend them a hand.'

Later still Jaruzelski, unhappy, embittered, became the target of another widespread joke which began with him complaining to his driver about his inexplicable unpopularity: 'It would take a miracle to make the Polish people love me,' he moaned.

The driver, in secret a devout Catholic and a member of Solidarity, relays the conversation to his guardian angel. The angel has a word with the general. 'Leave it to me, Mr President. I'll give you the power to perform a miracle. You will walk on water.' So early one morning the general and his driver go to the banks of the Vistula. Jaruzelski tries to put one foot in the water. To his surprise, the foot stays on the surface. He tries with the other foot. Same result. So he sets off, walking on the water. As they stand near by, enjoying a glass of beer, two fishermen, typically irreverent Varsovians, spot him. 'Hey look! That's Jaruzelski,' says one. 'So it is,' says the other. 'How pathetic! Can't even swim.'

In August 1982 Jaruzelski had stopped Wojtyla travelling to Poland to celebrate the 600th anniversary of the shrine of Our Lady of Czestochowa. Two months later on 10 October the Pope canonised Maximilian Kolbe, in St Peter's Square; the Russians saw the fevered response with which the Poles also honoured their martyr as a manifestation of growing Polish unrest. Tass, the official Soviet news agency, accused the Pope of fomenting subversive activity in Communist countries, causing the political crisis in Poland, and spreading anti-Communistic propaganda on a vast scale.

But all the while the Vatican negotiated with Poland's rulers, while Jaruzelski's line towards the church softened as he increasingly realised that the only way out of the deadlock or 'state of war' was, in spite of Soviet threats, to offer more concessions, and even to allow the planned but delayed papal visit to happen in 1983. So, surprisingly to the West, Lech Walesa was freed from internment, while the 'state of war' was put on hold if not formally ended.

Meantime a myth had formed, or begun to circulate, that in these years a 'holy alliance' between President Reagan and John Paul had been devised in secret, whose aim was nothing less than the collapse of Communism (what Reagan called the 'evil empire') in Eastern Europe. In later years this became the central contention of several papal biographies and countless commentators, but mainly Philip Schweizer in *Victory*, and Carl Bernstein and Marco Politi in *His Holiness: John Paul II and the Hidden History of Our Time*.

The thesis of Bernstein and Politi was that Reagan and the Pope had formed an intimate relationship to support Solidarity. Was there any truth in this? Five days after his British visit, and shortly before he left for Argentina, John Paul saw Reagan for forty-five minutes – a Vatican source says the meeting only 'lasted half an hour' – and Reagan dozed off during it. Bernstein, of Watergate fame, first claimed in a *Time* cover article that this meeting, in which the two leaders agreed to undertake a 'clandestine campaign to hasten the dissolution of the communist empire' was a turning-point in world history. It came just after Reagan failed to halt a pipeline bringing Soviet natural gas to Western Europe, and this setback supplied Reagan with strong motivation to take any anti-Soviet action he could (incidentally the Pope was against Reagan on the pipeline measure).

The Holy See denied the strong connection of the Pope with Reagan. Tad Szulc, reliable in his biography of John Paul on this issue, dismisses the theories about the Pope's close political involvement with Poland, but concedes the Vatican, with John Paul's knowledge, did contribute financially to Solidarity and other opposition forces in Poland. Cardinal Krol of Philadelphia vehemently denied he met, as was claimed, the then CIA director William Casey frequently 'to discuss support for Solidarity and covert operations' – 'I never sat independently with Casey,' he said. Zbigniew Brzezinski, retained as Reagan's national security adviser, said of Bernstein's article: 'Baloney! The pope wouldn't discuss that kind of stuff, and Reagan never got into that kind of detail.' As for Schweizer's 'leaked fabrication' about financial support ($8 million pumped into Solidarity by the CIA), the reverse was true: the United States, Polish-American private donations apart, refused to help, which awoke much fury among Poles. Apart from generous Italian and Vatican financial help, one of Solidarity's main backers was the anti-American French trade-union movement. Bohdan Cywinski, a Varsovian anti-Communist academic who skied with Wojtyla when he was a bishop, and disputed with him his tough standards of morality about sex, claimed that at this time the Pope 'was very distant from and distrustful of the United States'.

Some of Solidarity's support – no one knows how much, and how it was channelled – came from the Vatican Bank (the IOR or Institute of Religious Works), which became involved in the 1980s in shady operations with the Roman Banco Ambrosiano. This bank's chairman, Roberto Calvi, popularly known as 'God's Banker', was, on 18 June 1982, five days after John Paul's return from Argentina, found by an employee of the London *Daily Express*, hanging dead from scaffolding under Blackfriars Bridge. The sensational collapse of the Banco Ambrosiano swiftly followed the suicide or suspected murder of Calvi (still unsolved in 2005). The IOR was a guarantor for a huge amount of the bank's debts, and the Vatican head of the IOR, now Archbishop Marcinkus, the Pope's bodyguard and foreign-tour supremo (who famously said, 'You can't run the church on Hail Marys'), faced criminal charges which could not be pressed, as he was a Vatican employee and immune from Italian prosecution.

Calvi had undoubtedly been close to the Vatican, while some pointed out – in the abundance of speculation and fanciful conspiracy theories unleashed by the scandal – the symbolic choice of bridge ('black friar' = a Dominican priest, follower of St Thomas, therefore in some minds connected with Rome and the Vatican).

One reported episode was that the Pope was photographed naked beside his swimming pool installed in Castel Gandolfo. Licio Belli, leader of the P2 Masonic lodge that figures largely in the Calvi affair, allegedly told Vanni Nistico, a Socialist party press officer, on producing these photographs, 'Look at the problems the secret services have. If it's possible to take these pictures of the pope, imagine how easy it is to shoot him.' No one knew, if they really existed, what became of the pictures. John Paul was exposed to intimations of intrigue and insinuations that seemed bizarre when revealed in accounts of the Calvi mystery.

Calvi believed Marcinkus had given Solidarity money, and, according to him, that if the Soviets knew, it could provoke reprisals: it was reported that he told Marcinkus, 'If it comes out that you are giving money to Solidarity, there won't be a stone left of St Peter's.' The Pope stonewalled the various allegations at first, then reluctantly concurred with Marcinkus's 'retirement' to Phoenix, Arizona, where he played golf and refused to discuss the crash and his dismissal with anyone. He made no personal gain and had only the church's interests at heart, and was perhaps blamed too much for events over which he could have had little control. Later, in a rare admission, he told the *Catholic News Service* about the IOR scandal, 'There is no way I can get away from it. It is like the scarlet letter you carry around with you all the time. I sometimes felt I was a pariah, a leper.'

The scandal over these financial shenanigans, the large IOR debt and Calvi's death, put the church of John Paul's reign in its worst and most damaging light, although much, if not all, happened without his knowledge. But a characteristic reluctance on his part to be involved, or to find out what was happening, despite the fact that much of it had been before his time, resulted in a culpable degree of negligence. This episode could be interpreted as reflecting the unworldliness of Wojtyla's total dedication to spiritual life. It did not, however, diminish his sense of responsibility over the scandal and confusion, although the main player, Marcinkus, was quickly replaced. Szulc called it 'a serious blemish on John Paul II's reputation as an administrator', with the Holy See's 'dignified silence' adding 'fuel to the accusations'. But the Pope 'learned a valuable lesson, and Vatican finances are now under the most strict controls'.

Do we register the 1983 confrontation between the two leaders John Paul and Jaruzelski as a turning-point that owed its cause to the personalities and intentions of the two men? Or were they merely pawns of forces larger than themselves – who apparently brought about this astonishing reversal in the late-twentieth-century history of mankind – and under the direction of which they merely acted as passive, even predetermined, agents? It is rather in Wojtyla's favour that he did not summarise, or with hindsight either justify or claim credit for, what now was to happen on his second Polish journey.

In another paradox, the Pope's restraint and even submission ultimately advanced the cause of Polish independence and democracy that was so unexpected. He never hoped for more than an improvement and greater freedom under Communist control, although in the long term he did not believe the Communist empire would last. But how it would fall he had no inkling, while as for the timing he felt he would not live to see it.

The two men who met at the Belweder Presidential Palace in Warsaw on Friday 17 June 1983 could not have presented a stronger contrast. One was the tormented atheist, mainly seen as a tragicomic figure dressed in olive-green uniform with rows of ribbons on his chest, the stiff rigid back of a man in a corset for back injury, and of course with those large dark glasses for his sensitive eyes which concealed his long eyelashes, and much of his severe, schoolmasterly face. Those glasses themselves told a story, a harsh and punishing

Siberian captivity in his late teens after the Russians invaded Eastern Poland, and consequently a surprising identification and sense of affinity with ordinary suffering Russians. This led him to realise that they were 'not the monsters my education had led me to expect. Nor were they the monsters of traditional Polish literature or the stories told around the family fireside.' Captive in the isolated wastes of Siberia he had begun to read the great Russian authors, finding in the libraries the works of Chekhov, Tolstoy, Turgenev: 'I read at night,' he said, 'by a very feeble, low-powered light, sometimes only a candle. A practice that, combined with the blinding reflections of the Siberian snow, ruined my eyesight and forced me to wear, as an adult, these dark glasses with which I am always identified.'

In meeting Wojtyla he confronted everything that he was not. He confessed that his legs were trembling. The Pope also noticed that 'certainly his knees trembled' – but only in the beginning. Jaruzelski went on that 'it was a deep personal experience. I am a non-believer, but, you know, something remains in the genes from one's youth.' The figure of the Pope in white – 'it all affected me emotionally. Beyond all reason . . . I was deeply moved . . . I was even nervous . . . It was our first conversation, a get-acquainted conversation, but, at the same time, very important in substance.'

From now on the general was to remain under Wojtyla's spell: he felt subconsciously that he was 'in the presence of greatness'. With all the crowds, the millions falling on their knees, and the dignitaries and famous people kneeling, kissing his hand, it was 'a contagious mood'.

While being rationally 'very, very sober' and aware of the Pope's 'human dimension', Jaruzelski became acutely aware of their shared background, their common heritage. Wojtyla was of his generation, with the experience of an enslaved Poland the same as his. 'General,' the Pope told him, 'I always have in mind that terrible tragedy our nation suffered . . . the Great Partitions.' They swapped references to the heroic insurrections in 1830, 1846 and 1863. Although Jaruzelski could feel from the Pope a reserve, an official coolness, it soon vanished: 'There would be a citation from Norwid or Wyspianski . . . His pragmatism lives surrounded by romanticism, his very emotional approach to our history.' Jaruzelski told the Pope that his plays were being performed in ten cities, in eleven theatres and that the circulation of Catholic publications and bulletins had gone up from 800,000 to 1.9 million. He said further that he would not be establishing contacts with Solidarity, but 'that the dialogue with the Church was never interrupted. On the contrary, it gets stronger.'

Jaruzelski, after a recital of his own hard childhood exile in Russia, found he had impressed John Paul with his sincerity – 'I shall carry this burden until the end of my life' – and the Pope believed that he had the interests of the Polish people at heart. Ideologically they were enemies, but it was the presence of Wojtyla that disarmed this prickly, tormented man who has been listed among the world's worst seven dictators, whose public profile, when he assumed sole control of Poland, was almost a stereotype of the military leader of a banana republic.

There was an iron streak in the Pope, too, but it served a different end: here, remarked Jaruzelski, was 'a man who knows how to listen calmly even when he disagrees completely with what he hears . . . This touched me very much . . . Every meeting I have had with him brought us closer together in a purely human sense – not only in an intellectual format, but with warmth.'

Of course the dictator, by mentioning among other things the performance of his plays, did his best to flatter and appease the Pope, who must have been pleased, as well as diminish the political importance of aspects of his visit. But John Paul still stubbornly insisted on meeting Walesa, and the meeting duly took place in the Tatra Mountains, where he had often skied. What was said between the two men has not been reported, 'Nothing of substance,' says the Pope, while Walesa, in his autobiography, briskly recalls most

> the atmosphere of openness and simplicity – his words were like an invitation to remove the daily mask one wears to cope with life. One curious thing struck me during that meeting. I suddenly noticed the Pope's large feet, and I watched how he walked. Surprisingly, his steps were steady, measured and confident. They seemed to give me back my strength.

For Walesa the meeting was a resurrection. Like so many things in Wojtyla's life, it had symbolic value ('the son meets his father' and 'We all felt that behind him stood God'). Four months later Walesa was awarded the Nobel Peace Prize. For his part, John Paul would defend the increasingly embattled and isolated Jaruzelski, on one occasion interrupting a Polish bishop's denigration of the dictator and echoing

Jaruzelski's own sense of his commitment: 'Please, do not say anything critical about the general in my presence. He has put an enormous sack of stones on his back.' This 1983 visit was not only bravely undertaken on the Pope's part, but through his measured use of language he calmed the situation, adding his prestige to Jaruzelski's regime, which is what the general hoped for, and why he had allowed the visit.

Although improving, in 1984 relations between church and Polish state were once more rocked by the sensational murder of Jerzy Popieluszko, a popular young Warsaw parish priest. A Solidarity supporter, he inveighed from the pulpit against the abuses of Communism, which attracted crowds in their thousands. Discreetly the Pope let him know of his support, but Cardinal Glemp had been obliged by government pressure to ask him to be more moderate.

On 19 October state security officers abducted him, sealed him alive in a trunk and dumped him in the icy Wisla River not far from Wloclawek. Eleven days later, a passer-by found his body. The crime shocked the whole country, while in parliament the now increasingly clamorous opposition, no longer token, claimed the government had ordered the death of Popieluszko. Jaruzelski was identified with King Boleslaw, the tyrant who murdered St Stanislaw. As a young man Wojtyla had acted the symbolic role, and now in this new version of the epic story, history had come to life again.

Jaruzelski claimed that Popieluszko 'was killed by a crazy fanatic', though few believed him, but on 30 October the Ministry of the Interior admitted its involvement and some of those responsible were tried and sent to jail. (It is now known that this murder was arranged by hardliners in the security services in order to compromise Jaruzelski.) Nearly half a million Varsovians came to Father Popieluszko's funeral in St Stanislaw-Kostra, but Glemp downplayed the occasion.

Jaruzelski's subsequent alliance with Gorbachev, which – when the latter came to power and introduced reforms – drew the Pope into a triumvirate of Slavs, did much to ensure the implementation of reforms, not only in Poland, which was now the leader of these reforms, but in Hungary and in the Communist bloc as a whole. Until then, Jaruzelski continued to have a rough ride of transitional threats and denunciation from Moscow over his friendly dealings with the Polish church and the 'counter revolutionary' activities of Solidarity, only just stopping short of the use of force.

In 1985, with the Kremlin hardliners Andropov and Chernenko out of the way, the balance in the Kremlin swung in favour of Gorbachev, now in control, and *perestroika*, his policy of restructuring the Communist bloc by returning sovereignty to member countries and furthering reforms in Russia itself, was in the offing. On the initiative of Jaruzelski the 'alliance' with John Paul now widened to include Gorbachev: the general preened himself, 'in thinking that I was the one who, for the first time, brought the pope and Gorbachev together though without their physical presence . . . Because I was the one who knew Gorbachev well.'

During a 1986 meeting Gorbachev asked Jaruzelski what the Pope was like, and how he thought. Jaruzelski, close to playing devil's advocate, put the Pope's case, trying to communicate 'the personal dimension of the pope and, at the same time, his positive role'. He pointed out that he was the first pope to become so greatly committed to the cause of peace, 'and not only verbally, but through his great participation in many activities'. He was the first pope who emphasised strongly the question of social justice and whose social teachings were 'rather close to some concepts of socialist and communist ideology'. He told Gorbachev that this was 'a Slav pope' who knew the realities of their region, their history – and their dreams. 'I like to think that in my conversations with Gorbachev I was able to improve his view on the pope and the Roman Catholic Church.' He informed the Russian Communist leader that the Pope was 'a man of universal thought who was not at all uncritical about capitalism, in which he detected certain malaises and that he talked openly about it'. The Pope wanted to pursue an 'eastern policy' of *rapprochement*. Jaruzelski was making his bid to become an intermediary between the Pope and Gorbachev.

Gorbachev was, like Wojtyla, impressed by Jaruzelski's intelligence and grasp of the wider political situation, as well as his 'humanity' (he had already responded to the Pope's desire to see socialism 'with a human face'). Gorbachev relates in an autobiography that, from the very beginning, 'the greatest mutual understanding on the problems of *perestroika* was reached with Kádár and especially Jaruzelski, who fervently supported the changes in the Soviet Union'. They had formed a very close and an amicable relationship. He noted that Jaruzelski, too, was convinced that you cannot resolve a country's complex problems by force. Bitter opposition to change led to 'the most acute social and political crises, and mass popular demonstrations swept away the old regimes'.

Gorbachev was determined on reform, while from his favoured position Jaruzelski now adopted the role of an informal conduit and bearer of opinions from Gorbachev to the Pope, and from the Pope to Gorbachev. Jaruzelski interpreted each personality 'constructively', or so he claimed, telling the Pope what he knew about Gorbachev, and what role Gorbachev was playing,

> what were his intentions, what difficulties he faced, how important it was to support him, how to understand him, and what a great chance this was for Europe and the world – even if everything was not happening as smoothly as one may desire. And when I spoke with Gorbachev, I tried to convey to him the opinions of the pope, in which he was very much interested.

By the time of John Paul's third visit to Poland in June 1987, when the Pope met Jaruzelski in the Archbishop's Palace for a long session (eighty minutes), reconciliation between church and state was no longer a dream for, as the Pope said later, 'Providence had sent us Gorbachev.' The Soviet Union and the Holy See were now involved, said Gorbachev, 'in a period of massive change'. The new thinking spelt the end of the socialist system. From now on, Poland rapidly progressed towards its first free parliamentary election in June 1989, when, by an overwhelming majority, the Solidarity party was elected. Again, for the first time in over sixty years, Poland was a free country. For one and a half years more Jaruzelski remained as titular president while Tadeusz Mazowiecki, the Catholic intellectual, founder editor of *Wiez* and former Solidarity adviser, became prime minister.

But John Paul and Gorbachev still had not met although, from what they knew about one another and from their interchange of letters and documents, they had developed considerable sympathy for one another. A contact through Gorbachev's initiative, implemented through Patriarch Filaret of Kiev, of inviting the leaders of the world's religions to Moscow to commemorate a thousand years of Christianity in Russian lands, which as the Pope's deputy Cardinal Casaroli attended, led to perhaps the most extraordinary, unprecedented meeting held in the twentieth century.

On 1 December 1989, in the Vatican, at the Pope's invitation, the first general secretary of the Soviet Communist Party met the supreme pontiff of the Roman Catholic church.

Gorbachev had already, he said, been impressed by *On Social Concerns (Sollicitudo Rei Socialis)*, the Pope's most recent encyclical, which commented on the world's social and economic development in the light of new situations. The Pope had unequivocally declared what he (speaking for the church) did with those new situations, namely presented 'the Blessed Virgin difficult individual situations, so that she may place them before her Son', asking alleviation and change. Also presented to her were worrying '*social situations* and *the international crisis* itself', such as the arms race, contempt for human rights, and so on.

What could the leader of the atheist world answer to this? According to Gorbachev he provided the thrust in their twenty-minute conversation in John Paul's study. Facing each other across the small antique desk, Wojtyla sat in an armchair, Gorbachev in a straight-backed chair. Raisa, his wife, in a short red dress that made Vatican officials regret they had not given the Soviet embassy, when they asked, a specific and more seemly dress code, waited in the ante-room. When Gorbachev introduced her to the Pope he said, 'Raisa, I should like to introduce His Holiness, who is the highest moral authority on earth, but he's also a Slav.' For Gorbachev the 'but' tokened a friendly complicity, as did his own intense participation in amateur theatricals like Wojtyla earlier in life. Gorbachev wrote:

> I noted that there were many identical terms in my statements and his. 'This means that we must also have something in common "at the source" – in our ideas,' I said. As if in reply to my thoughts, John Paul II referred to perestroika as a process that 'allows us to search jointly for a new dimension of co-existence between people that will be better adapted to the needs of the individual, of different peoples, to the rights of individuals and nations'.
>
> 'The efforts you undertake,' he continued, 'are not merely of great interest for us. We share them.'
>
> The pope drew another important idea to my attention. 'Europe must breathe with both its lungs.'
>
> 'This is a very precise image,' I replied.

The Pope said that this was precisely what he had in mind when, in 1980, he proclaimed Cyril and Methodius – two representatives of the Eastern, Byzantine, Greek, Slav and Russian traditions – patron saints of Europe, together with St Benedict, who represented the Latin tradition.

'This is my European creed,' Gorbachev reported him as saying. They then dwelt on a number of questions connected with the situation of the Orthodox and Catholics in Russia. 'We focused on freedom of conscience, as one of the fundamental human rights, and on freedom of worship . . . I explained my approach to these issues. "We intend to realize our plans by democratic means," I said.'

Gorbachev had 'come to the conclusion that democracy alone is not enough. We also need morality.' While he believed that 'Democracy can bring both good and evil – there is no denying it. You have what you have.' For Russia it was 'essential that morality should become firmly established in society – such universal, eternal values as goodness, mercy, mutual aid'. He wanted to start from the principle that 'the faith of believers must be respected', and this applied both to Orthodox believers and to representatives of other religions, including Catholics. It would seem that John Paul had effected the most significant change of belief of his lifetime.

Cardinal Deskur adds further to this account that Gorbachev requested the Pope to 'pray for me and my plans'. The two men then left the study to be joined by interpreters, and deliver their formal exchanges of welcome and hope for future co-operation and contacts. These were more than fulfilled, for John Paul had been 'exalted', or so he remarked, by the historic meeting, commenting that Gorbachev had none of the usual Communist mentality – something he would have instinctively grasped at once – and that he was a man of principle prepared, on 'religious liberties and other freedoms', to go the whole way. He was, moreover, ready to accept 'whatever unpleasant consequences of his acts that may occur'.

At the end of the same year, 1989, the Berlin wall came down.

Archbishop Jean-Louis Tauran, a well-placed Vatican diplomat, later claimed the Pope was 'the detonator that set off the explosion of the [Communist] lies'.

When he received Tadeusz Mazowiecki in private audience, in response to the gratitude Mazowiecki expressed 'for the support you have given us in recent years', John Paul answered, 'I think that if I have done anything in this regard, I have done it as part of my universal mission; and that is the way it should be seen.'

Had Tolstoy to explain the unravelling of the Soviet Union he may well have said the causes of this lay in 'the collective will of the people transferred to the person'. Modern history, he wrote, cannot admit 'the conception of the ancients as to the direct participation of the deity in human affairs, and therefore history ought to give other answers'.

But, declared Gorbachev, 'What has happened in Eastern Europe would not have been possible without the presence of this pope, without the great role – even political – that he has played on the world scene.'

Part Four

THE NEARER WE ARE
TO THE MOUNTAIN,
THE SMALLER WE ARE

The nearer we are to the mountain, the smaller we are: the nearer we are to eternal Sanctity, the more sinful we seem ourselves to be, and the more sinful we truly are, in our own eyes. The protestations of the saints are not just hypocritical formulas. It is not by our virtues, but by our infirmities, that we have the right to God's intention.

Paul Claudel
Letter to André Gide

CLOV: Fit to wake the dead!
         The end is terrific!
HAMM: I prefer the middle.

Samuel Beckett
Endgame

25

Was He Losing the Plot?

(1990–93)

We live in the post-modern world where everything is possible and almost nothing is certain . . . Experts can explain everything in the objective world, yet we understand our own lives less and less.

Vaclav Havel, 1993

The enemy of Communism, at least in the dimension to which it was reduced in the end, was simple and had a human scale. It was very different from the new enemy which was tentacular and octopus-like, and destined never to stop spreading: corporate capitalism. The McDonald's golden arches was its symbol. In *Fast Food Nation* Eric Schlosser describes the telling antithesis:

A survey of American schoolchildren found that 96 per cent could identify Ronald McDonald. The only fictional character with a higher degree of recognition was Santa Claus. The impact of McDonald's on the way we live today is hard to overstate. The Golden Arches are now more recognized than the Christian Cross.

While at home in his Vatican apartment during these turbulent middle years of his papacy, Wojtyla generally was comfortable and rarely lost his temper. As before his serenity, his generosity to those who worked on a project with him, spread an impressive influence in every direction; only deliberate, callous acts of inhumanity provoked him to anger (the shelling of a marketplace in Sarajevo in 1993, for example). Life in Poland had made him permanently suspicious of telephone privacy, but he allowed a constant stream of old friends from Poland or the Angelicum easy access to his convivial presence. Many Polish clerics surrounded him to offer advice – his 'Polish Mafia' – but he was the boss, and his private staff of dedicated nuns, his Italian driver with the black Mercedes, remained always as wary and attentive staff. He used to watch soccer matches on television, but now rarely spent more than twenty minutes in front of a set, or watching a video. Once, when Polish bishops were visiting him, the nuns showed them that the Pope was 'wearing knickers that had been patched so often they couldn't be patched any more'. But he insisted on keeping them. The secretary of the Polish episcopate and former ethics student of Wojtyla told the nuns, no matter what the Pope said, to throw them out and get him some new ones.

John Paul's resistance to the new universal adversary, the 'virus' as he called it, of Western capitalism, became as challenging to him as earlier endgames. By 1991, when he visited Poland again, the vast crowds of the faithful had dwindled from filling parks to filling central squares, but he could express towards the vanquished enemy something of even generous nostalgia. 'The followers of capitalism,' he said, 'usually tend to refuse to admit of any "good" resulting from communism: the struggle against unemployment, a concern for the poor. In communism there is a preoccupation with social questions, while capitalism, on the contrary, is individualistic.'

With the eclipse of the most monstrous totalitarian systems of the twentieth century, the inward enemies of the church also swelled in significance. In the New Testament Christ was betrayed, the secret of his whereabouts sold for profit, by an intimate, a confidant, a disciple. In the larger scale of demonology, Lucifer was the brightest angel in heaven, who fell from grace through pride and resentment towards God. Many, likewise, of John Paul's most ardent and would-be damaging critics were people, for one reason or another, of disappointed faith, beginning with excessive expectations as to what one human being could deliver.

According to the arch-conservative views, Pope John Paul II had sold out, embraced the populist theology of 'roly-poly Roncalli' (John XXIII), whom as a 'wily, peasant monoglot' it was impossible to dislike. John, coming from the poor, had wanted to redress the balance between rich and poor, while liturgical 'reforms' in the Catholic mass abolished the Real Presence of Christ. 'Unfortunately, his piety was not sufficient to give him perception,' this line of stricture continued, and by March 1963 he had realised himself that something was going seriously wrong with Vatican Two, which he had initiated, saying, 'This is no longer my Council.'

For arch-conservatives, in the diabolical disorientation of the church that followed, especially in America with its 'covens' of homosexual priests and bishops, the attitude had become, 'We're going to commit adultery tomorrow: we're going to anyway so you might as well absolve us beforehand.' The rot set in even more in 1965–75 when 'Catholicity disappeared' and God 'withdrew his sanctifying grace'. Seeking to become popular, the church had sold out to Marxism, the essence of which was that the 'people are the source of power'. Absolution, salvation was open to all, in direct contradiction to Christ's teaching 'Many are called, but few are chosen'. To continue this scenario, Pius XII had foretold the coming destruction of the church, and refused a general council. As for John Paul II, the bumbling poet-philosopher who had 'wandered into the papacy by mistake', being too weak to re-establish papal authority he had decided according to this criticism on playing an endgame. So he thought and ate, 'and sleeps and dreams geopolitics', and as such 'had ignited the energies of one of the profoundest geopolitical changes in history'.

When not indulging his love of travel in this, the ultra-traditionalist view, he had been a prisoner of the Vatican, blocked and sitting impotently on the top of a pyramid of Curial dissent and intrigue. To sum up:

> From the close of the Second Vatican Council in 1965 to the end of the seventies – a solid, vibrant Church structure had been liquidated. It had been as if, say, the Panama Canal had suddenly been emptied of water. For in that brief period, the Roman structure – a vast organization built over the centuries at huge costs in blood and sacrifice – had suddenly been emptied of the spiritual and moral energy that had animated it and made it into the womb of a whole civilization and a formidable force among the nations.

By dissolving and subjecting its unique autocratic authority to popular election, he would destabilise the papacy, align papal power with worldwide, corporate enterprises. The next elected pope would be 'the anti-Christ'.

At the opposite end of the spectrum, the liberals were equally scathing. For John Spong, Episcopalian Bishop of New York, the church had to change or die. Hell and heaven had been 'incorporated into life here and now', while hierarchies and concepts such as God the Father were deemed anachronistic and even, a favourite word of Spong's, 'murky'. 'I would choose to loathe,' writes Spong, 'rather than to worship a deity who required the sacrifice of his son.' According to his supporters, Spong 'demolished the stifling dogma of traditional Christianity'. Catholic scholars like Garry Wills in his highly accusatory *Papal Sin* charged the Pope with intellectual dishonesty, maintaining that the Marian image so loved by him held women back, while gay priests had to learn a 'discipline of deceit lest their secret slip out'.

In between the immoderate views there was criticism. The raw nerve of the Catholic church under Wojtyla's pontificate, many commentators claimed, was that it perpetrated a view of sexuality that was 'out of sync' with modern orthodoxy. A delegation of French women who besieged the papacy in 1993 alleged that 'Thousands of women who are with priests (i.e. as secret lovers) are forced to live in the shadow of their companions.' In the early nineties appeared articles that argued Wojtyla was 'the shepherd out of step with his flock' as Peter Stanford, an English writer on religion, expressed it – betraying a widespread sentiment that, in the late twentieth century, it was the flock of sheep that should be leading the shepherd. Stanford quoted a poll showing how John Paul had presided over a fragmentation of faith: it revealed on the eve of his August 1993 visit to the United States 'the abyss between America's 59 million Catholics and their leader . . . 84 per cent opposed the Vatican's ban on the pill. Almost 60 per cent think you can divorce and remarry without the Church's sanction. Even on abortion, once the keystone of orthodoxy, 58 per cent rejected a total ban'.

Stanford didn't go on to quote statistics of other beliefs held by those American Catholics. Most practising Catholics supported the two Bush presidents' wars with Iraq, both of which, in 1991 and 2003, the Pope outspokenly opposed, while many voted for Bush's reelection in 2004. Had they voted, in their states, for capital punishment, also strongly opposed by the Pope? They paid as little attention to the Pope's pronouncements on military arms control, or ecology, as to those on birth control. Opinion polls were the current popular form of 'authority', but they had no claim to ethical truth. Martius in Shakespeare's *Coriolanus* calls the common voice

> no surer, no,
> Than is the coal of fire upon the ice,
> Or hailstone in the sun

while in Wojtyla's view opinion polls, like psychotherapy, were devices to escape responsibility for doing what was right. They tempted people to take these mere statistical studies 'as the standard for their discipline'. In the area of sex the statistical emphasis or biological urges driving men and women to satisfy immediate desire were like 'treating the human body as a raw datum, devoid of any meaning'.

At the same time, at the nadir of his popularity, in his encyclical *Veritatis Splendor* (*The Splendour of Truth*), 1993, he branded sex before marriage, contraception and homosexuality as 'intrinsically evil': in the cynical interpretation of this firm stand, by yet another commentator,

> These vices now rank beside tax dodging and passing false cheques in the Pope's list of iniquities which risk eternal damnation. Last year he broadened the scale of mortal sins to include abortion, euthanasia, drug-dealing and drug-taking – each incurring total alienation from God and everlasting punishment. To these he added the summary offences of drunken driving, eating too much, betting, reading horoscopes and the Italian peccadillo – also known to journalists worldwide – of falsifying expenses. (Rome fiddled and souls burned.)

He was censured for 'digging an even deeper pit for his church'. Biologists questioned his biology in his condemnations of euthanasia and abortion under the overriding excuse that, as one doctor put it, 'Even life itself is hard to define, and the precise transition point from non-living material to living organism is to some extent arbitrary'.

An old Krakow companion noted in 1995, 'He is not as joyful as he was before. He is witnessing a moral catastrophe throughout the world – the perversion of evil for good, and good for evil – and no one wants to hear about it.' He never became as depressed as Paul VI, who said to the diplomat who was trying to cheer him up, 'Now I understand St Peter, who came to Rome twice, the second time to be crucified.'

Bullying, threats, brutal extermination made him very angry, especially on his own doorstep. Generally speaking the church looked the other way at the mobster intimidation in Sicily. John Paul reversed this. On visits to Palermo he attacked the 'barbarous violence' of the city. In May 1993, celebrating mass in the famous Valley of the Temples of Agrigento, he lost his temper; with voice shaking he denounced those who went against God's law: 'God once said, "Don't kill!"' Man, any group of men, the Mafia, can't change and trample this most sacred law of God . . . Those who have on their consciences the weight of so many victims must understand . . . must understand!' 'Repent!' he cried out. 'One day you will come face to face with the judgment of God!'

The Mafia retaliated too, threatening the Pope, damaging St John Lateran, his diocesan cathedral in Rome with a bomb and in Sicily killing Father Giuseppe Paglisi, a notably anti-Mafia priest. In Catania, where John Paul later preached, a local priest found on his doorstep a lamb with slit throat and a note, 'It may happen to you!' But some Mafia chiefs publicly renounced their life in crime, and witnesses came forward in trials, attesting to the effectiveness of his intervention.

Barbarity abroad equally stirred up his wrath, as he denounced the bloodshed in the former Yugoslavia. 'Stop! Stop! Stop!' he shouted before the St Peter's Square crowd. But he produced mocking headlines later in that year when on his Baltic tour at Riga, Latvia, he claimed that Marxism's 'kernel of truth' was its recognition of the 'situation of exploitation to which an inhumane capitalism had subjected the proletariat'. He also criticised Poland and post-Communist democracies for accepting Western pure market economies.

So as the new decade wore on, far from being the acclaimed 'God's politician' of the 1980s Wojtyla was now cast as the isolated unheeded prophet crying in the wilderness. Western countries and peoples felt insulted to be called, as he continually told them, a poor role model for Eastern Europe after the fall of Communism. From 1990 onwards wrong-footing him became something of a competitive game, often personal, even vindictive. Some of the debates (as opposed to the horrific consequences, say, of sexual licence), seemed like the medieval theological debates on how many angels could balance on the head of a pin. From the view-point of newspaper editors, often the only important thing was that they provided superb photo opportunities, for example, the white-robed anti-abortion champion Wojtyla with right arm raised, printed against a background of thirty boxed human embryos in the various stages of gestation.

In 1991 David Willey, BBC Rome correspondent, described Wojtyla's pontificate as tired. 'He comes from a folksy nineteenth-century background, and it is beginning to show. I fear we are waiting for him to die.' The chant of 'It's time to go' persisted in periodic diatribes by religious and scientific author John Cornwell who, having attacked Pius XII as 'Hitler's Pope', was crafting papal demolition into lifelong habit. In 1995 Cornwell compared John Paul to the nineteenth-century Pope Pius IX, longest-reigning pope ever with thirty-two years, who was convinced the future of the church depended upon him alone and as such had become 'hyperactive, grandiose and unhinged'. Likewise the present pontiff had become isolated – and in essence mad. Cornwell quoted Jack Dominian, a 'Catholic psychotherapist', to the effect that in Wotyla's mind reality and delusion had merged: 'He is attached to false beliefs, and what he sees as a blazing truth is approaching a delusional level.'

For John Wilkins, former editor of the *Tablet* and dubbed a papal knight in 2003, the Catholic church had become a 'dysfunctional family. In themselves the members of it are happy, but there is a problem with Dad. Everyone knows it but no one can say, or he may throw a tantrum. Everyone is afraid of him.' Wilkins conceded that he was a great man, but not a great pope. For Margaret Hebblethwaite, religious writer and widow of Pope Paul VI's biographer, 'John Paul reminds me of that foot in the Monty Python series, that squelched anything in sight.'

These writers and many others complained in a way that made one believe the Pope should somehow be answerable to them, as a democratically elected leader is supposedly answerable to his or her electorate. Cornwell maintained, perhaps to sum up the attitude, that the Pope had 'a curiously "mystical" sense of entitlement to longevity': the inference being that he should have died long ago.

In Dorothy Sayers's *The Man Born to Be King*, her 1940s sequence of radio plays on the life of Jesus, it is Judas himself who feels betrayed: 'The noblest dreams I ever dreamed, the holiest prayer my heart could utter, all my hopes, all my ideals, seemed incarnate in him. Yet he has lowered himself to the measure of little minds, eating the applause of the ignorant . . . Why could he not listen to me?' All critics of the Pope unite in this theme, that he eats 'the applause of the ignorant'. As Cornwell comments on John Paul's 'gimlet-eyed' gaze on the coming of the third millennium, 'He had a weakness for synchronicities, predictions, anniversaries, red-letter feasts, hints that his life and times were not subject to coincidence, nor indeed to any earthly explanation.'

As Sayers says in her character notes, beneath Judas's idealism is a rooted egotism. He justifies himself: 'I was not really wrong . . . I was right all the time – it is Jesus who has deteriorated.' Judas makes it clear that what he admired in Jesus was not really Jesus at all, 'but only his own ideas in another person . . .' Like most of the Pope's articulate and intelligent critics did with the Pope, Judas, in Sayers's interpretation, wanted a Jesus who would interpret Judas to the world, under his guidance and direction. But Wojtyla would remain obstinately his own man.

Veritatis Splendor, John Paul's masterpiece encyclical, published on 3 October 1993, as a major church document of moral theology, came as a robust proclamation that the inner man was still alive and well, able to answer his critics, and carry the fight into the adversary's territory. 'Will the Prince of Darkness surrender,' he wrote, 'he who is the father of lies, who continually accuses the sons of man as he once accused Job. It is unlikely that he will surrender, but his arguments may weaken.' Over fifty years on he was still identifying with the protagonist of *Job*, the powerful play written when he was nineteen. The anger of *God's Own Brother* was also still intact.

It had taken six years for him to realise his stated intention in the apostolic letter *Spiritus Domini*, to probe the issues and deliver a full statement or reflection on the foundations of moral thought. By proclaiming a universal morality, *Veritatis Splendor* followed on also from the *Catechism of the Catholic Church* (1992) of specific directives for practice of the faith. Although the hand – or if not the hand, the influence – of others could be detected (Andrzej Szostek, the Polish theologian from Lublin; Joseph Ratzinger; other Swiss and Vatican theologians) the distinctive thrust and shape of *Veritatis Splendor* was Wojtyla's. Moral life is a drama, typically: in the introduction he states boldly, 'No one can escape from the fundamental questions: what must I do? How do I distinguish good from evil? The answer is only possible thanks to the splendour of truth.'

In a morally relativistic world that had successfully separated freedom from truth, to ask what truth is might seem a foolhardy question, but again he pointed out what the world neglected. The Pope addressed the overall crisis. He defined – or, as he has so often done – redefined the basic qualities and tools of the human being in relation to truth and goodness, and the path that should be followed, not only for redemption but for the fullest and most rewarding life on earth.

Similar to many other basic human qualities, conscience had been hijacked by the present-day notion that every human being had the right or even obligation to create his or her own truth: 'Conscience is no longer considered in its primordial reality as an act of a person's intelligence, the function of which is to apply the universal knowledge of the good in a specific situation . . . Instead there is a tendency to grant to the individual conscience the prerogative of independently determining the criteria of good and evil and then acting accordingly.' The conscience 'is man's sanctuary and most secret core, where he finds himself alone with God, whose voice resounds within him'.

As for the 'right to choose' abortion, and the *Brave New World* march towards designer babies and selective breeding, 'it is never lawful, even for the gravest reasons, to do evil that good may come out of it'. Paul Johnson pointed out that 'the pope's words [in *Veritatis Splendor*] remind us that Hitler started his road to Auschwitz murdering the incurable and the insane.'

But with such pronouncements *Veritatis Splendor* awoke hostility, as if critics were expecting a pope who was also an ethical philosopher to be putting forward something that would have been entirely out of character. He was upbraided for imposing his views, for being anti-culture, and anti-democratic. His greatest crime was that he would not change: he refused to reinvent himself, together with the Catholic church. One casuistical response was that, in the English *Times Higher Educational Supplement*, of a German academic: the Pope's encyclical showed 'that in post-modern times, you have only to remain old-fashioned long enough in order to become up-to-date in the end'. The academic added, 'A case for faith can still be made' – it apparently never crossed his mind that unchanging truth could be more than just a stratagem. On the other hand, the English novelist Malcolm Bradbury averred that people 'longed for uncomfortable truths and would sooner or later turn away from the modern vogue for moral relativism', where everything is equal and nothing is better, while any opinion about right and wrong came down to 'it depends on the circumstances', or 'it depends on your outlook'. This had created a 'world without landmarks', which was 'very unlikely to make anyone happy'.

Bradbury, confessing he had no religious beliefs and was a 'committed liberal', noted how, after fifteen years of Wojtyla's papacy, liberal Roman Catholics and liberals everywhere were throwing up their hands in despair at this backward document that refused to respond to the energies of modern change:

> The encyclical shows, we're told, the backward nature of the Roman Catholic Church, and how out of touch the present Pontificate is with the forces that are really changing the world.
>
> By what I am sure is a complete coincidence, this same weekend saw several new books appear on the plight of the Anglican Church. Take two of them. Their titles alone are instructive: *The Church Hesitant* and *Is There a Church of England?*

Bradbury also lauded John Paul's magnificently titled encyclical, deploring that our age has – as its only real standards of value – fashion, celebrity and the market place. As a powerful antidote to its times *Veritatis Splendor* became highly controversial, and would seem to have won wider recognition and praise from non-Catholics than from dissenting theologians such as Hans Küng ('Küng would make an excellent Lutheran,' wrote the English journalist Mary Kenny when in 1994 Küng called the Pope a 'disaster for our church', 'and I think it rather snobbish and sectarian of him not to become one.' There were many dissident Catholic theologians who thought it smarter to be 'a rebel Roman' than an 'honest Protestant'). 'You can't take it à la carte,' Cardinal Hume said of Roman Catholicism. John Paul also showed in this encyclical, Ann Widdecombe told this author, that he was 'a great and genuine successor of St Peter', although the encyclical 'could have done with being written in flock language'. He was not going to take even a step or two down the slippery path of 'endless compromise'.

When the 1994 population conference convened in Cairo, representatives from 185 countries met to curb world population growth; the explosive issue was proposed by the Clinton administration (to be endorsed by the conference in paragraph 8: 25 of the draft document)

– that the US believed 'access to safe, legal and voluntary abortion is a fundamental right of all women'. John Paul believed that for the first time in human history abortion was being proposed as a means of population control.

Navarro-Valls said, 'He put all the prestige of his office at the service of this issue,' and for nine days the Vatican delegates, under his direction, lobbied and filibustered; they kept their Latin-American bloc in line and struck up alliances with Islamic nations opposed to abortion. In the end the Pope won. The Cairo conference inserted an explicit statement that 'in no case should abortion be promoted as a method of family planning'; in return the Vatican gave partial consent to the document. These consuming issues now occupied Wojtyla so exhaustively that there was little time for inner creativity (apart from that devoted to prayer) or to think of writing poems or plays – or even, in what for most people are years of retirement and reflection, personal memoirs.

26

The Connection with Suffering

(1993–94)

In 1993 Italian television commissioned Vittorio Messori, a Catholic journalist, to conduct an interview with Wojtyla. The Pope agreed, and prior to this Messori sent him twenty questions to consider. The interview never happened. The Pope kept the questions by him, and responded to them in writing, heavily underlining certain passages. The title *Crossing the Threshold of Hope* was his own; 'Do with them what you like,' he told Messori: what could be more conclusive than the contact and proof of his 'humility, of his generous availability to hear our voices', wrote Messori later.

In it, he once again argued that 'This world, which appears to be a great workshop in which knowledge is developed by man, which appears as progress and civilization, as a modern system of communications, as a structure of democratic freedoms without any limitations, this world is not capable of making man happy.'

In essence the Pope and his critics now talked at cross-purposes, about different universes. Genuine belief in God did not sell newspapers or promote new products – nor did John Paul's admonition to 'Be not afraid' – but fear and anxiety, generated artificially, drove people to spend money, buy newspapers, and pursue selfish aims. As evidence emerged in the late 1990s of the tragic abuse of minors by paedophiliac priests the media had a new quarry to pursue on behalf of justice and victims claiming compensation, sometimes not entirely out of genuine concern for social and moral good.

The Pope reacted, 'One cannot acquiesce in treating moral evil as an occasion for sensationalism.' A person's fall was a painful experience, but sensationalism 'has become the particular style of the age'. In contrast, the spirit of the Gospel is one of compassion, with Christ's saying 'Go and sin no more.' Fuelled by sensational reporting, in the public eye the image of priests changed harshly. Monsignor Roderick Strange, rector of the Beda College, Rome, noted, 'A priest I know called in at his local supermarket', and held the door open, as he arrived, for a woman who was leaving. He had never seen her before. She looked at him, stopped, and spat in his face. ' "People like you should be in hell," she told him.'

In response to Messori's twenty questions, among which were 'If God exists why is he hiding?', 'Why does God tolerate suffering?' or the more personal 'Have you ever had doubts?' Wojtyla argued that the priest, the pope, as successor of St Peter, must not be afraid, because following his vocation is not only a human initiative 'but also an *act of God* [Wojtyla's italics] who walks and reveals himself through man'.

He agreed with his interrogator that the pope is a mystery and a sign of contradiction – a challenge or a 'scandal' to logic and good sense. He had, he might have added (but he did not, again with that restraint that defined him as 'unpolitical'), shown he himself was just that. The weight of being pope, together with those responsibilities, he answers – again revealing the inner man – he bore, through prayer. As he so visibly showed (even as a young man, even as a child, when he prayed he was standing or prostrating himself before God) in prayer you laid yourself open to God. You allowed God to take possession: in prayer you acknowledged that it was the one place where there was nowhere to hide. '*In prayer, then, the true protagonist is God,*' he wrote. 'The protagonist is *Christ*, who constantly frees creation from slavery to corruption and leads it toward liberty, for the glory of the children of god. The protagonist is the *Holy Spirit*, who "comes to the aid of our weakness" . . . we learn that it is always God's initiative within us.'

While you might pray for specific ends, you had also to pray in many different ways, which the Bible taught through a multitude of examples, so that prayer 'reflects all created reality'. But in prayer it was God, not man, who was centre-stage. It was again supportive of the creative theme of his life that John Paul sketched the cosmos as a dramatic critic might.

God was not transcendent but human, for he humiliated himself in the flesh (he suffered, in Herbert McCabe's phrase, 'death by public helplessness'). The Hebrews and then Islam, affirmed the Pope, could not accept a God who was so human. 'It is not suitable to speak of God in this way,' they protested. 'He might remain absolutely transcendent; He must remain pure Majesty.' But if 'He were not Mystery, there would be no need for Revelation, or more precisely, there would be no need for *God to reveal himself*'. Forcefully he expressed other important differences:

> Some of the most beautiful names in the human language are given to the God of the Koran, but He is ultimately a God outside the world, a God who is *only Majesty, never Emmanuel*, God-within-us. *Islam is not a religion of redemption*. There is no room for the Cross and the Resurrection. Jesus is mentioned, but only as a prophet who prepares for the last prophet, Muhammad. There is also mention of Mary, His Virgin Mother, but the tragedy of redemption is completely absent. For this reason not only the theology but also the anthropology of Islam is very distant from Christianity.

Yet he also much admired the fidelity to prayer, the image of believers falling to their knees who, disregarding all else, immersed themselves in prayer.

For a man who had lived through so much pain and suffering – both in himself, and seen and experienced them in others – how did, or could, he explain why, if God is omnipotent, He hadn't eliminated these? The answer here, given by John Paul, was not all that far away from Samuel Beckett's answer in *Endgame*.

Confronted with our human freedom, says the Pope, God decided to make himself 'impotent'. Because of this,

> one could say that God is paying for the great gift bestowed upon a being He created 'in his image, after his likeness' (Gn, 1:25). Before this gift, He remains consistent and [as his son Jesus] *places himself before the judgment of man*, before an illegitimate tribunal which asks Him provocative questions: 'Then you are a king?' (cf: Jn 18:37); 'Is it true that all which happens in the world, in the history of Israel, in the history of all nations, depends on you?'

We know Christ's response to this question before Pilate's tribunal: 'For this I was born and for this I came into the world, to testify to the truth' (Jn 18:37). But then: 'What is truth?' (Jn 18:38), and here ended the judicial proceeding, that tragic proceeding in which man accused God before the tribunal of his own history, and in which the sentence handed down did not conform to the truth. Pilate says: 'I find no guilt in him' (Jn 18:38), and a second later he orders: 'Take him yourselves and crucify him!' (Jn 19:6). In this way he washes his hands of the issue and returns the responsibility to the violent crowd.

Therefore, *the condemnation of God by man is not based on the truth, but on arrogance, on an underhanded conspiracy.* Isn't this the truth about the history of humanity, the truth about our century? In our time the same condemnation has been repeated in many courts of oppressive totalitarian regimes. And isn't it also being repeated in the parliaments of democracies where, for example, laws are regularly passed condemning to death a person not yet born?

'A book would penetrate the conscience', he had said of this publishing project. 'Pictures flee, a book stays.' *Crossing the Threshold of Hope*, an astonishing personal work, fast became a bestseller in twenty-two countries, including the UK and the United States. The Pope may have looked tired and ill, but there was no art to tell the mind's construction in the face.

Clov opens Samuel Beckett's *Endgame* by moaning, 'I can't be punished any more.' Hamm, at the start of his opening speech, asks, 'Can there be misery – (*he yawns*) – loftier than mine?' These beginning utterances suggest the uses to which suffering (or waiting), since we were taught to suffer, has been put, in order to end itself. Either it can make us good, worthy of pardon, or it can make us powerful, ascendant, worthy of praise.

'These are the endgames of suffering with which we begin . . . Each requires his audience: Clov, because his worthiness must be seen; Hamm, because his loftiness must be appreciated. And the giving up of audience must present itself, both to the theologian and to the artist, as death.'

In Wojtyla's life we can equate Hamm with the artist in himself that the Pope long before renounced as a secular ambition, but kept in his inner being. Hamm's vision of salvation is (as most secular Western or humanist vision of man today) through his art. Day after day, in all media in the non-religious West men and women were telling their story, hoping to move their audiences to gratitude through sharing their private guilts with self-justification, as well as exacting vengeance when believed it was due, hoping to share the burden of their guilty secrets, hoping above all when they were able to 'speak no more about it' to end their endgames.

This today was the only redemption that could be hoped for. The pessimistic and even narcissistic existentialist, isolated with just his own choices, creating himself (or self-creating himself as an object) was forever the hero of his own story.

Yet the danger remained in heaven, as the philosopher Stanley Cavell pointed out in his exposition of *Endgame*, for the audience of the play is God, and its object is the reverse of prayer. 'Its object is to show God not that he must intervene, bear witness to our efforts and aid and mitigate them, but that he owes it to us, to our suffering and our perfect faithfulness, to depart forever, to witness nothing more . . .' 'Lord, I believe; help thou my unbelief' now means 'Help me not to believe.' So Beckett, a fundamentally ascetic and spiritual (or spiritually atheistic) writer, submitted his beliefs to art.

But even in *Endgame* Beckett's vision could be encompassed in love – or so Cavell finally claims:

> With it, we could explain why we lack words, and have too many. We could re-understand the sense in which redemption is impossible, and possible: impossible only so long as we live solely in history, in time, so long as we think that an event nearly 2,000 years ago relieves us of responsibility rather than nails us to it – so long, that is, as we live in magic instead of faith. And we can reinterpret suffering yet again: I had occasion to complain that we take suffering as proof of connection with God; but a sounder theology will take *that* suffering to prove exactly that the connection has not been made, but resisted; for, as Luther's confessor had to remind him, God appears only in love.

Karol Wojtyla demonstrated this resistance to suffering not only in his response to early deprivation and loss of family, but to Nazism, Communism, and then the Western 'culture of death'. But above and beyond all that, he resisted suffering itself as proof of connection with God, while showing that continuing is what allows God's redemptive love to operate for his salvation.

'The man who shares in redemption,' he wrote in *Crossing the Threshold of Hope*, 'will have the advantage over the man who sets himself up as an unbending judge of God's actions in his life as well as in that of all humanity.'

27

Still Seeking To Heal

(1994–96)

At the age of seventy-five, when even cardinals retire (although many continue with a full workload until older), John Paul made, in the course of one year, his fourth papal visit to the United States; he travelled to Cameroon, the Republic of South Africa, Kenya; spent four days in Slovakia; made a second trip to Belgium; returned again to Poland and the Czech Republic; flew to the Philippines, Papua New Guinea, Australia and Sri Lanka.

In Manila his ceremonies of innocence were far from being drowned, attended probably by the largest crowd, estimated at five million, that had ever collected on this planet, for a World Day for Youth. 'We love you, Pope Lolek!' shouted the young audience. 'Lolek is a name for a baby, but I am an old man . . .' 'No! No!' . . . 'But John Paul is too serious. Call me Karol.'

But sex had remained, and would remain, the great stumbling block for the Catholic faith. In April 1987 in Santiago, he had asked a vast crowd of young people, 'Will you renounce the idolatry of wealth?' 'Yes!' they had roared back. 'Will you renounce the idolatry of power?' 'Yes!' 'Will you renounce the idolatry of sex?' 'No!'

As if his punishing itinerary was not enough, the Pope in 1995 beatified sixty-four martyrs of the French Revolution, and forty-five martyrs of the Spanish Civil War. In this same year he published two encyclicals, the first, *The Gospel of Life* (*Evangelicum Vitae*), stressing in magisterial terms his lifelong commitment and exposition of the dignity of the human person and the sanctity of human life; the second, *On Commitment to Ecumenism* (*Et Unium Sint*), dealing fully yet again with the ecclesiology of communion and how the

Catholic church should or could participate in ecumenical dialogue with other Christian churches.

For the international year of the woman he wrote his *Letter to Women*, and in this and on other occasions in 1995 he expressed sorrow and asked for forgiveness for the injustices the church had committed in the past against women.

> Unfortunately, we are heirs to a history which has conditioned us to a remarkable event. In every time and place this conditioning has been an obstacle to the progress of women . . . if objective blame, especially in particular historical contexts, has belonged to not just a few members of the Church, for this I am truly sorry . . . Women have contributed to . . . history as much as men, and more often than not they did so in much more difficult conditions . . . To this great, immense feminine 'tradition' humanity owes a debt which can never be repaid.

In the first Angelus address, on 10 June, he pointed out that equality between man and woman is stated in the Bible's opening pages, in its stupendous account of creation. Woman occupied a no less important place in his mystical vision. The Marian Year of June 1987–August 1988 – in John Paul's entrustment of the world of his own lifetime to Mary – had been a significant milestone. Mary had been from an early age the predominant 'sign of the woman', who was salvation for the world, and he continued to refer all things to Mary. Cardinal Ratzinger had expounded this when presenting John Paul's encyclical *Redemptoris Mater* (*Mother of the Redeemer*, 1987):

> 'I will put enmity between you and the woman' are the words [he said] in Genesis spoken to the serpent; the woman is pursued by the devil, but ultimately overcomes him. The last book of the New Testament speaks expressly of 'the sign of the woman' who at a determined moment of history, rises above it, to reconcile heaven and earth from that moment onwards. The sign of the woman is the sign of hope. She is the one who shows us the pathway of hope.

In *Crossing the Threshold of Hope*, John Paul had inveighed against male selfishness making women the victim in the conception of new life: 'When the woman most needs the man's support, he proves to be a cynical egotist, capable of exploiting her affection or weakness, yet stubbornly resistant to any sense of responsibility for his own action.'

In July 1995, in a second Angelus message, he remarked how too much attention had been paid to men's achievements, and not enough to women's faithful performance of the tasks of daily life: 'I would like to speak in the name of the church and pay homage to women for the multiple, immense but silent contributions by women in every phase and aspect of human existence.'

Again the appeal was passionate: earlier, when his apostolic letter *Mulieris Dignitatem* (*On the Dignity and Vocation of Women*) had been published (1988) a criticism was made that it lacked any suggestion of self-examination and confession of guilt – typical of official Catholic documents: 'The pope gives thanks but he neglects to ask forgiveness.' Now he was to go as far as he possibly could go in the other direction.

But in his *Letter*, although acknowledging the two did not necessarily come into conflict, he still preferred women to be Christians first and women second: 'All sisters have, as it were, conveyed to one another a password: "Let us first be Christians?" A certain number prefer to add the following, "Let us first be women." It is evident the two do not exclude each other.' Was there a hint of irony? If there was, the emphasis was clear: he was not going to open the church to the endless and unresolved uncertainties that the ordination of women would entail, helping as it has to fragment other churches built on already shaky – from a Catholic point of view – foundations.

In the *Catechism of the Catholic Church*, published the year before, in 1994 (in hardback alone it sold two million copies in the United States), the argument was cut and dried, stemming from the Canon Law principle, 'Only a baptized man (vir) validly receives sacred ordination' (The Code of Canon Law, can. 1024). This principle, as Roderick Strange maintained, was based upon what Jesus did.

All his apostles were men and when they in their turn appointed successors those successors were also men. As it says in the book of the Apocalypse, 'Jesus Christ is the faithful mistress, the First-born from the dead, the Ruler of the Kings of the east. He loves us and has washed away our sins with his blood, and made us a line of kings, priests to serve thy God and Father.' The *Catechism* then states crucially, 'The college of bishops, with whom the priests are united in the priesthood, makes the college of the twelve an ever-present and ever-active reality until Christ's return.'

The Pope did much, short of ordination, to make the church more inclusive of women and involve 'the feminine genius' in decision-making, in the higher reaches of church administration (diplomatic responsibilities, presidency of movements such as Focolare, a frater-nity to foster unity among all people, and in 2004 higher appoint-ments in the Curia), and in the celebration of mass. For many this was not enough. For example, Cherie Blair, wife of the British prime minister and a practising Catholic, in 2003 criticised the Vatican Curia for remaining, during his pontificate, basically a male preserve.

Karol (to distinguish the man from the function) always felt at ease with, and loved, women. His early life attested to their constant presence and influence. When feminists demonstrated against him, he suffered their interruptions with an indulgent if wry humour. When asked once if he could ever love these women, he answered, 'Yes, very much! It is necessary to have this love for people. But on the other hand one must speak the truth.' Another time when a woman, presented to him by name, refused to kiss his ring, he turned away with a humorous shrug. 'Ah, feminista!' he said knowingly.

Ann Widdecombe could not believe her luck when he gave her, as a new convert in 1996, a twenty-minute audience during which he asked her lots of questions – clearly more fluent in English than he had been early in his papacy – about the role of women in a secular society. She was amazed at his 'wide interest in the general fabric of life'. 'I've met only three genuinely holy people who provide a link with the early church: Cardinal Hume, Mother Teresa [canonised in 2003], and the Pope.'

The Pope's ultimate significance for her was that of Matthew 6: 19, 'Lay not up for yourselves treasures upon earth.' Her experience, as that of all women I talked to who had met him or known him over a long period, was that he loved women and instinctively understood them, seeing them as equals and not, as one woman from Krakow expressed it, 'Women in Catholic church is on the pedestal.'

In the latter part of his pontificate the controversial issue of women's ordination subsided as everyone seemed to know where the church stood, and like the equally explosive issue of gay rights and homosexual marriages, the Catechistic rules appeared worldwide to attract more people than they alienated. Under this pope the Catholic church sustained its refusal to change the basic rules, in order to avoid the risk of serious schism. Even more gentle modernisation had alienated millions of Catholics worldwide.

On various occasions the Pope had expressed his view that biography should convey the person's heart, soul and thoughts. By now the early outstanding actor had become at one with this extraordinary continuous performance as supreme pontiff: he had not only mastered the role of universal churchman, supreme witness as opposed to teacher or teller of the Gospel, and as such in keeping with the age in which he lived, but he had, to use the image of creation, created his own greatest character.

You could see, if so inclined, all those characters and mouthpieces he once wrote up in dialogue form, as well as all those parts he acted on stage, saints, heroes and sinners alike – but mostly saints and heroes – taking an active role in his life as pope, but rolled up into one, integrated, seamlessly unified and constant. His life as supreme pontiff had become his own supreme act of creation. He had learned to play himself, but in the playing had not lost himself.

From zero, from a dark nothingness, without thinking too much of himself, and by placing all his gifts, his whole being, in the service of God, he had made of his life an art, a role which, without losing energy through conflict, neurosis or any of the thousand other ills that modern man's psyche is heir to, he could play with zest and huge enjoyment: 'Blessed is he who expecteth nothing,' St Francis said, 'for he shall enjoy everything.'

So now it is, as a supreme example of the artist in life, that we approach Wojtyla in his last years: stage-manager, playwright, director and leading actor all in one, but all in the service of God, Jesus and the Holy Ghost, all – in those resounding words of Paul Claudel – in the celebration of creation: 'What is art, if not an exclamation and an acclamation, a counting and a conferring of Graces.'

'No one has ever urged the Pope to do what he does. He acts because he believes he ought to. On one occasion I heard him say, "We shall have all eternity to rest,"' reported Navarro-Valls in 1993 in the Italian magazine *Panyana*. To me in 2003 Navarro-Valls confirmed again,

He knows his own mind very well. He's not a sentimental man. He combines two main archetypes – the poet and the philosopher. As poet, very specific, sensitive, *sensible*, to the emotional aspects of reality. As philosopher he applied a conceptual abstract way of understanding – he sees things objectively. What is surprising is how these elements live together without any conflict in a very painless and natural way . . . *tout se tient* [everything holds together].

Wojtyla's concern with the dynamic of communication and the word, and his capacity for bringing the papacy close to common people resulted not only in a *Letter to Women*, but in a whole series of *mea culpas* or opportunities for asking forgiveness, which were expressive of the inner man, and an expansion of that early experience and sense of comfort brought by the confessional – both as father confessor and as penitent.

Karol described this driving, very personal quest of his to square the past as the 'purification of historical memory' and 'the confession of sin'. He had begun this process of admitting past mistakes of the church and asking pardon for them publicly (he had always been so inclined privately), as Metropolitan of Krakow in 1966. Years before his election as pope and as a key member of Polish and German bishops' initiatives of reconciliation between Poland and Germany, he had caused considerable outcry among Communist workers by his stance of not only forgiving, but *asking* forgiveness of, the German people: 'Let us try to forget! No polemics; no continuation of the cold war.'

When he became pope the process expanded considerably and he always travelled with the same underlying concern in mind to bring reconciliation, leading an Italian historian to claim, 'In this request for forgiveness we have the ultimate key to the travels of John Paul II.' The first to outline a coherent programme of this had been Hans Urs von Balthasar, the theologian and later cardinal, who as far back as 1967 presented a list of principal errors in *Who is a Christian?*:

Forcible baptisms, inquisitions and *auto-da-fé's*, the St Bartholomew's Day massacre, the conquest of new worlds with fire and sword as if the release of brutal exploitation were also the way of the religion of the cross and of love; unasked for and utterly absurd meddling in problems of developing natural science; proscriptions and excommunications by a spiritual authority which behaves as if it were political, and even demands recognition as such.

Von Balthasar put forward steps to be taken: no defence could be given; it was necessary to make a full confession; it would not be right to throw stones 'when no one is alive to stand up and plead for justification'.

In the second year of his papacy the Pope began a reinvestigation of the case of Galileo, condemned by Pope Urban VIII and forced to abjure the Copernican system. After lengthy examination the mistakes were frankly recognised by the commission John Paul had set up (although why it took so long to do so was not explained). In 1992 the Pope summed up the lesson that remained valid in relation to similar situations: depicting the world as lacking an absolute physical reference point in Galileo's time was, he said, inconceivable, while this reference point could only be situated in the earth or in the sun. 'Today, after Einstein and within the perspective of contemporary cosmology, neither of these two reference points has the importance they once had.' The new observation shows that often, beyond two partial and conflicting perceptions, 'there exists a wider perception which includes them and goes beyond both of them'.

The Spanish Inquisition, the wars fought by baptised Christians against one another, the inhumane treatment of Africans, for which the church bore some responsibility, the slave trade, mistreatment of indigenous peoples by European Colonists, the enmity between Christians and Muslims, and not least the injustice visited on the poor by the rich; these were only a few in the numerous, perhaps thirty or more, 'acts of atonement', acts of self-examination in the name of the church.

The Pope wrote these confessions, and the texts – sometimes arousing wide public interest but often passing unnoticed – were very personal. In his huge daily output of handwritten sheets he still would, by way of dedication at the top of each page, scribble by hand a few words of prayer: such as '*Totus tuus ego sum*', '*Adore te devote*', '*Magnificat anima mea Dominum*'. Invariably he asked forgiveness – a collection of quotations from these statements contains some twenty-five such supplications. (He even went as far, in *Mulieris Dignitatem (On the Dignity and Vocation of Women)*, as correcting the teaching of St Paul, who described the subjection of woman to man. 'All the suggestions in favour of the "subjection" of woman to man in marriage,' he writes, must be understood in the sense of 'mutual subjection' of both of them 'out of reverence for Christ'. No pope before him had ever corrected St Paul.)

The moving quality and personal sincerity of these avowals may be judged as they ranged from the direct and affectionate use of 'brothers and sisters' in inviting Muslims to his days of prayer at Assisi in 1986 and 1993: 'All of us, Christians and Muslims, live under the sun of the one merciful God. We both believe in the one God who is the Creator of man . . . Thus, in a true sense, we can call one another brothers and sisters in faith in the one God' – to the more emotional and timeless call to reflect on the sinful and unjust treatment of black people, and the historic barbarity of slavery.

When he visited the island of Gorée, Senegal, he spoke of the reality of injustice, and that he had come there to pay homage to 'all those victims, unknown victims; no one knows exactly how many there were; no one knows exactly who they were. Unfortunately our civilization, which calls itself Christian, returned to this situation of anonymous slaves in our century: we know what concentration camps were: here is a model for them.'

When he visited the 'house of slaves' on behalf of the Catholic people of Gorée, he implored heaven's forgiveness from 'this African shrine of black sorrow'. He recalled for his audience that Pius II, in 1462, writing to a missionary bishop who had been leaving for Guinea, described the enslavement of black people as the 'enormous crime', the *magnum sceles*.

Throughout a whole period of the history of the African continent, black men, women and children had been

> brought to this cramped space, uprooted from their land and separated from their loved ones to be sold as goods. They came from all different countries and, parting in chains for new lands, they retained as the last image of their native Africa Gorée's basalt rock cliffs. We could say that this island is fixed in the memory and heart of all the Black diaspora.

At Strasbourg in 1988, John Paul pronounced at the European Parliament that 'Medieval Latin Christendom, to mention only one example, while theoretically elaborating the concept of the state, following in the great tradition of Aristotle, did not always avoid the integralist temptation of excluding from temporal community those who did not profess the true faith.' In Poland in 1991 he condemned such a 'fanatical and fundamentalist attitude'.

In St Peter's, on 1 April 1993, Wojtyla commemorated the uprising in the Warsaw ghetto in 1943:

> The joy of this day must not prevent us from turning our attention to an event, so filled with human suffering, which took place 50 years ago: the uprising in the Warsaw ghetto . . . The days of the *Sho'ah* marked one of 'history's darkest nights', with unimaginable crimes against God and humanity. How could we not be with you, dear Jewish brothers and sisters, to recall in prayer and meditation, such a tragic anniversary?

One of Wojtyla's first actions on becoming archbishop in Krakow had been to have the macabre, anti-Semitic seventeenth-century painting in Kalwaria Monastery taken down to the basement, where it was eaten by rats. In April 1986, the first pope ever to do so, he had visited the Jewish synagogue in Rome, staying there an hour and fifteen minutes, embracing the Chief Rabbi twice and calling his hosts 'Hebrew brothers'. He admitted that in considering 'centuries-long cultural conditioning' we could not fail to recognise that 'the acts of discrimination, unjustified limitation of religious freedom, oppression also on the level of civil freedom in regard to the Jews were, from an objective point of view, gravely deplorable manifestations'. He re-stated, in the words of *Nostra Aetate*, the well-known declaration that the church 'deplores the hatred, persecutions, and displays of anti-Semitism directed against the Jews at any time and by anyone; I repeat: by anyone.'

He had brought together world religious leaders representing three billion worshippers for a World Day for Peace in 1986 at Assisi. Catholics, he acknowledged, 'had not always been peacemakers'. A year later he repeated: 'There is no doubt that the sufferings inflicted upon the Jews are also for the Catholic Church a reason for deep sorrow, especially if we think of the indifference and sometimes the resentment that in particular historical situations have divided the Jews and Christians.'

This scrutiny of the church's 'dark pages' was not to everyone's taste, and continued into the twenty-first century. As with his travels it provoked opposition, sometimes vocal criticism among senior church-men and members of the Curia, and best summarised as far back as 1949 by this Holy Office directive: 'Do not turn history against the Catholics by exaggerating their faults, nor in favour of the Reformers by concealing their faults. All things considered, that which constitutes the true essence of the events is the defection from the Catholic faith.' The criticism of his openness became so widespread that he had to go it alone.

He could well have been thinking back to his own experiences as a boy in Wadowice, when he played goalkeeper for a Jewish football team. He had to handle shots on the open (and often undefended) Catholic goal from whatever direction they came, and face the penalties, entailing

> a frank recognition of the facts, together with a readiness to forgive and to make amends for our respective mistakes. They prevent us from shutting ourselves up within preconceptions, so often a source of bitterness and fruitless recriminations. They prevent us from making groundless accusations against our brother, imputing to him intentions and aims which he does not have. Thus, when we are impelled by a desire to understand fully the other's position, disagreements are settled through patient and sincere dialogue, under the guidance of the Holy Spirit, the Paraclete.

Yet in his promotion of reconciliation and to maintain a balanced papacy in his quest for peace, he did not overlook militant Arab aspirations in the ongoing Arab–Israeli conflict over Palestine. In late 1982, Yasser Arafat visited the Pope in Rome, leaving in the ante-chamber the gun he always carried in his belt. He and the Pope spoke in English for 20 minutes without interpreters. A high-profile boost for the PLO, this scandalised the Israeli government, who accused Arafat of wanting 'to complete the work of Hitler and that the pope's meeting with him is indicative of a certain moral standard', while the Chief Rabbi of New York denounced collusion between 'the prince of peace and the prince of terror'.

He has continued to the very end to condemn the persecution of Jews.

The most chequered and unsatisfactory dealings of the Pope's ponti-ficate were with the Eastern Orthodox churches.

Eastern Orthodoxy and in particular Russian Orthodoxy had long-standing quarrels with the Roman Catholic churches, and with the end of Communism in Eastern Europe many of these old divisions, after long and often bitter attempts at burial, came to the surface.

In the newly independent Ukraine, for example, there was extreme hostility between the Uniates (five million Catholics of the Byzantine-Ukrainian rite), who owed their allegiance to Rome, and an Orthodox community split into three quarrelsome parts – one loyal to Moscow, and two fiercely independent: Father Ilarian, an Orthodox priest complained: 'The Uniates have seized back about a thousand of our Orthodox churches. Of course, it was a great injustice that Stalin abolished them in 1946 but you cannot cure one injustice with another.'

In front of the Pope at a St Peter's prayer service in 1991, Metropolitan Spyridon of Venice, Italy's Orthodox leader, ferociously condemned the Roman church for aggression in the Ukraine and Romania. Following the shocked silence that ensued, John Paul rose from his seat and 'without a word drew Metropolitan Spyridon into an embrace – the ancient kiss of peace'.

It changed little. Not only did most of the Eastern churches believe they had a far deeper union with God through heart and soul rather than the superficial intellect of Rome and its 'light-hearted rituals', but also they had never forgotten 1204 when the Catholics sacked Byzantium in their Fourth Crusade. Their view remained that if Orthodox belief was 'right', any other kind of belief must be 'wrong'. Religious pluralism and freedom of conscience did not make much sense to most Eastern Orthodox, while reasoning, as another Russian divine once declared, was 'the mother of all lusts'.

Humility about faith was not a noticeable Orthodox feature; Orthodox priests did not mince their words:

Jerusalem! That is an eternal drama they have there and history is what is produced out of this drama, by God and his people. This battle between all the religions to be the closest to God will last until the end of the world. But you know what delights me most? That Orthodoxy has remained the closest to God. Eighty per cent of the holiest places in the city are held by the Orthodox. The Greek priest who guards Christ's tomb, he's not going to give it up to anyone. Oh, no, not he! It's on this fire of faith that Christ's Church is built.

As for Anglican women priests? For the average Orthodox priest, they were, as one described it, 'a very disgusting phenomenon'. There may be moderates among the 200 million Orthodox believers, but – according to Victoria Clarke, who investigated the late-twentieth-century surge of Orthodoxy – not many in the heartland of Greece; or among the senior Orthodox clergy.

In Serbia an Orthodox patriot told Clark that in less than a decade after the end of the Cold War East and West were back to open schism. According to Orthodox belief, the Reformation had cost the West not only her rich monasteries and profiteering priests, but also its connection with the dead and with the fate of their souls. And here of course the Slav pope Wojtyla felt more sympathy with the Eastern church and its Slavophile observances of a relative's death, its ceaseless observations of anniversaries of the departed, and its rich celebration of hierarchies and great human beings, than with the cold levelling egalitarianism of much Western belief.

When visiting Istanbul in 1979 he had entertained high hopes of opening a constructive dialogue to reconcile the two churches. He had met Dimitrios in the patriarch's garden, the Pope wearing a red stole, Dimitrios a violet stole: 'This meeting is a divine gift,' John Paul had declared. But little had progressed at this time beyond exchanging views, and various trips and projected meetings were cancelled on the Orthodox side.

By June 1991, when he met with the Orthodox clergy at Bialystok, Poland, in spite of his appeal for reciprocal forgiveness – 'We have all made mistakes – let us, in a spirit of mutual reconciliation, forgive each other the wrongs we have suffered in the past' – the Eastern churches did not come closer.

In this, as in other causes, he persevered in the face of considerable personal danger. A bomb exploded just before his arrival in Athens on a 24-hour visit in 2001 as part of a pilgrimage to follow in the footsteps of St Paul. Monasteries were draped in black, and bells rang in mourning. 'When the Orthodox speak of the Fourth Crusade, you'd think it was an event of World War II,' commented Archbishop Nicholas of Athens, head of Greece's quarter million Catholics.

In spite of many and various initiatives – a joint document issued by the Pope and Patriarch of Constantinople when the latter visited Rome in 1995, John Paul's repeated exhortations and regrets ('The sin of our separation is very serious') – the conflict continued. This was not for want of trying on his part, or even for want of experiencing rebuffs and suffering severe humiliation. Appealing often for reciprocal forgiveness he never stopped in his efforts to make the Christian church, as he had told Gorbachev, 'breathe with both lungs'. Gorbachev had said in an aside to his wife, '. . . he is a Slav': in his love of pilgrimaging above all, Karol Wojtyla had the heart of a Slav. Dostoevsky writes in *The Brothers Karamazov* how the Russian peasant 'may suddenly . . . abandon everything and go off on a pilgrimage for his soul's salvation, or perhaps he will suddenly set fire to his native village, and perhaps do both. There are a good many "contemplatives" among the peasantry' – a view the Pope may have been tempted to share.

John Paul rounded off the St Paul voyage by stopping at Malta (where Paul was shipwrecked), and Syria (where Paul fled Damascus). Here when he visited the tomb of John the Baptist, which is located in a mosque, he become the first pope ever to set foot in a mosque. The Muslim world, equally, had become the target of John Paul's 'courage to forgive' – the phrase he used expressly of Islamic extremism, in particular the murder in May 1996 of seven Trappist monks by armed Muslims who cut their throats.

The real problem as regards Islam, was, as the writer of *When a Pope Asks Forgiveness*, Luigi Accattoli, pointed out, 'reciprocity'. In the assembly of world religious leaders at Assisi ten years earlier the Pope had called for a day of peace. Many had opposed that initiative but on the Pope's insistence it took place. Khaled Fouad Allam, a member of the Muslim delegation, reflected that during the interreligious day of prayer, 'I heard a phrase from Wojtyla that struck me: "We Catholics have not always been bearers of peace" . . . In Islam we have not yet reached this level; there are other problems, the first of which is the economic crisis and the Islamic extremism of Indonesia and Algeria.' Wojtyla himself had been a consistent bearer of peace, but reconciliation with other religions did not come easily.

28

True Protagonist of the Story

(1996–2000)

Christ remains before our eyes on his cross, in order that each human being may be aware of the strength that he has given him.

Pope John Paul, 1979

A German truck had knocked Karol Wojtyla down in 1944, and he subsequently recovered in a Krakow hospital; this had been the first major setback to his physical being. But until 1981 he had enjoyed, more or less, uninterrupted robust health. All this changed in that year, with the assassination attempt, although few would go so far as his anaesthesiologist at the Gemelli Hospital who maintained he never fully recovered from the psychological trauma which weakened him 'not due to senility but to interior suffering. If you are a person who loves, and someone shoots at you, the effect will be profound.'

In the subsequent eleven years of his pontificate there had been no evidence of this. There was no secrecy about his announcement, on 12 July 1992, when he told the crowd in St Peter's Square, 'Now I would like to tell you something confidential: this evening I shall go to the Gemelli Hospital for some diagnostic tests.'

Three days later Crucitti operated on the tumour found in the Pope's colon; the size of a fist or an orange, it was benign. The surgery lasted more than four hours, as they had to take extra care on account of the previous operation. The team also removed his gall bladder, which had gallstones.

John Paul recovered fully and quickly. He returned straight away to his room, where he was described as reacting 'perfectly, not like a man of his age, but like a young man'. From prison Agça sent him a get-well message. Although the growth was non-malignant, the operation triggered a spate of speculation that never abated over the next decade. When would he retire? Had he passed his peak (Communism was dead, he had served his purpose and now ought to go)? He was officially 'failing'.

His public visibility laid him open to having his image manipulated by the press. Often this was taken to absurd lengths as his detractors now saw him as sagging and stooping, with lustreless eyes, hand pressed to forehead – the photographs selected to fit the slant of the text. 'Tired and bitter' was the constant cry.

He was no such thing. The visits kept up. 'I travel to live, and I live to travel,' he once said. But he did honour his new rapport with interviewers and public over his health, often in a bantering form, telling reporters from his Alitalia flight to Kingston, Jamaica, in 1993, 'Up until now I have been able to walk on my own two feet, even in the mountains. I do everything possible to keep myself in shape, to avoid causing problems.' Much earlier, having the indoor pool installed in Castel Gandolfo, when critics questioned the cost, he had said, 'It's cheaper than a conclave.' Anyway it had been donated by Polish Americans.

At this time he began to suffer a tremor in his left hand. On 11 November 1993 he tripped or slipped on new carpeting in the Hall of Benedictions, falling down several steps and breaking his right shoulder. Gesturing with his left hand to the crowd he punned in Italian, '*Sono caduto ma non sono scaduto*' – 'I've fallen but not been downgraded.'

Henceforth, instead of writing by hand, he began dictating to Monsignor Rylko, his Polish assistant, who tapped his words into a laptop. Co-ordination was evidently failing, for only five months later he slipped taking a bath in his private quarters, breaking his right thigh bone, or femur, and again being taken to the Gemelli. The replacement hip was not entirely successful and he now had to use a cane. 'They are giving me a thorough examination,' he told the crowd from a Gemelli window, 'I never knew there were so many organs and so many possibilities.' But part of the press even falsely rumoured that through the 1981 blood transfusion he had contracted AIDS.

He could be mournful, wistful or humorous about these new and now permanent afflictions, themselves an effect not only of the shooting but of the remorseless discipline he had set himself. He remarked to doctors, 'I don't like to make a spectacle of myself, walking with a cane.' Another time when people in St Peter's Square were shouting, 'Viva il Papa! Viva il Papa!' he muttered, 'He lives – for the time being.' Aware journalists with binoculars were watching like hawks (or vultures) to see if he stumbled or his hand shook, he held out his hand, which clutched a sheaf of paper – 'See,' he said, 'not a single sheet has fallen! All the pages have stayed in my hand.' He self-mockingly quoted Galileo's famous comment on the earth's rotation to his bishop after a slow and painful walk to a Synod conference table '*Eppur' si muove*' – ('Yet it moves'). He told various crowds on different occasions that he checked in the papers to see if he was unwell or if he was better that day. More cheerfully he referred to death – upon exhortations to live – 'With this uproar it would be difficult to die, but the time will come.' Would he last to 2000?

'Neck down, not so good.' He began to comment that the millennium 'must also be introduced with suffering', assuming, that is, he would be there to do this. But on Easter Friday, 8 April 1994, he preached once more his passionate attachment to his theology of the body before the Michelangelo undraped nudes newly restored in the Sistine Chapel frescoes. He, according to the *New York Times*, 'seemed not the least embarrassed and, despite his frequent affirmations of the church's conservative teachings on sex' (in authorising the restoration he had half the loincloths from *The Last Judgment* removed). Again he was affirming his 'exuberant and readily roused sensuality' in his earlier words, and that this 'is the stuff from which a rich – if difficult – personal life may be made'. Once more, in the summer of 1996, the Gemelli became 'Vatican Number Three' when after prolonged and painful stomach upsets he returned for eleven days, his sixth medical treatment. This was for no more than the removal of a 'grumbling' appendix.

In 1996 he wrote the memoir *Gift and Mystery*, another very personal, even nostalgic book. In it he outlined, very simply, key moments and influences in his early vocation, and meditated on the priesthood. This gentle and affectionate manual or autobiography of priestly formation, in which he showed great warmth and gratitude towards those who freed him and enabled him to achieve his full stature, was penned with simplicity and lucidity.

Presence was the key. *Gift and Mystery* places you in Wojtyla's presence, as did his plays, poems and philosophical works, which seemed to have gathered layers of complexity as he grew into his middle years, and then successively peeled off the layers. The years peel away and you are back with Karol Wojtyla, the earnest, dedicated child. 'The gift is constantly growing!' he writes. 'It is wonderful that a man can never say that he has fully responded to the gift.'

Presence had always been the key. And attentiveness to the will of God. Here was a man who did not have a private life.

In 1997 the pope watchers discerned a deepening of the left-hand tremor. Speech thickened and slurred, face assumed a mask appearance, the whisperings began that he had Parkinson's disease, or a variant of it. The wear-and-tear of the job had caught up. Serious arthritis developed in his right knee; heavy loss of hearing in both ears.

He humorously reversed his previous attitude, now telling the cardinals, 'From the neck up I'm great': the cup was half full, no longer half empty. He had to figure out ways to fulfil appointments, cutting the reading of 100 documents a day to fifty, the thirty meetings down to ten. He inserted fifteen-minute breaks between appointments. From now on the physical impairment was evident, but there was no diminution in mental power, indeed sometimes an increase. Energy, health, vitality would fluctuate, come and go in cycles. The inscrutable and unblinking gaze with which he fixed people, said Dr Straiton the ophthalmologist, 'may be due to Parkinson's disease'. His punishing schedules and timetables were whittled down, but not that much; the much-touted reports of him losing control of the Vatican, of his enforced inactivity and early retirement to bed, of a period of acute and unprecedented danger for the church, were unfounded.

Moreover, he never became the lonely and isolated replica of many of his predecessors. In the privacy of his Vatican apartments he had his 'secret guardian angel' – Sister Tobiana, mother superior of the Congregation of the Heart of Jesus. A simple devout nun in her sixties, since joining his staff in the Archbishop's Palace in Krakow, she had dedicated her life to him. As nurse, closest friend and confidante she had become the family he lost so early in his life, while a Polish insider tells me that she had grown to become like a mother and sister to him. 'I would say she is the only person who can boss the Pope about. Like a mother she wants what is best for him and if that means taking his medicine or going to bed early then she makes him do it.'

On the table next to his bed at night now stood an electric alarm
button wired through to Tobiana's room. At work during daytime he
carried a pulse button linked to her, while on foreign tours, she
travelled behind him in a second vehicle.

In 1997 he set foot in Poland yet again, for the seventh time in his
pontificate. The immediate post-Communist trip had not been a
success: he had appeared angry, tired and reactionary, out of tune
with the new monster of freedom he had helped to bring into being.
Agitation for permissive abortion laws embittered him, as did the
hectic growth of the trashier aspects of consumerism. Purified in the
fire of conflict, Poland was selling its soul for a McDonald's burger.
Verbally brandishing the Ten Commandments the usurped Wojtyla
shook his fist and wept at Polish crowds.

But by 1997 tradition and good sense (as conservative forces might
say) had to some extent reasserted themselves and once again, and
with better communication from his entourage, at least the Pope
became restored as Papa Wojtyla, father of his country. Eight years
on from liberation and exposure to democracy and Western-style
entrepreneurism, the fading of the novelty and awareness of the
superficiality had helped to re-establish some of the basic values of
the Polish nation and soul, although materially it was following in the
footsteps of major European Union countries. It pleased him once
more to be there. 'Every return to Poland,' he said on arrival in
Wroclaw, 'is like a return to the family home, where the smallest
objects remind us of what is closest and dearest to our hearts.'

He made a further, more nostalgic visit to Poland in August 2002,
three years later, again strengthening his symbolic fatherhood of his
nation. Here he celebrated mass at the timbered Redemptorist church
in Podgorze, Krakow, where during the occupation, when he had
walked to work, he stopped on the journey to receive communion.

'Until this day,' he said, 'I remember this road from Borek Falecki to
Debniki. Every day I walked this road for different shifts in the
wooden shoes I used to wear in those days.'

He prayed at the tomb of his parents and his brother. He stopped
his popemobile at 10 Tyniecka Street where, when a seven-year-old
boy emerged from the building to give him a bunch of flowers, he
appeared close to tears. Lengthy searches after the end of Communism
had failed to find any heir to his uncle's house, so the Pope had been
told he was the inheritor. He refused this sole opportunity in his life for

the ownership of a property. The house went to the city. He did not visit Wadowice, where the house he was born in had now become a museum in his honour, and where his skis and boots were now exhibited.

In spite of never owning land or property, 'He's like every British aristocrat,' says a former Polish countess who fled the Russians from Eastern Poland, settled in Krakow, and as a child was confirmed by Wojtyla, who often visited her house. She now lives in London. 'He makes you feel at ease. You feel you met him 150 years ago . . . he's so great that he's ordinary. In Polish we say he gives you a "feeling of adequacy".' When finally he should come to die, she added, 'Krakow will be in mourning for the rest of time.'

On 31 August 1997 Diana, Princess of Wales died in a car crash in an underpass alongside the River Seine; five days later the Albanian nun, Mother Teresa of Calcutta, died at the age of eighty-seven. 'It was providential,' said John Paul, that Mother Teresa died at the same time as Diana. Both, according to him, as personalities pointed to a way beyond the self, to the demands of self-giving. 'I hope [Mother Teresa] will be a saint,' he said, and she became one, not instantly as the cry went up at the time, but with some waiving of formalities in 2002.

He had, throughout the 1990s, seen one world society after another muddying his vision of the sanctity of marriage, endorsing artificial fertilisation, homosexual unions, abortion. He railed, sometimes in a very personal way, as Timon of Athens did against flattery and ingratitude, against these developments, especially when it came to women and reproduction because, as his close friend Deskur remarked, this cathartic fury had a source in his own personal life: his mother's early death and the loss of Olga, the sister he had never known. The loss of something he could never have stung him into anguish.

But who was to judge if he was right or wrong? In Poland in 1991 he had scolded and berated Parliament and the people as if everything that came from the West in their new-won freedom was corrupt. It was as if he felt that if he did not hold to a rigid line everything would fall apart. He confessed sadly in the privacy of personal audiences, that 'I spent all my life on a concept of the person, and these problems.'

In *Evangelicum Vitae* (*The Gospel of Life*, 1995), his encyclical on the sanctity of life, John Paul claimed once again that society was excessively concerned with efficiency and looked upon as 'an enemy to be resisted or eliminated' those who not only were weak or ill, but simply existed. The facts bore him out – 1.6 million foetuses per year aborted by American women in the mid-1990s, while Moscow alone registered 137,000 abortions in 1994, more than double its 64,000 live births. The average Russian woman during her lifetime had five abortions. The uncomfortable vision of the costly freedom of the Gospel message, his thousands of encounters with the poor, the oppressed, had come up with some pretty extreme examples to test him. Someone in his household once asked, 'Does it make you weep?' 'No, not on the outside,' answered the Pope.

The interior man, the self-observer who watched the outward performer, still knew, with a supernatural instinct, that this defiance, this resistance, would to the very end continue to stimulate the vital forces within him and would serve to challenge not only the faithful, but the world at large with his presence. To him his brief was clear, 'I shall accomplish Peter's task for as long as Providence allows.'

Alone, of all the world leaders he had ever met over the past twenty-two years, President Clinton, with whom he said he was unable to make eye contact, was 'a bad listener . . . never paid much attention to what I said'. John Paul told this to Professor Fineschi, who had operated on his hip and with whom for a spell he had dined once a week: 'The only leader I never managed to have a proper conversation with was Clinton. While I was speaking he was always looking somewhere else, admiring the frescoes and paintings. He was not listening to me. But patience, patience.'

In 1995, before the World Youth Day when an estimated five million came to his closing mass (a Japanese company used aerial photography to calculate the number per acre, and claimed it was as much as seven million), a Manila apartment near John Paul's temporary residence in the Vatican embassy caught fire. Firefighters discovered plans and explosives for assassinating the Pope and blowing up a dozen Boeing 747s over the Pacific – as well as priests' cassocks for disguising the terrorists. Two Al Qaeda plotters of Islamic nationality were eventually arrested, one of whom, Banzy Yousef, had been convicted of the 1993 New York World Trade Center bombing.

In January 1998 he travelled to Cuba to visit a strangely humbled President Castro, icon of liberal Marxists and idealists in the 1960s. On the flight from Rome, Wojtyla said, 'I know well what I shall say about human rights. Human rights are the foundation of every civilization. I brought this conviction out of Poland, from my confrontation with the Soviet system and communistic totalitarianism. Nothing other than this can be expected from me.'

He displayed remarkable physical endurance on the five-day trip – which reminded him of his first return to Poland in 1979 – while unexpectedly Castro met him four times and, as an Italian commentator said, 'Over and over again, the most respected man in the world extended his hand to the man the U.S. government wished to banish from the world community.' At his palace reception the dictator presented his brothers, Raùl and Ramòn, and his sisters, Agnes and Agostina, to the Pope. 'My sister Agostina,' Castro explained, 'would like to embrace you as they do in Rome.' 'Let us do it,' agreed the Pope. They embraced and she wept.

John Paul inveighed against the American embargo of Cuba, saying that embargoes 'must always be condemned insofar as they are harmful to those who are most needy' (the U.S. subsequently reduced its embargo), but he also requested Castro to reform his country and ease its restrictions on liberty. He returned to Rome rejuvenated and, with a new confrontation with Communism, telling a general audience that the visit reminded him very much of his first papal trip to Poland in 1979.

On a trip to Bosnia, two years later, NATO officials alerted the papal party before landing, and had to call up an F16 plane escort. They told the Pope it was dangerous to land. Between the airport and Sarajevo, fifteen kilometres away, the underside of a bridge the popemobile had to cross had been packed with 100 kilos of plastic explosive. It had not been dismantled properly; the Pope asked the ones sent to tell him not to go, 'Are there people waiting for me?' 'Yes.' 'Then I will go.' This time the Islamic terrorists who planted the bomb were Iranian.

Beirut, too, was another conflict-torn city which after three cancelled attempts he visited in 1997. In advance of landing, he gave final absolution to everyone on his plane. On the ground 20,000 soldiers and police guarded him; the whole Catholic population of 1.3 million turned out to greet him.

As the measure of how much love we are capable of giving, he defiantly defined liberty, and while addressing the United Nations in 1995 as an apostle to hope, he stated: 'At the evening of our life we will be judged on love.'

So would he be himself. He adored meeting people, and called them to him, from all states and all classes, universal in his strength and breadth. He put on many costumes in many lands – Indian head-dresses, Mexican sombreros, African robes – just as he had sung and spoken in many tongues. He embraced all cultures but remained unified and one in himself.

In 1983, he had featured as the hero in a children's Marvel Comics book. He had become a grandiose personage, superlative in the celebrity hype he so obviously loathed. (Springer is dubbed in the satirical *Jerry Springer: The Opera*, thus: 'He's bigger than the fucking pope!') Crowds energised him, and not only crowds but writers and artists of all creeds and complexity – from a popular film he loved, such as Roberto Bemigmi's *Life is Beautiful*, to Nietzsche and Schopenhauer's nihilistic atheism. With every day punctuated and sustained by a pattern of intense prayer, unimpaired mental power and unswerving faith remained with him till the final days. He championed life itself, the whole span, beginning with the moment of conception, and ending with eternity. A Polish hero, he rode into battle as protector not only of the objects and aims of his love, but of all that was truly precious in fragile human nature. He was now a historic figure, and had he never lived the whole of the history of the twentieth century would have been different.

29

The Outward Husk of Mortality

(2000–03)

For nearly twenty years now we have become aware of the Papacy as the point of suffering, the needle of pain, and a certain love always arises for the man who suffers. Pain makes an individual, whether it is a Chinese woman weeping for her dead child or a patient figure in a hospital bed or this man in the Vatican.

Graham Greene on Pope Pius XII

Many heroes and great figures have but one turning-point and one death; Wojtyla had three main turning-points – his decision to become a priest, his assumption of papal authority, his near assassination – but he had also suffered as many as four near deaths. The ultimate destiny that he could be seen to embody was closely linked with the future of his church and, who knows, possibly humankind's future.

In his extreme old age he arrived at a further and final turning-point. He passed into the new millennium looking frail and weighed down even by his robes, and for the first time stood still on a mobile platform pushed by attendants. One Vatican analyst said the schedule he set himself was tantamount to suicide. Yet at a New Year audience in 2000 for ambassadors to the Holy See he remarked, 'God never asks us to do something which is beyond our powers . . . He gives us the strength to carry out what he expects of us.'

Two years later, in 2002, he still insisted on his full programme of foreign travel, that year to Azerbaijan and Bulgaria, then Canada, Mexico and Guatemala. Christ did not descend from the cross, he said, and nor would he fail to carry out his traditional three-hour masses over Easter. He denounced, face contorted from the persistent knee pain of arthritis, 'the spiral of hatred, revenge and abuse of power into which the Holy Land [had] fallen', pleading for peace. 'This is truly a great tragedy.'

He refused an electric wheelchair delivered to the Vatican. Variously he was reported as receiving – or not receiving, using natural cures and Hindu meditation – Levodopa, a conventional medication for Parkinson's disease needing increasingly close monitoring. Was he deliberately, even as a kind of moral or emotional blackmail, now using suffering as a weapon – 'his last bout as a great showman?' a reporter mockingly asked. 'I am desperately ill, yet I undertake these gruelling missions. With me suffer and believe.'

His critic Cornwell, reaching a climax of papal deconstruction, found him liable to the most alarming Parkinson's symptoms of all: acute depression and 'phases of paranoia'. If the first, he could take Prozac, but 'in the case of paranoia, who is to decide that he is psychotic rather than the victim of a genuine conspiracy to oust him?' But this 'spectre raised by specialists' was, according to Dr Richard Greenhall – a neurologist with an interest in Parkinson's disease – 'unusual' if arising from drug treatment. Greenhall distinguished between depression caused by the illness (in the Pope's case negligible), and other causes of dementia or cognitive trouble. The Pope appeared now to have reached a plateau of care in which the cocktail of therapies ensured competent but limited performance of his duties. The 'lapses' relished by commentators would be caused, Greenhall told me, by necessary adjustments to that cocktail, for progressively a patient becomes unpredictably responsive to treatment. According to well-informed Vatican sources John Paul had made provision for his retirement should he become mentally or physically handicapped to the extent that he could no longer be in charge. But otherwise retirement before death was just not an option.

He above all men knew the limits of theatrical gesture, and how it could rebound on its executant. He knew his brilliant stage-managed trip to the Holy Land in 2000, with its moving photo-opportunities of the Pope at the Wailing Wall, for all its magic, its drama of conflict and reconciliation, had not stopped the Church of the Nativity in Bethlehem, Christ's birthplace, from being profaned by bloodshed and armed occupation.

His old but sharp eyes and memory could see only too clearly Wawel Cathedral with Governor Frank still strutting at large over the desecrated images. As Palm Sunday arrived in 2000 and the Pope celebrated in St Peter's Square with 100,000 people, Mossad, the Israeli secret service, put Italian police on high alert, warning there could be an 'Islamic terrorist attack on the Holy Father'. Now Wojtyla had visited the Holy Land, shared intelligence between Israel and the Vatican had become one benefit. Between the Bernini columns, to screen visitors and the faithful, stood metal detectors. Both uniformed and plain-clothes police were strengthened to ward off any attack that, even if it did not reach the Pope himself, would be symbolic – to disrupt the Middle East peace process and discredit his triumphant visit to the Holy Land earlier in the year. But he had to do what he could, and while his resistance to evil vitalised him, while his passion still raged, while his anger of a lifetime could still be cherished and channelled, he would follow the path of peaceful acceptance, and not the artist's ego: 'Old age should burn and rage at close of day/Rage, rage, against the dying of the light.'

The old showman knew perfectly well what he was doing: 'making himself suffer' again countered the cynical press who accompanied him to Azerbaijan, where reputedly lived only 120 Catholics. He riposted, 'I'm sorry to be forcing you to travel once again.' But he, the inner Wojtyla, characteristically independent and his own man to the last, was not making himself suffer for the church. In terms of what he was doing the suffering was irrelevant. The fact now that people called him a symbol of the suffering Christ: that was purely incidental, it was never the intention.

The valid answer was that he still felt called to act as a witness to the truth – and he still had the opportunity to use his first-class philosophical mind for the benefit of mankind. This was *Veritatis Splendor* in action, this hard thing he now did, running counter to his own comfort and desire for security, but it brought him a terrible joy by joining him to Christ on the cross who was raised for all to see, a source of resurrection and of a more authentic existence in that presence. He had now taken on, in his own flesh and body, a persevering presence in the face of crippling adversity, as Eamon Duffy, Cambridge professor of the history of Christianity, wrote, a 'witness to the nobility of suffering and the value of the weak whom society prefers to sideline'.

As well as direct and divine inspiration, all through Wojtyla's life the Virgin Mary had been the platonic ideal, a supreme embodiment of virtue. Plato's theory of forms, expounded in *The Republic*, considered this whole life, like a shadow cast upon a wall, as an illusion, although that shadow itself was of an eternal form. No man more energetically devoted his life to a female historical figure who was for him a living presence, while he thought no religion – certainly not the Anglican and Nonconformist Christian churches, Judaism or Islam – proposed that balance and equality between the feminine world and way of thinking, and the male ethos, more than does Roman Catholicism.

Wojtyla's relationship with the mother of Christ had over his long life an extraordinary dramatic structure of its own. Wojtyla saw Mary's life as God's intervention in human history to save mankind from evil and the devil. To 'enlightened' Western ears this may sound ridiculous superstition, but on the basis of Karol's own life no one can prove or disprove it.

The bleak world picture of Stephen Hawking's *A Brief History of Time*, in which Hawking claimed to understand the mind of God, but in which the deity had become 'the merest whisper of an afterthought, a functionless grace-note to round off the theory', had lost credibility in the eyes of his scientific peers. It became increasingly evident that, as John Barrow, professor of the public understanding of mathematics at Cambridge, stated, 'No final theory of everything is possible.' The retreat of scientists with all-embracing explanations for the existence of the universe did not go as far as agreeing with Dante, who saw the cosmos as a machine 'constructed around the drama of salvation', but science backed down from claiming to be able to provide a spectacle of majestic forward projection, and increasingly mankind felt a deeper need for something else. As Ludwig Wittgenstein in 1951 said, 'We feel that even when all scientific questions have been answered, the problems of life remain completely untouched.'

No less individual and conclusive in Karol Wojtyla's integration of the Marian elements in his life, which he had underlined and emphasised whenever possible, was his decision, to reveal what the three popes before him had fallen short of revealing – many claimed with dire consequences. This was the chilling third secret of Fatima, believed to foretell the apocalypse.

In 1917 three Portuguese shepherd children had witnessed a visitation of Mary. They said the Virgin Mary appeared in their native village of Fatima above an olive tree and made three prophecies. The first was a vision of 'hell', seen as the First and Second World Wars; the second vision, uncannily fulfilled in the decade of the late 1980s, was the persecution of Christians under Russian Communist regimes that would ultimately be defeated. The fact that Ali Agça's assassination attempt happened on 13 May, the anniversary of the first Marian visitation at Fatima, replicated the Miracle of the Vistula in 1920 when the Polish armies defeated Russia. There were no accidents in human life (even the atheist Marxist Jean-Paul Sartre once pronounced, '*Il n'y a pas d'accidents*'). Wojtyla's election was not an accident. One of the church's obligations, as in Vatican Two, was to put over this truth: life had a purpose which extended beyond the grave.

The Pope had seen, so Cardinal Sodano, now Secretary of State since the retirement of Casaroli in 1990, revealed in 2000 on John Paul's third pilgrimage of thanks to Fatima after the shooting, a poster of Our Lady of Fatima in the St Peter's Square crowd on that near-fatal day. Sodano had quoted the Pope as saying that 'a motherly hand guided the bullet's path', and he 'was stopped at the threshold of death'. But the third Fatima secret, passed from pope to pope, had become a sticking-point, posing a dilemma. And then Wojtyla had it – and for twenty-two years kept it to himself.

Gorbachev, in his private meeting with the Pope (according to one diverting speculation), asked for a private reading of the third secret text, desperately needing as he did a miracle to stop the disintegration of his dream of a new federation of Russian states. Another notion, probably equally absurd, was that, from 1960, the popes kept silent because to reveal the second and third secrets would have given the Soviets a strategic long-term advantage over the non-Communist West.

The Pope went to Fatima in 2000 to beatify two of the three children, Tinta Marto and her brother Francisco, who were seven and nine at the time of the miracle, and who both died three years later in the worldwide influenza epidemic. The third child, ten at the time, was Lucia de Jesus dos Santos, cousin of the other pair, who had first revealed the visions to the public and written the secrets down. She was now 93, and a nun, and she and the Pope met and talked. The third secret had inspired many books, doomsday cults, and even, by a man who demanded the Vatican reveal it, a hijacking.

At this beatification mass, attended by more than 600,000 pilgrims,

Cardinal Sodano, but not Wojtyla himself, told the assembly that the third secret spoke of 'a bishop in white' who 'falls to the ground, apparently dead, under the burst of gunfire'. This referred to the attempted assassination. This was the third secret. In the full text, published later, the 'bishop' is the Holy Father who, traversing an apocalyptic landscape, is killed by soldiers. On this third commemorative trip, next to the offering he had already made of the bullet to the Virgin's statue, the Pope placed one of his most precious possessions, the ring given to him upon his election by Wyszynski. Veneration for the Blessed Virgin of Fatima provided a sweet respite for all tired, frightened and wavering souls.

The atmosphere of those three Fatima visits would never leave him:

> Fatima had become a darksome and velvet sea through which a winding stream of tiny flames moved to the rising and falling cadences of the Ave Maria voiced by the thousands of pilgrims, each carrying a lighted candle, who took part in the procession around the Basilica. It was a contrast between the dusty memories of long-dead men . . . and the living, breathing soul of a believing community renewing its quickened hopes and lively faith in the immortality guaranteed only by the all-powerful Son of the living God and delivered to mankind by the fiat of a village maiden now become the Queen of Heaven and the Mother of all human beings.

God (the protagonist) never promised Christians worldwide victory on earth. In imitation of his redeemer the 'Slavic Pope' had established himself as a symbol of human suffering. The final decision was not to step down.

30

Final Lighting of the Lamp

(2003–)

It is probably fair to assert that Europe, before 1914, produced virtually all of the ideas in which the twentieth century has traded; the rest being mere technical extensions of these ideas.

Norman Stone
Europe Transformed

The 2003 Iraqi war brought the question of the faith of Anthony Blair, the British prime minister, into the public arena. A devout Anglican with leanings towards Rome, Blair refused to discuss his religious practices ('We don't do God,' Alastair Campbell, his press secretary, said). Even so, with the robust condemnation by John Paul before the invasion began, it was generally perceived that Blair visited the Pope in February 2003 to put his case for a just war, although he knew he would be unlikely to succeed. But this was a private family visit, arranged long before, claimed his wife, and such it was.

John Paul had firmly opposed the first Iraqi war, which began in August 1990 with the Iraqi invasion of Kuwait. He wrote to the first President Bush to stress the devastating and tragic consequences that war would bring if the coalition of thirty-nine countries resorted to military action. He had gone to extraordinary lengths, with over fifty initiatives of diplomacy, meetings, letters and telephone calls to avoid hostilities, then later end them, then repair the damage. This unwavering dedication to peace has been much undervalued: Lech Walesa reacted with fury and regret that the Pope did not receive the Nobel Peace Prize for his efforts to stop the 2003 Iraqi war (the reason given was because of the church's stand on contraception).

I happened, two days before the arrival of Blair with his family, to be interviewing Monsignor Brian Chestle at the English College situated, sumptuously, in some of Rome's darkest and most tangled streets. In portraits hung on its walls the illustrious faces of persecuted bishops and martyrs proudly proclaimed the recently canonised saints of the English Catholic church.

The Monsignor, an extraordinary, quintessential English figure who might have stepped out of the pages of Evelyn Waugh, had just sat down in his study to talk with me when the phone rang. It was the English primate, Cardinal Cormac as he is known, calling from London. Near as I was to the Monsignor I could not but hear his brisk, business-like voice: 'I'm just with Cherie Blair,' he said amiably, 'and she wants to know the form when they meet the Pope. How should she play it?'

Chestle, who acted as usher and as master of ceremonies during private audiences with heads of state, explained the brief: 'The man goes into the library and has a talk; you wait outside, then you go in', and so on. 'She wants to know if anyone else is going.' 'The British Ambassador to the Holy See . . . But it's nothing to worry about. The Pope's very relaxed – just play it easy and speak up. The Pope has a deaf aid. Don't be like Mr Heath. "I used to be the British prime minister," he mumbled. The Pope went "huh" and turned away.'

Satisfied, Cardinal Cormac rang off. The Monsignor, clearly, was an old hand who had served this pope, and others before him. This one was 'approachable', he told me, always relaxed, never grows tense, 'switches from language to language. But if he gets irritated he bangs his hand on the table.'

The Blairs arrived in Rome. From Cherie Blair's perspective the visit was a high point, and she was delighted that they had come with a largely Catholic entourage. Blair likes the Catholic rites and had long attended mass, often on his own. Some years before he had been subject to criticism that he might convert: 'Can a modern, democratic leader really declare,' wrote Bishop Michael Nazir-Ali of Rochester in *The Times*, 'that he orders his spiritual life within such an autocratic framework?' Yet he might simply want to participate in the Eucharist.

The prime minister, who arrived with his wife and three of his children, spent twenty minutes with the Pope during which, over Iraq, John Paul told him, 'It is up to you to decide what to do.' Cherie joined him for a further ten minutes. Leo, their two-year-old son, had drawn a picture to give with the official gifts: Vatican Staff let him sit on one of the Pope's thrones. The Pope presented them with rosaries and medals and a fine icon.

The following morning, the second day of the visit, they attended mass in the new, brown marble-floored papal chapel at 8 a.m. (the time, as a concession to his age, had been moved from 7 a.m.). Here, as observed one of the Beda acolytes when they arrived, was the Pope sitting on a chair ten minutes before, facing the altar, absorbed in prayer. This image he gave was, for Cherie, a symbol of both suffering and the defeat of suffering. When he began to say mass he sprang to life: he said all of it, the first part in English but, when he came to the Eucharistic prayer, in Latin.

Blair, in off-the-peg suit and muted tie (taller and much younger-looking than he appeared in his photos), read the first reading from Isaiah, 'I it is who must blot out everything.' Euan, his eldest son, read the responsorial prayer 'Heal my soul for I have sinned against you . . .' and Kathryn, their daughter, the second reading, from Corinthians, 'Jesus was never yes and no: with him it was always yes.'

The Irish bishop, host at the Irish College where the Blairs were staying, read the Gospel from Mark, Chapter Two: 'The Son of Man has authority on earth to forgive sins.' There was no homily, while the Pope stood for the whole Eucharistic prayer.

The Pope then gave the family communion, while the other cele-brants gave communion to the rest of the congregation. The Pope, in spite of his strongly voiced opposition to the war, extended the warmest hospitality he could. 'Everyone had direct access to me,' he said of himself in Krakow and the same was true in Rome; to world leaders he was no different. 'A bishop must be a father.'

At the end of the mass the Pope sat in his chair, looking at the congregation. With those big blue eyes, Louis, one of seminarians from the Beda College who attended, said he 'doesn't miss a thing . . . He has that much power. He's saying, "I'm looking at all of you"'. The pope's diction had been distinct and clear – he'd been on new drugs since the previous summer: 'This guy will last for years,' had been Louis's verdict. At the end he stood – stooping to one side – and spoke, in English; 'God bless you all.' He shook everyone's hand, gave out rosaries, had his photograph taken holding Leo by the hand. The tone of the ceremony had been 'subdued and gentle', and of remark-able stillness. Later Cherie Blair surprised me by saying – meaning it seriously – that their visit was 'the highlight of my time here' (meaning 10 Downing Street).

In March 2003 John Paul unexpectedly published a final book of poetry entitled *Roman Triptych: Meditations*. Vincent Nichols, who much admired the Pope's ability to divide his mind, to listen and read a book at the same time – as Nichols observed him doing at a synod in the 1980s – had asked, 'Holy Father, you are not writing poetry any more?' To this he had answered, 'I don't have the context any more.' To others, after the publication of his poems and plays ended in the 1960s he had said that this side of him was 'now a closed chapter'.

But he kept in touch with his early plays even if he had not written another. He attended, as far back as 1980, a performance of *The Jeweller's Shop* played in the Vatican by an Italian company. In 1988 the Comédie-Française brought from Paris to Castel Gandolfo, during the summer vacation, a production of Charles Péguy's mystical and enchanting *Le Mystère de la charité de Jeanne d'Arc*, whose text had an immediate rapport with his own plays. Ten years later, in the Vatican private cinema, once a chapel, he attended a viewing of his fifty-year-old *Our God's Brother*, in Krzysztof Zanussi's film version, with Scott Wilson as Chmielowski. Zanussi had already directed *Job*, into which he inserted scenes depicting the assassination of Aldo Moro and Father Popieluszko. In 2004, watching in his kitchen on wide-screen TV Mel Gibson's *The Passion of the Christ* he said: 'That is what it was like.' Later Dziwisz denied he said it.

On the popular, more profane level of the pop world Ivan Michello and his group I Cugini di Campagna were singing '*La Nostra Terra*' – lyric by Karol Wojtyla – but in 1988 were disbarred from entering it into the San Remo pop festival. The jury refused it on the grounds that its lyricist was not Italian. 'But he's Bishop of Rome,' retaliated the group. The jury then said his fame would disadvantage the other contestants. Outraged, Michello responded, 'It's as if one said Brazil should not play football!' In 1999 a bestselling compact disc, *Abba Pater*, featured his prayers, homilies and psalms set against a musical background. It reached No. 53 in the British pop charts, ahead of the latest CD of Sinead O'Connor, who several years before on American TV's *Saturday Night Live* had torn up the Pope's picture.

Translated from Polish into English, again by Jerzy Peterkiewicz, the *Roman Triptych* created a new and moving dialogue, between Wojtyla and Michelangelo, between priest and pope, and former creative artist. It is no surprise the Sistine Chapel, Michelangelo's supreme creative act of his last years (he lived to the age of eighty-nine), housed and stimulated the meditation. This was where Karol was elected pope, and where the Last Judgment, in the great painter's vision, dominated the eye and the mind. Dante's imagery of hell in *The Inferno*, or the damnation of souls by an all-conquering God of justice in Michelangelo's Sistine Chapel vision, was still as real and pertinent to the present age as it had been to theirs. Michelangelo

> draws on the imagery of doom established since the so-called Dark Ages: the devils are as hairy, as bestial, as forked and cloven as any monstrous product of uncouth Romanesque fantasy. Christ, raising his right hand to strike down the damned, commands the full terror of absolute power so that even the elect seem to cower, while the fallen stream downwards convulsed in agony as the devils take them captive down to hell. Even the Virgin in this despairing painting cannot interpose, but curls herself under the figure of her son.

Wojtyla, like Michelangelo, was a man of vehemence, and while Michelangelo's work had not appealed to the Christian propagandists of the Enlightenment in the seventeenth century, neither had Wojtyla's papacy appealed to the progressive Catholic theologians in our time.

John Paul brought to that anguished and terrifying reality of judgment his own measured response. His triptych disclosed more calm, unleashing no vivid powers of violent self-dramatisation, but simplicity, sincerity, almost in awe of the place and its reverberations on his spirit.

'The Stream', the first part of *Roman Triptych*, reminds one of passages in *The Jeweller's Shop*, evoking a mountain landscape of the poet's hiking days, romantic in feel, Wordsworthian in its search for meaning and the sense of God's imprint on natural beauty:

> If you want to find the source
> You have to go up, against the current.
> Break through, search, don't yield,
> You know it must be here somewhere.

Going against the current repeated the defiant, resistant streak in his character. The second, 'Meditations on the book of Genesis at the

Threshold of the Sistine Chapel', was more physical, more personal: 'All this exuberance of vision, unleashed by human genius' (Adam and Eve in particular in their Garden of Eden) rekindled sexual innocence: although both were naked, 'They felt no shame in the presence of each other!'

Wojtyla, in these muted and heavily veiled revelations of the inner man, added a personal biographical detail when he quoted a Latin motto written above the gate of his Wadowice high school: 'for eight years I read these words every day . . . *Casta placent superis; pura cum veste venite/Et morubis puris sumite pontis aquam.*' Breaking a taboo, he contemplated his own death and the conclave for the election of a new pope. 'Meditations' became a rumination on his succession to the papacy as the cardinals assemble:

> They come here to this very place.
> And once more Michelangelo wraps them in his vision.
> In him we live and move and have our being.

What finer testimony could he leave of his own inner man – expressing faith and gratitude to his creator as manifest in the great artist, in himself, in the dramatic re-creation of Abraham's near sacrifice of his son, Isaac – subject of the third and final part of the triptych.

> Abraham, you who climb this hill in the land of Moriah,
> There exists a limit to fatherhood,
> A threshold you will never cross.
> Here another father will accept the sacrifice of his son.
> Do not be afraid, Abraham, go ahead,
> Do what you have to do.
> You will be the father of many nations.
> Do what you have to do, to the end.

To the very end he has kept his ability to surprise. Some believed his final return to Poland in the summer of 2002 may have sparked this revival. He followed this, published in Krakow in May 2004, on the occasion of his eighty-fourth birthday, with another prose work, *Wstancie chodzmy!* (*Rise, Let Us Be On Our Way!*), dealing with his years prior to his election and the critical importance of Brother Adam Chmielowski's model in leaving art and theatre behind. 'With the eyes of my heart I see the gigantic shape of my heart.' In March 2005 he published *Memory and Identity*, a last testament of 'auto-biographical, philosophical reflection on the horror of the twentieth century and his hopes for the future'. Drawing on transcriptions of discussions held over ten years earlier with the Polish philosopher Father Jozef Tischner and Krystztof Michalski in seminars at Vienna and Castel Gondolfo, *Memory and Identity* gathers together the threads of his perennial and never-failing thought, demonstrating again that in his life and work *'tout se tient'*. While *Rise, Let Us Be On Our Way* magnificently ennumerates the rites and symbols and his many friendships of his pre-papal days, with its main theme that 'God's love does not impose burdens on us that we cannot carry, *Memory and Identity* addresses the nature of ideologies and evil.'

In spite of worldwide visibility, in spite of superstar status and enormous celebrity, Karol Wojtyla's life has remained one of complete surrender and selfless dedication. As John Paul II he survived his bullet to implement his unique vision that God has entrusted the world to mankind as 'a gift', of which beauty is an intrinsic part, and also as 'a task'. With this vision he has raised awareness of what it means to be fully human. He might often have asked, as in that poem 'Actor', 'Did not the others, crowding in, distort the man that I am?' But ultimately he identified and lived his true self. He has remained subject and not object. As he wrote in another, earlier poem:

> I am a giver. I touch forces that expand the mind;
> Sometimes the memory of a starless night
> Is all that remains.

Epilogue

A pontificate in a complex age of unprecedented media explosion and suffocating information technology is made up of many strands; each one, separated, can be taken on its own and lengthy cases made for and against John Paul's effectiveness in dealing with it: all pronouncements may carry the papal stamp, but some may be far from reflecting the Pope's personal feeling or even immediate attention.

What is remarkable is that Wojtyla the man did not become swamped or sidetracked by the sheer volume of activity which, being at its centre, he found going on around him. Also that he remained unaffected by the many millions of words written about him by others. A modern pope has power through the influence of his response to events such as war or famine, and in the political realm he may also use his influence to warn or pre-empt. But his main and ultimate power is as a spiritual example to be followed. The church may prescribe and exhort, the pope may pronounce, but it is up to the individual what he or she does, and no one else is in charge of the navigation of his or her own soul.

John Paul's supreme achievement is that he has, through his millions of words and his living presence, made this more clear and more evident to more people on the globe than it is conceivable to imagine any one human being could. Over and again he has said – whether it be of nation or of group, or a single person – that destiny lies in the hands of each human being, to be worked out in relation to man's God-given freedom. His detractors have been the ones who argue against the human person as being deeply worthy of respect and capable of responsibility. They believe for a variety of reasons (e.g. socialism, Communism, imperialism, Fascism, utilitarianism, natural selection, situationism, determinism, scientism, etc.) that mankind is not capable of responsible choice. John Paul's assertion that the spiritual rights of mankind (ignoring for the moment the political and social rights) come only from the spiritual stature of man derived from and created by God. As such it is difficult to consider the life of Karol Wojtyla (or the history of Poland – 'God's playground') without reference to the divine dimension.

This pope never occupied the Vatican as landlord, material governor, or chief executive of Catholicism Worldwide Inc. 'I have always sensed,' he says in *Rise, Let Us Be On Our Way*, 'that Christ was the real owner of my episcopal residence, and that we bishops are just short-term tenants. That's how it was in Franciszkanska Street for almost twenty years, and that's how it is here in the Vatican.' He never set himself up to be a reformer ('My purpose is to conserve'). He ruled autocratically when he perceived the church to be in danger, but in most matters he has tempered his authority with compassion and moderation, and has striven above all to achieve a balance between serving and ruling.

His fundamental character has been a combination of apostle and genius, and in giving up the direction of the second in order to commit himself fully to the first he achieved a unique combination of both. He has steered a middle way, attempting with his chosen executives to balance a radical agenda with a liberal outlook, or – if you view it the other way – a liberal agenda (stemming from Vatican Two) with a radical conservative outlook. Listing the positions he has held under the headings 'conservative' or 'liberal', we find:

1. Conservative. Full of human sympathy as he is, how can he be so blind to so many human yearnings? For example, his reiterated rejection of contraception, women priests, divorce, married clergy and homosexual acts; according to liberals this has forced good Catholics into disobedience and desertion; the disciplining of dissident theologians has created a 'rule of fear'. He has been equally unyielding in his opposition to sexual freedom, to euthanasia, and to abortion; his readiness to reassert discipline over priests and nuns in what they wear, whether they married and what they taught, and his devotion to the Virgin Mary show attachment to out-of-touch and archaic principles.

2. Liberal. His opposition to war in whatever form has ignored
the principle of a 'just war'; his opposition to capital punishment, global capitalism, fundamentalism of all kinds, and
arms manufacture is unrealistic; his support of trades unions,
human rights, international organisations, the spirit of Vatican Two (he drafted some of the documents) has alienated
some of the traditionalists; his dialogue with other faiths,
apology for Catholic anti-Semitism, rehabilitation of thinkers
such as Galileo, and regret for other past church abuses have
weakened Vatican authority.

Many have drawn up such lists, but, as a cardinal in Rome said,
'conservative' and 'liberal' as terms applied to Karol Wojtyla's papacy
– though useful up to a point – were really 'categories of archaeology'.
The Pope has not been in some respects one, and in some respects the
other, but instead something else entirely.

In *Memory and Identity* the Pope sums up, 'the Lord God allowed
Nazism twelve years of existence, and after twelve years the system
collapsed'. A contention which he has striven to make good all his life
is that the experience of the Polish Catholic church during the period
of resistance to Communism has universal value. Deriving from an
exchange in Rome in 1948 with a young Flemish priest, he also reports
in *Memory and Identity* that this college companion told him that 'we
were spared [Communism] in the West, because perhaps we could not
have withstood so a great a trial. You [i.e. the Polish people] on the
other hand, could take it.'

From this he develops the argument that zealous but 'godless anti-
evangelisation', supported by the West's great financial resources, is
striking at the very foundation of human morality, and spreading
'another form of totalitarianism under the appearance of democracy'.
He heard the same view about the weakness of the West expressed by
an eminent European politician who told him at the time, 'If Soviet
Communism comes to the West we will not be able to defend
ourselves.'

This is radical expression from a pope in his eighty-fifth year. But in
the end the mystic inside Wojtyla, away from which Sapieha and
others steered him, has triumphed; part at least of his protracted but
not incapacitating illness has been functional in isolating him from the
business – the overloaded, pullulating Vatican corridors – so that he

could be alone in the presence of God. 'In my end is my beginning,' wrote Eliot, and here that phrase, as did the *Roman Triptych*, indicates how he has returned to the lonely core and mainspring of belief. Perhaps, too, there is a parallel in that the symptoms of Parkinson's disease, with its Beckettian lapses, stopping and starting, repeated gesture, its festination, changes of mood – used by the playwright to show the throes of a civilisation, or at least a culture, caught in the irresolution of its own endgame – have been resisted by the Pope. For Wojtyla resistance to, the solution of, the endgame comes through non-judgemental or disinterested love, in agape. 'A man,' wrote Chesterton, 'must have magnanimity of surrender, of which he only catches a glimpse in first love, like a glimpse of our first Eden.'

Karol Wojtyla's first love had been his mother, brother and father, then Mary the Virgin and celibate priests and mentors, possibly then, in short-lived passions, one or other of his fellow players in Krakow. This glimpse had expanded into magnanimity, sparing him from that symbol for all selfishness, the 'sort of woman . . . who ruthlessly exacted tribute in the form of flowers', or the avaricious creature 'who demanded solid gold in the form of a ring'. Chesterton continued, '[Men will ask] what cruel kind of God can have demanded sacrifice and self-denial? They will have lost the clue to all that lovers have meant by love; and will not understand that it was because the thing was not demanded that it was done.' Wojtyla knows what is meant by love.

Notes

List of Abbreviations

PRINCIPAL SOURCES CITED

By Karol Wojtyla (KW)

The Acting Person	*AP*
Love and Responsibility, published by JNKUL, Lublin, in 1960. English edition (London, 1982)	*L&R*
The Collected Plays and Writings on Theater, translated and with introductions by Boleslaw Taborski (Berkeley, 1987)	*CP*

By John Paul II (JPII)

JPII with Vittorio Messori, *Crossing the Threshold of Hope* (New York, 1994)	*Crossing*
Gift and Mystery (New York, 1996)	*G&M*

About John Paul II

Adam Boniecki, *The Making of the Pope of the Millennium: Kalendarium of the Life of Karol Wojtyla* (Stockbridge, Mass., 2000) – 994 pages in length. This is the most complete source of information and historical data on the life of Karol Wojtyla, a daily record of appointments, meetings, transcripts of speeches, homilies, as well as interviews, documents from others, until he became pope in 1978. A unique compilation, it contains a wide range of primary source material of all kinds.   *K*

PREFACE

1 'This hermit buried . . .
      Graham Greene, *Collected Essays*, 'Three Priests' (London, 1970), 294
2 'that he was certainly . . .
      Crossing, 228
    'Shall we blame Beckett . . .
      Stanley Cavell, *Must We Mean What We Say?* (Cambridge, 1976), 162

PART ONE

3 Had Pilsudski . . .
   'Quoted by Norman Davies, *God's Playground* (London, 1982) Vol. 1–2, pp. 400–4

5 Nothing in this world . . .
   K, 231
   'Horse-drawn buggies . . .
   Jerzy Kluger to author. His reminiscences are mainly recorded in Darcy O'Brien, *The Hidden Pope, The Personal Journey of John Paul II and Jerzy Kluger* (New York, 1999); see 52 ff.

7 'up a crooked flight . . .
   Mieczyslaw Malinski, *Pope John Paul II, The Life of My Friend, Karol Wojtyla* (London, 1979), 273

8 'It is only when alone . . .
   Donald W. Winnicott, *The Maturational Processes and the Facilitating Environment* (London, 1969), 29
   Your arms now remember . . .
   JPII, *The Place Within* (tr. Jerzy Peterkiewicz) (London, 1995), 'Space Which Remains in You', 46–7
   In that little town . . .
   Ibid., 'Her Amazement at Her Only Child', 43
   How attentive . . .
   Ibid., 'Embraced by New Time', 49

9 I stood for a moment . . .
   Ibid. 'Space Which Remains in You', 46
   first you had to penetrate . . .
   CP, 354

11 elevated sacrifice and sorrow . . .
   Geoffrey Myers, *Joseph Conrad* (London, 1988), 3
   like cavalrymen . . .
   Karol, aged twenty-one, refers passionately to this in one of the plays he wrote during the German occupation of Poland:
      There with your blood you sealed your deeds;
      you sealed them with your blood and life.
      On those bloody fields where you were reduced to dust,
      You won the greatest of your victories. *CP*, 140
   '. . . they were very patriotic'
   D.H. Lawrence, *The Rainbow* (London, 1949), 50

12 'based on peacock . . .
   Davies, *God's Playground*, (London, 1982), 5
   In exile the Pole . . .
   Other Polish outlooks in exile explored appropriately in plays: drunken aristocrat in Chekhov's *On the Highroad*; the violent Stanley Kowalski in *A Streetcar Named Desire* (Tennessee Williams)
   'which bound him . . .
   Iris Murdoch, *Nuns and Soldiers* (London, 1980)

to be buried alongside . . .
Malinski, *Pope John Paul II*, 272
13 **Austro-Hungarian German . . .**
Karol in old age, as pope, signed a decree conferring on the last Austrian
emperor, Karl von Habsburg, the title of 'venerable'. Karl ruled from 1916 to
1919 when Austria became a republic, but opinion was divided as to whether
he was an 'exemplary Austrian, husband, father and ruler', for he gave the go-
ahead for the use of poison gas on the Italian front during the First World
War. *Tablet*, 3 May 2003

Over this your . . .
JPII, *The Place Within*, ooo

a 'big' Poland . . .
One opinion held that in 1921 Poland, greedy and bellicose after three years of
fighting, expanded much more than expected. She had fought the Ukrainians,
the Czechs, secured her rights against the Germans by force both in the Baltic
and Silesia. She invaded Lithuania, occupying the mainly Polish Vilno and
incorporated it after a plebiscite. She waged war against Russia and persuaded
the Western powers to ratify her new frontiers in 1923. Britain, fearing
Bolshevism, and France, desirous of a powerful ally in the east (now its old
Tsarist alliance had gone for ever), both approved, but when Germany
invaded Poland in 1939 – both were powerless to help her.
  Besides Russia, Poland had the largest minorities problem in Europe in the
post-war period; out of twenty-seven million a third were minorities (West
Ukrainian, Belorussians, Germans, Lithuanians, all concentrated in their own
areas, as well as three million Jews). While at Versailles Poland had signed a
treaty guaranteeing minority rights, she did not keep to it, even during her
democracy in the twenties. Under the benevolent dictatorship of Pilsudski, she
maintained an enormous police force and huge, ill-equipped standing army to
defend indefensibly long frontiers.
14 **'I am slipping away . . .**
H. Roy Harrod, *Life of John Maynard Keynes* (London, 1951), 253–4
'raised for ever for . . .
G.K. Chesterton, *Collected Poems* (London, 1936), 85–6
15 **'So hard on himself . . .**
André Frossard, *Be Not Afraid!* (New York, 1984), 14. JPII refers to Frossard
in *Rise, Let Us Be On Our Way* (London, 2004) as 'My dear departed Friend',
147
'There was a moment . . .
Radiation of Fatherhood, CP, 357
16 **'Many women who have . . .**
Sigmund Freud, (Vol. 7) *On Sexuality* (London, 1972), 377
'these new parents . . .
Ibid., 224
pierogi
Meat, cheese, or sweet rolls
17 **a loaded revolver . . .**
Malinski, *Pope John Paul II*, 274

'When I was 10 or 12 years old . . .
André Frossard, *Portrait of John Paul II* (San Francisco, 1990), 74
. . . pray to the Holy Spirit . . .
'The end product from that lesson from my childhood is my encyclical
[*Dominum et Vivificantem*] on the Holy Spirit.' Pentecost is the feast of
the Holy Spirit, which led Wojtyla all his life. 'No law can touch you,' writes St
Paul, 'if you are guided by the Spirit. When self-indulgence is at work the
results are obvious: fornication, gross indecency and sexual irresponsibility;
idolatry and sorcery; feuds and wrangling, jealousy, bad temper and quarrels;
disagreements, factions, envy; drunkenness, orgies and similar things . . .
what the Spirit brings is very different: love, joy, peace, patience, kindness,
goodness, trustfulness, gentleness and self-control. There can be no law
against things like that, of course. You cannot belong to Jesus Christ unless
you crucify all self-indulgent passions and desires.'
St Paul to the Galatians, 5, 16–25
18 'I had not yet made . . .
    G&M, 20
19 'that it was as if God . . .
    O'Brien, *Hidden Pope*, 89
    'a prototype of . . .
    Ibid., 74
20 'Every child's desire to . . .
    Ibid., 74
    'bore in their bodies . . .
    André Frossard, *A Portrait of John Paul II*, 68
21 'a rather tall boy . . .
    K, 44
    'Thanks to him I grew . . .
    G&M, 25
22 'it internalised . . .
    Roger Scruton, *The West and the Rest* (London, 2002), 3, 21
    'And the Word became . . .
    John 1: 14, *G&M*, 7
    In records kept of his . . .
    K, 48–9
    Proceedings of the School Board, Marcin Wadowita secondary school, 1933/34,
    p. 18
23 'the saintly Queen Jadwiga . . .
    O'Brien, *Hidden Pope*, 95
    'how Aereas carried . . .
    Ibid., 96
24 'the nucleus of a drama . . .
    CP, 326
    If you are to be born of your father . . .
    Ibid. 354
    'his example was in a way . . .
    G&M, 20

embedded in me with . . .
   CP, 345
26 illusory, 'exotic' . . .
   Andrzej Paczkowski, *The Spring Will Be Ours* (Pennsylvania, 2003), 34; according to Iris Murdoch (*Nuns and Soldiers*) 232–3, Pilsudski wanted to invade Germany in 1933 – not alone but with Britain and France, but they wouldn't go along with him. According also to Murdoch, Stalin liquidated the feeble Polish Communist Party which he thought too patriotic (7)
27 'fact that the . . .
   quoted in O'Brien, *Hidden Pope*, 100
28 'As with all melodrama . . .
   Kluger quoted in O'Brien, *Hidden Pope*, 78
29 It showed Christ . . .
   Ibid., 79, 276
30 'As for what people call . . .
   7 November 1905, on the Feast of the Immaculate Conception: *The Correspondence between Paul Claudel and André Gide* (London, 1952), 42–3
31 'the conscience of . . .
   He records this when living in Rome, 1974
   Karol said how he enriched . . .
   Foreword to Mieczyslaw Kotlarczyk's 'The Art of the Living Word', *CP*, 380
   'In the same period . . .
   Ibid.
   'I got to know him . . .
   Ibid.
32 Amid discord God strikes . . .
   The Polish Review, Vol. 124 (1979) tr. Ludwik Krzyzanowski, 5–6
33 While still at school . . .
   K, 48
   'There was a lot of . . .
   Interview Bill Mouland, *Daily Mail*, 20 March 2000
34 'I must admit that . . .
   Ibid.
   Corriere della Sera.
   9 December 1978
35 'Fewer than seven . . .
   O'Brien, *Hidden Pope*, 107
   Mr Wojtyla was upset . . .
   Ibid., 108
   He just looked at me . . .
   Daily Mail, 20 March 2000
37 We liked being . . .
   Evening Standard, 28 February 2000
   claimed that Wojtyla . . .
   Daily Telegraph, 3 October 1998
   'He had girlfriends.
   Paul Johnson, *Pope John Paul II and the Catholic Restoration* (London, 1982), 118

38 the degree and kind . . .
      Laurence Schifano, *Luchino Visconti* (London, 1990), 378
    'the sign of the woman' . . .
      Genesis 3: 15. Revelation 12: 1
    'Poetry is a great lady . . .
      Preface by KW to *An Anthology of Poetry by Priests*, Poets and Priests Press
      (London, 1971)
39 'My religion teacher . . .
      G&M, 5
    'I believe the first . . .
      G&M, 35
    'Certainly,' he said . . .
      G&M, 6
40 'the inextricable bonds . . .
      K, 585–6
    'The sanctuary of the nation . . .
      Ibid.
42 And new Philosophy . . .
      John Donne, *Complete Poetry & Selected Prose* (London, 1990), 202
    Principles of Polish . . .
      K, 55
43 like a village boy . . .
      See Malinski, *Pope John Paul II*, (New York, 1979). See also *K* 56
    A Slav troubadour . . .
      The Place Within, (London, 1974), 186
44 Karol's birth-sign . . .
      Catechism of the Catholic Church (1992), proscribes horoscopes, saying they
      should not be followed
    'A steadfast and persevering . . .
      Zolar's Horoscope (New York, 1980), 45–61
    'Intensified religious consciousness . . .
      O'Brien, *Hidden Pope*, 134–5
45 The difference between young . . .
      Ibid.
    linen foot clouts . . .
      K, 54
46 'I will never forget . . .
      G&M, 26
    Over the next years . . .
      With Nikita Khrushchev in charge, the Soviets also eliminated sections of the
      population that might oppose Soviet rule
    'This first wartime Mass . . .
      K, 62
48 'The father constituting . . .
      The Black Book, Vol. 2, The German New Order in Poland 1939–41
      (London 1942), 26
49 'The Germans will take . . .
      Paczkowski, *The Spring Will Be Ours*, 38

50 The theatre is in operation . . .
   CP, Introduction; also *K*, 62–3
51 The Nazis placed . . .
   The Black Book, Vol. 2. 'A lower race needs less food', 470 ff.
   'Vita Cracoviensis' . . .
   K, 62
   'The blood of innumerable . . .
   The Black Book, 3
   'In her real truth . . .
   K, 63–4
53 'the gateway of Christ . . .
   Ibid.
   'In view of the fact . . .
   K, 64, and *The Black Book*, 435–7
54 The Germans allowed . . .
   Krakovians could still attend mass at most other churches
55 'What we need in England . . .
   Cardinal Cormac Murphy-O'Connor to author
56 clandestine existence . . .
   James Knowlson, *Damned to Fame* (London, 1996), 307, 309
57 'sacred text'.
   Quoted in A.N. Wilson, *Iris Murdoch as I knew Her* (London, 2003), 94
   'Let theatre be a church . . .
   K, 63
58 lost and secret content . . .
   One report is that KW wrote *David* for his mother Emilia
59 The point of departure . . .
   CP, 19
   Job still could not . . .
   K, 71
60 Thus he speaks . . .
   CP, 57
61 'next to outright . . .
   K, 63
   Act I takes place . . .
   CP, 80–1
62 'You are in the clutches . . .
   CP, 95–6
64 Slavs could be . . .
   George Huntston Williams, *The Mind of John Paul II* (New York, 1981),
   55
   'Whether food does you . . .
   Bo Lozoff, *We're All Doing Time* (North Carolina, 1985), 58
66 'importunate and bossy'.
   Malinski, *Pope, John Paul II*, 19
   'sort of strange . . .
   KW, *Tygodnik Powszechny* 5, 1949, 'The Apostle'

'I learned the basic . . .
> G&M, 24

69 first three poems . . .
> JPII, *The Place Within*, 63–9. 'The Quarry' was not in fact written until 1956 and although based on wartime experience, it marked the deaths of demonstrating workers in Poznan.

71 felt he was so distressed . . .
> Malinski, *Pope, John Paul II*, 12

'The dark period . . .
> G&M, 40

73 And a stone . . .
> JPII, *The Place Within*, 70–1

74 When the Nazis . . .
> George Weigel, *Letters to a Young Catholic* (Herefordshire, 2004), 226

75 'life or death . . .
> A phrase used by the French poet Paul Claudel: see p. 30

'Karol, you should . . .
> K, 76

76 The actor is a rhapsodist . . .
> In KW 1974 essay, 'On the theatre of the word', CP, 376

77 'playing the role' . . .
> K, 77, 79–80

Polish prisoners of war . . .
> Mikhail Gorbachev, *Memoirs* (London, 1996), 350–1.
> Massacres were also committed by the Russians, e.g. of Polish officers in Katyn Forest (1940): *Tass* 13 March 1990 stated that 'it represented one of the most heinous crimes of Stalinism'. The officers were captured in September 1939. According to Simon Sebag Montefiore, *Stalin: The Court of the Red Tsar* (London, 2004), 319, the depredations unleashed on the Poles were 'every bit as cruel and tragic as those of the Nazis'. See also Gerald Reitlinger, *The SS: Alibi of a Nation 1922–1945* (London, 1956), 377, regarding massacres of Poles by White Russian POWs serving as SS.
> Boris Yeltsin sent Lech Walesa, 14 October 1992, official papers documenting Stalin's order to liquidate 21,857 Polish officers.

78 'This God-loving boy . . .
> Stephania Koscielnok, K, 85

. . . the plant was a true . . .
> G&M, 21–2

79 'given an order . . .
> William Styron, *Sophie's Choice* (London, 1979), 205–6

80 Bruno Burgowiec . . .
> Elaine Murray Stone, *Maximilian Kolbe, Saint of Auschwitz* (New York, 1997), 74–89, 101

81 'Poles, the heroism . . .
> *The Black Book*, 571

'atavistic burden . . .
> K, 73

'I feel some resentment . . .
     K, 77, 79–80
82 'He scarcely moved . . .
     Interview, *Evening Standard*, 28 February 2000
85 Try to understand . . .
     CP, 169
86 I do not know . . .
     CP, 244
     I know for certain . . .
     CP, 248
     'he is revealed to himself . . .
     CP, 187
87 'I found in him . . .
     G&M, 33
     'memory, in his heart . . .
     Boleslaw Taborski's translation for author: *Wstancia chodzmy!* (Krakow, 2004); later in English as *Rise, Let Us Be On Our Way* (London, 2004)
88 'Yes, Mary . . .
     G&M, 29
     'I actually wept over . . .
     Reported in Rocco Buttiglione, *Karol Wojtyla, The Thought of the Man Who Became John Paul II* (Cambridge, 1997), 257, 265
89 The Germans infected Polish . . .
     Cf. JPII's later thinking about test-tube ideologies of the twentieth century
     'The greatest institution . . .
     Quoted in Paul Johnson, *A History of the Modern World: From 1917 to the 1980s* (London, 1983) 415
     As in a large-scale . . .
     Joseph Barking, *The Crime and Punishment of I.G. Farben* (London, 1979), 111–27
     German Armaments Incorporated . . .
     Martin Gilbert, *Final Journey: The Fate of the Jews in Nazi Europe* (London, 1979), 69–70
     Himmler announced in . . .
     Manvell and Fraenkel, *Heinrich Himmler* (London, 1965), 117
90 'deprived of all . . .
     Peter Hebblethwaite, *Paul VI, the First Modern Pope* (London 1993), 165
     The worst thing of all . . .
     Carlo Falconi, *The Silence of Pius XII* (London, 1970), 148–150
91 We entered the precincts . . .
     Malinski, *Pope John Paul II*, 35
93 'did not alter . . .
     K, 90
     'bloodiness alone . . .
     cf Wyszinski quoted by JPII in *Memory and Identity* (London, 2005): 'I think the Cardinal needed to conclude his daily labours with the golden lock of sleep and instead he closed them with the diamond of prayer.'
95 'to the Polish imagination . . .

Diary 2 February 1940, quoted in Lech Walesa, *The Struggle and the Triumph* (New York, 1992), 246

A German document . . .
Williams, *The Mind of John Paul II*, 87–8

98 'they found not . . .
O'Brien, *Hidden Pope*, 228–9. It could also be said that Dresden, Hamburg and Coventry suffered similar destruction

'But my begging . . .
Mrs Kotlarczyk to Boniecki and others, Tad Szulc, *Pope John Paul II* (New York, 1995), 128–9

'Hidden forces produce . . .
Letter to Mieczyslaw Kotlarczyk, November 1946; *K*, 109

Among Karol's new companions . . .
Malinski, *Pope John Paul II*, 219

100 Marshal Koniev . . .
Boleslaw Taborski to author

Two days later . . .
O'Brien, *Hidden Pope*, 228–9

'immense and horrible . . .
G&M, 36

102 'Death is only . . .
JPII, *The Place Within*, 'Song of the Inexhaustible God', 15

the Lord taking root . . .
Ibid., 'Shores of Silence', 7

103 'like his shadow . . .
G.K. Chesterton, *St Francis of Assisi* (London, 1960), 68

'The great painter . . .
Ibid., 92

'was a Lover . . .
Ibid., 18

'His religion was . . .
Ibid., 22

104 The impact of his . . .
G&M, 43–4

105 'has a wonderful . . .
Aprocryphal story related to the author

106 'Personally, I have . . .
JPII, *Rise, Let Us Be On Our Way*, 142

There was a brief lull . . .
Kingsbury Smith, Clark Kinnaird (eds.) *It Happened in 1946* (London, 1947)

PART TWO

107 A Catholic theologian . . .
Cross Currents, Winter 1973, No. 4, 426

109 'explains how, with . . .
G&M, 92

110 Writing to Kotlarczyk . . .
Letter to M.K., 1946, *K*, 114–15

'The second essential thing . . .
Letter to Mrs H. Szkocka, 21 March 1947, *K*, 112–13
'especially after touring . . .
JPII quoted in 1979, just after his election (Szulc, *Pope John Paul II* 140)
111 'You might make a . . .
G.K. Chesterton, *St Thomas Aquinas* (London, 1952), 13
that it is a privilege . . .
Ibid., 58
112 'the embodied ideal . . .
Williams, *The Mind of John Paul II*, 92–3, 104
113 Evasion was impossible . . .
Laurence Shifano, *Luchino Visconti, the Flames of Passion* (London 1990), 213
114 'Polish women . . .
Malgorzaga Hruzik Mazurkiewiecz to author
God created man . . .
JPII, *Roman Triptych: Meditations*, ts 9
115 'You can say whatever . . .
Quoted in Hebblethwaite, *Paul VI*, 245
Karol had arrived . . .
According to Malinski, Sapieha had intended first that Starowieyski should benefit from Rome, while KW was included as an afterthought to accompany the younger man
Karol's first sight . . .
G&M, 512
116 'the appearance of the Pope . . .
Peter Hebblethwaite, *The Year of Three Popes* (London, 1978), 29
'the systematic destruction . . .
Andrea Riccardi, *Il Potere del Papa* (*The Power of the Pope*) *Inside the Vatican* (Rome, 1993). Riccardi also reports 'no public protest' when the Vatican's sovereignty was violated by Italian Fascists, supported by the German forces, hunting for Jews (106)
'You must not forget . . .
Pius XII interview with Edoardo Senatro, *L'Osservatore Romano*, 1943
as his 'silence' . . .
'silence in the presence of the enemies of a cause encourages them,' smiles JPII. ' "Use of fear to enforce silence," is the first goal in the strategey of the wicked.' *Rise, Let Us Be On Our Way*, 190
117 'omitting to take up . . .
Letter to the *Tablet*, 29 June 1963
'Read Father Blet . . .
Inside the Vatican, issue October 1999 deals exhaustively and convincingly with the charges against Pius XII; Pierre Blet, *Pius XII and the Second World War: According to the Archives of the Vatican* (Paulist Press, New York, 1991)
118 'while exonerating Pius XII . . .
Damian Thompson, *Sunday Telegraph*, 7 November 2004
'We travelled through . . .
July 1947 letter to Mrs I. Szkocka

119 'did not think himself . . .
      Frossard, *Be Not Afraid!*, 19–20
    'You know, during these . . .
      K, 114
    It was then that . . .
      Frossard, *Be Not Afraid!*, 20.
      Cf also 'Man is a spiritual abyss', quoted in Frossard, *Portrait of John Paul II*, 90
    bearing witness . . .
      Malinski, *Pope John Paul II*, 92
    hard chapel floors . . .
      Jonathan Kwitny, *Man of the Century* (London, 1997), 103
    it was not printed . . .
      Published ultimately in an Italian version (Vatican City, 1979)
121 'They do not want to . . .
      Andrzej Micewski, *Cardinal Wyszynski: a biography* (Orlando, Florida, 1984), 394 ff.
122 'It was harvest time . . .
      G&M, 61–2
    'hilly with argillaceous . . .
      K, 118
    Over beaten path . . .
      Malinski, *Pope John Paul II*, 94–5
124 He especially loved . . .
      Frossard, *Be Not Afraid!*, 114. KW called Chesterton's words
      'Beautiful and true . . . shrewd and demanding'
125 'What does it mean to . . .
      K, 147
126 'O, the supernatural . . .
      Lublin retreat for priests, August 1954
    'I sometimes wonder . . .
      Malgorzaga Hruzik Mazurkiewiecz to author
    an ophthalmist . . .
      Dr M. Straiton to author
  1 Wojtyla, meantime . . .
      Jonathan Kwitny claimed a hitherto undiscovered work by Karol, published clandestinely in two volumes in 1953 and 1954, with each page of a limited edition rolled by hand over a typed matrix (112,750 sheets in all). Called *Catholic Social Ethics* it was subsequently confirmed as not being Wojtyla's material, but copies of lecture notes taken from a book written by a friend (Father Jan Piwowarczyk), to which Wojtyla contributed but was not the main transcriber. Kwitny, *Man of the Century*, 135–42, and George Weigel, *Witness to Hope* (New York, 1999), 898, note 32
    Dressed in lay clothes . . .
      Malinski, *Pope John Paul II*, 249
    'A small episode: . . .
      K, 135, 334
129 the Bronze Badge for Hiking . . .
      K, 146

'He cannot wait . . .
  W.H. Auden, *The Dyer's Hand* (London, 1963), 435–50
130 contrasting aspects of the human personality . . .
  In Ibsen's *Peer Gynt*, Act V, quoted by Auden, the Button Moulder and the
  Lean One tell Peer
  To be one self is: to slay oneself (Scene IX) . . . in two ways a man can be
  himself – there's a right and wrong side to the jacket (Scene X)
  Each of us carries two people . . .
  Retreat, 22–28 March 1954; *K*, 141
131 'Cleverness, quick . . .
  Max Scheler, *Ressentiment* (New York, 1972), 155
  what is really a peculiar . . .
  Ibid., 125
  When Francis of Assisi . . .
  Ibid., 91
132 To the extent that women . . .
  Ibid., Introduction by Lewis A. Coser, 25–6
  But while rejecting . . .
  See Williams, *The Mind of John Paul II*, 119, 140
133 Jerzy Turowicz . . .
  He had called KW a 'young priest with large wings'. The newspaper was
  suppressed in 1953
134 Sexual drive is a gift . . .
  K, 140
135 'Evil', he told his young . . .
  K, 168
136 in an outfit not . . .
  K, 152–3
137 Contemporary life . . .
  K, 171
138 'You educate a man . . .
  The magazine *Wiez*, No. 11, November 1978
  'My train for Krakow . . .
  He went on to see Baziak who said it would be inappropriate to return to
  Mazurio. Karol insisted, Baziak smiled, saying, "But come back in time for the
  ordination." ' JPII, *Rise, Let Us Be On Our Way*
140 I recall one month . . .
  KW, *The Jeweller's Shop*, tr. Boleslaw Taborski (San Francisco, 1992), 27
141 'complete stripping down . . .
  Jerzy Grotowski, *Towards a Poor Theatre* (Holstebro, Denmark, 1965), 18
142 Acting is mostly . . .
  Michael Frayn, David Burke, *Celia's Secret: An Investigation* (London, 2000)
  supplied by Monsignor Strange to author
143 'absorbed the whole secret . . .
  The Jeweller's Shop, 58
144 made into a feature film . . .
  Directed by Michael Anderson, music by Michel Legrand, the film went on
  general release in 1990

145 'his extraordinariness . . .
      Malinski, *Pope John Paul II.*
    Yet liberals in the West . . .
      See the reactions below to Wojtyla's visits, as pope, to France, Germany and
      Great Britain, pp. 235–8, 264–76
    'benighted inhabitants . . .
      Frossard, *Portrait of John Paul II*, op. cit., 48
    'is open to every . . .
      KW, *L&R*, 10
146 students reading aloud . . .
      July 1955, *K*, 150, and Dr. Navarro-Valls to author
    'One of our great . . .
      C.S. Lewis, *The Screwtape Letters* (London, 2002), 50
    The whole philosophy of . . .
      Ibid., 94
    'All great moralists . . .
      Ibid., 125
147 'a general misdirection of . . .
      Ibid., 106
148 to say that the sexual act is an . . .
      L&R, that, 232
    'Gandhi confesses . . .
      In his *Autobiography*, 232–3
149 'Man must take
      L&R, 272–3
    'Resentment', Wojtyla . . .
      Ibid., 143–4
150 a paradoxical pattern: . . .
      Ibid., 39
151 'The pope's a silly . . .
      Guardian, 5 August 1993
152 'A woman wants to be loved . . .
      L&R, op. cit., 179; see also 200, 223
    'Confession,' he told Malinski . . .
      Malinski, *Pope John Paul II*, 95–6
154 The puppet regime's belief . . .
      Szulc, *Pope John Paul II*, 256 ff.
    conveyed none of his . . .
      But did so indirectly later: see his reaction to Vatican Two, and his response to
      Wojtyla's selection as pope
    'Today,' he said in one . . .
      During Lenten Devotions, celebrated in Krakow, 15 March 1964
155 Secret police files . . .
      Dated 5 August 1967, Szulc, *Pope John Paul II*, 197
156 'a young Pole . . .
      Clifford Longley, *The Worlock Archive* (London, 2000), 162
157 'mysterious underground . . .
      Malinski, *Pope John Paul II*, 170, 180. One example was Cardinal Bea,
      accused of being leader of a Jewish-Masonic conspiracy

158 'the stony and desert-like . . .
   Letter to priests of the Archdiocese, December 1963
   'throughout the whole year . . .
   Sermon at Wawel, *K*, 225
   'seemed pleased that . . .
   To priests of the Krakow deanery, 13 January 1963
   'The style with which . . .
   KW to priests of Krakow deanery, ibid.
159 We need to live . . .
   Hebblethwaite, *Paul VI*, 290
160 'president of the assembly' . . .
   Peter Hebblethwaite, *The Runaway Church* (London, 1976), 32–3, 72
   'If there was one man . . .
   Johnson, *Pope John Paul II and the Catholic Restoration*, 27
   'You know,' Karol . . .
   Frossard, *Be Not Afraid!*, 171.
   'You could say . . .
   Weigel, *Witness to Hope*, 202
   Father, father, I am here! . . .
   CP, 321
163 'whose final words . . .
   Antoni Mackowski (*K*, 298)
164 'Many a time since . . .
   26 March 1967, Resurrection Mass, *K*, 287
165 This is not a city . . .
   Consecration sermon, 15 May 1977, *K*, 754
   She was serenaded . . .
   George Blazynski, *John Paul II: A Man from Krakow* (London, 1979), 74
166 original and positive content . . .
   Johnson, *Pope John Paul II and the Catholic Restoration*, 33
   'I cannot believe that . . .
   Hebblethwaite, *The Runaway Church*, 213
   'God bless you . . .
   London Weekend Television, December 1968. Father Rhonheimer ('The truth about condoms', *Tablet*, 10 July 2004) is the most sensibly reasoned judgement I have read on this subject
167 and killed forty-eight
   Walesa, *The Struggle and the Triumph*, 160
168 Not so long ago the Gospel . . .
   Homily at Jasna Gora, 1 September 1968, *K*, 330
   Sometimes it takes a greater . . .
   Ibid., 331
   He never went local . . .
   Malinski, *Pope John Paul II*, 233–4
169 'Having conquered . . .
   JPII, *The Acting Person* (Dordrecht, Holland, 1979), Introduction
   As Cardinal Heenan once . . .
   Cardinal Cormac Murphy-O'Connor to author

'I don't think he understood . . .
Quoted in Carl Bernstein and Marco Politi, *His Holiness: John Paul II and the Hidden History of Our Time* (New York, 1996), 135–40

'They found none . . .
Ibid.

170 multi-faceted . . .
Ibid.

'man can only govern . . .
AP, 108–9

Thomist explanations . . .
See above pp. 109–12

'The feeling of one's body . . .
AP, 230

'intellectual content but . . .
Leszek Kolakowski quoted in ed. John Whale, *The Pope from Poland: an Assessment* (London, 1980), 49

'he feels what determines . . .
AP, 230

171 'hidden theological tendency'
Rucco Buttiglione, Karol Wojtyla: *The Thought of the Man Who Became Pope John Paul II* (Cambridge, 1997)

'Not only does Wojtyla . . .
Williams, *The Mind of John Paul II*, 202

172 The world is charged . . .
The Man Within, 'A Bishop's Thoughts on Giving the Sacrament of Confirmation in a Mountain Village', 93

173 Many are the evils . . .
Sermon at Kalwaria, 18 August 1977, K, 768

177 I knelt, I prayed . . .
Vatican Radio, 21 August: 'My meetings with Paul VI'

179 'a simple infirmary . . .
Quoted in Hebblethwaite, *The Year of Three Popes* (London, 1980), 10

'The real protagonist . . .
Quoted in ibid., 56

181 . . . the name John Paul I . . .
Some felt the name was a clumsy way to show he combined the virtues of both John XXIII and Paul VI

182 'When I preach . . .
Il Tempo, 27, August 1978

'It's difficult to be pope . . .
Ibid.

183 'our request of forgiveness . . .
KW letter 13 January 1966, to Krakow daily *Dziennik Polski*, K, 258–9

184 'In the walled enclosure . . .
Jean-Claude Besret, quoted in Johnson, *John Paul II and the Catholic Restoration*, 37

'from a small ageing . . .
Quoted in John Cornwell, *A thief in the Night* (London, 1989), xxx

185 'There comes a time . . .
Quoted in Hebblethwaite, *The Year of Three Popes*.

185 I still have him before . . .
        1 October 1978, Mariacki Basilica Sermon, K, 834
187 'the votes for Wojtyla . . .
        Wilton Wynn, *Keepers of the Key* (New York, 1988), 39
187 'I obtained no . . .
        Quoted in Szulc, *Pope John Paul II*, 95
188 The hidden breath . . .
        'Stanislaw', *The Place Within*, 181
189 With his style so close . . .
        Hebblethwaite, *The Year of Three Popes*, 137
190 'No, he would . . .
        Quoted in Ibid., 134
        'One name was on . . .
        Guardian, 15 October 1978; much of what is quoted pp. 189–92 and 197–
        205 comes from contemporary press reports (see bibliography)
191 'We ate supper together . . .
        Wynn, *Keepers of the Keys*, 38
        'If they elect you . . .
        Reported in his homily on the Sistine Chapel, 8 April 1994, after the
        restoration of Michelangelo's paintings when JPII ordered the fleshy bodies
        to be revealed in all their glory (*Tablet*, 26 June 2004)
        'a decisive change of mind . . .
        Interview in magazine *Trenta Giorni* (*Thirty Days*), November 1978
        'When the number of votes . . .
        Hebblethwaite, *The Year of Three Popes*, 149
192 'Do you accept the . . .
        As reported by JPII in *Redemptor Hominis* (*The Redeemer of Man*) 4 March
        1979 (Boston, 1979) n. 2
        'Now you know who . . .
        Luigi Accatolli, *John Paul II, Man of the Millennium* (Boston, 2000), 34
193 May Jesus Christ be . . .
        JPII address, 16 October 1978
194 I do not know . . .
        Ibid.
        'There is no hope . . .
        JPII, *The Jeweller's Shop*, 73

PART THREE

197 'I say, Gertrude . . .
        Iris Murdoch, *Nuns and Soldiers*, 461
        'servant of the servants'
        Cardinal Wyszynski, 404
198 'This is our reward . . .
        Ed. John Whale, *The Pope from Poland*, 45
        'The soviets would . . .
        La Stampa, 17 October 1978

'He is certainly no mere . . .
The Tablet, 22 October 1978
199 Students tore . . .
Mary Craig, *Man from a Far Country* (London, 1982), 127
'making emotional . . .
Ibid., 126–7
'We feel great pride . . .
Ibid., 130
200 'He taught me how . . .
Quoted by Szulc, *Pope John Paul II*, 283. The Pope also said of Deskur 'He
does my suffering for me'
'Everything the Holy Father . . .
Deskur, quoted ibid., 284
who recorded in his diary . . .
Giulio Andreotti, *Giovanni Paulo II* (Milan, 1981)
'And this is what I thought . . .
Delivered Sunday, 5 November 1978
202 'identify with pope . . .
Cardinal Cormac Murphy-O'Connor to author
203 Then Simon Peter . . .
Matthew 16: 16–19
The Vatican is a court . . .
Quoted in John Cornwell, *A Thief in The Night* (London, 1978), 62–4
204 'You know what the . . .
O'Brien *Hidden Pope*, 274
205 To Sister Jadwiga . . .
Malinski, *Pope John Paul II*, 218–19
'Well, they're putting . . .
Ibid., 101–2
'You must never . . .
Jerzy Kluger to author
206 'The photograph is . . .
Roland Barthes, *Mythologies*, London 1972, 91–2
207 'So many colonnades . . .
JPII 'Marble Floor', *The Place Within*, 103
Dear Luisa, God . . .
K, 41
208 I have expressed a desire . . .
JPII, 24 January 1994
'The pope was praying . . .
Frossard, *Portrait of John Paul II*, 46
209 On Thursday, 25 January . . .
Marek Skwarnicki, in *Tygodnik Powszechny*, quoted in Boleslaw Wierbianski
(ed.), *Shepherd of All The People* (New York, 1982), 60
210 'The more difficult . . .
Frossard, *Be Not Afraid!*, 196
'exclusively as the . . .
4 May 1980, Malinski, op. cit., 168; Christopher Sluvinski, in *Tygodnik
Powszechny*, quoted in *Shepherd for All People*, 172

211 'cause of humble people . . .
    Ibid., 352
  'necessary to carry out . . .
    Ibid.
  'to the cry of . . .
    Ibid.
  'an excellent view . . .
    Wierzbianski, *Shepherd for All People*, 85
212 The church in Poland . . .
    Ed. John Whale, *The Pope from Poland*; Szulc, 289; Johnson, *Pope John Paul II and the Catholic Restoration*; *Cardinal Wyszynski*, 407
  'Without your faith . . .
    La Repubblica, 23 October 1978; previously he said, quoted in *Cardinal Wyszynski*, xiii–xiv, 'There would be no Polish pope . . . without your faith, never retracted during imprisonment and suffering, your heroic hope, your unceasing trust . . .'
  'skilful technique of . . .
    Ed. John Whale, *The Pope from Poland*, 136
213 The crowd would immediately . . .
    Ibid., 26, 35
  'It was so hot . . .
    Wierzbianski, *Shepherd for All People*, 19
  'One has only to . . .
    Ibid., 25
214 'Come closer to us . . .
    Timothy Garton Ash to author
  'The miners wore the . . .
    Mary Craig, *Man from a Far Country*, 154
  'The Second Coming . . .
    Letter to *Newsweek*, 9 July 1979
  'I have discovered in Rome . . .
    Wierzbianski, *Shepherd for All People*, 34–5
  'Every detail,' he . . .
    Ibid., 39
215 'Oswiecim is a *testimony* . . .
    Ibid., 324; also Ed. John Whale, *The Pope from Poland*, 162–5
  'Every time I see . . .
    Ibid., 165
216 'How can the Pope . . .
    Ibid., 48–9
217 'Christ will never approve . . .
    Ibid., 52–3
218 'He came at Pentecost
    Mary Craig, *Man from a Far Country*, 161
  'The first week of June . . .
    Newsweek, 9 July 1979
  'There's a divinity . . .
    William Shakespeare, *Hamlet*, V. ii. 10–11
220 The English Sunday Mirror . . .
    28 March 1982

'confirmed in the faith by . . .
Wierzbianski, *Shepherd for All People*, 355-7
'When the moral fibre . . .
Mass, 29 September 1979, Phoenix Park, ibid., 355-7
221 'I appeal to you . . .
Drogheda, 27 September, ibid., 361
222 In Derry he hugged a boy . . .
Ibid., 180
'They saw him . . .
Ed. John Whale, *The Pope from Poland*, 185
'Holy Father, I'm in charge . . .
Ibid., 185
To a tiny village . . .
Wierzbianski, *Shepherd for All People*, op. cit., 102
224 Wherever they have hit . . .
Elaine Pagels, *The Origin of Satan* (London, 1996) 163-4
225 'He can't handle . . .
Kwitny, *Man of the Century*, 264-5
when her husband . . .
Ibid., 332-3
Christ himself linked . . .
Wierzbianski, *Shepherd for All People*, 379
'Priesthood's for ever . . .
Ibid., 135
226 the right to life . . .
Ibid., 368-74
227 Your ancestors came . . .
Ibid., 387-8
With the usual civilities . . .
Ed. John Whale, *The Pope from Poland*, 212
228 'He himself is to blame . . .
Ibid., 215
229 'But perhaps he who . . .
Ibid., 216
230 For the Muslim, the . . .
Wierzbianski, *Shepherd for All People*, 248-9
231 'The Russian and American . . .
28 November 1979
232 Rome was dark when . . .
Wierzbianski, *Shepherd for All People*, 154
234 There is on the one hand . . .
Peter Hebblethwaite, *The Papal Year* (London 1981), 33
235 'gratitude to my Roman . . .
15 January 1999, quoted in Frossard, *Be Not Afraid!*, 22
236 Religion, Patrie . . .
Alfred Cobban, *A History of Modern France*, Vol. 3 (London, 1977), 183

'They say that the intellectuals . . .
Frossard, *A Portrait of John Paul*, 162
237 'There is no such thing as a . . .
Wierzbianski, *Shepherd for All People*, 236–7
The Pope's face . . .
Ibid., 236
238 'He is always traveling . . .
Cardinal Tucci to author
239 'I have to go, I have . . .
Ibid.
advised General Pinochet . . .
The Times, 5 January 2001
240 'The pope looked surprised . . .
Wynn, *Keepers of the Keys*
'War is an act . . .
Wierzbianski, *Shepherd for All People*, 447
'as if it were a matter . . .
Ibid., 449
241 'The future of man . . .
Ibid., 447
243 'I had the feeling . . .
Frossard, *Be Not Afraid!*, 223
243 The Holy Father . . .
Dziwisz to Frossard, ibid., 226–7
'the very basis . . .
Alexandre de Marenches, *The Evil Empire* (London, 1988), 152–3
244 'The terrorist assassin's . . .
Time, 25 May 1981
245 I ran to scrub my hands . . .
Frossard, *Be Not Afraid!*, Prof. Crucitti to Frossard, 230
'One hand fired the gun . . .
Ibid., 231
I saw blood . . .
Ibid., Prof. Crucitti to Frossard, 235–9
246 Earth felt the wound . . .
John Milton, *Paradise Lost*, Book IX, lines 780–3
'I am afflicted . . .
This and the following from various press sources
247 too visible presence . . .
Cf. 'Wisdom and goodness to the vile seem vile/Filths savour but themselves':
Shakespeare, *King Lear*, IV. ii. 37–8
248 'by an unknown . . .
David Wise, report in *New York Times* magazine, 1944
'The question of whether . . .
Robert M. Gates, *From the Shadows* (London, 1996) 252–3
249 'He found the bed a bit short . . .
Ibid., unnamed nun to Frossard, 241–6
250 'I remember,' said one doctor . . .
Ibid., Prof. Sanna to Frossard, 247–8

'came down with a . . .
   Ibid.
'can persist in an organism . . .
   Ibid.
'The real cross
   Basil Hume, *Basil in Blunderland* (London, 1992)
251 'Don't forget that . . .
   Prof. Crucitti to Frossard, *Be Not Afraid!*, 243–7
'useful reminder'
   Ibid.
'He was tenacious . . .
   Prof. Sanna to Frossard, ibid.
'A journalist claimed . . .
   Prof. Crucitti to Frossard, ibid. Crucitti died in 2003, and JPII visited his
   widow to express condolence
253 'I assure you, Your . . .
   Cardinal Tucci to author
'Now I rejoice . . .
   Part to the Colossians 1: 29
'great divine trial'
   Frossard, *Be Not Afraid!*, 251
'As soon as I . . .
   David Willey, *God's Politician: Pope John Paul II, The Catholic Church, and
   the New World Order* (London, 1991), 24
254 'to unite one . . .
   Crossing, 214
'She never fails us . . .
   Letter 11 December 1907, F.J. Sheed, *The Mary Book* (London, 1954), 305
'suffering's refined jealousy . . .
   Frossard, *Be Not Afraid!*, 251
'sick people used . . .
   Frossard, *Portrait of John Paul II*, 68
If the Lord consents . . .
   Salvifici Dolores, 11 February 1984
vision of concrete . . .
   CP, 396
257 A month-long synod . . .
   Hebblethwaite, *The Papal Year*, 103–7
258 'Served unceasingly . . .
   JPII, Rise, *Let Us Be on Our Way* 50
'It's his personal . . .
   John Allen, *Tablet*, 18 September 2004
'I should have . . .
   JP, *Rise, Let Us Be on Our Way*, 49
'small, compact . . .
   John Cornwell, *The Pope in Winter* (London, 2004), 90
'seeks transcendence . . .
   John Allen, *Tablet*, 18 September 2004

259 'first example of . . .
     Witness to Hope, 356
     'Under this pope . . .
     Quoted in *Daily Telegraph*, 3 October 1988
260 'The theologian knows . . .
     Hebblethwaite, *The Papal Year*, 53
     'The Church is the . . .
     Charles Moore, op. cit., 3 October 1998
261 'It is throught this mystery . . .
     Williams, *The Mind of John Paul II*, 296
262 A later, highly bizarre . . .
     Austen Ivereigh, 'Milingo and Maria', *Tablet*, 23 November 2002
263 'infested with careerism' . . .
     Richard Owen, *The Times*, 20 January 2000
     'Peter, you are . . .
     JP, *The Place Within*, 103
264 'by divine will . . .
     Dennis Sewell, *Catholics* (London, 2002), 12, 17
     'Dost thou seek after . . .
     John Donne, *Complete Poetry and Selected Prose*, ed. John Hayward (London, 1929), 357
     'equal the licentiousness . . .
     Ibid., 378
266 'The Men of Harlech'
     Quoted in Sewell, *Catholics*.
     'the foundations of . . .'
     Marina Warner, *Alone of All Her Sex* (London, 2000), 77, preface xvii
     'Christ's birth . . .
     Joan Smith, *Misogynies* (London, 1989) 45–6
     'The Bolshevists are advancing . . .
     Evelyn Waugh, *Sword of Honour* (London, 1980), 670
     'post-tridentine . . .
     Roderick Strange to author
267 'Newman in his Catholic . . .
     The Worlock Archive, op. cit., 36; appropriately for JPII it was Newman who also wrote, 'Without the support of a strong papacy the Christian hierarchy would have long ago degenerated into a feudal, semi-clerical, semi-secular caste, endowed with hereditary benefices and more and more a slave to civil authority'
     'the general feeling in Rome . . .
     Archbishop MacDonald to author
     'England doesn't like certainty . . .
     Ann Widdecombe to author
     'great sympathy and outreach . . .
     MacDonald to author
     'truth about the great . . .
     'On the Theatre of the Word', CP, 371

268 'Christian discussion . . .
      Quoted in (and with following) Humphrey Carpenter, *Robert Runcie* (London, 1996), 207–30. Also Humphrey Carpenter to author
269 They had been in Rome . . .
      Longley, *The Worlock Archive*, 287
270 'papal allocution in . . .
      Runcie to Hume, 17 November 1980, *Robert Runcie*, 236–7
    I explicitly mentioned . . .
      Ibid., 238–42
271 'extreme anti-Catholicism . . .
      Hugo Young, *One of Us* (London, 1981), 288–9, 552
    'The English are cold . . .
      Frossard, *Portrait of John Paul II*, 159
272 'We must make sure . . .
      Carpenter, *Robert Runcie*, 231
    'Peace is an obligation . . .
      Longley, *The Worlock Archive*, 311
273 'fully understand her . . .
      Carpenter, *Robert Runcie*, 224–5
    'Here was an immediate . . .
      Archbishop Nichols to author
    'His sheer energy and . . .
      Dame Joanna Jamieson, Abbess of Stanbrook Abbey, to author
274 'The two men knelt . . .
      Kentish Gazette, 3 June 1982
275 It was a slightly . . .
      Carpenter, *Robert Princie*, 254
    (subsequently unmasked . . .
      In J.D.F. Jones, *Laurens van der Post* (London, 1999)
    the Duke of Kent sent . . .
      Sunday Telegraph, 8 January 1995
    a royal servent . . .
      Sunday Times, 22 January 1995
276 'did not appreciate . . .
      Carpenter, *Robert Runcie*, 371
    One might have said . . .
      Frossard, *Portrait of John Paul II*, 58–9
    On the plane back . . .
      Kwitny, *Man of the Century*, 444–5
    he admitted the Pope . . .
      In the *Independent* Magazine, 'Heroes and Villains', 2002
    'characters from a Fellini . . .
      Tablet, 20 April 1985
279 'What do they think . . .
      Frossard, *Portrait of John Paul II*, 61
279 The Pope neither confirmed . . .
      Later JPII confirmed 'the attack was not his own initiative, it was someone else's idea'. Dziwisz said he did not hear Agça ask forgiveness, 'He was only

interested in the secret of Fatima.' JPII *Memory and Identity* (London, 2005), 184–5

281 **It is God . . .**
See JP, *Crossing*, 127–34
'the activity of these people . . .
Leo Tolstoy, *War and Peace* (London, 1944), 489–91

282 **'it could prove to be . . .**
John Miller, *Daily Telegraph*, 31 October 1978
Like all other . . .
Jaruzelski interview with Riccardo Grizio, *Talk of the Devil: Encounter With Seven Dictators* (London, 2003), 79

283 **'two religious leaders . . .**
Zbiegniew Brzezinski *Power and Principle* (London, 1986), 461
'It was moving to see . . .
Ed. John Whale *The Pope from Poland*, 174
'Heavens,' she said . . .
Ibid., 174
The central question . . .
Ibid., 131

284 **'They saw themselves . . .**
Norman Davies, *Rising '44: 'the Battle for Warlaw'* (London, 2004), 601
'survives under . . .
Lech Walesa, *The Struggle and the Triumph*, 16
'I shall not allow the use of . . .
Quoted in Szulc, *Pope John Paul II*, 346–7

285 **'he would relinquish . . .**
Gordon Thomas and Max Morgan-Witts, *Pontiff* (London, 1983), 429–30

286 **'There does not exist . . .**
Quoted in *The Pope from Poland*, 000
'emotional blackmail'
Ed. John Whale *From the Shadows*, 253

287 **'In this situation, Wojciech . . .**
Gorbachev, *Memoirs*, 618

288 **subsequently maintained Jaruzelski . . .**
Grizio, *Talk of the Devil*, 72–3

289 **'Our Polish comrades are not . . .**
Quoted in Timothy Garton Ash, *The Polish Revolution: Solidarity* (London, 1999), 181–2

290 **Reagan dozed off . . .**
His Holiness (New York, 1996), 734; Kwitny, *Man of the Century*, 446
'clandestine campaign . . .
Time, 24 February 1992
'I never sat . . .
Kwitny, *Man of the Century*, 445
'was very distant . . .
Ibid., 445–63, Kwitny quotes a dozen Polish and American sources to the effect that little help came from the CIA

291 one reported episode . . .
      The Pope was changing from trunks into his clothes. Some nakedness is visible
      from a distance but not his private parts. Boleslaw Taborski to the author. The
      photos were published in a German magazine
      'Look at the problems . . .
      Larry Gurwin, *The Calvi Affair* (London, 1984), 51, 183, 178 See also
      L'Espresso, 6 July 1981
292 'There is no way . . .
      CNS, Kwitny, *Man of the Century*, 617
      'a serious blemish on . . .
      Szulc, *Pope John Paul II*, 380
293 'not the monsters my education . . .
      Largely under the Marian Fathers in Warsaw, Orizio, *Talk of the Devil*, 68–9
      his legs were trembling
      Szulc, *Pope John Paul II*, 389
293 'a contagious mood'.
      Ibid.
294 his plays were . . .
      Our God's Brother was premiered in Krakow in December 1980
      'a man who knows how . . .
      Quoted in Szulc, *Pope John Paul II*, 398
      the atmosphere of openness . . .
      Lech Walesa, *A Way of Hope: An Autobiography* (New York, 1987)
      'the son meets . . .
      Ibid.
295 'was killed by a crazy . . .
      Orizo *Talk of the Devil*, 88
296 'in thinking that I . . .
      Quoted in Szulc, *Pope John Paul II*, 405–7
      'the greatest mutual . . .
      Gorbachev, *Memoirs*, 617
297 what were his intentions . . .
      Quoted in Szulc, *Pope John Paul II*, 391
      'in a period of massive . . .
      Walesa, *The Struggle and the Triumph*, 246
      A contact through . . .
      Szulc, *Pope John Paul II*, 655
      On Social Concerns . . .
      Issued 30 December 1987
298 'Raisa, I should like . . .
      Daily Telegraph, 3 October 1998
      I noted that there were . . .
      Gorbachev, *Memoirs*, 655–7
299 'come to the conclusion that . . .
      Ibid.
      John Paul had been . . .
      JPII, quoted in Accatoli, *Man of the Millennium*, 192. John Casey, the English
      philosopher, who spoke to members of the Curia, wondered if the Pope asked

Gorbachev about his attempted assassination: 'One of them surely suspected, and the other (with his close KGB connections . . .) certainly knew . . . I wonder if President Gorbachev took the opportunity to express regret.'
Sunday Telegraph, [undated] May 1990

'the detonator that set . . .
Accatoli, *Man of the Millennium*, 192

'for the support you have . . .
Ibid., 104

300 'the collective will . . .
Tolstoy, *War and Peace*, 489–91

'What has happened in . . .
Gorbachev, quoted in *La Stampa*, Turin, 3 March 1992

PART FOUR

303 A Survey of . . .
Eric Schlosser, *Fast Food Nation* (London, 2002)

304 'wearing knickers that had . . .
Bishop Tadeusz Pieronek, quoted in Kwitny, 501

'The followers of capitalism . . .
J. Gavronski, *Il Mundo di Giovanni Paulo II* (Milan, 1994), 13

'roly-poly Roncalli' . . .
Malachi Martin, *The Windswept House* (New York, 1998), 188–9

305 'wandered into the papacy . . .
Ibid., 32–4

From the close of the . . .
Ibid., 595

306 'incorporated into life here . . .
John Selby Spong, *Why Christianity Must Change or Die* (San Francisco, 1999), 95

'discipline of deceit lest . . .
Garry Wills, *Papal Sin: Structures of Deceit* (London, 2000), 202

'Thousands of women who . . .
Bruce Johnson, Suzanne Lewis, *Daily Telegraph*, 23 September 1993

'the shepherd out of . . .
Independent on Sunday, 15 August 1993

'the abyss between America's . . .
Ibid.

Most practising Catholics supported . . .
According to Richard Major, *Tablet*, 22 March 2003: Americans have 'become adept at evading certain papal pronouncements . . . This Pope in particular is not consistently congenial to either Left or Right'

307 'No surer, no . . .
Shakespeare, *Coriolanus*, I. ii. 170–2

'as the standard for their . . .
JPII, *Veritatis Splendor* (London, 1993), 72

'treating the human body . . .
Ibid.

These vices now rank . . .
   Sunday Times, Profile of JPII, 26 September 1993
'He is not as joyful . . .
   Quoted in *Sunday Times*, 17 September 1995
308 God once said . . .
   Cardinal Tucci to author
'kernel of truth . . .
   Riga, September 1993
309 Wojtyla with right arm . . .
   Independent, 20 April 1995
'hyperactive, grandiose and . . .
   Sunday Times, 4 January 2004
'dysfunctional . . .
   Quoted in *Sunday Times*, 12 September 1995
'John Paul reminds me . . .
   Ibid.
'The noblest dreams I ever . . .
   Dorothy L Sayers, *The Man Born to Be King* (London, 1943), 230
310 'gimlet-eyed' gaze . . .
   Cornwell, *The Pope in Winter*, 145
'I was not really wrong . . .
   Sayers, *The Man Born to Be King*, 208
'Will the Prince of Darkness . . .
   JP II, quoting John 8: 44 and Job 1: 9ff; Graham Greene wrote, 'Rob human beings of their heavenly and their infernal importance, and you rob your characters of their individuality' (Introduction to John Gerard's *Autobiography*)
'No one can escape . . .
   JPII, *Veritatis Splendor*, 4
311 'Conscience is no longer . . .
   Ibid., 86–7; *Gaudium et Spes*, 16 ff.
'it is never lawful . . .
   JPII, *Veritatis Splendor*, 123
'the pope's words . . .
   Sunday Telegraph, 26 September 1993
'that in post-modern . . .
   Times Higher Education Supplement, 18 February 1994
312 The encyclical shows, we're told . . .
   Daily Mail, 10 October 1993
'a great and genuine . . .
   Ann Widdecombe to author
'endless compromise'
   A.N. Wilson (*Evening Standard*, 25 January 2000), reversing an earlier view, celebrated the Pope, saying, 'No one is more difficult or more cursed than Wojtyla, which is why I have come not merely to revere him, but to love him.' He added, 'Wojtyla makes us wonder about deep things, about who and what we are – we strange creatures on this revolving planet in the middle of space, who fashioned gods in our own image and then found that we had a God who told us words we did not hear'

'He put all the . . .
    Dr. Navarro-Valls to author
314 'Do with them what you like,' . . .
    Crossing, vi
    'humility, of his generous . . .
    Ibid.
    'One cannot acquiesce . . .
    JPII statement to visiting US bishops, Rome, 1987
315 'A priest I know . . .
    Quoted in Roderick Strange, *The Risk of Discipleship* (London, 2004)
    'reflects all created . . .
    Crossing, 17
316 'He were not Mystery . . .
    Ibid., 38
    Some of the most beautiful . . .
    JPII *Crossing*, 92–3
    (Adel Smith, the president of the Muslim Union of Italy, sued the Pope March
    2004 under Italian equality-of-religion law. Smith cited this and other
    passages which claim that the 'richness of God's self-revelations' in the Bible
    has been set aside. Smith had already fought a court battle to have a crucifix
    taken down from his son's classroom. *Tablet*, 6 March 2004)
    one could say . . .
    Ibid., 64–5
317 'These are the endgames . . .
    Stanley Cavell, *Must We Mean What We Say?* (Cambridge, 1976), 151
318 'Its object is to show God . . .
    Ibid., 154
    With it, we could explain . . .
    Ibid., 162
    'The man who shares . . .
    Crossing, 87
320 Unfortunately, we are heirs . . .
    JP II, *Letter to Women* (Boston, 1993), *Tablet*, 29 June 1995
    'I will put enmity . . .
    Accattoli, *Man of the Millennium*, 130
    'When the woman most . . .
    Crossing, JPII, 206
321 'I would like to speak . . .
    JPII, Angelus address, July 1995
    'Let us first be . . .
    JPII to International Union of Superiors General of Women Religious, 16
    November 1978
    All his apostles . . .
    Strange, *The Risk of Discipleship*, Ch. 12, 3
322 'Yes, very much! . . .
    9 September 1984, Accattoli, *Man of the Millennium*, 182
    'Ah, feminista!' . . .
    Private source. Since he became pope the ordination of women had been an

important issue, while his opposition to it resulted in considerable unpopularity. Tom Stacey wrote in the *Daily Telegraph*, 13 November 1992, quoting historical precedents, that the introduction of women priests led inevitably to religious decline and ultimately to the demise of those religions in which it had been adopted: 'a living church enshrines the paradigm of sexuality which is integral to the spiritual meaning of love. To have "democratised" that [male/female] polarity away will murk the secret spring of its truth, maybe fatally.' Some years after the ordination of women in the Church of England, Clifford Longley (*Daily Telegraph*, 21 May 1999) assessed the effect: 'The latest Church of England figures – down yet again – show that ordaining women was no more the magic button which would reverse the Church's fortune than was the new Bible, the new prayer book, or calling bishops "Jim". Even in terms of women's issues the post-feminist focus has changed. Younger women no longer see the Church of England as high moral ground to be captured. Most never think about it at all. A few see it as a problematical career choice or at best an interesting irrelevance.'

'Wide interest . . .
Ann Widdicombe to author

323 'Blessed is he who . . .
St Francis, quoted in *St Francis of Assisi*, 88–9
'What is art . . .
See p. 30 for full quotation

324 He knows his own mind . . .
Dr Navarro-Valls to author
'Let us try to forget! . . .
K, 258–60
'In this request . . .
Albert Monticone, quoted in Luigi Accattoli, *When a Pope Asks Forgiveness* (Boston, 1998), xxiii
Forcible baptisms . . .
Hans Urs von Balthasar, *Who is a Christian?* (New York, 1967), 14–15

325 'Today, after Einstein . . .
Accattoli, *When a Pope Asks Forgiveness*, 135
In his huge daily output . . .
Some claim JPII was the most prolific Polish writer of his time

326 'All the suggestions . . .
JPII, *Mulieris Dignitatem*, 9: 24
'All of us, Christians . . .
JPII address to government authorities, Kaduna, Nigeria, 14 February 1982
the island of Gorée . . .
Visit of 22 February 1992
Throughout a whole period . . .
Accattoli, *When a Pope Asks Forgiveness*, 240–41
'Medieval Latin Christendom . . .
JPII, 11 October 1988

327 The joy of this day . . .
Accattoli, *When a Pope Asks Forgiveness*, 117
'centuries-long cultural . . .
JPII, 13 April 1986, quoted in Accattoli, *When a Pope Asks Forgiveness*, 14;

in 1999 a group of cardinals, including Accattoli; König, felt JPII was wrong to apologise for the church's sins of the past (*Tablet*, 29 March 1999)

'There is no doubt . . .

Letter to the US bishops, *When a Pope Asks Forgiveness*, 117–18

328 a frank recognition of . . .

JPII at the ecumenical celebrations at the close of the Synod of Europe, St Peter's, 7 December 1991

who accused Arafat . . .

Kwitny, *Man of the Century*, 457. The Vatican responded by calling the Israeli statement 'an outrage against the truth'

'the prince of peace . . .

Monsignor Chestle to author

329 'The Uniates have seized . . .

Victoria Clark, *Why Angels Fall* (London, 2000), 306

'without a word drew . . .

Witness to Hope, 849

Jerusalem! That is an . . .

Why Angels Fall, Clark, 99

330 'When the Orthodox . . .

BBC News, 4 May 2001

'May suddenly . . .

Dostoevsky, *The Brothers Karamazov* (London, 1992), 256–7

333 'Sono caduto ma non . . .

La Repubblica, 1 December 1993

'They are giving me a . . .

22 May 1994, Accattoli, *Man of the Millennium*, 214

234 'He lives – for the . . .

Ibid., 215

'seemed not the least . . .

Weigel *Letters to a Young Catholic*, 121–38

'Neck down . . .

John Allen to author

335 'The gift is constantly . . .

G&M, 79

Presence had always . . .

'First of all you have the pope sitting across from you you, like a great white bird with folded wings; if the silence continues and permits you to go on with your study, you will see, beyond the pope, the indelible character of the priest; beyond the priest, you will find the man, and the man's fundamental modesty will lead you directly to the child he once was, and from whom he was never separated and even still seems to be leading along by the hand; after the child there is nothing but the light of God, that he does not see, but that enlightens us all.' Frossard, *Portrait of John Paul II*, 171–2

'From the neck up I'm . . .

John Allen to author

'May be due . . .

Dr Straiton to author

'I would say she . . .
Private source; Tobiana's real name is not known
336 'Every return to Poland . . .
JPII, quoted in *The Times*, 1997
'Until this day . . .
Quoted in *The Times*, 19 August 2002. This was his eighth trip
337 'He makes you feel . . .
Malgorzaga Hruzik Mazurkiewiecz to author
'I spent all my life . . .
Kwitny, *Man of the Century*, 627. Cardinal Jozef Tomko told Weigel (*Witness to Hope*, 857): 'People mistake his respect for persons as weakness. It isn't . . . He trusts his collaborators, and he is not a worrier. He is neither afraid of making a decision nor does he force a decision if the situation is not mature.'
338 **1.6 million foetuses**
Nearly a third of all babies conceived: figures from Allan Gutmacher Institute (httpl/womensissues.about.com)
'Does it make you . . .
JPII, quoted by Eamon Duffy in *Financial Times* magazine, 8 November 2003
'a bad listener . . .
The Times, 5 January 2001
'I know well what . . .
Accattoli, *Man of the Millennium*, 232
339 'Over and over again . . .
Ibid.
a general audience . . .
28 January 1998
'Are there people . . .
Dr Navarro-Valls to author
'At the evening . . .
JP II, quoting Saint John of the Cross: see Karol Wojtyla, *The Way To Christ* (San Francisco, 1984), 100
341 **For nearly twenty years** . . .
Graham Greene, *Collected Essays*, 286
tantamount to suicide . . .
Richard Owen, *The Times*, 28 May 2002
342 'the spiral of hatred . . .
See 'Newspaper Articles' listed p. 417
'unusual . . .
Dr Greenhall to author; Humphrey Carpenter to author
'well-informed Vatican sources . . .
Cardinal Jorge Mejia of Argentina, quoted in *The Times*, 18 October 2003; on 1 February 2005 the Pope was rushed to the Gemelli Hospital with severe breathing problems and nearly died. Speculation restarted on whether or not he should step down (Associated Press, 8 February 2005)
343 'Old age should burn . . .
Dylan Thomas, *Collected Poems, 1934–52* (London, 1952), 116
'making himself suffer'
Richard Owen, *The Times*, 28 May 2002

'I'm sorry to be . . .
　　Ibid.
'witness to the nobility . . .
　　Financial Times magazine, 8 November 2003
344 'the merest whisper . . .
　　In Stephen Hawking, *A Brief History of Time* (London, 1988), there was in
　　space-time no boundary, which 'means it had no beginning, no moment of
　　creation' (116). JPII told Hawking and other scientists at an audience that they
　　should not inquire into the Big Bang itself 'because that was the moment of
　　Creation and therefore the work of God'
'No final theory of . . .
　　Quoted by John Cornwell, '*U-Turn* on Universe', *Tablet*, 27 March 2004
'constructed around the drama . . .
　　Quoted in Bryan Appleyard, *Understanding the Present*, op. cit., 178–9
'We feel that even . . .
　　Ludwig Wittgenstein, (1951) *Tractatus Logico-Philosophicus* (London,
　　1978), 187
345 'a motherly hand . . .
　　See above, p. 245
346 'a bishop in white'
　　Daily Telegraph, 15 May 2000. The Pope ordered a full account, finally made
　　public on 26 June by Cardina Ratzinger on the Vatican website: of 'a Bishop
　　dressed in white "We had the impression it was the Holy Father" . . . the Holy
　　Father passed through a big city half in ruins and, half trembling with halting
　　step, afflicted with pain and sorrow, he prayed for the souls of the corpses he
　　met on his way; having reached the top of the mountain, on his knees at the
　　foot of the big cross he was killed by a group of soldiers who fired bullets and
　　arrows at him, and in the same way there died one after the another . . .
Fatima had become . . .
　　Windswept House, 118–19
347 'It is probably fair . . .
　　Norman Stone, *Europe Transformed, 1878–1919* (London, 1983), 390. A
　　report in 2004 stated traffic in London travels on average at the same speed it
　　did a hundred years ago.
From Cherie Blair's perspective . . .
　　Cherie Blair to author
349 'I it is who must blot . . .
　　Isaiah 43: 18–19, 21–2, 24–5
'The Son of Man . . .
　　Mark 2: 1–12
'doesn't miss a thing . . .
　　Private source to author, Beda College
350 'Holy Father, you are not . . .
　　Archbishop Nichols to author
'now a closed chapter . . .
　　Ibid.
350 . . . the *Roman Triptych* . . .
　　In this first poetical work published under the name John Paul II, introduced
　　by Cardinal Ratzinger with six other cardinals in attendance at a Vatican press

conference, he descended again into the depths both of the personal, the inner man, and the archetypal spiritual being. Translated into English by Jerzy Peterkiewicz. See also *The Times*, 7 March 2003

draws on the imagery . . .
Marina Warner, *Alone of All Her Sex*, 329

If you want to find the source . . .
JPII, *Roman Triptych: Meditations*, Typescript, 4

352 **'They felt no shame . . .**
Ibid., 9

Casta placent superis; . . .
Ibid., 12, trans: 'Heaven is pleased with what is pure; come with pure robes, and with unsullied hands drink water from this source.'

They come here . . .
He also joked (14 June 1994), about this succession: 'It is nice to have so many cardinals at the Vatican when there is no conclave'

Abraham, you who climb . . .
Ibid., 20

. . . Brother Adam Chmielowski . . .
The new work, a 'varied book style' of anecdotal passages (Boleslaw Taborski to author). It covers his appointment as bishop when he told Archbishop Baziak, 'I will return to my boat trip' and the Archbishop, who had not thought it proper said, 'Go – but be sure you come back for me for your consecration'). He reflects on the history of Poland, in the sacraments and his attitudes towards an assortment of Polish saints. He quotes extensively also from his poetry, notably from 'St Stanislaw' and 'The Quarry'

'With the eyes of . . .
Boleslaw Taborski to author. JPII proclaimed him saint 12 November 1989, the first time an author has ever later as pope canonised the subject of a play he has written

353 **'autobiographical, philosophical . . .**
The Times, 7 October 2004

I am a giver . . .
JP, *The Place Within*, 93

355 **'I have always sensed . . .**

356 **'Categories of archaeology . . .**
Quotes in *Daily Telegraph*, 3 October 1998

'The Lord God . .
JPII, *Memory and Identity*, 16

'We were spared . . .
Ibid., 50–2

'A man,' . . .
Chesteron, *St Francis of Assisi*, 95

'sort of woman . . .
Ibid.

Chronology

1920
18 May   Birth of Karol Jozef Wojtyla, Wadowice, Poland, to Karol Wojtyla and Emilia Kaczorowska

1929
13 April   Death of mother

1932
5 December   Death of Edmund, elder brother, a doctor, age 26, from scarlet fever

1938
August   Move, aged 18, with father to Krakow to study at Jagiellonian University

1940
September   Start of work at Zakrzowek stone quarry

1941
18 February   Death of Karol's father
March   Founding of Krakow theatrical group
August–October   Transfer from Solvay stone quarry to factory

1942
October   Acceptance by Archdiocese of Krakow as clandestine seminarian; start of secret attendance at Jagiellonian University classes in theology.

1944
29 February   Serious accident from being struck down by German army truck; two weeks in hospital
August   Goes into hiding in Archbishop Sapieha's residence, Franciszkanska Street, and continues studies

1946
1 November   Ordination as priest; beginning of visit to Rome for further graduate studies

1948

June   Completion of first doctorate thesis, *Faith according*
                                      to St John of the Cross, and return to Poland
8 July   Assigned as curate to the country parish of
                                      Niegowic

1949

August   Appointment as curate in the Krakow parish of St
                                      Florian

1953

1 December   Qualified as teacher at Jagiellonian University
                                      with thesis on Max Scheler

1956

1 December   Professor of Ethics at Lublin Catholic University,
                                      a post held until election as pope

1958

28 September   Ordination as auxiliary bishop of Krakow

1960   Publication of *Love and Responsibility*, first book

1962

October   Attendance at Pope John XXIII's Vatican Two
                                      Council in Rome

1963

30 December   Appointment by Pope Paul VI as Archbishop of
                                      Krakow

1967

28 June   Elevation to cardinal

1969

28 February   Visit to synagogue in the Kazimerz quarter of
                                      Krakow.
September–October   Participation in his first Synod of Bishops in Rome

1971

5 October   Election to the Council of the Secretary General
                                      of Bishops (re-elected in 1974 and 1977)

1972

8 May   Archdiocesan Synod at Krakow. Publication
                                      of *Sources of Renewal*

1974

27 September–26 October   Appointment as relator at the Synod of Bishops
on evangelisation

1976

February   Preacher of Lenten spiritual exercises at the Vatican
to Paul VI

1978

6 August   Death of Paul VI

19 September   Visit to Germany with delegation of Polish bishops

29 September   Death of Pope John Paul I

16 October   Election as Pope John Paul II

22 October   Celebration to mark the inauguration of papal
ministry at St Peter's

1979

25 January–1 February   Papal trips to the Dominican Republic, Mexico
and the Bahamas; address to the third general
conference of Latin-American bishops, Puebla,
Mexico

4 March   Publication of inaugural encyclical *Redemptor
Hominis*

28 April   Appointment of Agostino Casaroli as Secretary
of State

2–10 June   First visit to Poland

29 September–8 October   Visits to Ireland and the United States. Speech to
the United Nations 2 October

10 November   Announcement of re-examination of the Galileo
case

28–30 November   Visit to Turkey and meeting with Dimitrios I,
Ecumenical Patriarch of Constantinople

1980

2–12 May   First African pilgrimage, Zaire, Congo, Kenya,
Ghana, Upper Volta, Ivory Coast

30 May–2 June   First pastoral trip to France

30 June–12 July   First pastoral visit to Brazil

26 September–25 October   Exploration by the International Synod of Bishops
of role of the family in the modern world

15–19 November   First papal visit to Germany

30 November   Publication of the encyclical *Dives in Misericordia*

1981

16–27 February   First pastoral visit to Asia: Pakistan, the Philippines,
Guam and Japan

13 May   Attempted assassination in St Peter's Square by
Ali Agça

14 September	Publication of encyclical *Laborem Exercens*
25 November	Appointment of Cardinal Ratzinger as Prefect of the Congregation for the Doctrine of the Faith

1982

12–19 February	Second visit to Africa: Nigeria, Benin, Gabon, Equatorial Guinea
12–15 May	Visit to Portugal (pilgrimage to Fatima on anniversary of assassination attempt)
28 May–2 June	Visit to Great Britain (meeting with Anglican primate, Archbishop Runcie)
10–13 June	Visit to Argentina
15 June	Visit to Geneva
29 August	Visit to the Republic of San Marino
31 October–9 November	First pastoral visit to Spain

1983

25 January	Promulgation of the revised *Code of Canon Law*
2–10 March	Visits to Central America: Costa Rica, Nicaragua, Panama, El Salvador, Guatemala, Honduras, Belize, Haiti
25 March	Opening of the Holy Year of the Redemption
16–23 June	Second pastoral visit to Poland (under martial law since December 1981)
14–15 August	Pastoral visit to Lourdes
10–13 September	First visit to Austria
29 September	Synod of Bishops on the theme of reconciliation and penance opens
11 December	Visit to the Lutheran church in Rome
27 December	Visit to Ali Ağça in prison

1984

11 February	Publication of the Apostolic Letter *Salvifici Doloris*, on the Christian meaning of suffering
9 April	Appointment of the Secretary of State to represent him in the exercise of power over Vatican City state
2–12 May	Second pastoral visit to Asia and Oceania: Fairbanks, Alaska, South Korea, Papua New Guinea, Solomon Islands, Thailand (in Seoul, canonisation of 103 Korean martyrs)
12–17 June	Visit to Switzerland (in Geneva, address to the World Council of Churches)
9–21 September	First pastoral visit to Canada
10–13 October	Pastoral visit to Spain, Dominican Republic, Puerto Rico

2 December	Publication of the Apostolic Exhortation, *Reconciliatio et Paenitentia* (a basis for the examination of conscience later proposed in 1994)

1985

26 January	Sets off on pastoral visits to Venezuela, Ecuador, Peru, Trinidad and Tobago
31 March	Apostolic Letter *To the Youth of the World*
11–21 May	Visit to the Netherlands
2 June	Publication of the encyclical *Slavorum Apostoli*
8–19 August	Pastoral visits to Togo, Ivory Coast, Cameroon, Republic of Central Africa, Zaire, Kenya, Morocco (on 19 August speaks to 50,000 young Muslims in Casablanca)
8 September	Visit to Lichtenstein

1986

31 January–11 February	Visit to India (on 4 February meets with Mother Teresa of Calcutta)
13 April	Meets with the Jewish community in the Synagogue of Rome
18 May	Publication of the encyclical *Dominum et Vivificantem*
1–8 July	Visits to Colombia and Santa Lucia
4–7 October	Third pastoral visit to France
27 October	World Day of Prayer and Fasting for Peace at Assisi, Italy
18 November–1 December	Visits to Bangladesh, Singapore, Fiji Islands, New Zealand, Australia, Seychelles

1987

25 March	Publication of the encyclical *Redemptoris Mater*
31 March–13 April	Pastoral visits to Latin America: Uruguay, Chile, Argentina (on 12 April to Buenos Aires for World Youth Day)
30 April–4 May	Second visit to Germany
6 June	Opening of the Marian Year in Rome
8–14 June	Third pastoral visit to Poland
10–21 September	Second pastoral visit to the United States
1–30 October	The Synod of Bishops on the vocation and mission of the laity
22 November	Beatification of eighty-five English martyrs
3–7 December	Visit by Ecumenical Patriarch Dimitrios to the Vatican
30 December	Publication of the encyclical *sollicitudo Rei Socialis*

1988

7–19 May	Pastoral visit to Uruguay, Bolivia, Peru, Paraguay
19 June	Canonisation of 117 Vietnamese martyrs
23 June	Second pastoral visit to Austria
2 July	Excommunication of Marcel Lefebvre and followers
15 August	Apostolic Letter *Mulieris Dignitatem*
10–19 September	Pastoral visit to Zimbabwe, Botswana, Lesotho, Swaziland, Mozambique
8–11 October	Fourth pastoral visit to France
30 December	Apostolic Exhortation *Christifideles Laici*

1989

28 April–6 May	Pastoral visit to Madagascar, La Réunion, Zambia, Malawi
1–10 June	First papal visits to Norway, Iceland, Finland, Denmark, Sweden
19–21 August	Third pastoral visit to Spain (including Compostela, for World Youth Day)
30 September–3 October	Reception of Robert Runcie, Anglican Archbishop of Canterbury
6–16 October	Fifth visit to Asia: South Korea, Indonesia, Mauritius
1 December	Reception of Mikhail Gorbachev at the Vatican; invitation to Russia

1990

25 January–1 February	Pastoral visit to Africa: Capo Verde, Guinea-Bissau, Mali, Burkina Faso, Chad
21–22 April	Visit to Czechoslovakia (announcement of the European Bishops' Synod)
6–14 May	Visit to Mexico
25–27 May	Visit to Malta
1–10 September	Pastoral visit to Tanzania, Burundi, Rwanda, Ivory Coast
30 September–28 October	Synod of Bishops on priestly formation
1 December	Cardinal Casaroli replaced by Archbishop Angelo Sodano as Secretary of State
7 December	Publication of the encyclical *Redemptoris Missio*

1991

15 January	Letters to Saddam Hussein and President George Bush to prevent the Gulf War
13 April	Appointment of bishops for the territory of the former Soviet Union, which provokes protest from the Orthodox Patriarch of Moscow
1 May	Publication of the encyclical *Centesimus Annus*
10–13 May	Third papal visit to Portugal (visit to Fatima on the tenth anniversary of attempted assassination)

1–9 June	Fourth pastoral visit to Poland (first after the end of Communist regime)
13–20 August	Travelled to Czestochowa for World Youth Day and later to Hungary
12–21 October	Third pastoral visit to Brazil
28 November–14 December	Meeting of Special Assembly of the European Synod of Bishops in Rome

1992

19–26 February	Pastoral visit to Senegal, Gambia, Guinea
4–10 June	Pastoral visit to Angola, Sao Tome, Principe
12–28 July	Admission to Gemelli Hospital for removal of tumour in colon
9–14 October	Pastoral visit to the Dominican Republic for fifth centenary of the evangelisation of Latin America
31 October	Conclusion of the examination of the Galileo case: urged new dialogue between science and religion
7 December	Presentation of the *Catechism of the Catholic Church*

1993

9–10 January	World Day of Prayer and Fasting for Peace in the Balkans at Assisi
3–10 February	Pastoral visit to Benin, Uganda, Sudan (in Khartoum requested Islamic government to respect religious freedom)
25 April	Visit to Albania
8–10 May	Visit to Sicily; made vehement protest against Mafia
12–17 June	Fourth pastoral visit to Spain
9–16 August	Sixtieth international journey: Jamaica, Mexico, United States (in Denver participation in the World Day for Youth)
4–10 September	Papal visit to Lithuania, Latvia, Estonia
3 October	Publication of the encyclical *Veritatis Splendor*
11 November	Fall and fracture of shoulder

1994

2 February	Publication of *Letter to Families* (for International Year of the Family)
10 April–8 May	Special Assembly of Bishops' Synod for Africa
29 April–27 May	Second fall and again hospitalisation with fracture of right femur
22 May	Publication of Apostolic Letter *On Reserving Priestly Ordination to Men Alone*
13–14 June	Convened an extraordinary consistory to prepare for the Great Jubilee

17 June	First time in twenty-three years: announcement by the Prefecture of Economic Affairs of a favourable balance for the year 1993
10–11 September	Visits to Zagreb, Croatia
19 October	Publication of *Crossing the Threshold of Hope*
10 November	Publication of Apostolic Letter *Tertio Millennio Adveniente*, in preparation for the Great Jubilee

1995

11–21 January	Pastoral visit to the Philippines, Papua New Guinea, Australia, Sri Lanka (in Manila, attendance at the World Day for Youth)
25 March	Publication of John Paul's eleventh encyclical, *Evangelicum Vitae*
20–22 May	Second visit to the Czech Republic and sixth to Poland
25 May	Publication of the encyclical *Ut Unum Sint*
3–4 June	Second visit to Belgium
27–29 June	Reception of Patriarch Bartholomew of Constantinople at the Vatican
29 June	Publication of *Letter to Women*, for the International Year of the Woman
30 June–3 July	Visit to Slovakia
14–20 September	Visit to Africa and issue of an Apostolic Letter on the Bishops' Synod for Africa: Cameroon, Republic of South Africa, third visit to Kenya
1 October	Beatification of sixty-four martyrs of the French Revolution and forty-five martyrs of the Spanish Civil War
4–9 October	Sixth papal visit to the United States
26 November–14 December	Special Assembly for Lebanon of the Synod of Bishops in Rome

1996

5–12 February	Visit to Latin America: Guatemala, Nicaragua, El Salvador, Venezuela
14 April	Visit to Tunisia
17–18 May	Papal visit to Slovenia
21–23 June	Third pastoral visit to Germany
6–7 September	Second visit to Hungary
19–22 September	Fifth visit to France
6–15 October	In hospital for a sixth time, for appendectomy
15 November	Publication of *Gift and Mystery* for the fiftieth anniversary of ordination as a priest
3–6 December	Reception of Anglican primate Archbishop George Carey at the Vatican

1997

12–13 April	Papal visit to Bosnia-Herzegovina (Ssrajevo)
25–27 April	Third visit to the Czech Republic
10–11 May	Papal pilgrimage to Lebanon (Beirut)
31 May–10 June	Seventh visit to Poland
21–24 August	Sixth visit to France (World Day of Youth in Paris)
2–6 October	Third papal visit to Brazil (Rio de Janeiro)
16 November–12 December	Special Assembly of the Synod of American Bishops in Rome

1998

21–26 January	First papal visit to Cuba
16 March	Publication of Holy See's document: *We Remember: A Reflection on the Shoah*
21–23 March	Second visit to Nigeria
19 April–14 May	Special Assembly for Asia of the Synod of Bishops in Rome
25 May	Became longest-reigning pontiff of the twentieth century
31 May	Publication of the Apostolic Letter *Dies Domini*
19–21 June	Third papal visit to Austria
25 June	Text released of joint Lutheran/Roman Catholic statement on the doctrine of justification
4 September	Publication of John Paul's thirteenth encyclical, *Fides et Ratio*

1999

22 January	Publication of the Apostolic Exhortation *Ecclesia in America*
22–28 January	Visit to Mexico and, on return trip to Rome, St Louis, Missouri
4 April	Publication of *Letter to Artists*
7–9 May	Papal visit to Romania
5–17 June	Eighth papal visit to Poland
19 September	Pastoral trip to Slovenia
1 October	Publication of *Letter to the Elderly*
5–9 November	Pilgrimage to India and Georgia
6 November	Publication of the Apostolic Exhortation *Ecclesia in Asia*
11 December	Inauguration of restored Sistine Chapel
24 December	Opening of Holy Door, St Peter's Basilica, for Jubilee Year 2000

2000

24–26 February	Trip to Mt Sinai on first Egypt visit
20–26 March	Visit to Holy Land
12–13 May	Pilgrimage to Fatima

18 May   Eightieth birthday
13 June   Ali Agça granted clemency by Italian president;
                                extradited to Turkey
15 June   5th World Youth Day in Rome

2001
21, 28 January   Named 43 new cardinals
11 March   Beatified 233 Spanish martyrs
4–9 May   Visits to Greece, Syria and Malta
23–27 June   Visit to Ukraine
1 August   Thousandth general audience of the papacy held in
                                St Peter's Square
22–26 September   Papal visits to Kazakhstan and Armenia
22 November   Publication of Post-synodal Apostolic Exhortation
                                Ecclesia in Oceania

2002
22–26 May   Apostolic visits to Azerbaijan and Bulgaria
16 June   Canonisation of Padre Pio
23 July–1 August   Papal visit to Toronto (third), Guatemala City (third)
                                and Mexico City
16–19 August   Ninth visit to Poland

2003
6 March   Publication of *Roman Triptych: Meditations*
17 April   Publication of encyclical *Ecclesia de Eucharistia*
3–4 May   Fifth apostolic visit to Spain
5–9 June   Visit to Croatia
22 June   Visit to Bosnia–Herzegovina
                                Publication of Apostolic Exhortation *Ecclesia in
                                Europa*
11–14 September   Third apostolic visit to Slovakia
28 September   Created thirty-one new cardinals
16 October   Twenty-fifth anniversary of election as pope

2004
5–6 June   Fourth visit to Swizerland (Berne)
14–15 August   Pilgrimage to Lourdes (Seventh visit to France)
30 September   Publication of *Rise, Let Us Be On Our Way*

2005
25 February   Publication of *Memory and Identity*

Documents of John Paul II

Encyclicals

Redemptor Hominis (The Redeemer of Man)
   4 March 1979
   The new pope outlines the programme for his pontificate. The document centres on Christ the Redeemer, the human person and the church's mission today.

Dives in Misericordia (On the Mercy of God)
   30 November 1980
   This encyclical focuses on God the Father. It is 'God, who is rich in mercy' whom Jesus Christ has revealed to us as Father.

Laborem Exercens (On Human Work)
   14 September 1981
   John Paul draws on his experience as a worker and develops a spirituality of human work, relating it to the redemption.

Slavorum Apostoli (Eleventh Century Saints Cyril and Methodius)
   2 June 1985
   The Apostles of the Slavs, Saints Cyril and Methodius, are remembered with the great work of evangelisation through eleven centuries.

Dominum et Vivificantem (On the Holy Spirit in the Life of the Church and the World)
   18 May 1986
   This encyclical draws on Scripture and on the teaching of the Second Vatican Council.

Redemptoris Mater (Mother of the Redeemer)
   25 March 1987
   The Pope presents Mary as a figure of the pilgrim church and explains her role of maternal mediation.

Sollicitudo Rei Socialis (On Social Concern)
   30 December 1987
   Written for the twentieth anniversary of Paul VI's *Populorum Progessio*, this encyclical prescribes answers for world's social and economic development.

Redemptoris Missio (Mission of the Redeemer)
>   7 December 1990
>   The permanent validity of the church's missionary mandate, and a call for a
>   new evangelisation.

Centesimus Annus (On the Hundredth Anniversary of *Rerum Novarum*)
>   1 May 1991
>   On the centenary of Leo XIII's social encyclical, this document addresses
>   issues in view of the collapse of Communism.

Veritatis Splendor (The Splendour of Truth)
>   3 October 1993
>   Jesus Christ, the true light that enlightens everyone.

Evangelicum Vitae (The Gospel of Life)
>   25 March 1995
>   The dignity of the human person and the sanctity of human life.

Ut Unum Sint (On Commitment to Ecumenism)
>   25 May 1995
>   The call for Christian unity.

Fides et Ratio (On the Relationship Between Faith and Reason)
>   4 September 1998
>   Faith and reason are like two wings on which the human spirit rises to the
>   contemplation of truth.

Ecclesia de Eucharistia (The Church for the Eucharist)
>   17 April 2000
>   A celebration of the mystery and importance of the Eucharist.

Post-synodal Apostolic Exhortations
Catechesi Tradendae
>   October 16, 1979
>   On the role and importance of catechetics

Familiaris Consortio
>   November 22, 1981
>   On the role of the Christian family in the modern world

Reconciliatio et Paenitentia
>   December 2, 1984
>   On and penance in the church today reconciliation

Christifideles Laici
>   December 30 1998
>   On the role of the laity in the church and the world

Pastores Dabo Vobis
   25 March 1992
   I will give you shepherds On priestly formation and ministry

Ecclesia in Africa
   14 September 1995
   On the church's mission in Africa towards the year 2000

Vita Consecrata
   25 March 1996
   On the nature of consecrated life and the choice of total self-giving

A New Hope for Lebanon
   10 May 1997
   In preparation for the year 2000

Ecclesia in America
   22 January 1999
   Conversion, communion and solidarity

Ecclesia in Asia
   6 November 1999
   On the church's mission in Asia
Ecclesia in Oceania
   22 November, 2001
   On the church's mission in Oceania
Ecclesia in Europe
   28 June 2003
   Signs of hope and challenges for the church of Europe
Pastores Gregis
   16 October 2003
   For the hope of the world

Apostolic Letters
Rutilans Agmen
   8 May 1979
   For Cardinal Wyszynski and Archbishop Markarshi and the Polish church,
   to mark the ninth centenary of the martyrdom of St Stanislaw

Patres Ecclesiae
   2 January 1980
   To commemorate the sixteenth centenary of the death of St Basil

On the Mystery and Worship of the Eucharist (*Dominicae Cenae*)
   24 February 1980
   On the Eucharist and the priesthood

Amantissima Providentia
    29 April 1980
    To mark the sixth centenary of the death of St Catherine of Siena

Sanctorum Altrix.
    11 July 1980
    To mark the fifteenth centenary of the death of St Benedict, patron of
    Europe

Egregiae Virtutis
    31 December 1980
    Commemorates Leo XIII's encyclical *Grande Munus* on Saints Cyril and
    Methodius

A Concilio Constantinopolo I
To the bishops for the Sixteen-Hundredth Anniversary of the First Council of
Constantinople and the Fifteen-Hundredth Anniversary of the Council of Ephesus
    25 March 1981
    On the Christological and Marian power of salvation

Salvifici Doloris
    11 February 1984
    On the Christian meaning of human suffering

Redemptionis Donum
    25 March 1984
    To men and women religious on their Consecration in the light of the
    mystery of the Redemption. Issued for the Jubilee Year of the Redemption

Redemptionis Anno
    20 April 1984
    An appeal for peace in Jerusalem and the Middle East

Les Grandes Mystères
    1 May 1984
    On the situation in the Lebanon

Dilecti Amici
    31 March, 1985
    To world youth on the occasion of the international youth year

Augustinum Hipponensem
    28 August 1986
    On the significance of St Augustine, the great teacher of the church

Sescentesima Anniversaria
    5 June 1987
    For the sixth centenary of the 'Baptism' of Lithuania

Spiritus Domini
> 1 August 1987
> For the bicentennial of the death of St Alphonsus

Duodecimum Saeculum
> 4 December 1987
> On the Twelve-Hundredth Anniversary the Second Council of Nicaea, which dealt with the lawfulness and veneration of icons

Euntes in Mundum Universum
> 25 January 1988
> The millennial celebration of the baptism of St Vladimir and the conversion of Russia to Christianity

Mulieris Dignitatem
> 15 August 1988
> On the dignity and vocation of women in light of the Pope's 'theology of the body'

Vicesimus Quintus Annus
> 4 December 1988
> On the twenty-fifth Anniversary of Vatican Two's *Constitution on the Sacred Liturgy* with guidelines for liturgical renewal

Fiftieth Anniversary of the Beginning of World War II
> 27 August 1989
> On the necessity to avoid future conflict

On the Situation in Lebanon
> 7 September 1989
> An appeal for reconciliation between waring factions

For the Centenary of the Work of St Peter the Apostle
> 1 October 1989
> The promotion of vocations and seminaries through this organisation

Fifth Centenary of Evangelization of the New World
> 29 June 1990
> The growth of the church in Latin America

Ordinatio Sacerdotalis
> 22 May 1994
> On reserving priestly ordination to men alone. Expounding the teaching of the church on this matter

Tertio Millennio Adveniente
> 10 November 1994
> On preparation for the Jubilee of the year 2000

Orientale Lumen
  2 May 1995
  To mark the significance of Eastern traditions of the church and the need to
  embrace them

Fourth Centenary of the Union of Brest
  12 November 1995
  The historic crossroads of the Greek Ukrainian Church and its relations
  with Rome

Three-Hundred-Fifty Years of the Union of Uzhorod
  18 April 1996
  Celebrating the reunion of the Ukrainian eparchy of Mukacheve with Rome
  as a result of the Council of Florence (1439)

Operosam Diem
  1 December 1996
  To mark the sixteenth centenary of the death of St Ambrose of Milan

Laetamur Magnopere
  15 August 1997
  Approval and promulgation of the Latin edition of the *Catechism of the
  Catholic Church*

Divini Amoris Scientia
  19 October 1997
  Proclaims St Thérèse of Lisieux a Doctor of the Universal Church

Dies Domini
  31 May 1998
  On keeping the Lord's Day holy

Inter Munera Academiarum
  28 January 1999
  On the Pontifical Academy of St Thomas Aquinas

Apostolic Constitutions
Sapientia Christiana
  29 April 1979
  Instruction to Catholic universities and faculties on the teaching of
  theology

Magnum Matrimonii Sacramentum
  7 October 1982
  On the Pontifical Institute for Studies of Marriage and Family

Sacrae Disciplinae Leges
    25 January 1983
    For the promulgation of the new *Code of Canon Law*

Divinus Perfectionis Magister
    25 January 1983
    On new legislation instructing the causes of the canonisation

Spirituali militum curae
    21, April 1986
    On new legislation regulating the causes of the saints

Pastor Bonus
    28 June 1988
    On the Roman Curia

Ex Corde Ecclesiae
    15 August 1990
    On the mission of Catholic universities

Fidei Depositum
    11 October 1992
    On the publication of the *Catechism of the Catholic Church*

Universi Dominici Gregis
    22 February 1996
    New regulations for the orderly election of a new pope

Ecclesia in Urbe
    1 January 1998
    On the vicariate of Rome

Letters

Letter to Families
    2 February 1994
    On the occasion of the Year of the Family

Letter to Children
    13 December1994
    On the occasion of the Year of the Family

Letter to Women
    29 June 1995
    On the occasion of the Fourth World Conference on Women, held in
    Beijing

Letter to Artists
>   4 April 1999
>   Those who search for new 'epiphanies' of beauty

Letter to the Elderly
>   1 October 1999
>   Personal reflections on shared age and a review of the past

Select Bibliography

By Karol Wojtyla

Sign of Contradiction, New York: Seabury, 1979

The Acting Person, Dordrecht: D. Reidel Publishing Company, 1979

Sources of Renewal: The Implementation of Vatican II, San Francisco: Harper and Row, 1980

Faith According to St John of the Cross, San Francisco: Ignatius Press, 1981

Love and Responsibility, London: Fount Paperbacks, 1982

The Collected Plays and Writings on Theater, trans. and with introductions by Boleslaw Taborski, Berkeley: University of California Press, 1987

The Jeweller's Shop, trans. and with introduction by Boleslaw Taborski, San Francisco: Ignatius Press, 1992

The Place Within: The Poetry of Pope John Paul II, trans. by Jerzy Peterkiewicz, London: Hutchinson, 1994

The Way to Christ: Spiritual Exercises, San Francisco: HarperCollins, 1994

The Word Made Flesh: The Meaning of the Christmas Season, New York: Harper-Collins 1994

By Pope John Paul II

The Theology of Marriage and Celibacy, Boston: St Paul Editions, 1986

Crossing the Threshold of Hope, London Jonathan Cape, 1994

The Encyclicals of John Paul II, edited with introductions by J. Michael Miller, CSB. Huntingdon, Ind: Our Sunday Visitor Publishing Division, 1996; London: Catholic Truth Society

Gift and Mystery: On the Fiftieth Anniversary of My Priestly Ordination, New York: Doubleday, 1996

The Theology of the Body: Human Love in the Divine Plan, Boston: Pauline Books and Media, 1997

Roman Triptych: Meditations, trans. by Jerzy Peterkiewicz, London: Catholic Truth Society, 2003

Rise, Let Us Be On Our Way!, London: Jonathan Cape, 2004

Memory and Identity, London: Weidenfeld & Nicolson, 2005

Further Sources

Accattoli, Luigi, *Karol Wojtyla: L'uomo di fine millennio (Man of the Millenium)* Milan: San Paolo, 1998; English edition, 2000, Pauline Books, Boston.

  When a Pope Asks Forgiveness: The Mea Culpa's of John Paul II, Boston: Pauline Books, 1998

Allen, John L., Jr., *Conclave*, New York: Doubleday, 2002

Anonymous, *To the Priests, Our Lady's Beloved Sons*, Dublin: The Marian Movement of Priests, 1998

Anscombe, G.E.M., *Intention*, London: Harvard University Press, 1963

Arnold, Anthony, *The Fateful Pebble*, London: Presidio, 1993

Auerbach, Erich, *Mimesis, the Representation of Reality in Western Literature*, New Jersey: Princeton University Press, 1991

Baron-Cohen, Simon, *The Essential Difference: Men, Women and the Extreme Male Brain*, London: Allen Lane, 2003

Barthes, Roland, *Mythologies*, London: Jonathan Cape, 1974

Bernstein, Carl, and Marco Politi, *His Holiness: John Paul II and the Hidden History of Our Time*, New York: Doubleday, 1996

The Black Book, Vol. 2, *The German New Order in Poland 1939–41*, London and Melbourne: Hutchinson, 1942

Boniecki, Adam, MIC, *Kalendarium zycia Karola Wojtyly*, Krakow: Znak, 1979. *The Making of the Pope of the Millennium: Kalendarium of the Life of Karol Wojtyla* English translation by Irena and Thaddeus Mirecki et al., Boston: Marian Press, 2000

Bradley, Ritamary, *Julian's Way*, London: HarperCollins, 1992

Brother Michel de la Sainte Trinité, *The Third Secret of Fatima*, Devon: Augustine Publishing Co, 1988

Brzezinski, Zbiegniew, *Power and Principle*, London: Polomia, 1986

Buttiglione, Rocco, *Karol Wojtyla: The Thought of the Man Who Became Pope John Paul II*, Cambridge: Eerdmans, 1997

Cavell, Stanley, *Must We Mean What We Say?*, Cambridge: Cambridge University Press, 1996

Carey, George, *Know the Truth*, London: Fount, 1997

Chesterton, G.K., *Collected Poems*, London: Methuen, 1937
  St Thomas Aquinas, London: Hodder & Stoughton, 1952
  St Francis of Assisi, London: Hodder & Stoughton, 1960
  What's Wrong With The World, San Francisco: Ignatius Press, 1994

Clark, Victoria, *Why Angels Fall*, London: Picador, 2000

Clostermann, Pierre, *Flames in the Sky*, London: Penguin, 1958

Cornwell, John, *A Thief in the Night*, London: Viking, 1989
  Hitler's Pope, London: Viking, 1999
  Breaking Faith, London: Viking, 2001
  The Pope in Winter, London: Viking, 2004

Craig, Mary, *Man from a Far Country: A Portrait of Pope John Paul II*, London: Hodder & Stoughton, 1982

Davies, Norman, *God's Playground: A History of Poland*, 2 vols. Oxford: Oxford University Press, 1982
  Rising '44: 'The Battle for Warsaw', London: Pan, 2004

de Marenches, Alexandre, and Christine Ockvent, *The Evil Empire*, London: Sidgwick and Jackson, 1988

Dulles, Avery, *The Splendour of Faith*, New York: The Crossroad Publishing Company, 1999

Falconi, Carlo, *The Silence of Pius XII*, London: Faber, 1970

Freud, Sigmund, Vol. 7, *On Sexuality*, London: Penguin, 1972

Frossard, André, *Portrait of John Paul II*, San Francisco: Ignatius Press, 1990

Frossard, André, and Pope John Paul II, *Be Not Afraid!*, New York: St Martin's Press, 1984

Gaeta, Saverio, *Giovanni Paolo II: Autobiographia del cuore*, Rome: Piemme, 2003

Garton Ash, Timothy, *The Polish Revolution: Solidarity*, London: Penguin, 1999
 The Uses of Adversity, London: Penguin, 1999
 We the People, London: Penguin, 1999

Gates, Robert M., *From the Shadows*, New York: Simon & Schuster, 1996

Gorbachev, Mikhail, *Memoirs*, New York: Doubleday, 1996

Granfield, Patrick, *The Limits of the Papacy*, New York: The Crossroad Publishing Group, 1987

Gromyko, Andrei, *Memoirs*, London: Hutchinson, 1989

Gurwin, Larry, *The Calvi Affair*, London: Pan, 1984

Hebblethwaite, Margaret, *Motherhood and God*, London: Geoffrey Chapman, 1984

Hebblethwaite, Peter, *The Runaway Church*, London: Collins, 1975
 The Year of Three Popes, London: Collins, 1978
 The Papal Year, London: Geoffrey Chapman, 1981
 Introducing John Paul II, London: Fount, 1982
 In the Vatican, London: Sidgwick & Jackson, 1986
 John XXIII: Pope of the Council, London: Fount, 1994
 Paul VI: The First Modern Pope, London: Fount, 1994
 The Next Pope, London: Fount, 2000

Hebblethwaite, Peter, and Ludwig Kauffman, *John Paul II: A Pictorial Biography*, New York: McGraw-Hill, 1979

Henze, Paul B., *The Plot to Kill the Pope*, New York: Scribner's, 1983

Hughes, Gerard W., *God, Where Are You?* London: Darton, Longman & Todd, 1997

Hume, Basil, *Basil in Blunderland*, London: Darton, Longman & Todd, 1992

Jenkins, David, *God, Politics and the Future*, London: SCM Press, 1988

Johnson, Paul, *A History of the Modern World: From 1917 to the 1980s*, London: Weidenfeld & Nicolson, 1983
 Pope John Paul II and the Catholic Restoration: London, Weidenfeld & Nicolson, 1982

Kelly, J.N.D., *Oxford Dictionary of Popes*, Oxford: Oxford University Press, 1996

Klein, Emma, *The Battle for Auschwitz: Catholic–Jewish Relations under Strain*, London: Vallentine Mitchell, 2001

Knowlson, James, *Damned to Fame*, London: Bloomsbury, 1996

Kostor, Vladimir, *The Bulgarian Umbrella*, New York: St Martin's Press, 1985

Küng, Hans, *My Struggle for Freedom*, London: Continuum, 2003

Kwitny, Jonathan, *Man of the Century: The Life and Times of Pope John Paul II*, London: Warner, 1997

Lewis, C.S., *Letters to Malcolm: Cheifly on Prayer*, London: Geoffrey Bles, 1964
 Miracles, London: Fontana, 1976
 The Pilgrim's Regress, London: HarperCollins, 1977
 The Screwtape Letters, London: HarperCollins, 2002

Longley, Clifford, *The Warlock Archive*, London: G. Chapman, 2000

Lorenz, Konrad, *Civilized Man's Eight Deadly Sins*, London: Methuen, 1974

Malinski, Mieczyslaw, *Pope John Paul II: The Life of My Friend Karol Wojtyla*, New York: Seabury, 1979

Micewski, Andrzej, *Cardinal Wyszynski: A Biography*, Orlando (Fl): Harcourt Brace Jovanovich, 1984

Mindszenty, Joseph, *Memoirs*, New York: Macmillan, 1974

Moore, Sebastion, *Let This Mind Be In You*, London: Dartman, Longman & Todd, 1985

The Crucified Is No Stranger, London: Darton, Longman & Todd, 1977

Morgan, Ted, *A Covert Life*, New York: Randon House, 1999

Nichols, Peter, *The Pope's Divisions: The Roman Catholic Church Today*, New York: Penguin Books, 1982.

O'Brien, Darcy, *The Hidden Pope: The Personal Journey of John Paul II and Jerzy Kluger*, New York: Daybreak Books, 1998

Oddie, William (ed.), *John Paul the Great*, London: The Catholic Herald and the Catholic Truth Society, 2003

Orizio, Riccardo, *Talk of the Devil: Encounter with Seven Dictators*, London, Secker & Warburg, 2003

Paczkowski, Andrzej, *The Spring Will Be Ours*, University Park: The Pennsylvania State University Press, 2003

Pagels, Elaine, *The Origin of Satan*, London: Allen Lane, 1996

Petrisco, Thomas W., *The Fatima Prophecies*, McKees Rocks, PA: St Andrews Productions, 1998

Poltawska, Wanda, *And I Am Afraid of My Dreams*, London: Hodder & Stoughton, 1987

Quinn, John R., *The Reform of the Papacy*, New York: The Crossroad Publishing Company, 1999

Rahner, Karl, *Visions and Prophecies*, London: Burns & Oates, 1966

Ratzinger, Cardinal Joseph, and Messori, Vittorio, *The Ratzinger Report*, London: Fowler Wright, 1985

Rees-Mogg, William, and James Dale Davidson, *The Sovereign Individual*, London: Macmillan, 1997

Reese, Thomas, J., *Inside the Vatican*, Cambridge: Harvard University Press, 1996

Rico, Herminio, *John Paul II and the Legacy of Dignitatis Humanae*, Washington, DC: Georgetown University Press, 2002

Ruane, Kevin, *To Kill a Priest*, London: Gibson Square, 2004

Schifano, Laurence, *Luchino Visconti, the Flames of Passion*, London: Collins, 1990

Schofield, Nicholas (ed.), *A Roman Miscellany*, Herefordshire: Gracewing, 2002

Scruton, Roger, *The West and the Rest*, London: Continuum, 2002

Sebag Montefiore, Simon, *Stalin: The Court of the Red Tsar*, London: Pan, 2004

Seed, Michael, *Will I See You In Heaven?* London: Blake, 1999

Sewell, Dennis, *Catholics: Britain's Largest Minority*, London: Penguin, 2002

Sheed, F. J., *The Mary Book*, London: Sheed and Ward, 1954

Stone, Elaine Murray, *Maximilian Kolbe, Saint of Auschwitz*, New York: Paulist Press, 1997

Strange, Roderick, *The Catholic Faith*: Oxford: Oxford University Press, 1986

The Risk of Discipleship, London: Darton, Longman & Todd, 2004

Szulc, Tad, *Pope John Paul II: The Biography*, New York: Scribner, 1995

Thomas, Gordon and Max Gordon-Witts, *Pontif*, London, Granada, 1983

Thompson, Damian, *The End of Time*, London: Sinclair-Stevenson, 1996

Tischner, Jozef, *The Spirit of Solidarity*, San Francisco: Harper and Row, 1984

Vidler, Alec R., *Prophecy & Papacy*, London: SCM Press, 1954

Vircondelet, Alain, *Jean-Paul II: La biographie*, Paris: First Editions, 2004

Walesa, Lech, *A Way of Hope: An Autobiography*, New York: Henry Holt, 1987

The Struggle and the Triumph, New York: Arcade Publishing, 1992

Walsh, Michael, *John Paul II: A Biography*, London: Fount, 1995

Weigel, George, *Witness to Hope, The Biography of John Paul II*, New York: Cliff Street Books, 1999

The Courage to Be Catholic, New York: Basic Books, 2002

Letters to a Young Catholic, Herefordshire: Gracewing, 2004

Weiner, Tim, *Betrayal*, London: Richard Cohen Books, 1996

Whale, John (ed.), *The Pope from Poland: An Assessment*, London: Collins, 1980

Wierzbianski, Boleslaw (ed.), *Shepherd for All People*, New York: Bicentennial Publishing Corporation, 1982

Willey, David, *God's Politician: Pope John Paul II, The Catholic Church and the New World Order*, London: Faber and Faber, 1992

Williams, George Huntston, *The Mind of John Paul II: Origins of His Thought and Action*, New York: Seabury, 1982

Wills, Garry, *Papal Sin: Structures of Deceit*, London: Darton, Longman & Todd, 2000

Wittgenstein, Ludwig, *On Certainty*, Oxford: Basil Blackwell, 1977

Tractatus Logico-Philosophicus, London: Routledge & Kegan Paul, 1978

Woodward, Kenneth L., *Making Saints*, New York: Simon & Schuster, 1990

Wynn, Wilton, *Keepers of the Keys*, New York: Random House, 1988

Young, Hugo, *One of Us*, London: Macmillan, 1981

Newspaper Articles

George Armstrong, 'Church asked to honour Galileo'
Guardian, 5 November 1964
Leslie Childe, 'Rome honours hero priest'
Sunday Telegraph, 17 October 1971
Peter Greig, 'Now, a Pope to put the fear of God in the persecutor'
Daily Mail, 17 October 1978
'Cardinals turn to Poland for new pope'
Guardian, 17 October 1978
John Miller, 'Gierek weighs the number of the Pope's divisions'
Daily Telegraph, 31 October 1978
Paul Johnson, 'Tough Pope with the simple touch'
Sunday Telegraph, May 1981 [day unknown]
Sam White, 'The Warning I gave the Vatican'
Evening Standard, May 1981 [day unknown]
Lance Morrow, 'Hand of Terrorism'
Time, 25 May 1981
'Nuclear alert by the Pope'
Daily Mail, 4 April 1983
Aleksandr Solzhenitsyn, 'Godlessness, the first step to the Gulag'
The Times, 11 May 1983
Leslie Childe, 'Pope-plot man on trial'
Sunday Telegraph, 26 May 1985
Mary Kenny, 'Future women priests, beware'
Sunday Telegraph, 6 July 1986
John Casey, 'A Pole apart'
Sunday Telegraph, May 1990 [day unknown]
Mary Kenny, 'Sex explosion gets the world into trouble'
Sunday Telegraph, 27 May 1990
Jonathan Petre, 'This is why you will not forget me'
Guardian, 6 September 1990
'God's politician cries out in the wilderness'
Daily Telegraph, 1 April 1991
Ian Traynor, 'Pope likens abortion to Holocaust'
Sunday Times, date unknown, 1991
John Casey, 'Why the Pope is not a Thatcherite'
Sunday Times, 5 May 1991
Bruce Johnson, 'Pope's move to the right rattles Italy'
Sunday Times, 14 July 1991

Anthony Gardner, 'The Network'
    Evening Standard, 30 May 1992
Mary Kenny, 'Let the punter in the pew decide'
    Sunday Times, 31 May 1992
Bruce Johnson, 'Pope "like man of 20 after surgery"'
    Daily Telegraph, 16 July 1992
Clare Pedrick, 'The 20th Century sins'
    Daily Mail, 23 September 1992
Tom Stacey, 'Reverence yes: Reverends no'
    Daily Telegraph, 13 November 1992
Piers Paul Read, 'How the Church found its militant'
    The Times, 15 January 1993
Pope John Paul II, 'I am writing to you my brothers . . .'
    The Times, 5 August 1993
'Of sex and sin'
    Guardian, 5 August 1993
Mark Palmer, 'Battle for soul of Rome'
    Sunday Telegraph, 8 August 1993
'The Vatican's compassionate reaction'
    Sunday Telegraph, 15 August 1993
David Willey, 'Pilgrim pope has lost his way'
    Observer, 12 September 1993
Profile: 'A tired old campaigner still waging war on sin'
    Sunday Times, 26 September 1993
Ferdinand Mount, 'No pontification in this realm of England'
    Spectator, 29 January 1994
Peter Hebblethwaite, 'How many divisions has the Pope?'
    Guardian, 10 July 1994
Auberon Waugh, 'When to stop'
    Daily Telegraph, 7 September 1994
Tom Wilkie, 'Pope needs a biology lesson'
    Independent, 12 January 1995
Phillip Sherwell, 'Terror gang "sent to kill the pope"'
    Daily Telegraph, 14 January 1995
'Scarlet Women'
    Sunday Times, 22 January 1995
Clifford Longley, 'Pope condemns "culture of death"'
    Daily Telegraph, 31 March 1995
'Mixed views on "culture of death"'
    Letters, *Daily Telegraph*, 3 April 1995
John Habgood, 'The meaning of life – and death'
    Independent, 20 April 1995
Ruth Gledhill, 'Pope condemns prejudice against women'
    The Times, 11 July 1995
John Paul II, 'Letter to Women'
    Tablet, 15 July 1995

Mary Kenny, 'Future women priests, beware'
    Sunday Times, 17 September 1995
John Cornwell, 'The Pope: A man possessed?'
    Sunday Times, 17 September 1995
Andrew Brown, 'Pope accused of abusing power'
    Independent, 2 December 1995
Ian Gallagher, 'Pope stirs up the mother of all rows'
    Daily Express, 7 December 1995
'Man of the Year'
    The Times, 26 December 1995
Obituary: The Most Reverend Derek Worlock
    The Times, 9 February 1996
Cardinal Basil Hume, 'The Death of Trust'
    The Times, 27 November 1997
Kieran Cooke, 'In Heaven's name'
    Financial Times, 31 January 1998
Clifford Longley, 'The Pope's mission'
    Daily Telegraph, 25 August 1998
Charles Moore, 'The Man of the World',
    Daily Telegraph, 3 October 1998
Victoria Combe, 'Catholics embarrassed by the revival of indulgences'
    Daily Telegraph, 30 November 1998
John Hooper, 'Pope equates consumerism with fascism in angry attack on markets'
    Guardian, 16 December 1998
John Hooper, 'Pope falters as Holy Year beckons'
    Guardian, 28 December 1998
Tom Stacey, 'Reverence yes, Reverends no'
    Evening Standard, 12 January 1999
'Plea by Pope saves triple killer from death sentence'
    The Times, 26 January 1999
Richard Owen, 'Cinema is blessed by "Pope's Oscars"'
    The Times, 2 February 1999
'Papal trips are paid for by host states'
    Night and Day, Mail on Sunday, 12 February 1999
Ruth Gledhill, 'Catholic Church divided on Pinochet extradition'
    The Times, 20 February 1999
Frances Kennedy, 'The Pope cuts war remarks from speech'
    Independent, 3 April 1999
Peter Stanford, 'A paradoxical Pope'
    Independent on Sunday, 4 April 1999
Christopher Morgan, 'Pope speaks out against "culture of death"'
    Sunday Times, 4 April 1999
Bruce Solmton, 'Pope asks Serbs to open "humanitarian corridor"'
    Daily Telegraph, 5 April 1999
Tom Stacey, 'Reverence yes, Reverends no'
    Daily Star, 9 April 1999

'Pope is a Fulham fan'
      Daily Star, 9 April 1999
'Trimble's handshake with the Pope'
      Daily Mail, 23 April 1999
John Phillips, 'Unemployed spies sought to protect the Pope'
      The Times, 27 April 1999
Kate Connolly, 'Romania set for unorthodox visit'
      Guardian, 6 May 1999
'Miracle monk a step nearer sainthood'
      Daily Mail, 9 May 1999
Victoria Combe, 'Pope salutes the courage of Hume'
      Daily Telegraph, 22 June 1999
Philip William, 'Schedule is killing Pope, says expert'
      Guardian, 29 June 1999
Jude Webber, 'Pope damns idea of Hell fire'
      Independent, 29 July 1999
Christopher Leake, 'Fury at Carey's attack on the church'
      Mail on Sunday, 1 August 1999
Richard Owen, 'Pope "taking wrong road to Abraham's city"'
      The Times, 2 August 1999
John Follain, 'Pope foils hopes of old pretenders'
      Sunday Times, 15 August 1999
Rembert Weakland, 'A Polished life'
      America, 13 November 1999
Bruce Johnstone, 'Uproar in Rome over pressure on Pope to resign'
      Daily Telegraph, 11 January 2000
Richard Owen, 'Critics join chorus for Pope to quit'
      The Times, 12 January 2000
Rory Carroll, 'Agile Pope defies rumour mill at unity ceremony'
      Guardian, 19 January 2000
Richard Owen, 'The Cardinals who would be Pope'
      The Times, 20 January 2000
A.N. Wilson, 'An oldie but still a goodie'
      Evening Standard, 25 January 2000
Roland White, 'Ailing Pope loses control of Vatican'
      Sunday Times, 12 March 2000
John Casey, 'When the fatuous cult of youth means nothing'
      Mail on Sunday, 12 March 2000
Bill Mouland, 'The Pope's sweetheart'
      Daily Mail, 20 March 2000
Rebecca Fowler, 'At a shrine of horror, the Pope lays his healing touch on the wounds of history'
      Daily Mail, 24 March 2000
Bruce Johnstone, 'Vatican defends Haider meeting with the Pope'
      Daily Telegraph, 17 April 2000
Paul House, 'I was the Pope's first girlfriend'
      Evening Standard, 28 April 2000

Bruce Johnstone, 'Pope celebrates 12,000 martyrs of 20th century'
  Daily Telegraph, 8 May 2000
Rebecca Fowler, 'Three shepherd children, boiling oil, and the Vatican's best kept secret'
  Daily Mail, 12 May 2000
Christopher House, 'Fascinating Third Secret'
  Daily Telegraph, 15 May 2000
Gordon Heald, 'The Soul of Britain'
  Tablet, 3 June 2000
Richard Owen, 'Pope in attack on Clinton'
  Times, 5 January 2001
Patrick Sawer, 'Holy Pontiff! The Pope's become a comic book hero'
  Evening Standard, 15 January 2001
John Follain and Simon Caldwell, 'Pope takes fight to Satan with third exorcism'
  Sunday Times, 3 March 2002
'Pope gives blessing to a patron saint of Harry Potter'
  Sunday Times, 31 March 2002
Richard Owen, 'Frail Pope says he will serve to the end "like Jesus"'
  The Times, 1 July 2002
Rory Caroll, 'Cardinals smoke out the next pope'
  Guardian, 26 May 2002
Richard Owen, 'See him suffer, and believe'
  Times, 28 May 2002
Nick Pisa, 'Multitude for a Saint'
  Daily Mail, 17 June 2002
Richard Owen, 'Pope to canonise "saint who never was" despite protests'
  The Times, 27 July 2002
'Two million attend papal Mass in Poland'
  New York Times, 19 August 2002
Richard Owen, 'Go for it and multiply, Pope urges Italians'
  Times, 15 November 2002
Austen Ivereigh, 'Milingo and Maria'
  Tablet, 23 November 2002
'Pope's global despair'
  Sunday Telegraph, 22 December 2002
Andrzej Stylinski, 'Poetic return for John Paul II, the Vatican's amateur actor'
  Independent, 31 December 2002
Richard Owen, 'Testament in verse to the life of the Poetic Pope'
  The Times, 1 January 2003
'Catholics must resist a modern morality'
  Daily Mail, 17 January 2003
'Pope in saints for sale outrage'
  News of the World, 2 May 2003
Peter Stothard, 'A Portrait of Power'
  The Times, 2 May 2003

Papal document: 'Gay unions defy God' says Vatican; and Clifford Longley, 'This is a fight the Vatican can't win'
    Guardian, 12 August 2003
Peter Stanford, 'Saints for Sale'
    Daily Mail, 11 October 2003
Kevin Rafferty, 'Cardinal Sin – prince and king-maker'
    Tablet, 11 October 2003
Richard Owen, 'Pope "has plan if illness worsens"'
    The Times, 16 October 2003
Eamon Duffy, 'A giant among popes'
    Tablet, 18 October 2003
John Cornwell, 'The dying of the light'
    Sunday Times, 4 January 2004
'Third longest Pope, 9,281 days'
    Daily Telegraph, 15 March 2004
John Allen, 'Cardinal Paradox'
    Tablet, 18 September 2004
Richard Owen, 'Pope ready to publish his "last testament"'
    The Times, 7 October 2004

Acknowledgements

There is an uncomfortable saying that whoever eats pope, dies of it, and as the faithful Archbishop Dziwisz is reported as observing, 'Many of those who have predicted the early demise of the Holy Father are now in heaven.' I began collecting material for this biography in 1995, when I also began interviewing people. Some of the biographers and commentators I read between then and the completion of the book are now dead: I must acknowledge with gratitude the work especially of the late André Frossard, who with his two books made a priceless collection of John Paul's feelings and thoughts on a wide range of subjects, and who was on the spot as crucial witness in the early years of the papacy. I am also grateful to other biographers who have died: Tad Szulc, Darcy O'Brien, Jonathan Kwitny. As well as the many writers of source material I have drawn on, and cite in this book, I have a particular debt of gratitude to pay the late Martin Page, and his widow Katherine. Just before his final illness Martin introduced me to his set of Roman friends and colleagues, and their contribution has been invaluable. I would never have been able to employ the 'endgame' imagery had I not, while researching an earlier book, spent some time in Paris with Samuel Beckett, whom I admired, and has remained for me a figure of quasi-papal authority (in the literary and dramatic field). I also acknowledge that other Irish writer whose work and life I know, Sean O'Casey, who was described to me by Harold Macmillan as 'a saintly kind of man'. In the lives of both these writers religion (or its absence) played an important, if not the most important, part.

Pope John Paul II excites comment from everybody, so many have contributed unwittingly to this book. In particular I must thank the following whom I have interviewed or chatted informally to, or who have helped in a variety of different ways. Monsignor Graham Adams, Peter Alegi, John Allen, Lord David Alton, the late Elizabeth Anscombe, Louis Beasley-Suffolk, Lord Belhaven and Stenton, Roger Bolton, Cherie Blair, Giles Brandreth, Adam Bujak, Monsignor

Charles Burns, David Came, the late Humphrey Carpenter, Monsignor Brian Chestle, Peter Conradi, the late Betty Coxon, Father Tim Dean, John and Mary Finnis, Archbishop Michael Fitzgerald, Archbishop John Foley, Anna Frazer, Saverio Gaeta, Timothy Garton Ash, Susan Geddes, Adrian Giaglinski, Jim Gillespie, Dr Richard Greenhall, Don Claudio Gugerotti, Father Mark Hargreaves, the late Peter and Margaret Hebblethwaite, Maciek Hrybowicz, Austen Ivereigh, Dame Joanna Jamieson, Jerzy Kluger, Judith Landry, Roger Lewis, Joe Loughlin, Denis MacShane, Archbishop Kevin McDonald, Allesandra Maggiorani, Malgorzaga Hruzik Mazurkiewiecz (Lady Belhaven), Krzysztof Michalski, Tom Monaghan, Cardinal Cormac Murphy-O'Connor, Ana O'Connor, Dr Joachin Navarro-Valls, Archbishop Vincent Nichols, Richard and Julia Owen, Reginald Piggot, Piers Paul Read, Kate and Marcellin Rice, Brother Dunstan Robertson, Wendy Robinson, Paul Scofield, Father Michael Seed, Dennis Sewell, Sir Sigmund Sternberg, David Stevens, Dr Michael Straiton, Monsignor Roderick Strange, Boleslaw Taborski, Cardinal Roberto Tucci, Irving Wardle, Father Philip Whitmore, Ann Widdicome, Sister Pru Wilson, Cindy Wooden, Janet Zmroczek.

For permission to quote from Adam Boniecki's *Kalendarium* my thanks to David Came and the Marians of the Immaculate Conception and Association of Marian Helpers, Stockbridge, Massachusetts. For assistance with the Chronology and Documents I thank Cindy Wooden of the Catholic News Service, Rome, as well as www.vatican.va/holy_father.

My thanks to Mark Loftus, Monsignor Roderick Strange, Ana O'Connor, for reading the book in manuscript. To Boleslaw Taborski for reading it in proof.

My especial thanks to my editor Bill Swainson who has encouraged and monitored the book at all stages, to Nigel Newton, Pascal Carris, Hugo de Klee, Sarah Barlow, Sarah Marcus, Polly Napper and Lisa Birdwood and everyone else at Bloomsbury who has contributed to its production. Also my thanks to my agent Christopher Sinclair-Stevenson and to Samantha Hill for her endless typing and word-processing as I progressed through numerous drafts.

Finally, not least, to Vicky and my family.

Index